A New Star-Rating System & Other Exciting News from Frommer's!

In our continuing effort to publish the savviest, most up-to-date, and most appealing travel guides available, we've added some great new features.

Frommer's guides now include a new **star-rating system.** Every hotel, restaurant, and attraction is rated from 0 to 3 stars to help you set priorities and organize your time.

We've also added **seven brand-new features** that point you to the great deals, in-the-know advice, and unique experiences that separate travelers from tourists. Throughout the guide, look for:

Finds	Special finds—those places only insiders know about
Fun Fact	Fun facts—details that make travelers more informed and their trips more fun
Kids	Best bets for kids—advice for the whole family
Moments	Special moments—those experiences that memories are made of
Overrated	Places or experiences not worth your time or money
Tips	Insider tips—some great ways to save time and money
Value	Great values—where to get the best deals

We've also added a **"What's New"** section in every guide—a timely crash course in what's hot and what's not in every destination we cover. Here's what the critics say about Frommer's:

Frommer's®

Montréal & Québec City

2003

by Herbert Bailey Livesey

WILEY

Wiley Publishing, Inc.

About the Author

Herbert Bailey Livesey has written about travel and food for many publications, including *Travel & Leisure, Food & Wine,* and *Playboy.* He's the coauthor of several guidebooks, including *Frommer's Canada, Frommer's Europe from $70 a Day,* and *Frommer's New England.*

Published by:

Wiley Publishing, Inc.

909 Third Ave.
New York, NY 10022

ISBN 0-7645-6714-4
ISSN 1084-418X

Editor: Elizabeth Albertson
Production Editor: Heather Wilcox
Cartographer: Nicholas Trotter
Photo Editor: Richard Fox
Production by Wiley Indianapolis Composition Services

Front cover photo: The Changing of the Guard at La Citadelle in Québec City.
Back cover photo: The promenade on Place Jacques-Cartier in Montréal.

For information on our other products and services or to obtain technical support, please contact our Customer Care Department within the U.S. at 800-762-2974, outside the U.S. at 317-572-3993 or fax 317-572-4002.

Wiley also publishes its books in a variety of electronic formats. Some content that appears in print may not be available in electronic formats.

Manufactured in the United States of America

5   4   3   2   1

Contents

List of Maps

An Invitation to the Reader

In researching this book, we discovered many wonderful places—hotels, restaurants, shops, and more. We're sure you'll find others. Please tell us about them, so we can share the information with your fellow travelers in upcoming editions. If you were disappointed with a recommendation, we'd love to know that, too. Please write to:

Frommer's Montréal & Québec City 2003
Wiley Publishing, Inc. • 909 Third Ave. • New York, NY 10022

An Additional Note

Please be advised that travel information is subject to change at any time—and this is especially true of prices. We therefore suggest that you write or call ahead for confirmation when making your travel plans. The authors, editors, and publisher cannot be held responsible for the experiences of readers while traveling. Your safety is important to us, however, so we encourage you to stay alert and be aware of your surroundings. Keep a close eye on cameras, purses, and wallets, all favorite targets of thieves and pickpockets.

New! Frommer's Star Ratings & Icons

Every hotel, restaurant, and attraction listing in this guide has been ranked for quality, value, service, amenities, and special features using a star-rating scale. In country, state, and regional guides, we also rate towns and regions to help you narrow down your choices and budget your time accordingly. Hotels and restaurants in the Very Expensive and Expensive categories are rated on a scale of one (highly recommended) to three stars (exceptional). Those in the Moderate and Inexpensive categories rate from zero (recommended) to two stars (very highly recommended). Attractions, towns, and regions are rated according to the following scale: zero stars (recommended), one star (highly recommended), two stars (very highly recommended), and three stars (must-see).

In addition to the rating system, we also use seven icons to highlight insider information, useful tips, special bargains, hidden gems, memorable experiences, kid-friendly venues, places to avoid, and other useful information:

(Finds   (Fun Fact   (Kids   (Moments   (Overrated   (Tips   (Value

The following abbreviations are used for credit cards:

AE American Express	DISC Discover	V Visa
DC Diners Club	MC MasterCard	

FROMMERS.COM

Now that you have the guidebook to a great trip, visit our website at **www.frommers.com** for travel information on nearly 2,500 destinations. With features updated regularly, we give you instant access to the most current trip-planning information available. At Frommers.com, you'll also find the best prices on airfares, accommodations, and car rentals—and you can even book travel online through our travel booking partners. At Frommers.com, you'll also find the following:

- Online updates to our most popular guidebooks
- Vacation sweepstakes and contest giveaways
- Newsletter highlighting the hottest travel trends
- Online travel message boards with featured travel discussions

What's New in Montréal & Québec City

After the economic malaise of the 1990s, when unemployment went into the double digits and "For Sale" signs papered stores and office buildings, Montréal continues its muscular recovery. Optimism and prosperity have returned, and a billion-dollar construction boom is filling downtown's empty spaces. One big change for residents was the creation of a new megacity, effective January 2002. The 28 towns and cities that occupy the Island of Montréal were merged into a metropolis of 1.8 million inhabitants, making it the second largest city in Canada after Toronto.

PLANNING YOUR TRIP Even in the face of a slide against several of the world's major currencies, the U.S. dollar continues to be strong compared to the Canadian version, making Québec an increasingly rare travel bargain for American travelers.

While Montréal is one of the easier cities to get around by private car, it also has an excellent subway system, the Métro, which reaches every attraction and neighborhood of interest to visitors. Note that the name of the stop formerly known as Ile Ste-Hélène is now **Parc Jean-Drapeau.**

ACCOMMODATIONS A perhaps irrational exuberance has caused a surge in hotel construction, notably in the historic riverside district known as Vieux-Montréal (Old Montréal). An unprecedented taste for boutique hotels got underway in 2001 with the hyper-stylish, 48-room **Hôtel Place d'Armes,** 701 Côte de la Place d'Armes

(© 888/450-1887). Coming on board in 2002 were the **Hôtel St-Paul,** 355 rue McGill (© 514/935-4758); the **Hôtel Le Saint-Sulpice,** 48 rue Le Royer (© 514/282-9942); the **Hôtel XIXe siècle,** 262 rue St-Jaques (© 514/985-0019); the **Hôtel Gault,** 447–449 rue Ste-Hélène (© 514/904-1616); the **Hôtel Nelligan,** 106 St-Paul ouest (© 514/842-1887); and the **Hôtel Le St-James,** 354 rue St-Jacques ouest (© 514/847-0015). The largest has 120 rooms, the smallest 30. In an admirable trend, all seven are housed in rehabilitated structures dating from the 19th and early 20th centuries. See chapter 4 for more details.

In Québec City, a similar but less explosive trend has seen a surge of boutique hotels in recycled buildings in the Lower Town. One of the first, the superb **Dominion 1912,** 126 rue St-Pierre (© 888/833-5253), has been so successful that the owners purchased the building next door, adding a bistro and 20 more rooms. A more modest (and cheaper) effort is the new **Hôtel des Coutellier,** 253 rue St-Paul (© 888/523-9696). Quiet rooms—and six suites—have all the expected conveniences and go for as little as US$86 a night. See chapter 12 for details.

DINING Quebecois were a little slow to open up to the food revolution that swept most of North America in the '80s and '90s. Montréal's better restaurants were good to excellent, but they were French, with a few Italian options throw in. That's changed, with a vengeance. Eat at a place like **Area,** 1429 rue Amherst (© **514/890-6691**), and see. The "fusion" umbrella is the only label that will contain its cuisine, which hops around the world for inspiration, with techniques and ingredients from several continents piled high on each plate. **Le Blanc,** 3435 bd. St-Laurent (© **514/288-9909**), seems to have beaten the jinx of its location, which had seen three previous efforts fail in the last decade. The global cuisine is attractively put together, and jazz combos often give the Art Deco space a supper-club ambience. A local enthusiasm for Thai cookery has prompted the success of **Chao Phraya,** 50 av. Laurier (© **514/272-5339**), where you can partake of dishes that range from slightly peppery to incendiary, all invariably flavorful. Not far away, **Leméac,** 1045 av. Laurier (© **514/270-0999**), is getting attention for its fresh takes on bistro reliables—salmon *pot au feu,* for one. See chapter 5 for details.

Culinary changes are less frequent in smaller Québec City, but we're pleased to report that one of its most romantic eateries, **Le Saint-Amour,** 48 rue Ste-Ursule (© **418/694-0667**), has regained its footing after a couple of years of decline that saw changes in ownership and the kitchen. The main room has been expensively redecorated and the waitstaff trained to a finer edge. For the hot-hot-*hottest* recent entry, though, make time for the **Voodoo Grill,** 575 Grand Allée (© **418/647-2000**). Geopolitical references are a little confused, with a decor of African masks and food from around the Pacific Rim, but the eats are surprisingly good, and assuming you don't require Bach and quietude with your dinner, you'll enjoy the energy of the good-looking young clientele. See chapter 13.

Incidentally, new regulations now require nonsmoking sections in restaurants throughout the province—no small thing in heavy-puffing Québec.

SIGHTSEEING Utilizing a variety of technological tricks and displays, the **Science Centre,** King Edward Pier, Vieux-Port, Montréal (© **514/496-4724**), intends to enlighten visitors, especially young ones, about science. Its most popular component by far is its IMAX Theater, with powerful images on a screen at least four stories high. **La Ronde Amusement Park,** Parc des Iles, Ile Ste-Hélène, Montréal (© **514/872-4537**), home to 35 rides and the annual international fireworks competition, was teetering on the edge of bankruptcy when it was rescued in 2001 by the Six Flags empire. Improvements in maintenance and attractions are slowly becoming apparent. See chapter 6.

AFTER DARK Montréal's racy nightlife reputation dates from the 1920s Great Experiment south of its border. Hearty partiers still pour into the city for the season of summer festivals that celebrate jazz, comedy, ethnic cultures, and the event that kicks it all off in June, the Grand Prix. Fashion shows, dances, and general merriment enliven the Formula One race, and native son and driver, Jacques Villeneuve, recently opened **Newtown,** 1476 rue Crescent (© **514/284-6555**). The instantly trendy nightspot contains a disco, a big barroom, and a restaurant. See chapter 9.

On Québec City's boisterous Grande Allée, two grungy new bar/dance clubs are the **Liquid Bar,** 580 Grande Allée (© **418/524-1367**), and the **Living Lounge,** 690 Grande Allée (no phone). Crowds are in their late teens and early twenties, and T-shirts and jeans, or the cold-weather equivalent, make up the dress code. For chic adult crowds, **Chez Dagobert,** 600 Grande Allée (© **418/522-0393**), and **Maurice,** 575 Grande Allée (© **418/640-0711**), still rule. See chapter 17.

The Best of Montréal & Québec City

The duality of Canadian life has been called the "Twin Solitudes." One Canada, English and Calvinist in origin, tends to be staid, smug, and work-obsessed. The other, French and Catholic, is more creative, lighthearted, and inclined to see pleasure as the end purpose of labor. Or so go the stereotypes.

These two peoples live side by side throughout Québec and in the nine provinces of English Canada, but the blending occurs in particularly intense fashion in Québec province's largest city, Montréal. French speakers, known as Francophones, constitute 66% of the city's population, while most of the remaining population are speakers of English—Anglophones. (The growing number of residents who have another primary tongue, and speak neither English nor French, are called Allophones.) Although both groups are decidedly North American, they are no more alike than Margaret Thatcher and Charles de Gaulle.

Montréal is a modern city in every regard. Its downtown bristles with sky-scrapers, but many of them are playful, almost perky, with unexpected shapes and uncorporate colors. The city above ground is mirrored by another below, where an entire winter can be avoided in coatless comfort. To the west and north of downtown are Anglo commercial and residential neighborhoods, centered around Westmount. To the east and north are Francophone *quartiers,* notably Plateau Mont-Royal and Outremont. In between are the many dialects and skin tones of the immigrant rainbow.

Over the past decade, there was an undeniable impression of decline in Mon-tréal. A bleak mood prevailed, driven by lingering recession and uncertainty over the future. After all, it still remained possible that Québec would choose to fling itself into independence from the rest of Canada. Secession would be a seismic event accompanied by even greater Anglo flight, loss of federal subsidies, and grievous economic uncertainty. Lately, though, passions have cooled, especially since Québec's premier, Lucien Bouchard, a devout separatist, abruptly resigned in 2001.

Something else is going on: Ripples of optimism have become waves, spreading through the province and its largest city. Unemployment in Québec, long in double digits, shrank to under 7% in 2000, the lowest mark in more than 2 decades and below that of archrival Toronto. In another (perhaps connected) trend, crime in Montréal, already one of the safest cities in North America, hit a 20-year low. Favorable currency exchange and the presence of skilled workers have made the city a favored site for Hollywood film and TV production. The rash of "For Rent" and "For Sale" signs that disfigured the city in the 1990s has evaporated, replaced by a welcome shortage of store and office space and a bil-lion-dollar building boom that's filling up vacant plots all over downtown. The beloved old hockey arena was converted to a dining and entertainment center called Forum Pepsi, and La Ronde, a popular amusement park that was experiencing a sharp decline that threatened to end in bankruptcy, was saved by its sale to the Six Flags empire. A new convention center opened in 2002. Somewhat controversial in its vividly colorful design, it nonetheless is expected to enhance the city's desirability as a meeting place.

To be sure, not every project has enjoyed smooth sailing. A plan to build a downtown baseball stadium collapsed soon after it was proposed, as did a plan for a new theme park. But those stumbles won't matter to American visitors, for whom Montréal already might seem an urban near-paradise. The subway system, called the Métro, is modern and swift. Streets are clean and safe. Montréal's best restaurants are the equal of their south-of-the-border compatriots in every way, yet they are as much as 30% to 40% cheaper. And the government gives visitors back most of the taxes it collects from them.

Québec City is less sophisticated, more conservative, and more French. With its impressive location above the St. Lawrence River and its virtually unblemished Old Town of 18th- and 19th-century houses, it even looks French. Probably 95% of its residents speak French, and far fewer are bilingual, as most Montréalers are. (In the province as a whole, about 81% of citizens are Francophone.) With that homogeneity and its status as the putative capital of a future independent nation, citizens seem to suffer less angst over what might happen down the road. They are also aware that a critical part of their economy is based on tourism, and they are far less likely to vent the open hostility that American visitors not infrequently experience in English Canada.

1 Frommer's Favorite Montréal & Québec City Experiences

MONTREAL

- **Exploring Vieux-Montréal.** The old city is filled with old-world flavor. Wander Place Jacques-Cartier, the most engaging of the old city's squares; explore museums and the stunning architecture of the churches; and stroll along the revitalized waterfront. See chapter 6, "Exploring Montréal," and the walking tour of Vieux-Montréal in chapter 7.

- **Feasting on Table d'Hôte Specials.** Indulge in three or four courses for a fixed price that is only slightly more than the cost of an a la carte main course alone. Most full-service restaurants offer the table d'hôte, if only at midday. See chapter 5, "Where to Dine in Montréal."

- **Listening to Jazz.** Downtown, Old Town, the Latin Quarter, all over, this is a favorite pastime of

locals and visitors alike, especially in late June and early July during the renowned Montréal Jazz Festival. See chapter 9, "Montréal After Dark," and p. 141.

- **Savoring French and International Cuisine.** Dine in true French style, and in all of French Cuisine's permutations—haute, bistro, original Quebecois. Also sample the city's Cal-Asian hybrids and the legion of ethnic restaurants representing dozens of foreign cuisines, notably Italian, Mexican, Thai, Chinese, Greek, Polish, and Indian. See chapter 5, "Where to Dine in Montréal."

- **Shopping.** Browse the shops of world-class domestic designers, from the up-and-coming to the well established; search for Inuit (Eskimo) sculptures of the highest order (with prices to match); and take in the dozens of eclectic antique shops along rue Notre-Dame between rue Guy and rue Atwater. See chapter 8, "Montréal Shopping."

QUEBEC CITY

- **Admiring the Skyline from the Lévis Ferry.** The ferry provides quite a view for very little money, and passengers can stay on board and come right back without disembarking. See p. 221.
- **Discovering the Blossoming Lower Town.** All but abandoned to shipping and grimy industry, the old riverside neighborhood is being reborn, filling with antique shops, bistros, boutique hotels, and rehabilitated 18th- and 19th-century buildings. See chapter 14, "Exploring Québec City," and the walking tour of the Lower Town in chapter 15, "Québec City Strolls."
- **Lingering at an Outdoor Cafe.** Tables are set out at place

d'Armes, in the Quartier du Petit-Champlain, and along the Grande-Allée—a quality-of-life invention the French and their Quebecois brethren have perfected. See chapter 13, "Where to Dine in Québec City."
- **Relaxing in Battlefields Park (Parc des Champs-de-Bataille).** This park is beautifully situated, overlooking the St. Lawrence River, and is particularly lively on weekends, when families and lovers come here to picnic and play. See p. 217.
- **Strolling and Lounging on the Terrasse Dufferin.** Captivating Québec is at its best here, with the copper-spired Château Frontenac rearing up behind, the Lower Town below, and ferries, freighters, and pleasure craft moving on the broad, silvered river. See p. 221.

2 Best Hotel Bets

MONTREAL

- **Best Historic Hotel:** No contest. **The Ritz-Carlton Montréal,** 1228 rue Sherbrooke ouest (© **800/363-0366** or 514/842-4212), has been around since 1913, giving it a half-century lead on the nearest competition. See p. 52.
- **Best for Business Travelers:** A closer call, with several worthy candidates, but **Fairmont The Queen Elizabeth,** 900 bd. René-Lévesque ouest (© **800/441-1414** or 514/861-3511), gets the nod for its central location atop the railroad station, concierge floors, fully equipped health club, and excellent bus connections to the airport. See p. 53.
- **Best for a Romantic Getaway:** With ancient cut-stone walls, swags of velvet and brocade, and tilting floors that were once trod

by Benjamin Franklin, as well as a baronial dining room and a breakfast nook under a peaked glass roof, **La Maison Pierre du Calvet,** 405 rue Bonsecours (© **866/544-1725** or 514/282-1725), provokes memories of lovers' hotels by the Seine. See p. 58.
- **Best Boutique Hotels: Hôtel Le Germain,** 2050 rue Mansfield (© **877/333-2050** or 514/849-2050), brings a needed jolt of panache to the too-often stodgy corps of downtown business hotels. Similar in style, but employing a handsome 19th century building in Vieux-Montréal, is the shiny new **Hôtel Place d'Armes,** 701 Côte de la Place d'Armes (© **888/450-1887** or 514/842-1887). See p. 53 for Hôtel Le Germain and p. 58 for Hôtel Place d'Armes.

- **Best Lobby for Pretending That You're Rich:** A tie—the woody, hushed **Ritz-Carlton Montréal** (see "Best Historic Hotel," above) exudes old money, while the **Loews Hôtel Vogue,** 1425 rue de la Montagne (© **800/465-6654** or 514/285-5555), caters to the cellphone and Armani set. See p. 52 for the Ritz-Carlton Montréal and for Loews Hôtel Vogue.

- **Best for Families:** The **Delta Montréal,** 475 avenue du President-Kennedy (© **877/286-1986** or 514/286-1986), keeps the kids blissfully waterlogged with *two* pools—one inside, one outside. The young ones can also be placed under watchful eyes in the play center, giving their parents a break. See p. 53.

- **Best Moderately Priced Hotel:** True, there are no surprises here, but the management keeps tinkering with the formula and the cheapest rooms dip into the budget category (as low as US$80 for a double) at the **Holiday Inn Montréal-Midtown,** 420 rue Sherbrooke ouest (© **800/387-3042** or 514/842-6111). See p. 55.

- **Best Budget Hotel:** Rates at the **Lord Berri,** 1199 rue Berri (© **888/363-0363** or 514/845-9236), start low (a double goes for just US$55 in low season) and get lower the longer you stay. It's near St-Denis and just a 5-minute walk from Vieux-Montréal. See p. 57.

- **Best B&B:** Located in a 1723 house in Vieux-Montréal, **Auberge Les Passants du Sans Soucy,** 171 rue St-Paul ouest (© **514/842-2634**), is more upscale and stylish than most of its peers, and it's near top restaurants and clubs in the old town. See p. 60.

- **Best Service:** It's tough to choose among the troops at the **Loews Hôtel Vogue** (see "Best Lobby for Pretending That You're Rich," above), the **Ritz-Carlton Montréal** (see "Best Historic Hotel," above), and the **Hôtel Inter-Continental Montréal,** 360 rue St-Antoine ouest (at Bleury; © **800/361-3600** or 514/987-9900). All three display an almost equal amount of grace and care when it comes to tending to their guests. See p. 52, p. 52, and p. 57 for each hotel, respectively.

- **Best Location:** Airport buses leave regularly from the front door of **Fairmont The Queen Elizabeth** (see "Best for Business Travelers," above). The main railroad station is just a couple of levels down in the hotel elevator, and most of the major corporate buildings are accessible through the corridors of the underground city. See p. 53.

- **Best Health Club: Hôtel Omni Mont-Royal,** 1050 rue Sherbrooke ouest (© **514/284-1110**), lays on aerobics classes with instructors, free weights *and* weight machines and Exercycles, as well as saunas, a steam room, whirlpools, and massages to recover from the workout. See p. 49.

- **Best Hotel Pool:** Most of the big downtown hotels have heated pools, but at the **Hilton Montréal Bonaventure,** 1 place Bonaventure (© **800/267-2575** or 514/878-2332), you can slip into the pool indoors and stroke into the outdoors without leaving the water, even in January. See p. 49.

- **Best Views:** With 32 stories, the **Hôtel Omni Mont-Royal** (see "Best Health Club," above) has some of the loftiest rooms, with the most panoramic views, in town. See p. 49.

The Best of Montréal & Québec City Online

You can find lots of information on Montréal and Québec City on the Internet. Here are a few of our favorite planning and general information sites.

- **Bonjour Québec** (www.tourisme.gouv.qc.ca), the official site of the government of the Province of Québec, endeavors to be a comprehensive information bank about all things Québec, and nearly succeeds. You'll find information on upcoming events and ongoing attractions, and you can search for hotels and reserve online.
- **Bonjour à la Montréal** (www.tourisme-montreal.org), another official tourism site, constitutes a first source that hits the highlights rather than delves at depth. Click the "traveler" box for a directory of attractions, guided tours, entertainment, accommodations, and restaurants. Be sure to scope the "Sweet Deals" on lodging and activities from October to May.
- **Montréal Online** (www.montrealonline.com) is a site packed with festival schedules, a slew of theater and dance reviews, interactive music listings, a bar guide, and movie listings. Can't decide? Let the site's condensed "The Very Best of Montréal" section guide you.
- **Hour** (www.hour.ca) is a Montréal culture magazine that highlights local happenings. Read entertainingly grumpy and often profane takes on current events from several columnists, as well as updated restaurant and film reviews.
- **Québec: Une Histoire d'Amour** (www.quebecregion.com) is sponsored by the Greater Québec Area Tourism and Convention Bureau. They provide a site full of information about Québec City's accommodations, attractions, sports, shopping, dining, history, and culture.

QUEBEC CITY

- **Best Historic Hotel: Fairmont Le Château Frontenac,** 1 rue des Carrières (© **800/828-7447** or 418/692-3861), is more than a century old. It was one of the first hotels built to serve railroad passengers and to encourage tourism at a time when most people stayed close to home—and it still rewards a visit. See p. 194.
- **Best for Business Travelers:** A tie. Both the **Hilton Québec,** 1100 bd. Rene-Levesque est (© **800/445-8667** or 418/647-6508), and the **Radisson Québec,** 690 bd. René-Lévesque est (© **800/463-2820** from eastern Canada and Ontario, 418/647-1717 or 800/333-3333 from elsewhere), are as central as can be found, with good fitness centers and executive floors with concierges and business services. See p. 198 for the Hilton Québec and p. 199 for the Radisson Québec.
- **Best for a Romantic Getaway:** It's hard to beat curling up with a glass of wine beside the fire in the country-chic great room of the **Auberge Saint-Antoine,** 10 rue St-Antoine (© **888/692-2211** or 418/692-2211). See p. 200.
- **Best Boutique Hotel:** The sleek **Dominion 1912,** 126 rue Saint-Pierre (© **888/833-5253** or 418/692-2224), infuses a pre–World War I building with modernist

design, continuing a trend in designer hotels and inns in the Basse-Ville. It is especially fashionable among the younger business set. See p. 201.

- **Best Location:** Where else? For tourists, nothing can beat **Fairmont Le Château Frontenac** (see "Best Historic Hotel," above) for proximity to all the sights. In fact, the Château *is* one of the sights. See p. 194.
- **Best Health Club and Pool:** At the **Radisson Québec** (see "Best for Business Travelers," above), weights, Exercycles, and a workout room with instructors, as well as a whirlpool and sauna, will help you ease out the kinks. Slip into the heated pool inside and swim out to the open air. See p. 199

3 Best Dining Bets

For a discussion of dining in Québec, see "Cuisine Haute, Cuisine Bas: Smoked Meat, Fiddleheads & Caribou," in the appendix.

MONTREAL

- **Best Spot for a Business Lunch:** The classic power place since 1958 has been **Le Beaver Club** in The Queen Elizabeth hotel, 900 bd. René-Lévesque ouest (☎ **514/861-3511**), but because its men's-club air might be unpalatable to some women business travelers who have to entertain while on the road, the elegantly neutral **Restaurant le Paris** at the Ritz-Carlton, 1228 rue Sherbrooke ouest, at rue Drummond (☎ **514/842-4212**), won't disappoint, at least in its deluxe setting and polished service. See p. 65 for Le Beaver Club and p. 68 for Restaurant le Paris.
- **Best Spot for a Celebration:** No need to rake in stacks of chips at the gambling tables in the casino to join the festive gatherings at **Nuances,** 1 av. du Casino (5th floor of the casino; ☎ **514/392-2708**), the gracious multi-starred *temple de cuisine* on the top floor. You'll get superb service, astonishing food, and spectacular views of the skyline to boot. See p. 80.
- **Best Wine List: Les Halles,** 1450 rue Crescent, between rue Ste-Catherine and boulevard de Maisonneuve (☎ **514/844-2328**), has a selection of more than 400 labels, carefully arranged not simply by such broad regional categories as Bordeaux and Burgundy, but by appellation. Prices run well into three figures, but more moderately priced bottles are also available. See p. 65.
- **Best Decor:** With its exposed brick and stone walls, ceiling-high shelves of wine behind the handsomely turned-out center bar, and candle flames flickering in the breezes through the big open windows along the front and side, **Modavie,** 1 St-Paul ouest in Vieux-Montréal (☎ **514/287-9582**), pleases the eye at every turn. See p. 72.
- **Best Value:** At lunch, the all-you-can-eat Indian buffet at **Le Taj,** 2077 rue Stanley, near rue Sherbrooke (☎ **514/845-9015**), is a wonder. At dinner, even the *expensive* four-course table d'hôte at **Le Bourlingueur,** 363 St-François-Xavier, near rue St-Paul (☎ **514/845-3646**), comes in under C$16 (US$10). See p. 68 for Le Taj and p. 75 for Le Bourlingueur.
- **Best for Kids:** On the assumption that a kid who doesn't like pizza is as rare as fish feathers, get over to **Pizzédélic,** on The Main at 3509 bd. St-Laurent, near rue

Sherbrooke (℃ **514/282-6784**). They have all manner of toppings, from the utterly conventional to just short of odd, and pastas, too—all to be eaten while looking out at the street or under umbrellas on the terrace in back. See p. 80.

- **Best French Cuisine: Les Halles** (see "Best Wine List," above) has best expressed the glories of traditional French cuisine for more than a quarter century with judicious evolution in its cookery rather than wrenching overhauls. See p. 65.

- **Best Italian Cuisine:** Super-chic **Buona Notte,** 3518 bd. St-Laurent, near rue Sherbrooke (℃ **514/848-0644**), may look as if it's more concerned with being a place to be seen than with what it sends out of the kitchen, but the pastas, focaccias, and risottos rival the occasional celebrity sightings. See p. 77.

- **Best Mexican Cuisine:** There's a party every night at **Casa de Matéo,** 440 rue St-François-Xavier, near rue St-Paul (℃ **514/ 844-7448**), starting with the birdbath margaritas and dancing on through fried cactus, ceviche, and fish Veracruz. The infectious enthusiasm of the staff is often heightened by live mariachi music. See p. 73.

- **Best Thai Cuisine: Chao Phraya,** 5 Laurier ouest, near bd. St-Laurent (℃ **514/272-5339**), purveys examples of a most complex Asian cooking style at good value in a sophisticated setting that eschews snarling gold temple dogs. See p. 81.

- **Best Seafood:** Fish is the mainstay of Greek cooking, and is best when preparations are simplest. Grills are paramount at **Milos,** 5357 av. du Parc (℃ **514/272-3522**), and

the fish is mere hours from the sea. See p. 75.

- **Best Pizza:** The name says it all: **Pizzédélic** (see "Best for Kids," above), where they do anything from same-old, same-old tomato and cheese to forward-edge designer concoctions with unlikely toppings like snails. See p. 80.

- **Best Desserts:** With patisseries on every other corner, indulging in creamy, gooey, blissfully caloric sweets doesn't require a difficult search. But along boulevard St-Laurent, make the effort to seek out heavenly **Kilo,** 5206 bd. St-Laurent, between rue Maguire and rue Fairmount (℃ **514/277-5039**). See p. 83.

- **Best Late-Night Dining:** Plateau Mont-Royal's most Parisian bistro, **L'Express,** 3927 rue St-Denis, near Rue Roy (℃ **514/845-5333**), doesn't need a sign out front, because it stays full nightly until 3am (Sun only until 2am). Simple but toothsome recipes with the freshest ingredients keep the night owls coming. See p. 77.

- **Best Outdoor Dining:** Serious food isn't the lure at **Le Jardin Nelson,** 407 place Jacques-Cartier (℃ **514/861-5731**). Instead, you get music—classical or jazz—as you partake of sweet or savory crêpes or very good pizzas under the crabapple tree in the garden. See p. 75

- **Best People-Watching:** Any of a dozen cafes along St-Denis will fit this bill, especially on weekends, when the Plateau Mont-Royal boulevard comes alive. But **Café Cherrier,** 3635 rue St-Denis, at rue Cherrier (℃ **514/843-4308**), might be the most fun, if you can find a seat on the wraparound terrace. See p. 82.

- **Best Afternoon Tea:** Gentility and correctness prevail at the **Restaurant le Paris** in the Ritz-Carlton (see "Best Spot for a Business Lunch," above), where high tea is sublimely reassuring at any time of year, but best in spring and summer, when they move outdoors next to the duck pond. See p. 68.

- **Best Brunch:** Crêpes with multitudes of fillings make for Frenchified brunches at **Le Jardin Nelson,** 407 place Jacques-Cartier, near rue de la Commune (℗ 514/861-5731), in the garden, inside, or on the terrace facing place Jacques-Cartier. See p. 75.

- **Best Smoked Meat:** It'll only throw another log on a local battle for the title of "best smoked meat," which has blazed for at least a century, but **Chez Schwartz Charcuterie** on The Main at 3895 bd. St-Laurent, north of rue Prince-Arthur (℗ 514/842-4813), serves up the definitive version of this untransplantable deli treat. See p. 79.

- **Best Fast Food:** Where else but **Chez Better,** 160 rue Notre-Dame, near place Jacques-Cartier (℗ 514/861-2617), where sausages and schnitzels dominate the menu, washed down with any of dozens of foreign beers. Six branches and growing. See p. 74.

- **Best New Restaurant:** The young chef at **Area,** 1429 rue Amherst, near rue Ste-Catherine (℗ 514/890-6691), is making waves with his updated bistro food and *huge* portions. See p. 76.

- **Best Restaurant, Period:** Ever-questing Normand Laprise and partner Christine Lamarche keep **Toqué!,** 3842 rue St-Denis, near rue Roy (℗ 514/499-2084), in a league of its own. It's postmodern, it's postnouvelle, it's dazzling! Nipping at their heels, though, is **Nuances** (see "Best Spot for a Celebration," above). See p. 76 for Toqué! and p. 80 for Nuances.

QUEBEC CITY

- **Best Spot for a Romantic Dinner:** Stars above, tables illuminated by the flutter of candlelight, unobtrusive service, and even the name, **Le Saint-Amour,** 48 rue Ste-Ursule (℗ 418/694-0667), bespeak romance. See p. 205.

- **Best View:** Revolving rooftop restaurants rarely dish out food as elevated as their lofty venues. **L'Astral** in the Loews Le Concorde hotel (see chapter 12), 1225 cours du Général-de Montcalm (℗ 418/647-2222), doesn't challenge that perception, but neither is the kitchen inept. You may not notice, anyway, with that unobstructed 360° vista. See p. 208.

- **Best Bistro:** In a city that specializes in the informal bistro tradition, **L'Echaudé,** 73 rue Sault-au-Matelot, near rue St-Paul (℗ 418/692-1299), is a star. Classic dishes are all in place, from confit de canard to steak frites. The dining terrace is on a pedestrian-only street. See p. 210.

- **Best Contemporary Cuisine: Laurie Raphaël,** 117 rue Dalhousie (℗ 418/692-4555), is named for the owners' children, a choice that isn't lost on those diners who devote great care to things they hold important—family, friends, and the tables around which they gather. See p. 210.

- **Best Really Really Hot Spot:** You don't have to be young, gorgeous, and hip to get into the **Voodoo Grill,** 575 Grande-Allée (℗ 418/647-2000), but there seems to be a lot of self-selection going on. As part of a complex that includes two bars and the Maurice disco, the noise level is brutal and the pace frantic, making the surprisingly good food all the more remarkable. See p. 209.

- **Best Seafood:** The owner of **Le Marie-Clarisse,** 12 rue du Petit-Champlain (© **418/692-0857**), selects all the just-off-the-boat ingredients served at his comfortable bistro at the bottom of Breakneck Stairs. There's a fireplace inside and a terrace outside. See p. 211.

- **Best Pizza:** For conventional and unusual toppings on crispy-thin crusts that work better with a knife and fork than fingers, hit **Les Frères de la Côte,** 1190 rue St-Jean (© **418/692-5445**). See p. 205.

- **Best People-Watching:** Le Marie-Clarisse's few outdoor tables—perched above the main pedestrian intersection of Quartier du Petit-Champlain—monopolize an unsurpassed observation point. See "Best Seafood," above, and see p. 211.

- **Best Place to Take a Teenager:** Tasty pizzas and inventive pastas coupled with a thumping stereo and the noise level of a 20-lane bowling alley make **Les Frères de la Côte** (see "Best Pizza," above) a logical choice for parents with teens. See p. 205.

2

Planning Your Trip to Montréal & Québec City

Montréal and Québec City have a stronger foreign flavor than other cities in Canada, and the first language of most residents is French. But once you decide to go, pulling together information on ways to get there, border formalities, exchanging money, climate, lodging possibilities, and related details is almost as easy as getting from Illinois to Florida. The information below and in the "Fast Facts" sections in chapters 3 and 11 should help speed the process along.

1 Visitor Information

Québec tourism authorities produce volumes of detailed and highly useful publications, and they're easy to obtain by mail, by phone, or in person. To contact **Tourisme Québec,** write C.P. 979, Montréal, Québec H3C 2W3, call © **877/266-5687,** e-mail info@ tourisme.gouv.qc.ca, or visit their website at **www.bonjourquebec.com**.

The Québec government maintains a number of offices in the United States and abroad, which can provide specific tourism information about the province:

In the U.S.: Délégation du Québec, 1 Rockefeller Plaza, 26th Floor, New York, NY 10020-2201 (© 212/397-0200).

In the U.K.: Délégation du Québec, 59 Pall Mall, London SW1Y 5JH, England (© **071/930-8314**); High Commission of Canada, Canada House, Cockspur Street, Trafalgar Square, London SW1Y 5BJ, England (© **071/258-6600**).

In France: Délégation du Québec, 4 av. Victor-Hugo, 75116 Paris, France (© **144/17-32-40**); Canadian Embassy, 35 av. Montaigne, 75008 Paris, France (© **14/143-2900**).

Besides these offices outside Québec, the province has a large office in Montréal (contact information above), and there are convenient regional offices in Montréal and Québec City as well. See "Visitor Information," in chapters 3 and 11 for more details.

2 Entry Requirements

U.S. citizens or permanent residents of the United States require neither passports nor visas but will need some proof of citizenship, such as a birth certificate, plus a photo ID, to enter Canada and to reenter the United States. A passport is the logical and preferred document, even though it

isn't specifically required. Permanent U.S. residents who are not citizens must have their Alien Registration Cards (green cards) with them. If you plan to drive into Canada, be sure to have your car's registration handy as well.

An important point for teenage travelers: All persons under 19 require a letter from a parent or guardian granting them permission to travel to Canada. The letter must state the traveler's name and the duration of the trip. It is also essential that teenagers carry proof of identity with photo. Otherwise, the letter from Mom and Dad is useless at the border.

Citizens of Australia, New Zealand, the United Kingdom, and Ireland need only carry a valid passport. Citizens of many other countries must have visas, applied for well in advance at their nearest Canadian embassy or consulate. Questions can be addressed to the **Canadian Immigration Division,** place du Portage, 140 Promenade du Portage, Phase 4, Hull, Québec K1A 1L1; © **819/994-2424;** www.cic.gc.ca.

CUSTOMS
WHAT YOU CAN BRING INTO CANADA

Regulations are flexible in most respects, but visitors can expect at least a probing question or two at the border or airport. Normal baggage and personal possessions should be no problem, but tobacco and alcoholic beverages face limitations. Individuals 18 years or over are only allowed 50 cigars, 200 cigarettes, and 400 grams of loose tobacco. In addition, an Imperial quart (just over a liter) of wine or liquor may be brought in, or a curiously generous case (24 cans) of beer, assuming the bearer is at or over the minimum drinking age in Québec, which is 18.

Pets with proper vaccination records may be admitted, but inquire in advance about necessary procedures at one of the Délégation du Québec offices listed above and see "Pets" in "Fast Facts: Montréal," in chapter 3. Talk to U.S. Customs (see below) about bringing pets back home.

There are strict regulations regarding the import of plants, food products, and firearms. Hunters with valid licenses can bring in some gear, but handguns and fully automatic firearms are prohibited. Fishing tackle poses no problem as long as the proper nonresident license is obtained.

For more detailed information concerning Customs regulations, write to the **Canada Customs Office,** 400 place d'Youville, 2nd floor, Montréal, PQ H2Y 2C2 (© **514/283-2949** or 514/283-2959), or check out the customs website at www.ccra-adrc.gc.ca.

A car that is driven into Canada can stay for up to a year, but it must leave with the owner or a duty will be levied. The possession or use of a radar detector is prohibited, whether or not it is connected. Police officers can confiscate it and fine the owner C$500 to C$1,000 (US$323–US$645).

WHAT YOU CAN TAKE HOME

Returning **U.S. citizens** who have been away for at least 48 hours are allowed to bring back, once every 30 days, $400 worth of merchandise duty-free. You'll be charged a flat rate of 4% duty on the next $1,000 worth of purchases. Be sure to have your receipts handy. On mailed gifts, the duty-free limit is $100. You cannot bring fresh foodstuffs into the United States; tinned foods, however, are allowed. For more information, contact the **U.S. Customs Service,** 1300 Pennsylvania Ave., NW, Washington, DC 20229 (© **877/287-8867**) and request the free pamphlet *Know Before You Go.* It's also available on the Web at www.customs.gov. (Click on traveler information, then Know Before You Go.)

Citizens of the U.K. who are **returning from a European Union (EU) country** will go through a separate Customs Exit (called the "Blue Exit") especially for EU travelers. In essence, there is no limit on what you can bring back from an EU country, as long as the items are for personal use (this includes gifts), and you have already paid the necessary duty and tax. However, customs law sets out guidance levels. If you bring in more than these levels, you may be asked to prove that the goods are for your own use. Guidance levels on goods bought in the EU for your own use are 800 cigarettes, 200 cigars, 1kg smoking tobacco, 10 liters of spirits, 90 liters of wine (of this not more than 60l can be sparkling wine), and 110 liters of beer. For more information, contact **HM Customs & Excise,** Passenger Enquiry Point, 2nd Floor Wayfarer House, Great South West Road, Feltham, Middlesex, TW14 8NP (© **0181/ 910-3744;** from outside the U.K. 44/181-910-3744), or consult their website at www.open.gov.uk.

U.K. citizens returning from a non-EU country have a customs allowance of 200 cigarettes; 50 cigars; 250g of smoking tobacco; 2 liters of still table wine; 1 liter of spirits or strong liqueurs (over 22% volume); 2 liters of fortified wine, sparkling wine or other liqueurs; 60cc (ml) perfume; 250cc (ml) of toilet water; and £145 worth of all other goods, including gifts and souvenirs. People under 17 cannot have the tobacco or alcohol allowance. For more information, contact **HM Customs & Excise,** Passenger Enquiry Point, 2nd Floor Wayfarer House, Great South West Road, Feltham, Middlesex, TW14 8NP (© **0181/910-3744;** from

outside the U.K. 44/181-910-3744), or consult their website at www.open.gov.uk.

The duty-free allowance in **Australia** is A$400 or, for those under 18, A$200. Upon returning to Australia, citizens can bring in 250 cigarettes or 250 grams of loose tobacco and 1,125ml of alcohol. If you're returning with valuable goods you already own, such as foreign-made cameras, you should file form B263. For more information, contact **Australian Customs Services,** GPO Box 8, Sydney NSW 2001 (© **02/6275-6666** in Australia; 202/797-3189 in the U.S.), or go to **www.customs.gov.au**.

The duty-free allowance for **New Zealand** is NZ$700. Citizens over 17 can bring in 200 cigarettes, or 50 cigars, or 250 grams of tobacco (or a mixture of all three if their combined weight doesn't exceed 250g); plus 4.5 liters of wine and beer, or 1.125 liters of liquor. New Zealand currency does not carry import or export restrictions. Fill out a certificate of export, listing the valuables you are taking out of the country; that way, you can bring them back without paying duty. Most questions are answered in a free pamphlet available at New Zealand consulates and Customs offices: *New Zealand Customs Guide for Travellers, Notice no. 4.* For more information, contact **New Zealand Customs,** 50 Anzac Ave., P.O. Box 29, Auckland (© **09/359-6655**).

3 Money

CURRENCY

Canadian money comes in graduated denominations of dollars and cents. The exchange rate is great for Americans, because the Canadian dollar is worth about 67¢ in U.S. currency, give or take a couple of points' daily variation. This is the exchange rate used to convert prices in this book. Put another way, one U.S. dollar buys

about C$1.55 in Canadian money. This means that U.S. dollars gain substantially more spending power the moment they are changed for local currency (a return, for example, of approximately C$543 Canadian for every US$350). And because prices are roughly on par with those in the U.S., the difference is real, not imaginary. Prices in this book, unless otherwise indicated, are given in both Canadian and U.S. dollars.

Visitors can bring in or take out any amount of money they wish, but if U.S. citizens import or export sums of US$5,000 or more, a report of the transaction must be filed with U.S. Customs.

Aside from the $2 coin, Canadian coins are similar to their American counterparts: 1¢, 5¢, 10¢, 25¢. Bills—$2, $5, $10, $20, $50, $100—are all the same size but have different colors, depending on the denomination. The gold-colored $1 coin (called a "loonie" by Canadians because of the depiction of a loon on one side) has replaced the $1 bill. A $2 coin has appeared, with a bronze center surrounded by a nickel disk, meant to replace the old $2 bill, which is still found in circulation. (The $2 coin is sometimes called a "twonie," a reference to the next-smaller coin.) French speakers sometimes refer to a dollar as a "piastre."

Many stores accept U.S. dollars, often posting a sign to that effect that gives the percentage rate they offer. Usually, that amount is less than what banks offer, but sometimes it is more favorable because many establishments are eager to attract U.S. tourist dollars. As a rule, though, it's more advantageous to change money and traveler's checks at a bank, and better still to obtain cash at ATMs (see below).

It's a good idea to exchange at least some money—just enough to cover airport incidentals and transportation to your hotel—before you leave home, so you can avoid the less-favorable rates you'll get at airport currency exchange desks. Check with you local American Express or Thomas Cook office or your bank. American Express cardholders can order foreign currency over the phone at © **800/807-6233.** It's best to exchange currency or traveler's checks at a bank, not a currency exchange, hotel, or shop.

ATMS

As ubiquitous in Québec as in the United States, ATMs are found in most of the same places, outside or inside bank branches, but also increasingly at other locations, including the province's new casinos. Look for signs reading GUICHET ATOMATIQUE or SERVICES ATOMATISES.

The principal networks are **Cirrus** (© **800/424-7787**) and **PLUS** (© **800/843-7587**) for withdrawing funds from home checking accounts. A four-digit PIN (personal identification number) is required, so people with fewer or more digits need to have another PIN assigned to their account(s) before leaving home. The exchange rate at ATMs is usually more favorable than the rate offered by banks. This advantage can be wiped out, however, if your home bank charges high transaction fees, so check with your bank before departing. When using ATMs to obtain cash advances on credit cards, remember that interest is charged beginning on the day of withdrawal.

CREDIT CARDS

Credit cards are accepted as widely in Québec as in the United States. Visa and MasterCard dominate the market, followed by the American Express card, Diners Club, and its Canadian cousin, enRoute. The Discover and Carte Blanche cards fall well behind the others in usage. Charge slips are written up in Canadian dollars, and card companies convert the amount to U.S. dollars when they credit the transaction to your account.

You can also withdraw cash advances from your credit cards at any bank (though you'll start paying hefty interest on the advance the moment you receive the cash). At most banks, you don't even need to go to a teller; you can get a cash advance at the ATM if you know your PIN access number. If you've forgotten yours, or didn't even know you had one, call the

The Canadian Dollar, the U.S. Dollar & the British Pound

For U.S. Readers   The rate of exchange used to calculate the dollar values given in this book was US$1 = approximately C$1.50 (or C$1 = US$0.67).

For British Readers   The rate of exchange used to calculate the pound values in the accompanying table was £1 = approximately C$2.50 (or C$1 = 40p)

C$	US$	UK£	C$	US$	UK£
0.10	.07	.04	35.00	23.45	14.00
0.25	.17	.10	40.00	26.80	16.00
0.50	.34	.27	45.00	30.15	18.00
1.00	.67	.40	50.00	33.50	20.00
2.00	1.34	.80	55.00	36.85	22.00
3.00	2.01	1.20	60.00	40.20	24.00
4.00	2.68	1.60	65.00	43.55	26.00
5.00	3.35	2.00	70.00	46.90	28.00
6.00	4.02	2.40	75.00	50.25	30.00
7.00	4.69	2.80	80.00	53.60	32.00
8.00	5.36	3.20	85.00	56.95	34.00
9.00	6.03	3.60	90.00	60.30	36.00
10.00	6.70	4.00	95.00	63.65	38.00
15.00	10.05	6.00	100.00	67.00	40.00
20.00	13.40	8.00	150.00	100.50	60.00
25.00	16.75	10.00	200.00	134.00	80.00
30.00	20.10	12.00	250.00	167.50	100.00

number on the back of your credit card and ask the bank to send it to you. It usually takes 5 to 7 business days, though some banks will provide the number over the phone if you tell them your mother's maiden name or pass some other security clearance. Keep in mind that your credit card company will likely charge a commission (1% or 2%) on every foreign purchase you make.

WHAT TO DO IF YOUR WALLET GETS STOLEN

Odds are that if your wallet is gone, the police won't be able to recover it for you. However, after you realize that it's gone and you cancel your credit cards, it is still wise to inform them. Your credit-card company or insurer may require a police-report number.

Almost every credit-card company has an emergency toll-free number to call in the event your wallet or purse is stolen. They may be able to wire a cash advance immediately, and in many places, they can deliver an emergency credit card in a day or two. The issuing bank's toll-free number is usually on the back of the credit card—though of course that doesn't help much if the card is stolen. Making photocopies of credit cards, key passport pages, and other important documents therefore makes sense. Emergency numbers for the four major cards mentioned in this guide are as follows: **Visa,** © **800/847-2911** in the U.S. and Canada; **MasterCard,**

ⓒ **800/307-7309** in the U.S. and Canada; **American Express,** ⓒ **800/554-2639** in the U.S. or ⓒ **301/214-8228** collect outside the U.S.; and **Diners Club,** ⓒ **303/799-1504** collect outside the U.S. For other cards, call toll-free directory assistance at ⓒ **800/555-1212** and ask for your card company.

If you choose to carry traveler's checks, be sure to keep a record of their serial numbers separate from your checks. You'll get a refund faster if you know the numbers.

If you need emergency cash over the weekend when all banks and American Express offices are closed, you can have money wired to you from **Western Union** (ⓒ **800/325-6000;** www.westernunion.com/). You must present valid ID to pick up the cash at the Western Union office. However, in most countries, you can pick up a money transfer even if you don't have valid identification, as long as you can answer a test question provided by the sender. Be sure to let the sender know in advance that you don't have ID. If you need to use a test question instead of ID, the sender must take cash to his or her local Western Union office, rather than transferring the money over the phone or online.

4 When to Go

High season is late May through early September, when hotels are most likely to be full and charge their highest tariffs. Even then, though, weekends are cheaper and package plans reduce the bite, so advance planning has its rewards. The period from Christmas to New Year's is also busy (and more expensive), as are the days given to winter festivals in both Montréal and Québec City.

CLIMATE

Temperatures are usually a few degrees lower in Québec City than in Montréal. Spring, short but sweet, arrives around the middle of May. Summer (mid-June through mid-Sept) tends to be humid in Montréal, Québec City, and other communities along the St. Lawrence River, and drier at the inland resorts of the Laurentians and Estrie. Intense but usually brief heat waves mark July and early August, but temperatures rarely remain oppressive in the evening.

Autumn (Sept and Oct) is as short and changeable as spring, with warm days and cool or chilly nights. Canadian maples blaze with color for weeks. Winter brings dependable snows for skiing in the Laurentians, the Cantons-de-l'Est, and Charlevoix. After a sleigh ride or a ski run in Parc Mont-Royal, Montréal's underground city is a climate-controlled blessing. Mid-February is the time for Québec City's robust Carnaval d'Hiver (Winter Carnival). Snow and slush are more-or-less constantly present from November to March.

Montréal's Average Monthly Temperatures (°F/°C)

	Jan	Feb	Mar	Apr	May	June	July	Aug	Sept	Oct	Nov	Dec
High	21	25	34	52	65	74	78	77	70	56	43	26
	-6	-4	1	11	18	23	26	25	21	13	6	-3
Low	8	12	23	37	48	57	62	60	53	43	32	15
	-13	-11	-5	-3	9	14	17	16	12	6	0	-9

Québec City's Average Monthly Temperatures (°F/°C)

	Jan	Feb	Mar	Apr	May	June	July	Aug	Sept	Oct	Nov	Dec
High	19	21	32	46	60	70	76	74	65	52	39	23
	-7	-6	0	8	16	21	24	23	18	11	4	-5
Low	5	8	19	32	43	53	57	56	48	37	28	12
	-15	-13	-7	0	6	12	14	13	9	3	-2	-11

HOLIDAYS

In Québec province, the important public holidays are New Year's Day (Jan 1); Good Friday and Easter Monday (late Mar or Apr); Victoria Day (May 24 or nearest Mon); St-Jean-Baptiste Day, Québec's "national" day (June 24); Canada Day (July 1); Labour Day (1st Mon in Sept); Canadian Thanksgiving Day (2nd Mon in Oct); Remembrance Day (Nov 11); and Christmas (Dec 25 and 26).

MONTREAL & QUEBEC CITY CALENDAR OF EVENTS

From June to September, only a serious misadventure in planning might allow visitors to miss a celebration of some sort in Montréal and Québec City. If something's not going on in one city, it's bound to be happening in the other, and it's easy to get from one to the other.

February

Carnaval D'Hiver (de Québec), Québec City. Usually Québec is courtly and dignified, but all that is cast aside when the symbolic snowman called Bonhomme (Good Fellow) appears to preside over these 10 days of merriment in early February every year. During the event, more than a million revelers descend upon the city, eddying around the monumental ice palace and ice sculptures and attending a full schedule of concerts, dances, and parades. The mood is heightened by the availability of plastic trumpets and canes filled with a concoction called "Caribou," the principal ingredients of which are cheap whisky and sweet red wine. Perhaps its presence explains the eagerness with which certain Quebecois participate in the canoe race across the treacherous ice floes of the St. Lawrence.

Much of the Carnival is held in front of the Parliament Building—just outside the walls to the Old City—in early February. Hotel reservations must be made far in advance. Scheduled events are free. Call © **418/626-3716** for details.

La Fête des Neiges (Snow Festival), Montréal. Montréal's answer to Québec City's Carnaval d'Hiver (Winter Carnival) features outdoor events such as harness racing, barrel jumping, racing beds on ice, canoe races, snowshoeing, skating, and cross-country skiing. The less athletically inclined can cheer from the sidelines and then inspect the beautiful snow and ice sculptures. The event, held during the first 2 weeks of February, takes place mostly on Ile Notre-Dame, in the Port and Vieux-Montréal, and in Parc Maisonneuve. Call © **514/872-4537** for details.

Festival Montréal en Lumière. Filling a hole in the yearly schedule, the self-dubbed City of Festivals has created this "High Lights" celebration. It brings together a somewhat disparate collection of creative and performing events, from nearly 200 culinary competitions and special museum exhibitions to multimedia light shows and classical and pop concerts by international musical greats. Call © **888/515-0515** or see www.montrealhighlights.com for more information. Three long weekends in February.

May/June

Festival de Théâtre des Amériques, Montréal. Two weeks of contemporary theater works from artists throughout the Americas, many on the cutting edge of creativity. Performances are held at theaters throughout the city. Call © **514/842-0704** or see www.fta.qc.ca for details. Late May to early June.

Montréal Museums Day. On this day museums are free for all visitors, and free shuttle buses carry visitors to most of them. Call the tourism office (© **877/266-5687**) for details. Last Sunday in May.

Montréal Bike Fest. Early in June, more than 45,000 enthusiasts converge on Montréal to participate in a variety of cycling competitions, including a nocturnal bike ride, a 26km (16-mile) outing for up to 10,000 children, and the grueling Tour de l'Ile, a day-long 66km (41-mile) race around the rim of the island before more than 120,000 spectators. The Tour de l'Ile, which began in 1984, attracts 30,000 participants, almost as many of them women as men. Call © **888/899-1111** for details. First Sunday in June.

Grand Prix Air Canada, Montréal. The festival season kicks into screaming high gear when international drivers lay rubber for 70 laps around the Gilles-Villeneuve racetrack on Ile Notre-Dame. It's the only Formula I race in the country, and glamour attends, with celebs and models visiting the pits and revving up the après-race venues. Call © **514/457-5754** or check www.grandprix.ca for details. Second weekend in June.

Montréal Fringe Festival. In performance spaces clustered along or near bd. St-Laurent, about 60 theater groups perform in highly esoteric productions that often defy classification. As in all such endeavors, satisfaction cannot be guaranteed, but then, tickets are only C$10 and you may find a gem. Call © **514/849-3378** or check www.montrealfringe.ca. Ten days starting in mid-June.

Festival Mondial de la Bière, Montréal. Yes, brew fans, this is a 5-day festival devoted to your favorite beverage. From world brands to boutique microbreweries, over 70 companies showcase over 250 brands of their pride-and-joys, employing workshops, cooking demos, musical performances, and, of course, pub food and tastings, tastings, tastings of the featured hoppy tipple. For info and tickets, call © **514/722-9640** or check www.festivalmondialbiere.qc.ca.

Mosaïcultures Internationales Montréal. The resourceful minds of Québec's promoters never stop churning. This fragrant horticultural event has gardeners and floral designers from up to 50 countries and cities creating (sometimes large) three-dimensional floral sculptures and carpets for prizes in several categories. The Vieux-Port (Old Port) is the venue. Call © **514/868-4000** or check www.mosaiculture.ca. Late June to early October.

Jean-Baptiste Day. Honoring Saint John the Baptist, the patron saint of French Canadians, this *fête nationale* is marked by more festivities and far more enthusiasm throughout Québec province than Canada Day on July 1. It's Québec's "national" holiday. In the past, its hallmark parade had been marred by considerable drunkenness and vandalism in both Montréal and Québec City. A couple of years ago, in a successful effort to control such problems, the parade was held along the streets of Vieux-Montréal on the night of June 23, the day before the actual holiday. Call ✆ **418/849-2560** for details. June 24.

International Competition d'Art Pyrotechnique (International Fireworks Competition), Montréal. The open-air theater in La Ronde amusement park on Ile Ste-Hélène is the best place to view this fireworks extravaganza, although fireworks can be enjoyed from almost any point overlooking the river. Tickets to the show also provide entrance to the amusement park. Kids, needless to say, love the whole explosive business. The 90-minute shows are staged by companies from several countries. Because parking is limited, it's best to use the Métro. Call ✆ **514/872-4537** for details. Saturdays in late June, Sundays in July.

July

Festival International de Jazz de Montréal. Montréal has a long tradition in jazz, and this enormously successful festival has been celebrating America's one true art form since 1979. Miles Davis, Chet Baker, and Dizzie Gillespie have been among the many headliners in past years, but it costs money to hear stars of such magnitude. Fortunately, hundreds of other concerts are free, and are often presented on the streets and plazas of the city. You can see events along rue Ste-Catherine and rue Jeanne-Mance. For information and tickets, call ✆ **888/515-0515** or 514/871-1881; www.montrealjazz fest.com. Late June to early July.

Festival d'Eté International (International Summer Festival), Québec City. The largest cultural event in the French-speaking world, this festival has attracted artists from Africa, Asia, Europe, and North America since it began in 1967. There are more than 250 events showcasing theater, music, and dance, with 600 performers from 20 countries. One million people come to watch and listen. Jazz and folk combos perform free in an open-air theater next to City Hall; visiting dance and folklore troupes put on shows; and concerts, theatrical productions, and related events fill the days and evenings. Call ✆ **418/532-4540** for details or check www.infofestival.com. Ten days in mid-July.

Festival International Nuits d'Afrique, Montréal. This World Beat musical event showcases nearly 300 musicians from the Caribbean, the Americas, and Africa. Performances take place in Club Soda, Club Balattou, and Place Berri. Call ✆ **514/499-9239** or check out www.festnuitafric.com for details. Ten days in mid-July.

Festival Juste pour Rire (Just for Laughs Festival), Montréal. This celebration strives to do for humor what the more famous jazz festival has done for that musical form. Comics perform in many venues, some free, some not. Both Francophone and Anglophone comics, jugglers, and other funny acts from many countries participate. It's held along rue St-Denis and elsewhere in the Latin Quarter. Call ✆ **514/790-4242** for details or check www.hahaha.com. Ten days in mid-July.

Grands Feux Loto-Québec, Québec City. The capital has its own fireworks festival, overlapping the one in Montréal, and using the highly scenic Montmorency Falls as its setting. Five pyrotechnical teams are invited from as many different countries in this international competition. Their explosive displays are coordinated with appropriate music, as in Montréal. Call ✆ **418/692-3736** or check www.lesgrands feux.com. Wednesdays and Saturdays in late July to mid-August.

August

Les Medievales de Québec (Québec Medieval Festival), Québec City. Hundreds of actors, artists, entertainers, and other participants from Europe, Canada, and the United States converge on Québec City in period dress to recreate daily scenes from 5 centuries ago, playing knights, troubadours, and ladies-in-waiting during this event, a giant costume party. Parades, jousting tournaments, recitals of ancient music, and the Grand Cavalcade (La Grande Chevauchée), featuring hundreds of costumed equestrians, are just a few highlights. Fireworks are the one modern touch during this 5-day festival. Come in medieval attire if you wish. Held in Québec City only in odd-numbered years. (In even-numbered years, its sister event, the Festival des Remparts, takes place in Dinan, France.) Held in the streets and public grounds of Old Québec. Call ✆ **418/692-1993** for details. Early to mid-August.

Festival des Films du Monde (World Film Festival), Montréal. An international film event since 1976. Some 500 indoor and outdoor screenings take place over 12 days, including 200 feature films from more than 50 countries, drawing the usual throngs of directors, stars, and wannabes. It isn't as gaudy or as media-heavy as Cannes, but it's taken almost as seriously. Various movie theaters play host. Call ✆ **514/848-3883** for details. Late August to early September.

September

Fall Foliage. The maple trees blaze with color and a walk in the parks and squares of Montréal and Québec City is a refreshing tonic. It's a perfect time for a drive in the Laurentians or the Eastern Townships (near Montréal) and Ile d'Orléans or up into Charlevoix from Québec City. Mid- to late September.

October

Festival International de la Nouvelle Danse, Montréal. This 12-day showcase, held every 2 years (in odd years), invites troupes and choreographers from Canada, the United States, and Europe to various performance spaces. Call ✆ **514/287-1423** for details. Early October.

Festival du Nouveau Cinéma, Montréal. Screenings of new and experimental films ignite controversy and forums on the latest trends in film and video at halls and cinemas throughout the city. Call ✆ **514/843-4725** for details. Ten days in mid-October.

December/January

Christmas/New Year's. Celebrating the holidays a la Française is a particular treat in Québec City, with its streets banked with snow and almost every ancient building sporting wreaths and decorated fir trees.

5 Insurance & Health

TRAVEL INSURANCE AT A GLANCE

Check your existing insurance policies before you buy travel insurance to cover trip cancellation, lost luggage, medical expenses, or car rental insurance. You're likely to have partial or complete coverage. But if you need some, ask your travel agent about a comprehensive package or contact one of the following popular insurers:

- **Access America** (℡ **800/284-8300;** www.accessamerica.com/)
- **Travel Guard International** (℡ **800/826-1300;** www.travel guard.com)
- **Travel Insured International** (℡ **800/243-3174;** www.travel insured.com)
- **Travelex Insurance Services** (℡ **800/228-9792;** www.travelex-insurance.com)

CAR RENTAL INSURANCE (LOSS/DAMAGE WAIVER OR COLLISION DAMAGE WAIVER)

If you hold a private auto insurance policy, you probably are covered in the U.S., but not abroad, for loss or damage to the car, and liability in case a passenger is injured. The credit card you use to rent the car also may provide some coverage.

Car rental insurance probably does not cover liability if you caused the accident. Check your own auto insurance policy, the rental company policy, and your credit card coverage for the extent of coverage: Is your destination covered? Are other drivers covered? How much liability is covered if a passenger is injured? (If you rely on your credit card for coverage, you may want to bring a 2nd credit card with you, as damages may be charged to your card and you may find yourself stranded with no money.)

Car rental insurance costs about $20 a day.

MEDICAL INSURANCE

Most health insurance policies cover you if you get sick away from home—but check, particularly if you're insured by an HMO. With the exception of certain HMOs and Medicare/Medicaid, your medical insurance should cover medical treatment—even

hospital care—overseas. However, most out-of-country hospitals make you pay your bills up front, and send you a refund after you've returned home and filed the necessary paperwork. Members of **Blue Cross/Blue Shield** can now use their cards at select hospitals in most major cities worldwide (℡ **800/810-BLUE** or www.blue cares.com for a list of hospitals). If you require additional insurance, try one of the following companies:

- **MEDEX International,** 9515 Deereco Rd., Timonium, MD 21093-5375 (℡ **888/MEDEX-00** or 410/453-6300; fax 410/453-6301; www.medexassist.com).
- **Travel Assistance International** (℡ **800/821-2828;** www.travel assistance.com), 9200 Keystone Crossing, Suite 300, Indianapolis, IN 46240 (for general information on services, call the company's Worldwide Assistance Services, Inc., at ℡ **800/777-8710**).

LOST-LUGGAGE INSURANCE

On domestic flights, checked baggage is covered up to $2,500 per ticketed passenger. On international flights (including U.S. portions of international trips), baggage is limited to approximately $9.10 per pound, up to approximately $635 per checked bag. If you plan to check items more valuable than the standard liability, you may purchase "excess valuation" coverage from the airline, up to $5,000. If you file a lost luggage claim, be prepared to answer detailed questions about the contents of your baggage, and be sure to file a claim immediately, as most airlines enforce a 21-day deadline. You will only be reimbursed for what you lost, no more. Once you've filed a complaint, persist in securing your reimbursement; there are no laws governing the length of time it takes for a carrier to reimburse you. If you arrive at a destination without your bags, ask the airline to forward them to your hotel or to your next destination; they will usually comply. If your bag is delayed or lost, the airline may reimburse you for reasonable expenses, such as a toothbrush or a set of clothes, but the airline is under no legal obligation to do so.

Lost luggage may also be covered by your homeowner's or renter's policy. Many platinum and gold credit cards cover you as well. If you choose to purchase additional lost-luggage insurance, be sure not to buy more than you need. Buy in advance from the insurer or a trusted agent (prices will be much higher at the airport).

THE HEALTHY TRAVELER
WHAT TO DO IF YOU GET SICK AWAY FROM HOME

If you worry about getting sick away from home, consider purchasing **medical travel insurance** and carry your ID card in your purse or wallet. In most cases, your existing health plan will provide the coverage you need. See the section on insurance on p. 21 for more information.

If you suffer from a chronic illness, consult your doctor before your departure. For conditions like epilepsy, diabetes, or heart problems, wear a **Medic Alert Identification Tag** (© 800/ 825-3785; www.medicalert.org), which will immediately alert doctors

to your condition and give them access to your records through Medic Alert's 24-hour hot line.

Pack **prescription medications** in your carry-on luggage, and carry prescription medications in their original containers. Also bring along copies of your prescriptions in case you lose your pills or run out. Carry the generic name of prescription medicines, in case a local pharmacist is unfamiliar with the brand name.

And don't forget sunglasses and an extra pair of contact lenses or prescription glasses.

Contact the **International Association for Medical Assistance to Travelers (IAMAT; © 716/754-4883** or 416/652-0137; www.iamat.org) for tips on travel and health concerns in Canada, and lists of local, English-speaking doctors. Any foreign consulate can provide a list of area doctors who speak English. If you get sick, consider asking your hotel concierge to recommend a local doctor—even his or her own. You can also try the emergency room at a local hospital; many have walk-in clinics for emergency cases that are not life-threatening. You may not get immediate attention, but you won't pay the high price of an emergency room visit (usually a minimum of C$300 just for signing your name).

6 Tips for Travelers with Special Needs

FOR TRAVELERS WITH DISABILITIES

When calling to make an airline reservation or talking with a travel agent, inquire where a wheelchair will be stowed on the plane or train, or confirm that a Seeing Eye dog or hearing dog may accompany you. Remember that special meals can be pre-ordered when making airline reservations.

Québec regulations regarding accessibility for wheelchairs are similar to

those in the United States, including curb cuts, entrance ramps, designated parking spaces, and specially equipped bathrooms. However, access to the restaurants and inns housed in 18th- and 19th-century buildings, especially in Québec City, is often difficult or impossible.

Advice for travelers with physical limitations is provided in a brochure, *Accès Tourisme*. It lists hundreds of accessible hotels, restaurants, theaters, and museums. The price is C$15 (US$10) from Kéroul, 4545 av. Pierre de Coubertin, P.O. Box 1000, Station M, Montréal, Québec H1V 3R2 (© **514/252-3104**; www.keroul. qc.ca).

AGENCIES/OPERATORS

- **Flying Wheels Travel** (© **800/ 535-6790**; www.flyingwheels travel.com) offers escorted tours and cruises that emphasize sports and private tours in minivans with lifts.
- **Access Adventures** (© **716/889-9096**), a Rochester, New York–based agency, offers customized itineraries for a variety of travelers with disabilities.
- **Accessible Journeys** (© **800/ TINGLES** or 610/521-0339; www.disabilitytravel.com) caters specifically to slow walkers and wheelchair travelers and their families and friends.

ORGANIZATIONS

- **The Moss Rehab Hospital** (© **215/456-9603**; www.moss resourcenet.org) provides friendly, helpful phone assistance through its **Travel Information Service.**
- **The Society for Accessible Travel and Hospitality** (© **212/447-7284;** fax 212/725-8253; www. sath.org) offers a wealth of travel resources for all types of disabilities and informed recommendations on destinations, access guides, travel agents, tour operators, vehicle rentals, and companion services. Annual membership costs US$45 for adults; US$30 for seniors and students.
- **The American Foundation for the Blind** (© **800/232-5463;** www.afb.org) provides information on traveling with Seeing Eye dogs.

PUBLICATIONS

- **Mobility International USA** (© **541/343-1284;** www.miusa. org) publishes *A World of Options,* a 658-page book of resources, covering everything from biking trips to scuba outfitters, and a biannual newsletter, *Over the Rainbow.* Annual membership is $35.

FOR SENIORS

Senior discounts of 10% or 15% are offered by many airlines, but aren't necessarily the cheapest fares available. Check to see if there are limited promotional fares that might constitute even greater savings. Amtrak offers seniors 62 and older a 15% discount on the U.S. segment of some of its fares between New York City and Montréal, a trip that takes 10 to 12 hours. Carry proof of age in order to obtain possible discounts at hotels, restaurants, and most museums and other attractions—driver's license, passport, Medicare card, and/or AARP membership card. While hotels, airlines, Amtrak, and car-rental agencies routinely give discounts to AARP members, you must ask. For membership, write to the **AARP,** 601 E St. NW, Washington, DC 20049 (© **800/424-3410** or 202/434-2277; www.aarp.com). Most museums, cinemas, theaters, and other attractions in Québec have lower admission prices for seniors, usually defined as 65 and over, but sometimes as 60 or 62.

AGENCIES/OPERATORS

- **Grand Circle Travel** (© **800/ 221-2610** or 617/350-7500; www.gct.com) offers package deals for the 50-plus market, mostly of the tour-bus variety, with free trips thrown in for those who organize groups of 10 or more.
- **Elderhostel** (© **877/426-8056;** www.elderhostel.org) arranges study programs for those aged 55 and over (and a spouse or companion of any age).

- **Interhostel** (© 800/733-9753; www.learn.unh.edu/interhostel), organized by the University of New Hampshire, also offers educational travel for seniors. On these escorted tours, the days are packed with seminars, lectures, and field trips, with sightseeing led by academic experts. **Interhostel** takes travelers 50 and over (with companions over 40), and offers 1- and 2-week trips, mostly internationally.

FOR SINGLE TRAVELERS

Two problems crop up most often for solo travelers: added costs and feelings of isolation, especially on Friday and Saturday nights, when everyone else seems to be out and about in numbers divisible by two. Check the sections in this book on popular local bars (see chapters 9 and 17), for possibilities for meeting locals and engaging in some lively conversation. Jazz and folk music spots, especially those that charge no cover—and most in Montréal and Québec City do not—are also fertile grounds for meeting and chatting with Quebecois.

Bed-and-breakfast inns are often a good choice for meeting people, and both Montréal and Québec City have them. Guests come together over breakfast and might end up going out to explore or dine together. Prices are often (but not always) lower than those at hotels, many of which charge the same rate for a room whether it's occupied by one or two people. Guided walking tours are another excellent way to explore the city and enjoy a couple of hours of social interaction at the same time.

FOR GAY & LESBIAN TRAVELERS

In Montréal, gay and lesbian travelers enjoy the Gay Village, primarily along rue Ste-Catherine est between rue St-Hubert and rue Papineau, where there are numerous meeting spots, shops, cafes, bars, and clubs. Useful telephone services are the **Gay Line** (© 514/866-5090 or 888/505-1010 outside the 514 area code), which describes current events and activities in English, daily from 7 to 10pm. To increase the chances of meeting people, try to visit the city during the annual Diver/Cité, the Gay & Lesbian Pride Festival; it takes place in late July to early August, with a parade, concerts, parties, and art shows (© 514/285-4011). During the second week of October in Montréal, the **Black & Blue Festival** is 7 days of gay benefit parties at various locations throughout the city (© 514/875-7026). Two websites that may prove useful are www.gaywired.com and www.fugues.com. The latter is a leisure guide to gay life in Montréal and other Québec cities; you can find the printed version in bars and hotels in and around the Village. Additional information is available at **The Village Tourist Information Centre** at 1260 rue Ste-Catherine est opposite the Bleury métro station (© 514/522-1885; www.infovillagegai.com).

The gay community in Québec City is relatively small, centered in the Upper Town just outside the city walls, near Porte Saint-Jean. At the end of August, a 5-day gay festival, **Fête Arc-en-Ciel,** is held in the city. Call © 418/264-3365 for information.

AGENCIES/OPERATORS

- **Above and Beyond Tours** (© 800/397-2681; www.above beyondtours.com) offers gay and lesbian tours worldwide and is the exclusive gay and lesbian tour operator for United Airlines.
- **Now, Voyager** (© 800/255-6951; www.nowvoyager.com) is a San Francisco–based gay-owned and operated travel service.

PUBLICATIONS

- *Out and About* (℅ **800/929-2268** or 415/644-8044; www.outandabout.com) offers guidebooks and a newsletter 10 times a year packed with solid information on the global gay and lesbian scene.
- *Spartacus International Gay Guide* and *Odysseus* are good, annual English-language guidebooks focused on gay men, with some information for lesbians. You can get them from most gay and lesbian bookstores, or order them from **Giovanni's Room** bookstore, 1145 Pine St., Philadelphia, PA 19107 (℅ **215/923-2960;** www.giovannisroom.com).
- *Gay Travel A to Z: The World of Gay & Lesbian Travel Options at Your Fingertips,* by Marianne Ferrari (Ferrari Publications; Box 35575, Phoenix, AZ 85069) is a very good gay and lesbian guidebook series.

FAMILY TRAVEL

Montréal and Québec City offer an abundance of family-oriented activities, many of them outdoors, even in winter. Dog-sledding, watersports, river cruises, and frequent festivals and fireworks displays are among the family-friendly attractions. The walls and fortifications of Québec City are fodder for imagining the days of knights and princesses, and both cities have horse-drawn sightseeing carriages, a surefire hit with most youngsters. Many museums make special efforts to address children's interests and enthusiasms. For more details, see the "Especially for Kids" sections in chapters 6 and 14.

AGENCIES/OPERATORS

- **Familyhostel** (℅ **800/733-9753;** www.learn.unh.edu/familyhostel) takes the whole family on moderately priced domestic and international learning vacations. For kids

ages 8 to 15 accompanied by their parents and/or grandparents.

PUBLICATIONS

- *How to Take Great Trips with Your Kids* (The Harvard Common Press) is full of good general travel advice.

FOR STUDENTS

Many of the tips that apply to single travelers apply to students (who may or may not be traveling solo). Always carry a university or similar ID card to obtain the many available discounts, especially at museums and other attractions. Both Montréal and Québec City have their designated Latin Quarters, centrally located university areas filled with students.

To save money on lodging, consider the YMCA or the YWCA in Montréal and hostels in Québec City. For information about hostels in Québec and the rest of Canada, contact **Hostelling International,** 400–205 Catherine St., Ottawa, ON K2P 1C3 (℅ **613/237-7884;** www.hihostels.ca).

If you're planning to travel outside the U.S., you'd be wise to arm yourself with an **international student I.D. card,** which offers substantial savings on rail passes, plane tickets, and entrance fees. It also provides you with basic health and life insurance and a 24-hour help line. The card is available for $22 from the **Council on International Educational Exchange,** or CIEE (www.ciee.org). The CIEE's travel branch, **Council Travel Service** (℅ **800/226-8624;** www.counciltravel.com), is the biggest student travel agency in the world. If you're no longer a student but are still under 26, you can get a **GO 25 card** from the same people, which entitles you to insurance and some discounts (but not on museum admissions). **STA Travel** (℅ **800/781-4040;** www.statravel.com) is another travel agency catering especially to young travelers, although their bargain-basement prices are available to people of all ages.

In London, **Campus Travel** (© 020/7730-2101), opposite Victoria Station, is Britain's leading specialist in student and youth travel.

7 Getting There

Served by highways, transcontinental trains and buses, and three international airports, Montréal and Québec City are easily accessible from any part of the United States and Europe.

BY PLANE

TO MONTREAL   Dorval International Airport serves most of the world's major airlines, nearly 50 in all. (Mirabel Airport, farther from the city, now accepts only airfreight and some charter flights.) Most visitors fly into Dorval from other parts of North America on **Air Canada** (© 888/ 247-2262), **American** (© 800/433- 7300), **Continental** (© 800/231- 0856), **Delta** (© 800/221-1212), or **US Airways** (© 800/432-9768). In the United States, Air Canada flies out of New York (Newark and LaGuardia), Miami, Tampa, Chicago, Los Angeles, and San Francisco.

Other carriers that serve Montréal include **Air France** (© 800/847- 1106) and **British Airways** (© 800/ 243-6822). Regional airlines, such as Air Atlantic, American Eagle, and Inter-Canadian, also serve the city.

For details on getting from the airport to downtown and the city center, see page 34.

TO QUEBEC CITY   Québec City is served from the United States by a number of major airlines, notably Air Canada, but most air traffic comes by way of Montréal (see above) or Toronto. Direct flights are available from New York (Newark) on **Air Alliance,** a connector airline for Air Canada (© **800/361-8620** in Canada, or 800/776-3000 outside Canada). **Continental** flies into Québec City from international destinations outside the U.S. (© **800/525-0280**). **Air Canada** (© **800/361-8620**), and **Tango** (© **800/315-1390**), a new, low-fare subsidiary of Air Canada, are good choices for flying from Montréal to Québec City and vice versa.

For details on getting from the airport to downtown and the city center, see page 185.

AIR TRAVEL SECURITY MEASURES

In the wake of the terrorist attacks of September 11, 2001, the airline industry implemented sweeping security measures in airports. Expect a lengthier check-in process and possible delays. Although regulations vary from airline to airline, you can expedite the process by taking the following steps: Arrive at the airport at least 2 hours before your scheduled flight. Try not to drive your car to the airport because parking may be limited. Be sure to carry plenty of documentation (a government-issued photo ID is now required). Check The Transportation Security Administration (TSA) website at www.tsa.gov to find out what you can carry on and what you can't.

FLYING FOR LESS: TIPS FOR GETTING THE BEST AIRFARE

Passengers within the same airplane cabin rarely pay the same fare for their seats. Business travelers who need to purchase tickets at the last minute, change their itinerary, or get home before the weekend pay the premium rate, the full fare. Passengers who can book their tickets long in advance, who don't mind staying over Saturday night, or who are willing to travel on a Tuesday, Wednesday, or Thursday after 7pm will pay a fraction of the full fare. On most flights, even the shortest hops, a 7-day or 14-day advance purchase ticket can save you hundreds of dollars. Here are a few other easy ways to save:

- Periodically airlines lower prices on their most popular routes. Check your newspaper for advertised discounts, or call the airlines directly and ask if any **promotional rates** or special fares are available. If your schedule is flexible, ask if you can secure a cheaper fare by staying an extra day or by flying midweek. (Many airlines won't volunteer this information.) If you already hold a ticket when a sale breaks, it may even pay to exchange your ticket, which usually incurs a $50 to $75 charge.

  Note that the lowest-priced fares are often nonrefundable, require advance purchase of 1 to 3 weeks and a certain length of stay, and carry penalties for changing dates of travel.

- **Consolidators,** also known as bucket shops, are a good place to find low fares. Consolidators buy seats in bulk from the airlines and then sell them back to the public at prices below even the airlines' discounted rates. Their small ads usually run in the Sunday travel sections of most major newspapers. Before you pay, however, ask for a confirmation number from the consolidator, and then call the airline itself to confirm your seat. Be prepared to book your ticket with a different consolidator—there are many to choose from—if the airline can't confirm your reservation. Also be aware that bucket-shop tickets are usually nonrefundable or rigged with stiff cancellation penalties, often as high as 50% to 75% of the ticket price.

- **Council Travel** (② 800/228-6245; www.counciltravel.com) and **STA Travel** (② 800/781-4040; www.statravel.com) cater especially to young travelers, but their bargain-basement prices are available to people of all ages. Other reliable consolidators include FlyCheap.com (② 800/FLY-CHEAP); **TFI Tours International** (② 800/745-8000 or 212/736-1140; www.lowestairprice.com), which serves as a clearinghouse for unused seats; and "rebators" such as **Travel Avenue** (② 800/333-3335 or 312/876-1116; www.travelavenue.com), which rebate part of their commissions to you.

- Search the **Internet** for cheap fares—but know that it's still best to compare your findings with the research of an experienced travel agent. For full details on surfing the Web, see "Planning Your Trip Online," later in this chapter.

The way to get the cheapest flight of all may be to book an escorted tour or a package that includes airfare and accommodations. See "Package & Escorted Tours," below, for details.

BY TRAIN

For **VIA Rail** information, call ② 888/VIA-RAIL (842-7245) or log on to www.viarail.ca.

TO MONTREAL Montréal is a major terminus on Canada's **VIA Rail** network, with its station, **Gare Centrale,** at 935 rue de la Gauchetière Ouest (② 514/871-1331). The city is served by comfortable VIA Rail trains—some equipped with dining cars, sleeping cars, and cellphones—from other cities in Canada. There is scheduled service to Québec City via Trois-Rivières, and to and from Ottawa, Toronto, Winnipeg, and points west. Although there have been threats that the company might be closed down, at this writing, **Amtrak** (✆ **800/USA-RAIL [872-7245];** www.amtrak.com) has one train a day to Montréal from Washington and New York that makes intermediate stops. While it is a no-frills, coach-only affair, its scenic route passes along the eastern shore of the Hudson River and west of Lake Champlain. The Adirondack takes about 10½ hours from New York if all goes well, but delays aren't unusual.

Passengers from Chicago can get to Montréal most directly by taking Amtrak to Toronto, then switching to VIA Rail.

Fairmont The Queen Elizabeth (Le Reine Elizabeth) hotel is located directly above the train station in Montréal, and less expensive lodging is only a short cab or Métro ride away. Seniors 62 and older are eligible for a 15% discount on some Amtrak trains on the U.S. segment of the trip. VIA Rail has a 10% senior discount. Don't forget to bring along proof of citizenship (a passport or birth certificate) to use when crossing the border.

TO QUEBEC CITY   Québec City's train station, the **Gare du Palais,** is in the Lower Town at 450 rue de la Gare-du-Palais (✆ **418/692-3940**). At least four trains run between Montréal and Québec City daily between 7am and 11pm, and they have snack and beverage services. Travel time between the two cities is about 3 hours. One-way fares vary substantially, with many kinds of discounts for seniors, students, and different fares for different days of departure, but prices generally run from about C$37 (US$24) for supersaver economy class to around C$105 (US$52) for first-class, which provides meal service and more legroom.

BY BUS

TO MONTREAL   Montréal's main bus terminal is the **Terminus Voyageur,** 505 bd. de Maisonneuve

Est (✆ **514/842-2281**). The Voyageur company operates buses between here and all parts of Québec, with frequent runs through the Cantons-de-l'Est to Sherbrooke, to the various villages in the Laurentians, and to Québec City. Morning, noon, early afternoon, and midnight buses cover the distance between Toronto and Montréal in less than 7 hours. From Boston or New York, there is daily bus service to Montréal on **Greyhound** (✆ **800/229-9424** or 514/843-8495; www.greyhound.com) and between New York and Montréal on **Adirondack Trailways** (✆ **514/843-8495**). The trip from Boston takes about 8 hours; from New York City, with five departures daily, it takes 9 hours.

TO QUEBEC CITY   From New York or Boston, take **Greyhound** (✆ **800/231-2222**) to Montréal and change for the bus to Québec City, a 3-hour ride away. The bus traffic between Québec City and Montréal is frequent, with express buses from **Orléans Express** (✆ **514/842-2281** in Montréal, or **418/524-4692** in Québec City), running almost every hour on the hour from 7am to 1am. The bus line also links Québec City to the rest of Québec province, with connections to the rest of Canada. Ask about excursion tickets and discounts for seniors and children.

BY CAR

Highway distances and speed limits are given in kilometers (km) in Canada. The speed limit on the autoroutes (limited-access highways) is 100km per hour (62 mph), although enforcement is lax. In the unlikely event you are stopped, there is a stiff penalty for not wearing seatbelts. And if you possess a radar detector, it can be confiscated, even if it isn't connected. Passengers must buckle up in the backseat as well as in the driver's and passenger's seats up front.

Members of the **American Automobile Association (AAA)** should bring along their membership cards. The 24-hour hot line for emergency service provided by the **Canadian Automobile Association (CAA),** which is affiliated with AAA, is *©* **514/861-7575** in Montréal and *©* **418/624-0708** in Québec City. Headquarters for CAA-Québec is 444 rue Bouvier, Québec City, PQ G2J 1E3.

For information on road conditions in and around Québec City from November through mid-April, there is a 24-hour hot line (*©* **418/643-6830**). For the same information in Montréal, call *©* **514/284-2363;** outside Montréal, call *©* **514/636-3248.**

TO MONTREAL Interstate 87 runs due north from New York City to link up with Canada's Autoroute 15 at the border, and the entire 644km (400-mile) journey is on expressways. Likewise, from Boston, I-93 north joins I-89 just south of Concord, New Hampshire. At White River Junction there is a choice between continuing on I-89 to Lake Champlain, crossing the lake by roads and bridges to join I-87 and Canada Autoroute 15 north, or picking up I-91 at White River Junction to go due north toward Sherbrooke, Québec. At the border, I-91 becomes Canada Route 55 and joins Canada Route 10 west through Estrie to Montréal. The Trans-Canada Highway, which connects both ends of the country, runs right through Montréal. From Boston to Montréal is about 515km (320 miles); from Toronto, 540km (350 miles); from Ottawa, 190km (120 miles). Once you're in Montréal, Québec City is an easy 3-hour drive.

TO QUEBEC CITY Québec City is slightly more than 805km (500 miles) from New York, and less than 644km (400 miles) from Boston. Coming from New York and points farther south, pick up Interstate 91 at New Haven, and follow it right up to the Canadian border. From Boston, take I-93 out of the city and link up with I-91 at St. Johnsbury, Vermont. After crossing the border, I-91 becomes Québec Autoroute 55, to Sherbrooke and Drummondville. From Sherbrooke, there is a choice. To make the trip quickly, take Autoroute 55 to Autoroute 20. But Route 116, which heads northeast from Richmond, midway between Sherbrooke and Drummondville, is more scenic, if a bit slower.

On the approach to the city, follow signs for Pont Pierre-Laporte. After crossing the bridge, turn right onto boulevard Wilfrid-Laurier (Rte. 175), which later changes names and becomes the Grande-Allée. Past the Old City walls it becomes rue St-Louis, which leads straight to the Château Frontenac. For the most scenic entrance into the city, take an immediate exit onto boulevard Champlain after crossing the bridge, and turn left at the entrance to Parc des Champs-de-Bataille (Battlefields Park), up a steep hill to follow Chemin Grande-Allée to the Musée du Québec. Drive halfway around the circle in front of the museum, and then take avenue Montcalm-Wolfe to the Grande-Allée and turn right.

When you're driving to Québec City from Montréal (a car can be rented in the train station), Autoroute 40, which runs along the north shore of the St. Lawrence, is faster than Autoroute 20, on the south shore. The trip takes less than 3 hours without stops.

8 Package & Escorted Tours

Before you start your search for the lowest airfare, you may want to consider booking your flight as part of a travel package such as an escorted tour or a package tour. What you lose in adventure, you'll gain in time and money saved when you book accommodations, and maybe even food and entertainment, along with your flight.

ESCORTED TOURS & CRUISES

There are ample reasons for taking an escorted tour: to save money, to have someone else make the arrangements and deal with glitches in a foreign language, and to travel with built-in companions. There are disadvantages, too, however: rising, eating, and sleeping on someone else's schedule; abiding by the decisions of the group and the tour guide; and traveling in a unilingual bubble that works against interplay with members of the native population. In Québec, the pros aren't as strong as they might be in, say, India or Egypt. While French is the dominant language, there's almost always someone nearby who speaks English. The money is easy to comprehend, because it uses essentially the same denominations as in the United States, and prices are lower than at home. And the Québec tourism authorities are some of the most helpful and forthcoming in the world.

The following are some reputable escorted-tour operators. Make sure to ask as many questions as necessary, especially to find out exactly what is included in the price and what the cancellation policy is.

- **Air Canada** (© **800/925-4016,** ext. 8097) assembles custom packages that include round-trip air, lodging, sightseeing, and some meals in Québec City, Montréal, and Laurentian resorts.
- **Tauck Tours** (© **800/468-2825** or 203/226-6911; www.tauck. com) has a 7-day, 6-night tour that includes Vermont, New Hampshire, Montréal, and Québec City. It's offered spring to mid-October, and it is recommended

for providing the opportunity to view the fall foliage in both countries. For different perspectives, the company has a 7-night St. Lawrence River cruise from Rochester, NY to Kingston, Montréal, and Québec City, as well as a week's combined rail, boat, and coach tour from Montréal around the Gaspé Peninsula to Charlevoix and Québec City.

- **Yankee Holidays** (© **978/922-0461;** www.yankee-holidays.com) has packages of 2 to 5 nights in Montréal and Québec City. Dinners at prominent restaurants are often included, as is VIP admission to the Montréal Casino, plus bus tours and harbor cruises. Airfare is optional.
- **Cruises** from New York and New England through the Maritime Provinces and down the St. Lawrence to Québec City and Montréal are increasingly popular, especially from June through the foliage season. Among the lines offering these cruises, which are usually 6 to 12 days long, are **Clipper** (© 888/278-4732), **Crystal Cruises** (© 310/785-9300), **Holland America** (© 800/426-0327), **Norwegian** (© 800/327-7030), **Princess** (© 800/774-6237), **Seabourn** (© 800/528-6273), and **Silversea** (© 888/313-8883).
- Finally, railroad buffs may want to look into the new luxury train tour offered by **The Acadian Railway** (© **800/659-7602** or 866/91-TRAIN; www.Acadian Railway.com). Trains made up of about 10 rebuilt cars from the 1940s and 1950s, including domed dining cars, make trips of varying lengths through Québec and Nova Scotia, from June to early September.

PACKAGE TOURS

Package tours aren't the same thing as escorted tours. They are simply a way to buy airfare and accommodations at the same time. For popular destinations like Montréal and Québec City, they are a smart way to go, because they can save you a lot of money.

FINDING A PACKAGE DEAL

The best place to start your search is the travel section of your local Sunday newspaper. Also check the ads in the back of national travel magazines like *Travel & Leisure, National Geographic Traveler,* and *Condé Nast Traveler.* **Liberty Travel** (© **888/271-1584** for the agent closest to you; www. libertytravel.com), one of the biggest packagers in the Northeast, often runs a full-page ad in the Sunday papers. **American Express Vacations** (© **800/241-1700;** http://travel. americanexpress.com) is another option. Check out the "Last Minute Specials" on the website for deeply discounted vacation packages and reduced airline fares.

Another good resource is the airlines themselves, which often package their flights with accommodations. Fly-by-night packagers are uncommon, but they do exist; when you buy your package through the airline, however, you can be pretty sure that the company will still be in business when your departure date arrives. Among the airline packagers, options include **American Airlines FlyAway Vacations** (© 800/321-2121), **Delta Dream Vacations** (© 800/872-7786), and **US Airways Vacations** (© 800/455-0123).

9 Planning Your Trip Online

With a mouse, a modem, and a certain do-it-yourself determination, Internet users can tap into the same travel-planning databases that were once accessible only to travel agents. Sites such as **Travelocity, Expedia,** and **Orbitz** allow consumers to comparison shop for airfares, book flights, learn of last-minute bargains, and reserve hotel rooms and rental cars.

Check out:

- **Last-minute specials,** known as "E-savers," such as weekend deals or Internet-only fares, are offered by airlines to fill empty seats. Most of these are announced on Tuesday or Wednesday and must be purchased online. They are only valid for travel that weekend, but some can be booked weeks or months in advance. Sign up for weekly e-mail alerts at airline websites or check megasites that compile comprehensive lists of E-savers, such as Smarter Living (www.smarterliving.com) or Web-Flyer (www.webflyer.com).

- Some sites will send you **e-mail notification** when a cheap fare becomes available to your favorite destination. Some will also tell you when fares to a particular destination are lowest.

TRAVEL PLANNING & BOOKING SITES

The best travel planning and booking sites cast a wide net, offering domestic and international flights, hotel and rental-car bookings, plus news, destination information, and deals on cruises and vacation packages. Keep in mind that free (one-time) registration is often required for booking. Because several airlines are no longer willing to pay commissions on tickets sold by online travel agencies, be aware that these online agencies will either charge a $10 surcharge if you book a ticket on that carrier—or neglect to offer those air carriers' offerings.

Remember: This is a press-time snapshot of leading websites—some undoubtedly will have evolved or moved by the time you read this.

- **Travelocity** (www.travelocity. com) and **Expedia** (www.expedia. com) are the most longstanding and reputable sites, each offering excellent selections and easy searches for complete vacation packages. Travelers search by destination and dates coupled with how much they are willing to spend.

- The latest buzz in the online travel world is about **Orbitz** (www. orbitz.com), a site launched by United, Delta, Northwest, American, and Continental airlines. It shows all possible fares for your desired trip, offering fares lower than those available through travel agents.

- **Qixo** (www.qixo.com) is another powerful search engine that allows you to search for flights and hotel rooms on 20 other travel-planning sites (such as Travelocity) at once. Qixo sorts results by price, after which you can book your travel directly through the site.

SMART E-SHOPPING

The savvy traveler is one armed with good information. Here are a few tips to help you navigate the Internet successfully and safely.

- **Know when sales start.** Last-minute deals may vanish in minutes. If you have a favorite booking site or airline, find out when last-minute deals are released to the public. (For example, Southwest's specials are posted every Tues at 12:01am Central time.)

- **Shop around.** Compare results from different sites and airlines—and against a travel agent's best fare, if you can. If possible, try a range of times and alternate airports before you make a purchase.

- **Follow the rules of the trade.** Book in advance, and choose an off-peak time and date if possible. Some sites will tell you when fares to a particular destination tend to be cheapest.

- **Avoid online auctions.** Sites that auction airline tickets and frequent-flier miles are the number-one perpetrators of Internet fraud, according to the National Consumers League.

- **Maintain a paper trail.** If you book an e-ticket, print out a confirmation, or write down your confirmation number, and keep it safe and accessible—or your trip could be a virtual one!

10 Recommended Reading

Writing from the perspective of a minority within a minority, the late Jewish Anglophone Mordecai Richler inveighed against the excesses of Québec's separatists and language zealots in a barrage of books and critical essays in newspapers and magazines. His outrage and mordant wit can be sampled in *Oh Canada! Oh Québec!* (Knopf, 1992) and *Home Sweet Home: My Canadian Album* (Knopf, 1984; paperback, Penguin, 1985). An amusing, less caustic look at the Anglophone-Francophone conflict is provided by *The Anglo Guide to Survival in Québec* (Eden Press, 1983). A serious, relatively balanced view—with a slight lean to the French-Canadian side of the issue—is given by Brian Young and John A. Dickinson in *A Short History of Québec: A Socio-Economic Perspective* (Copp Clark Pitman Ltd., 1988). One of the authors taught at McGill University, the other at the Université de Montréal.

3

Getting to Know Montréal

For a city of 1.8 million inhabitants, getting to know and getting around Montréal is remarkably easy. Dorval Airport is only 23km (14 miles) away, and once you're in town, the Métro (subway) system is fast and efficient. Walking, of course, is the best way to enjoy and appreciate this vigorous, multidimensional city, neighborhood by neighborhood.

1 Orientation

ARRIVING

BY PLANE The **Aéroport de Dorval** (© **800/465-1213** or 514/394-7377; www.admtl.com) is 22km (14 miles) southwest of downtown, and accepts nearly all commercial flights. A new $145 million annex is planned for international flights, with completion expected by 2003. The ride into town takes less than 30 minutes if traffic isn't tangled, and a taxi trip costs about C$28 (US$18) plus tip. Montréal's **Aéroport Mirabel,** 55km (34 miles) northwest of the city, used to accept most international carriers from outside North America, but now receives only freight and charter flights. You'll need to take a taxi from Mirabel.

Dorval is served by **L'Aérobus** (© **513/931-9002**), which shuttles between the airport and the company's downtown terminal at 777 rue de la Gauchetiére ouest, near The Queen Elizabeth (Fairmont Le Reine Elizabeth) hotel. Free minibuses take passengers from the terminal to 41 major hotels. Schedules are changed frequently, but buses usually operate daily every 20 to 30 minutes from Dorval between 5:10am and 11:10pm. One-way fares are C$11 (US$7.10) for adults, C$7.50 (US$4.85) for children ages 5 to 12, and free for kids under 5.

BY TRAIN Montréal has one intercity rail terminus, **Gare Centrale** (Central Station), situated directly beneath The Queen Elizabeth (Fairmont Le Reine Elizabeth) hotel at the corner of boulevard René-Lévesque and rue Mansfield. Gare Centrale (© **514/871-1331**) is part of the underground city and is connected to the Métro (Bonaventure Station).

BY BUS The bus station, called **Terminus Voyageur** (© **514/842-2281**), has a bar, a cafeteria, and a travel agency. There is a rental-car desk and an information booth. Beneath the terminal is the Berri-UQAM Métro station, the junction of several important Métro lines and a good starting point for trips to most quarters of the city. (UQAM—pronounced "*oo*-kahm"—stands for Université de Québec à Montréal.) Alternatively, taxis usually line up outside the terminal building.

BY CAR For driving directions to Montréal, see "Getting There," in chapter 2.

VISITOR INFORMATION

The main information center for visitors in Montréal is the large and efficiently organized **Infotouriste Centre,** at 1001 rue du Square-Dorchester (© **877/266-5687** from anywhere in Canada and the U.S., or 514/873-2015), between rue Peel and rue Metcalfe in the downtown hotel and business district. To get there, take the Métro to the Peel stop. The office is open daily from late June through early September from 8:30am to 7:30pm, and early September through May from 9am to 5pm (closed Christmas, New Year's Day, and Easter Sun). Employed by the Québec Ministry of Tourism, the bilingual staff workers are quite knowledgeable, and the center is a useful information resource for dining, accommodations, and attractions throughout the province and in Montréal itself. In addition to the large number of brochures and publications on hand, there are counters for tour companies, hotel reservations, currency exchange, and car rental. There is an Internet terminal for use with cash or credit cards. You'll find a cafeteria and restrooms downstairs.

The city has its own convenient **information bureau** in Vieux-Montréal (Old Montréal) at 174 rue Notre-Dame (corner of place Jacques-Cartier), near the monument to Lord Nelson (© **514/871-1595**). It's open daily early June through early October from 9am to 7pm; mid-October through June from 9am to 5pm.

CITY LAYOUT

For the duration of your visit, it makes sense to accept local directional conventions, strange as they may seem. The city borders the **St. Lawrence River.** As far as its citizens are concerned, that's south, looking toward the United States, although the river in fact runs almost north and south at that point, not east and west. For that reason, it has been observed that Montréal is the only city in the world where the sun rises in the south. Don't fight it: Face the river. That's south. Turn around. That's north. When examining a map of the city, note that such prominent thoroughfares as rue Ste-Catherine and boulevard René-Lévesque are said to run "east" and "west," the dividing line being boulevard St-Laurent, which runs "north" and "south." To ease the confusion, the directions given below conform to local directional tradition. However, the maps in this book have the true compass on them rather than the Montreal-specific compass.

MAIN ARTERIES & STREETS   In **downtown Montréal,** the principal streets running east–west include boulevard René-Lévesque, rue Ste-Catherine (*rue* is the French word for "street"), boulevard de Maisonneuve, and rue Sherbrooke; the north–south arteries include rue Crescent, rue McGill, rue St-Denis, and boulevard St-Laurent, which serves as the line of demarcation between east and west Montréal (most of the downtown area of interest to tourists and businesspeople lies to the west). In **Plateau Mont-Royal,** northeast of the downtown area, major streets are avenue du Mont-Royal and avenue Laurier. In **Vieux-Montréal,** rue St-Jacques, rue Notre-Dame, and rue St-Paul are the major streets, along with rue de la Commune, which hugs the park that borders the St. Lawrence River.

Neighborhood street plans are found inside the free tourist guide supplied by **Tourisme Montréal** (© **514/844-5400;** www.tourisme-montreal.org) and distributed at the information bureau described in "Visitor Information," above. The Infotouriste Centre (also described above) provides a free large foldout city map.

Impressions

You cannot fancy you are in America; everything about it conveys the idea of a substantial, handsomely built European town, with modern improvements of half English, half French architecture.
    —Lt. Col. B. W. A. Sleigh, *Pine Forests and Hacmatack Clearings* (1853)

Greater Montréal

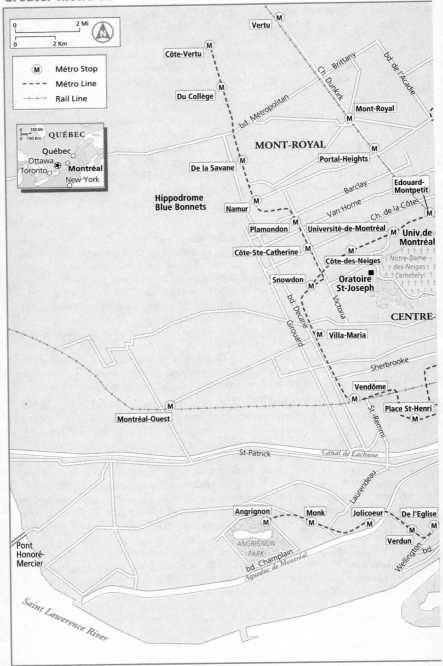

Vertu

Côte-Vertu

Du Collège

Brittany

Ch. Dunkirk

bd. de l'Acadie

bd. Métropolitan

Mont-Royal

MONT-ROYAL

Portal-Heights

De la Savane

Barclay

Van Horne

Edouard-Montpetit

Hippodrome
Blue Bonnets

Namur

Ch. de la Côte

Plamondon

Université-de-Montréal

Univ.de
Montréal

Côte-Ste-Catherine

Côte-des-Neiges

Notre-Dame-
des-Neiges
Cemetery

Snowdon

Oratoire
St-Joseph

CENTRE-

bd. Decarie

Girouard

Victoria

Villa-Maria

Sherbrooke

Vendôme

St-Remmi

Place St-Henri

Montréal-Ouest

St-Patrick

Canal de Lachune

Laurendeau

Angrignon

Monk

Jolicoeur

De l'Eglise

ANGRIGNON
PARK

Verdun

Pont
Honoré-
Mercier

bd. Champlain

Aqueduc de Montréal

Wellington bd.

Saint Lawerence River

Legend

0 ____ 2 Mi
0 ____ 2 Km

M — Métro Stop
- - - — Métro Line
+-+-+ — Rail Line

0 ___ 150 Mi
0 ___ 150 Km

QUÉBEC

Québec

Ottawa
Toronto

Montréal

New York

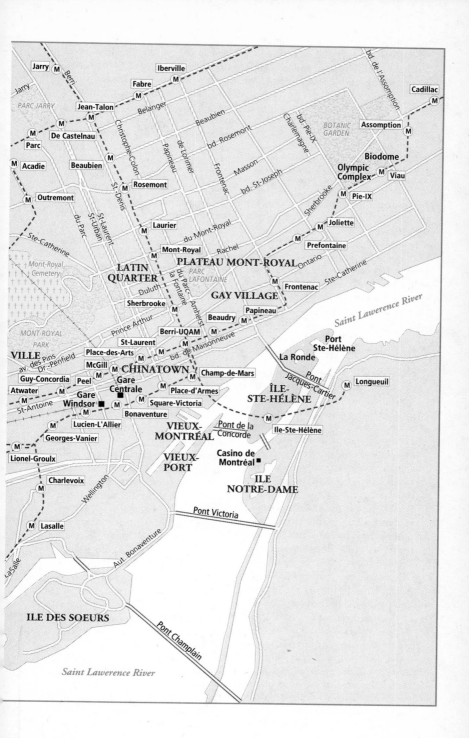

FINDING AN ADDRESS   Boulevard St-Laurent is the dividing point between east and west (*est* and *ouest*) in Montréal. There's no equivalent division for north and south (*nord* and *sud*)—the numbers start at the river and climb from there, just as the topography does. When you're driving along boulevard St-Laurent and passing number 500, that's Vieux-Montréal, near rue Notre-Dame; number 1100 is near boulevard René-Lévesque; number 1500 is near boulevard de Maisonneuve; and number 3400 is near rue Sherbrooke. Even numbers are on the west side of north–south streets and the south side of east–west streets; odd numbers are on the east and north sides, respectively.

In earlier days, Montréal was split geographically along ethnic lines: Those who spoke English lived predominantly west of bd. St-Laurent, and French speakers were concentrated to the east. Things still do sound more French as you walk east: Street names and Métro station names change from Peel and Atwater to St-Laurent and Beaudry. While boulevard St-Laurent is the east–west dividing line for the city's street-numbering system, the "ethnic split" comes farther west, roughly at avenue de Bleury/avenue de Parc.

THE NEIGHBORHOODS IN BRIEF

DOWNTOWN   This area contains the most striking elements of the dramatic Montréal skyline and includes the main railroad station, as well as most of the city's luxury and first-class hotels, principal museums, corporate headquarters, and largest department stores. This area is loosely bounded by rue Sherbrooke to the north, boulevard René-Lévesque to the south, boulevard St-Laurent to the east, and rue Drummond to the west. Downtown Montréal incorporates the neighborhood formerly known as "The Golden Square Mile," an Anglophone district once characterized by dozens of mansions erected by the wealthy Scottish and English merchants and industrialists who dominated the city's politics and social life well into this century. Many of those stately homes were torn down when skyscrapers began to rise here after World War II, but some remain, often converted to institutional use. At the northern edge of the downtown area is the urban campus of prestigious McGill University, which retains its Anglophone identity.

THE UNDERGROUND CITY   During Montréal's long winters and humid summers, life slows on the streets of downtown as people escape down escalators and stairways into *la ville souterraine,* which amounts to a parallel subterranean universe. Down there, in a controlled climate that's eternally spring, it's possible to arrive at the railroad station, check into a hotel, go out for lunch at any of hundreds of fast-food counters and full-service restaurants, see a movie, attend a concert, conduct business, go shopping, and even take a swim—all without unfurling an umbrella or donning an overcoat.

This underground "city" evolved when major building developments in the downtown area such as Place Ville-Marie, Place Bonaventure, Complexe Desjardins, Palais des Congrès, and Place des Arts put their below-street-level areas to profitable use, leasing space for shops and other enterprises. Over time, in fits and starts and with no master plan in place, these spaces became connected with Métro stations and with each other. It became possible to ride long distances and walk the shorter ones, through mazes of corridors, tunnels, and plazas. There are now more than 1,600 shops, 40 banks, 200 restaurants, 10 Métro stations, and about 30 cinemas down there.

Admittedly, the term "underground city" is not entirely accurate, because some parts—such as Place Bonaventure and Complexe Desjardins—define their own spaces, which may have nothing to do with "ground level." In Place Bonaventure, passengers may leave the Métro and then wander around on the same level only to find themselves, at one point, peering out a window several floors above the street.

The city beneath the city has obvious advantages, including the elimination of traffic accidents and avoidance of the need to deal with winter slush or summer rain. Natural light is let in wherever possible, which drastically reduces the feeling of claustrophobia that some malls evoke. However, the underground city covers a vast area, without the convenience of a logical street grid, and can be confusing at times. There are plenty of signs, but it's wise to make careful note of landmarks at key corners along your route in order to get back to your starting point. Expect to get lost anyway—but, being that you're in an underground maze, that's part of the fun.

RUE CRESCENT One of Montréal's major dining and nightlife districts lies in the western shadow of the massed phalanxes of downtown skyscrapers. It holds hundreds of restaurants, bars, and clubs of all styles between Sherbrooke and René-Lévesque, centering on rue Crescent and spilling over onto neighboring streets. From east to west, the Anglophone origins of the quarter are evident in the surviving street names: Stanley, Drummond, Crescent, Bishop, and MacKay. The party atmosphere that pervades after dark never quite fades, and it builds to crescendos as weekends approach, especially in warm weather, when the quarter's largely 20- and 30-something denizens spill out into sidewalk cafes and onto balconies in even greater numbers than during the winter months.

VIEUX-MONTREAL The city was born here in 1642, down by the river at Pointe-à-Callière, and today, especially in summer, activity centers around place Jacques-Cartier, where cafe tables line narrow terraces and sun worshipers, flower sellers, itinerant artists, street performers, and strolling locals and tourists congregate. The area is larger than it might seem at first, bounded on the north by rue St-Antoine, once the "Wall Street" of Montréal and still home to some banks, and on the south by the recently developed Vieux-Port (Old Port), a linear park bordering rue de la Commune that gives access to the river and provides welcome breathing room for cyclists, in-line skaters, and picnickers. To the east, Vieux-Montréal is bordered by rue Berri, and to the west by rue McGill. Several small but intriguing museums are housed in historic buildings, and the architectural heritage of the district has been substantially preserved. The restored 18th- and 19th-century structures have been adapted for use as shops, studios, galleries, cafes, bars, offices, and apartments. Take a walk through the district in the evening, when many of the finer buildings are illuminated.

ST-DENIS Rue St-Denis, from rue Ste-Catherine est to avenue du Mont-Royal, is the thumping central artery of Francophone Montréal, running from the Latin Quarter downtown and continuing north into the Plateau Mont-Royal district. Thick with cafes, bistros, offbeat shops, and lively nightspots, it is to Montréal what boulevard St-Germain is to Paris, and indeed, once you're here, it isn't difficult to imagine that you've been transported to the Left Bank. At the southern end of St-Denis, near the concrete campus of the Université du Québec à Montréal (UQAM), the avenue is decidedly student-oriented, with indie rock cranked up in the inexpensive bars and clubs, and kids in jeans and leather swapping philosophical insights and telephone numbers. Farther north, above Sherbrooke, a raffish quality persists along the facing rows of three- and four-story Victorian row houses, but the average age of residents and visitors nudges past 30 here. Prices are higher, too, and some of the city's better restaurants are located here. This is a district for taking the pulse of Francophone life, not for absorbing art and culture of the refined sort, for there are no museums or important galleries on St-Denis, nor is most of the architecture notable. But, then, that relieves visitors of the chore of obligatory sightseeing and allows them to take in the passing scene— just as the locals do—over bowls of café au lait at any of the numerous terraces that line the avenue.

PLATEAU MONT-ROYAL Northeast of the downtown area, this may be the part of the city where Montréalers feel most at home—away from the chattering pace of downtown and the crowds of heavily touristed Vieux-Montréal. Bounded roughly by boulevard St-Joseph to the north, rue Sherbrooke to the south, avenue Papineau to the east, and rue St-Dominique to the west, this area has a vibrant ethnicity that fluctuates with each new surge in immigration. Rue St-Denis (see above) runs the length of the district, but boulevard St-Laurent, running parallel to rue St-Denis, has more polyglot flavor. Known to all as "The Main," it was the boulevard first encountered by foreigners tumbling off ships at the waterfront. They simply shouldered their belongings and walked north on St-Laurent, peeling off into adjoining streets when they heard familiar tongues, saw people who looked like them, or smelled the drifting aromas of food they once cooked in the old country. New arrivals still come here to start their lives in Montréal, and in the usual pattern, most work hard, save their money, and move to the suburbs. But some stay on. Without its people and their diverse interests, St-Laurent would be another urban eyesore. But ground-floor windows here are filled with glistening golden chickens, collages of shoes and pastries and aluminum cookware, curtains of sausages, and even the daringly farfetched garments of those designers on the edge of Montréal's active fashion industry. Many warehouses and former tenements have been converted to house this panoply of shops, bars, and high- and low-cost eateries, and their often-garish signs draw eyes from the still-dilapidated upper stories above. (See chapter 7 for a detailed walking tour of this fascinating neighborhood.)

PARC DU MONT-ROYAL Not many cities have a mountain at their core. Okay, reality insists that it's just a tall hill, not a true mountain. Still, Montréal is named for it—the "Royal Mountain"—and it's a soothing urban pleasure to drive, walk, or take a horse-drawn calèche to the top for a view of the city, the island, and the St. Lawrence River, especially at dusk. The famous American landscape architect Frederick Law Olmsted, who created New York City's Central Park and Brooklyn's Prospect Park, among others, designed Parc du Mont-Royal, which opened in 1876. On its far slope are two cemeteries— one Anglophone and Protestant, one Francophone and Catholic— silent reminders of the linguistic and cultural division that persists in the city. With its skating ponds and trails for hiking, running, and cross-country skiing, the park is well used by Montréalers, who refer to it simply and affectionately as "the mountain."

CHINATOWN Just north of Vieux-Montréal, south of boulevard René-Lévesque, and centered on the intersection of rue Clark and rue de la Gauchetière (pedestrianized at this point), Montréal's pocket Chinatown is mostly restaurants and a tiny park, with the occasional grocery, laundry, church, and small business. For the benefit of outsiders, most signs are in French or English as well as Chinese. Community spirit is strong—it has had to be to resist the bulldozers of commercial proponents of redevelopment—and Chinatown's inhabitants remain faithful to their traditions despite the encroaching modernism all around them. Concerned investors from Hong Kong, wary of their uncertain future as part of mainland China, have

poured money into the neighborhood, producing signs that the neighborhood's shrinkage has been halted, even reversed. Signaling that optimism, there are new gates to the area on boulevard St-Laurent, guarded by white stone lions.

THE VILLAGE The city's gay and lesbian enclave, one of North America's largest, runs east along rue Ste-Catherine from rue St-Hubert to rue Papineau. A small but vibrant district, it's filled with clothing stores, antique shops, bars, dance clubs, and cafés, and houses the Gay and Lesbian Community Centre, at 1301 rue Ste-Catherine est. A rainbow, symbolic of the gay community, marks the Beaudry Métro station, in the heart of the neighborhood. Two major annual celebrations are the Diver/Cité (the gay pride festival) in August and the Black & Blue Party in October.

ILE STE-HELENE AND ILE NOTRE-DAME St. Helen's Island in the St. Lawrence River was altered extensively to become the site of Expo '67, Montréal's very successful world's fair. In the 4 years before the Expo opened, construction crews reshaped the island and doubled its surface area with landfill, then went on to create beside it an island that hadn't existed before, Ile Notre-Dame. Much of the earth needed to do this was dredged up from the bottom of the St. Lawrence River, and 15 million tons of rock from the excavations for the Métro and the Décarie Expressway were carried in by truck. The city built bridges and 83 pavilions. When Expo closed, the city government preserved the site and a few of the exhibition buildings. Parts were used for the 1976 Olympics, and today Ile Ste-Hélène is home to Montréal's popular casino and an amusement park, La Ronde.

2 Getting Around

BY METRO

For speed and economy, nothing beats Montréal's Métro system for getting around. Clean, relatively quiet trains whisk passengers through an expanding network of underground tunnels, with 65 stations at present and more scheduled to open. **Single rides** cost C$2.25 (US$1.45), a **strip of 6 tickets** is C$9 (US$5.80), a **1-day pass** permitting unlimited rides for 24 hours is C$7 (US$4.50), a **3-day pass** is C$14 (US$9.05). Buy tickets at the booth in any station, and then slip one into the slot in the turnstile to enter the system. Take a transfer *(correspondence)* from the machine just inside the turnstiles of every station, which allows transfers from a train to a bus at any other Métro station for no additional fare. Remember to take the transfer ticket at the station where you first enter the system. When starting a trip by bus and intending to continue on the Métro, ask the bus driver for a transfer. Connections from one Métro line to another can be made at the Berri-de Montigny, Jean-Talon, Lionel-Groulx, and Snowdon stations. The orange, green, and yellow Métro lines run from about 5:30am to 1am, and the blue line runs from 5:30am to 11pm on.

BY BUS

Buses cost the same as Métro trains, and Métro tickets are good on buses, too. Exact change is required to pay bus fares in cash. Although they run throughout the city (and give riders the decided advantage of traveling above ground), buses don't run as frequently or as swiftly as the Métro. If you start a trip on the bus and want to transfer to the Metro, ask the bus driver for a transfer ticket.

BY TAXI

There are plenty of taxis run by several different companies. Cabs come in a variety of colors and styles, so their principal distinguishing feature is the plastic sign on the roof. At night, the sign is illuminated when the cab is available. Fares aren't too expensive, with an initial charge of C$2.50 (US$1.60) at the flag drop, C$1.20 (US80¢) per kilometer (⅔ mile), and C45¢ (US30¢) per minute of waiting. A short ride from one point to another downtown usually costs about C$5 (US$3.25). Tip about 10% to 15%. Members of hotel and restaurant staffs can call cabs, many of which are dispatched by radio. They line up outside most large hotels or can be hailed on the street.

BY CAR

Montréal is an easy city to navigate by car. Visitors arriving by plane or train, however, will probably want to rely on public transportation and cabs rather than rent a car. A rental car can come in handy, though, for trips outside of town or if you plan to drive to Québec City.

RENTALS Terms, cars, and prices for rentals are similar to those in the United States. All the larger U.S. companies operate in Canada. Basic rates are about the same from company to company, although a little comparison shopping can unearth modest savings. A charge is usually levied when you return a car in a city other than the one in which it was rented. All of the companies listed below also have counters at Dorval Airport.

Major car-rental companies include **Avis,** 1225 rue Metcalfe (© **800/321-3652** or 514/866-7906); **Budget,** Gare Centrale (© **800/268-8900** or 514/938-1000); **Hertz,** 1073 rue Drummond (© **800/263-0678** or 514/938-1717); **Thrifty,** 1076 rue de la Montagne (© **800/367-2277** or 514/845-5954); and **National,** 1200 rue Stanley (© **800/287-4747** or 514/878-2771).

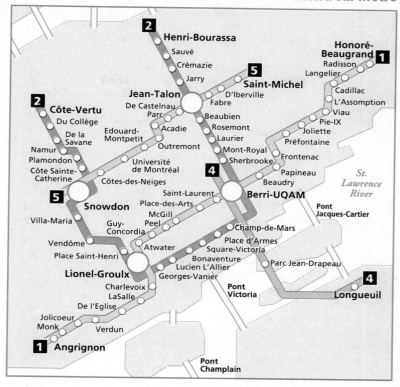

GASOLINE Gasoline and diesel fuel are sold by the Imperial gallon or, more often, the liter, at prices somewhat higher than those in the United States. One Imperial gallon equals 1.2 U.S. gallons, or 4.546 liters. In Québec, it costs about C$30 (US$19) to fill the tank of a small car with the lowest grade of unleaded gasoline. To convert the approximate cost of Canadian gas to familiar U.S. standards, multiply the cost per liter in Canadian dollars by four. Then convert the price to U.S. dollars.

PARKING It can be difficult to park on the heavily trafficked streets of downtown Montréal, but there are plenty of metered spaces, with varying hourly rates. (Look around before walking off without paying. Meters are set well back from the curb so they won't be buried by plowed snow in winter.) Check for signs noting restrictions, usually showing a red circle with a diagonal slash. The words *"livraison seulement,"* for example, mean "delivery only." Most downtown shopping complexes have underground parking lots, as do the big downtown hotels. Some of the hotels don't charge extra to take cars in and out of their garages during the day, which can save money for those who plan to do a lot of sightseeing by car.

DRIVING RULES The limited-access expressways in Québec are called *autoroutes,* and distances and speed limits are given in kilometers (km) and kilometers per hour (kmph). Some highway signs are in French only, although Montréal's autoroutes and bridges often bear dual-language signs. Seat-belt use is required by law while driving or riding in a car in Québec. Turning right on a red light has been prohibited in Montréal and the province of Québec, except where specifically allowed by an additional green arrow, but there is discussion about changing the law.

Note: Too many Québec drivers take perverse pride in their reputation as dangerously fast at the wheel and are prone to such maneuvers as making sudden U-turns and cutting across two lanes to snare a parking space. Growing indignation with such practices, with newspapers decrying excess speed and the accidents that result from it, doesn't seem to have curbed the behavior.

 FAST FACTS: Montréal

American Express Offices of the American Express Travel Service are located at 1141 bd. de Maisonneuve ouest near rue Stanley (✆ **514/ 284-3300**), and in La Baie (The Bay) department store, 585 rue Ste-Catherine ouest (✆ **514/281-4777**). For lost or stolen cards, call ✆ **800/268-9824.**

Babysitters Nearly all large hotels offer babysitting services *(garderie des enfants)*. In the smaller hotels and guesthouses, managers often know of sitters they believe to be reliable. Give as much notice as possible, and make certain about rates and extra charges, such as carfare, before making a commitment.

Business Hours Most **stores** are open from 9 or 10am to 6pm Monday through Wednesday, 9am to 9pm on Thursday and Friday, and 9am to 5pm on Saturday. Many stores are now also open on Sunday from noon to 5pm. **Banks** are usually open Monday through Friday from 8 or 9am to 4pm.

Currency Exchange There are currency-exchange offices (sometimes called "bureaux de change") near most locations where they're likely to be needed: at the airports, in the train station, in and near Infotouriste on Dorchester Square, and near Notre-Dame Basilica at 86 rue Notre-Dame. The **Bank of America Canada,** 1230 rue Peel, also offers foreign-exchange services Monday through Friday 8:30am to 5:30pm and Saturday 9am to 5pm.

Doctors & Dentists The front desks at hotels can contact a doctor quickly. If it's not an emergency, call your country's consulate and ask for a recommendation (see "Embassies & Consulates," below). Consulates don't guarantee or certify local doctors, but they maintain lists of physicians with good reputations. Even if the consulate is closed, a duty officer should be available to help. For dental information, call the hot line at ✆ **514/288-8888** or the 24-hour dental clinic at ✆ **514/342-4444.** In an emergency, dial ✆ **911.**

Drugstores Open 24 hours a day, 365 days a year, the branch of **Pharmaprix** at 5122 Côte-des-Neiges, at Chemin Queen Mary (✆ **514/ 738-8464**), has a fairly convenient location.

Electricity Canada uses the same electricity (110–120 volts, 60 cycles) as the United States and Mexico, with the same flat-prong plugs and sockets.

Embassies & Consulates All embassies are in Ottawa, the national capital. In Montréal, the American consulate general is located at 1155 rue

St-Alexandre (℃ **514/398-9695**). The United Kingdom has a consulate general at 1000 rue de la Gauchetière ouest, Suite 4200 (℃ **514/866-5863**). Other English-speaking countries (Australia and New Zealand) have their embassies or consulates in Ottawa.

Emergencies Dial ℃ **911** for the police, firefighters, or an ambulance.

Hospitals Hospitals with emergency rooms are Hôpital Général de Montréal, 1650 rue Cedar (℃ **514/937-6011**), and Hôpital Royal Victoria, 687 av. des Pins ouest (℃ **514/842-1231**). Hôpital de Montréal pour Enfants (℃ **514/934-4400**) is a children's hospital with a poison center. Other prominent hospitals are Hôtel-Dieu, 209 av. des Pins ouest (℃ **514/843-2611**), and Hôpital Notre-Dame, 1560 rue Sherbrooke est (℃**514/281-6000**).

Internet Access The **CyberGround NetCafé**, 3672 bd. St-Laurent (℃ **514/842-1726**), has 16 computers with big 21-inch monitors for e-mailing, word processing, or just surfing. Time at the keyboard costs C$3.50 (US$2.35) per half-hour, plus tax. Hours are Monday through Friday from 10am to 11pm; Saturday and Sunday from 11am to 11pm. Another possibility is **Cybermac Café Internet**, 1425 rue Mackay (℃ **514/287-9100**).

Liquor Laws All hard liquor and spirits in Québec are sold through official government stores operated by the Québec Société des Alcools (look for maroon signs with the acronym "SAQ"). Wine and beer can be bought in grocery stores and convenience stores, called *dépanneurs*. The legal drinking age in the province is 18. Liquor is sold every day of the week in SAQ stores.

Mail All mail posted in Canada must bear Canadian stamps. That might seem painfully obvious, but apparently large numbers of visitors use stamps from their home countries, especially the United States. To receive mail in Montréal, have it addressed to you, c/o Poste Restante, Station "A," 1025 rue St-Jacques ouest, Montréal, PQ H3C 1G0, Canada. It can be claimed at the main post office (see below). Take along valid identification, preferably with a photo.

Newspapers & Magazines Montréal's primary English-language newspaper is the *Montréal Gazette*. (To familiarize yourself with events in the city and province before your arrival, log on to the paper's website, **www.montrealgazette.com**.) Most large newsstands and those in the larger hotels also carry the *Wall Street Journal*, the *New York Times*, *USA Today*, and the *International Herald Tribune*. These papers are available at several branches of the **Maison de la Presse Internationale**, two of which are at 550 and 728 rue Ste-Catherine ouest. In Plateau Mont-Royal, a similar operation called **Multimags**, at 3550 av. St-Laurent, sells hundreds of foreign newspapers and magazines. For information about current happenings in Montréal, pick up the Friday or Saturday edition of the *Gazette*, or the free bimonthly booklet called *Montréal Scope*, available in some shops and many hotel lobbies.

Pets Dogs and cats can be taken into Québec, but the Canadian Customs authorities at the frontier will want to see a rabies vaccination certificate less than 3 years old signed by a licensed veterinarian. If a pet is less than 3 months old and obviously healthy, the certificate isn't likely to be required. Check with U.S. Customs about bringing your pet back into the

United States. Most hotels in Montréal do not accept pets or require that they be kept in cages, so inquire about their policy before booking a room.

Police Dial ✆ **911** for the police. There are three types of officers in Québec: municipal police in Montréal, Québec City, and other towns; Sûreté de Québec officers, comparable to state police or the highway patrol in the United States; and RCMP (Royal Canadian Mounted Police), who are similar to the FBI and handle cases involving infraction of federal laws. RCMP officers speak English and French. Other officers are not required to know English, though many do.

Post Office The main post office is at 1250 rue University, near Ste-Catherine (✆ **514/395-4909**), open Monday through Friday 8am to 6pm. A convenient post office in Vieux-Montréal is at 155 rue St-Jacques (at rue St-François-Xavier). At this writing, it costs C47¢ (US30¢) to send a first-class letter or postcard within Canada, and C60¢ (US40¢) to send a first-class letter or postcard from Canada to the United States. First-class airmail service to other countries costs C$1.05 (US70¢) for the first 20 grams (about ⅔ oz.). These prices are increased by the astonishing imposition of a *sales tax,* another C8¢ (US5¢) for a first-class stamp! See "Mail," above, for information on having mail sent to you in Montréal.

Safety Montréal is a far safer city than its U.S. counterparts of similar size, but common sense insists that visitors stay alert to their surroundings and observe the usual urban precautions. There are reports of escalating road-rage incidents, so expressions of impatience and anger with the actions of other drivers can be unwise.

Taxes Most goods and services in Canada are taxed 7% by the federal government. On top of that, the province of Québec has an additional 7.5% tax on goods and services, including those provided by hotels. In Québec, the federal tax appears on the bill as the TPS, and the provincial tax is known as the TVQ. Non-resident tourists can receive a rebate on both the federal and provincial tax on items they have purchased but not used in Québec, as well as on lodging. To take advantage of this refund, request the booklet called *Tax Refund for Visitors to Canada* at duty-free shops, hotels, and tourist offices. It contains the necessary forms. Complete and submit them, with the original receipts, within a year of the purchase. If you leave Canada by plane, train, bus, ferry, or boat, you'll have to attach your original boarding pass or travel ticket to the application. New procedures are being phased in, so contact the Canadian consulate or Québec tourism office for up-to-the-minute information about taxes and rebates.

Telephones The telephone system, operated by Bell Canada, closely resembles the American model. All operators (dial ✆ **00** to get one) speak French and English, and respond in the appropriate language as soon as callers speak to them. Pay phones in Québec require C25¢ (US15¢) for a 3-minute local call. Directory information calls (dial ✆ **411**) are free of charge. Both local and long-distance calls usually cost more from hotels—sometimes a lot more, so check. Directories *(annuaires des téléphones)* come in White Pages (residential) and Yellow Pages (commercial).

Time Montréal, Québec City, and the Laurentians are all in the eastern time zone. Daylight saving time is observed as in the U.S., moving clocks ahead an hour in the spring and back an hour in the fall.

Tipping Practices are similar to those in the United States: 15% to 20% of restaurant bills, 10% to 15% for taxi drivers, C$1 per bag for porters, C$1 per night for the hotel room attendant. Hairdressers and barbers expect 10% to 15%. Hotel doormen should be tipped for calling a taxi or other services.

Transit Information Call **STCUM** (© **514/288-6287**) for information about the Métro and city buses. For airport transportation, call **L'Aérobus** (© **514/931-9002**).

Useful Telephone Numbers For Alcoholics Anonymous, call © 514/376-9230; for the Institute for the Blind, call © 514/529-2040; for transport for disabled persons, call © 514/280-5341; for the Poison Centre, call © 800/463-5060; for 24-hour pharmacies, call © 514/738-8464; for the Sexual Assault Center, call © 514/934-4504; for Canadian Customs, call © 514/283-9000; for U.S. Customs, call © 514/636-3875.

4

Where to Stay in Montréal

Montréal hoteliers go the extra mile (or km, in this case) to make guests feel welcome, at least in part because there are proportionally more hotel rooms here than in other North American cities of similar size, still more are constructed every year, and all these hotels are hoping to have their rooms (there are more than 25,000 in the city) filled throughout the year. With that competition and the continued favorable exchange rate of the U.S. dollar in relation to its Canadian counterpart, this is the place to splurge, or at least step up in class.

Accommodation options range from soaring glass skyscrapers to grand boulevard hotels to converted row houses. Stylish inns and boutique hotels are appearing in increasing numbers, especially in Vieux-Montréal, and several of them are recommended below. Except in bed-and-breakfasts, visitors can almost always count on discounts and package deals, especially on weekends, when the hotels' business clients have packed their bags and gone home.

Though they don't usually offer discounts, B&Bs boast cozier settings, often at lower prices than comparable hotels, and give visitors the opportunity to get to know a Montréaler or two. By the nature of the trade, bed-and-breakfast owners are among the most outgoing and knowledgeable guides one might want. For information about downtown B&B's, contact **Bed & Breakfast Downtown Network,** 3458 av. Laval (at rue Sherbrooke), Montréal, PQ H2X 3C8 (✆ **800/267-5180** or 514/289-9749;

www.bbmontreal.qc.ca; bbdtown@cam.org). As a referral agency for homeowners who have one or more rooms available for guests, this company represents about 30 properties with 50 guest rooms. Doubles are typically C$80 to C$120 (US$52–US$77). Rooms with private baths are more expensive than those that share facilities. Accommodations and the rules of individual homeowners vary significantly, so it's wise to ask all pertinent questions up front, such as if children are welcome, if smoking is permitted, or if all guests share bathrooms. Deposits are usually required, with the balance payable upon arrival. American Express, Visa, and MasterCard are accepted.

Québec's tourist authorities have drawn up a six-level rating system for all establishments offering six or more rooms to travelers. No star is assigned to hotels or inns meeting only basic minimum standards and five stars are reserved for establishments deemed to be exceptional in terms of facilities and services. An ochre-and-brown shield bearing the assigned rating is found near the entrance to most hotels and inns. Most of the recommendations listed below are in the three- or four-star categories. The Québec system, however, is based necessarily on quantitative measures, while the new Frommer's star ratings are more subjective, taking into account such considerations as price-to-value ratios, quality of service, location, helpfulness of staff, and the presence of such facilities as spas and fitness centers. Stars in the reviews found below are of the zero to three-star Frommer's system (see the 1st page of this guide for an explanation of the Frommer's star system).

You'll find the highest hotel rates during Montréal's busiest times, from May through October, reaching a peak in July and August. High rates also pop up during the frequent summer festivals, during annual holiday periods (Canadian or American), and when Montréal and Québec City hold their winter carnivals in February (p. 18). At those times, reserve well in advance, especially if you're looking for special rates or packages. Most other times, expect to find plenty of available rooms.

Four useful websites for exploring lodging possibilities and making reservations online are www.tourisme-montreal.org, http://celestia.all-hotels.com, www.hospitality-canada.com, and www.hebergementquebec.com. There is also a **free hotel reservation hot line,** © **800/665-1528** or 514/287-9049.

Note: Nearly all hotel staff members, from front-desk personnel to porters, are reassuringly bilingual.

CATEGORIES For convenience, the recommendations below have been categorized first by neighborhood, then by price. At most hotels and inns, the price differential from low to high season is rarely more than 15% or 20%, so in the listings below, the lowest price is usually for a January stay, the highest for a room in the peak summer months. All rooms have private bathrooms unless otherwise noted.

TAXES The provincial government imposes a 7.5% tax on accommodations (TVQ) in addition to the 7% federal goods and services tax (TPS). Foreign visitors can get most of the hotel tax back, assuming they save their receipts and file the necessary refund form. Unless specifically noted, prices given here do *not* include taxes—federal or provincial.

1 Downtown

VERY EXPENSIVE

Hilton Montréal Bonaventure ★★ The Hilton's main entrance is at de la Gauchetière and Mansfield, but the lobby is on the 17th floor. The hotel constitutes what amounts to a penthouse above the Place Bonaventure Exhibition Hall. It has elevator access to Central Station and the underground city. From aloft, the hotel looks as if it has a square hole in its top. That's the 1 hectare (2½-acre) rooftop garden, with strolling pheasants, paddling ducks, and a year-round swimming pool. Many guest rooms have black-and-white televisions in the compact bathrooms; views are of the city or the garden. All rooms, public and private, have recently undergone renovation.

1 place Bonaventure (corner of Gauchetière and Mansfield), Montréal, PQ H5A 1E4. © **800/267-2575** or 514/878-2332. Fax 514/878-1442. www.hiltonmontreal.com. 395 units. C$149–C$380 (US$96–US$245) double. Children 18 and under stay free in parents' room. Weekend packages available. AE, DC, MC, V. Valet parking C$24 (US$16); self-parking C$16 (US$10). Métro: Bonaventure. **Amenities:** 2 restaurants (French, International) with summer dining terraces; bar; year-round heated outdoor pool; health club; concierge; substantial business center; 24-hr. room service; babysitting; laundry service; same-day dry cleaning; nonsmoking rooms; executive floor. *In room:* A/C, TV w/pay movies, dataport, minibar, coffeemaker, hair dryer, iron.

Hôtel Omni Mont-Royal ★★ This hotel is a worthy competitor to the nearby Ritz-Carlton, especially because of an ongoing all-floors multimillion-dollar renovation by the most recent owners. The coolly austere lobby, lined with marble, is softened by banks of plants and flowers. Rooms are large, with new-looking furnishings, offered in escalating categories of relative luxury, from standard to premium. Robes are available in each room. There are 12 nonsmoking

Downtown Montréal Accommodations

Auberge Bonaparte **22**
Auberge du Vieux-Port **26**
Auberge Les Passants du San Soucy **23**
Castel St-Denis **29**
Château Versailles/Hôtel Versailles **1**
Courtyard Marriott Montréal **13**
Delta Centre-Ville **15**
Delta Montréal **10**
Four Points Montréal Centre-Ville **11**
Hilton Montréal Bonaventure **9**

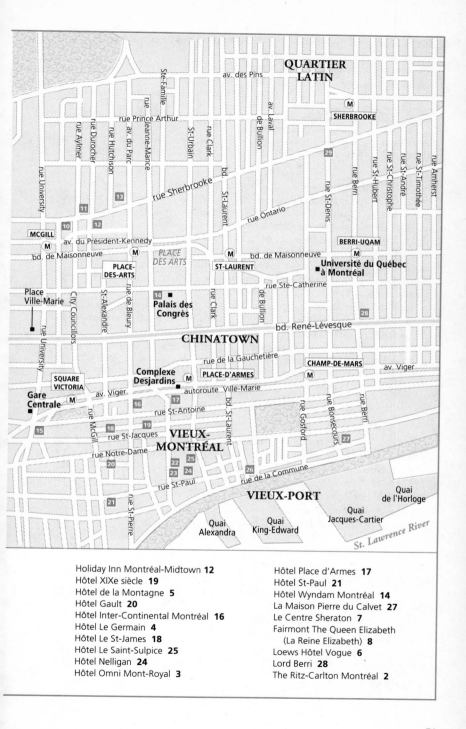

Holiday Inn Montréal-Midtown **12**
Hôtel XIXe siècle **19**
Hôtel de la Montagne **5**
Hôtel Gault **20**
Hôtel Inter-Continental Montréal **16**
Hôtel Le Germain **4**
Hôtel Le St-James **18**
Hôtel Le Saint-Sulpice **25**
Hôtel Nelligan **24**
Hôtel Omni Mont-Royal **3**

Hôtel Place d'Armes **17**
Hôtel St-Paul **21**
Hôtel Wyndam Montréal **14**
La Maison Pierre du Calvet **27**
Le Centre Sheraton **7**
Fairmont The Queen Elizabeth
    (La Reine Elizabeth) **8**
Loews Hôtel Vogue **6**
Lord Berri **28**
The Ritz-Carlton Montréal **2**

floors, an unusually large number. Buffet breakfasts and lunches are served in the lobby bar, which features piano music in the evenings. This is a great place for businesspeople, honeymooners, and well-to-do families.

1050 Sherbrooke ouest (at rue Peel), Montréal, PQ H3A 2R6. © **514/284-1110.** Fax 514/845-3025. www.omnihotels.com. 300 units. C$180–C$320 (US$116–US$206) double. Children under 14 stay free in parents' room. Weekend rates and special packages available. AE, DC, MC, V. Valet parking C$22 (US$14); self-parking C$16 (US$10). Métro: Peel. **Amenities:** 2 restaurants (Chinese, International); bar; heated outdoor pool; impressive health club and spa featuring aerobics classes; children's programs; concierge; complete business center; shopping arcade; 24-hr. room service; in-room massage; babysitting; laundry service; same-day dry cleaning; executive floors. *In room:* A/C, TV/VCR w/pay movies, fax, dataport, minibar, coffeemaker, hair dryer, iron, safe.

Loews Hôtel Vogue ★★★   The Vogue, a stunning conversion of a previously undistinguished office building, created quite a stir when it opened in late 1990. The hotel, whose interior was done over in Spring 2001, instantly joined the Ritz-Carlton at the apex of the local luxury-hotel pantheon. Confidence resonates from every member of its staff, and luxury permeates from the lobby to the well-appointed guest rooms. Feather pillows and duvets dress the oversized beds, fresh flowers accent the cherrywood furniture, and marble bathrooms are fitted with Jacuzzis—double-sized in suites—and separate shower stalls. Extra room amenities include TVs in the bathroom, high-speed Internet connection, and robes. The lobby bar has piano music on the weekends and opens an outdoor terrace in the summer. All of this suits the international Armani-and-cellphone clientele to a tee.

1425 rue de la Montagne (between bd. de Maisonneuve and rue Ste-Catherine), Montréal, PQ H3G 1Z3. © **800/465-6654** or 514/285-5555. Fax 514/849-8903. www.loewshotels.com/vogue. 142 units. C$169–C$500 (US$109–US$323) double. Children under 16 stay free in parents' room. Lower weekend rates. AE, DC, DISC, MC, V. Valet parking C$25 (US$16). Métro: Peel. **Amenities:** Restaurant (International); bar; small exercise room; concierge; business center; 24-hr. room service; babysitting; coin-operated washers and dryers; same-day dry cleaning. *In room:* A/C, TV w/pay movies, fax, dataport, minibar, hair dryer, safe.

The Ritz-Carlton Montréal ★★★   In 1912, the Ritz-Carlton opened its doors to the carriage trade, and that clientele has remained faithful. Over the years, however, their Pierce-Arrows gave way to Rolls-Royces and Mercedes, and a few of these are always parked in readiness near the front door. A much-needed $10-million renovation, completed in 1999, has restored the gloss and excellence of service that the hotel possessed in its early days. Rooms are large and traditional. Bathrooms are equipped with robes and speakers carrying TV sound. High-speed Internet connections are provided in every room. An umbrella is stashed in the closet. The famed Café de Paris is favored for its high tea, weekend brunches, and weekday power breakfasts, but serves all meals on the terrace in summer, next to the famous duck pond. There's piano music in the Ritz Bar and Le Grand Prix, with dancing nightly in the latter.

1228 rue Sherbrooke ouest (at rue Drummond), Montréal, PQ H3G 1H6. © **800/363-0366** or 514/842-4212. Fax 514/842-3383. www.ritzcarlton.montreal.com. 240 units. C$225–C$625 (US$150–US$417) double; C$395–C$675 (US$263–US$469) suite. Children under 14 stay free in parents' room. Packages available. AE, DC, MC, V. Valet or self-parking C$24 (US$16), with in/out privileges. Pets accepted (deposit required). Métro: Peel. **Amenities:** 2 restaurants (International); bar; modest fitness room; concierge; business center; 24-hr. room service; in-room massage; babysitting; laundry service; same-day dry cleaning; executive floors. *In room:* A/C, TV w/pay movies, fax on request, dataport, minibar, hair dryer, iron, safe.

EXPENSIVE

Delta Centre-Ville ★★   Within walking distance of Gare Centrale (the train station), downtown offices, and Vieux-Montréal, this Delta (Delta is a Canadian chain), formerly a Radisson, serves both businesspeople and families well, with facilities to keep everyone happy. Twenty-eight floors up is the city's only revolving restaurant, fun for a drink at sunset even if you eat elsewhere. One floor down, the once-public bar has become a private lounge for the executive Signature Club. There is a direct connection with the underground city and the Métro.

777 rue University (at rue St-Antoine), Montréal, PQ H3C 3Z7. ⓒ **800/268-1133** or 514/879-1370. Fax 514/879-1761. www.deltahotels.com. 711 units. C$195–C$235 (US$126–US$152) double. AE, DC, DISC, MC, V. Garage parking. Métro: Square Victoria. **Amenities:** 2 restaurants (International); 2 bars; heated indoor pool; well-equipped health club; sauna, children's center; concierge; business center; limited room service; massage; babysitting; laundry service; same-day dry cleaning; executive floors. *In room:* A/C, TV w/pay movies, dataport, minibar, coffeemaker, iron.

Delta Montréal ★★ *Kids*   This carefully maintained unit of Delta, a Canadian hotel chain, is targeted to the business traveler, but its supervised children's crafts and games center, two squash courts, indoor pool, and in-room Nintendo make it clear that families are welcome, too. Rooms in the 23-story tower have angular dimensions, getting away from the boxiness that defines many contemporary hotels. Most rooms have small balconies. A new wave of renovations was scheduled for late 2002.

475 av. du President-Kennedy (at rue City Councillors), Montréal, PQ H3A 1J7. ⓒ **877/286-1986** or 514/286-1986. Fax 514/284-4342. www.deltamontreal.com. 456 units. C$149–C$290 (US$96–US$187) double; from C$350 (US$226) suite. Children under 19 stay free in parents' room. Weekend packages available. AE, DC, DISC, MC, V. Valet parking C$18 (US$12). Métro: Place des Arts or McGill. **Amenities:** 2 restaurants (International, Bistro); bar; 2 pools (outdoor pool open July–Aug; indoor lap pool open year-round); superior health club and spa w/ aerobics instruction and 2 squash courts; game room; concierge; courtesy car; expansive business center w/ translation service; limited room service; laundry service; same-day dry cleaning; executive floors. *In room:* A/C, TV w/pay movies, dataport, coffeemaker, hair dryer.

Fairmont The Queen Elizabeth (Le Reine Elizabeth) ★★   Montréal's largest hotel has lent its august presence to the city since 1958. Its 21 floors sit atop VIA Rail's Gare Centrale (the main train station), with the Métro and popular areas like place Ville-Marie and place Bonaventure all accessible by underground arcades. This desirable location makes "the Queenie" a frequent choice for heads of state and touring celebrities, even though other hotels in town offer higher standards of personalized pampering. The Entree Gold 19th floor has a private concierge and check-in and a lounge serving complimentary breakfasts and cocktail-hour canapés to go with the honor bar. Less exalted rooms on floors 4 through 17 are entirely satisfactory, with most of the expected comforts and gadgets, in price ranges to satisfy most budgets. The rooms range from smallish to large (ask when reserving) and are furnished traditionally. Le Beaver Club (see chapter 5) features a band for dancing on Saturday nights.

900 bd. René-Lévesque ouest (at rue Mansfield), Montréal, PQ H3B 4A5. ⓒ **800/441-1414** or 514/861-3511. Fax 514/954-2258. www.fairmont.com. 1,050 units. C$189–C$299 (US$122–US$193) double; from C$325 (US$210) suite. Children 18 and under stay free in parents' room. Various discounts (including weekend discounts) and excursion packages available. AE, DC, MC, V. Valet parking C$21 (US$14). Métro: Bonaventure. **Amenities:** 3 restaurants (International); 3 bars; heated indoor pool; large health club and spa w/ Jacuzzi, steam room, and instructors; concierge; large business center; shopping arcade; salon; 24-hr. room service; in-room massage; babysitting; laundry service; same-day dry cleaning; executive floors. *In room:* A/C, TV w/pay movies, dataport, minibar, coffeemaker, hair dryer, iron.

Hôtel Le Germain ★★★   This latest undertaking by the owner of equally desirable boutique hotels in Québec City and Toronto brings a shot of panache to the downtown lodging scene. The hotel features a magical mix of Asian minimalism combined with all the Western comforts international executives might anticipate—and a few they might not. Discover three polished apples sitting in designated depressions on their shelves opposite the elevators—help yourself. In the capacious rooms, check out the vase containing an orchid, CD players, big wicker chairs with fat cushions, and beds so comfortable they can cure insomnia. Self-serve breakfasts, with perfect croissants, excellent café au lait, and choices of newspapers in French and English, are set out on the mezzanine. This is not an ideal place for families but it would be perfect for any other travelers.

2050 rue Mansfield (west end of av. President Kennedy), Montréal, PQ H3A 1Y9. ⓒ 877/333-2050 or 514/849-2050. Fax 514/849-1437. www.hotelgermain.com. 101 units. C$210–C$450 (US$136–US$290). Rates include breakfast. AE, DC, MC, V. Valet parking C$15 (US$9.70). Métro: Peel. **Amenities:** Restaurant (Eclectic); bar; exercise room; limited room service; babysitting; laundry service; same-day dry cleaning. *In room:* A/C, TV, dataport, minibar, coffeemaker, hair dryer, iron.

Hôtel Wyndham Montréal ⭐ *(Kids)* Its owners and names have changed with some frequency, but not much else has. This hotel is still an integral part of the striking Complexe Desjardins, across the street from the Place des Arts, which houses many theaters. Ask for one of the rooms that have been graced by the recent $25 million in renovations. Glass-enclosed elevators glide up to bedrooms and down to the lower levels of the complex, which contains a shopping plaza and a pool cantilevered over garden terraces. Vieux-Montréal, the downtown district, and the ethnic neighborhoods along The Main are within easy walking distance. The hotel is often the official headquarters of Montréal's annual jazz festival. The classy Le Bar has piano music nightly.

1255 rue Jeanne-Mance, Montréal, PQ H5B 1E5. ⓒ 800/361-8234 or 514/285-1450. Fax 514/285-1243. www.wyndham.com/hotels/YULMH/main.wnt. 600 units. C$119–C$250 (US$77–US$161) double; from C$350 (US$226) suite. Children under 18 stay free in parents' room. Packages available. AE, DC, MC, V. Valet parking C$19 (US$13); self-parking C$14 (US$9.35). Métro: Place des Arts or Place d'Armes. Small pets are accepted. **Amenities:** Restaurant (International); bar; heated indoor pool; health club; concierge; business center; shopping arcade; limited room service; in-room massage; babysitting; laundry service; same-day dry cleaning; executive floors. *In room:* A/C, TV/VCR w/pay movies, fax, dataport, minibar, coffeemaker, hair dryer, iron, safe.

Le Centre Sheraton ⭐⭐ This Sheraton rises near Gare Centrale (the city's main train station) a few steps off Dorchester Square, and within a short walk of the hopping rue Crescent dining and nightlife district. A high glass wall transforms the lobby atrium into a huge greenhouse that shelters royal palms. The staff is efficient and the rooms are comfortably corporate in style. That figures, since earnest people in suits make up most of the clientele. They gravitate to the separate Towers section, which bestows upon its guests complimentary breakfast and a private lounge with great views and free evening hors d'oeuvres. Half of the rooms have minibars and all have robes. Half of the 35 floors are nonsmoking. Jazz is performed evenings in the Impromptu Bar. Unfortunately, previously reasonable room rates have been raised to the higher levels of U.S. Sheratons.

1201 bd. René-Lévesque ouest (between rue Drummond and rue Stanley), Montréal, PQ H3B 2L7. ⓒ 800/325-3535 or 514/878-2000. Fax 514/878-3958. www.sheraton.com/lecentre. 825 units. C$339–C$475 (US$219–US$307) double; club floors C$70 (US$45) additional. Children under 17 stay free in parents' room. Weekend packages available. AE, DC, DISC, MC, V. Valet parking C$22 (US$14); self-parking with in/out privileges C$17 (US$11). Pets accepted, but they must be caged while owner is out. Métro: Bonaventure or Peel. **Amenities:** Restaurant (International); 2 bars; indoor pool; health club and spa; concierge (in Towers); airport limo; complete business center; shopping arcade; 24-hr. room service; babysitting; laundry service; same-day dry cleaning; executive floors. *In room:* A/C, TV w/pay movies, coffeemaker, hair dryer, iron.

MODERATE

Château Versailles/Hôtel Versailles ⭐⭐ This two-part facility underwent a remarkable transformation from a popular but dowdy inn to a full member of the growing local ranks of snappy boutique hotels. The Château portion of the property began as a European-style pension in 1958, expanding into adjacent pre–World War I town houses. Rooms have been given the full decorator treatment, with voluptuous colors, fine modern furnishings with faint Deco tinges, and some Second Empire touches. Only one deficiency remains: the lack of an elevator to deal with the three floors.

Some years ago, a modern tower was acquired across the street and made into a motel-ish hotel. Guest rooms in both sections are of good size. A few antiques pepper the public rooms. Breakfast, afternoon tea, and cocktails are served in a small dining room with a fireplace in the Château, and the tower unit has a full-service restaurant. Price and location (near Sherbrooke shopping and the Museum of Fine Arts) are competitive, so reserve well in advance.

1659 (north side) and 1808 (south side) rue Sherbrooke ouest (at St-Mathieu), Montréal, PQ H3H 1E5. ℂ 888/933-8111 or 514/933-3611. Fax 514/933-8401. www.versailleshotels.com. 65 units in town houses, 107 units in hotel. C$129–C$254 (US$83–US$164) double. Children under 17 stay free in parents' room. Special packages available Nov–May. AE, DC, MC, V. Valet parking C$15 (US$9.70). Métro: Guy. **Amenities:** Restaurant (French); lounge; limited room service; laundry service; same-day dry cleaning. *In room:* A/C, TV, dataport, minibar, coffeemaker, hair dryer, safe.

Courtyard Marriott Montréal *(Kids)*   Formerly La Citadelle, this hotel fulfills the Marriott chain's promise of providing lodging for business travelers at a moderate cost. But with its pool and self-service laundromat, the Courtyard also appeals to families on tight budgets. While the mid-rise slab can hardly be described as grand, necessary renovations have perked it up. The restaurant sets out a buffet breakfast (not included in the room rate) each morning.

410 rue Sherbrooke ouest (at av. du Parc), Montréal, PQ H3A 1B3. ℂ 800/449-6654 or 514/844-8855. Fax 514/844-0912. www.courtyard.com. 181 units. C$139–C$299 (US$90–US$193). AE, DC, MC, V. Valet parking C$16 (US$10). Métro: Place des Arts. **Amenities:** Restaurant (Italian); bar; heated indoor pool; compact health club w/ sauna and steam room; concierge; limited room service; coin-op washers and dryers; same-day dry cleaning. *In room:* A/C, TV w/pay movies, dataport, coffeemaker, hair dryer, iron.

Four Points Montréal Centre-Ville   Representing a new brand of the Starwood hotel colossus (which also owns the Westin and Sheraton chains), this mid-priced business hotel is a refurbished Howard Johnson. It accomplishes its mission without breathing hard. That is, it provides roomy suites for businesspeople (and families) on longer stays, with fax machines, copiers, and computers on call—all at reasonable prices. Rooms have Sony PlayStations and the newspaper of your choice is made available.

475 Sherbrooke ouest (at rue Aylmer), Montréal, PQ H3A 2L9. ℂ 800/842-3961 or 514/842-3961. Fax 514/842-0945. www.fourpoints.com. 195 units. C$155–C$250 (US$100–US$161) double. Children under 17 stay free in parents' room. Packages available. AE, DC, MC, V. Parking C$12 (US$7.75). Métro: McGill. **Amenities:** Restaurant (International); bar; modest exercise room; limited room service; laundry service; same-day dry cleaning. *In room:* A/C, TV w/pay movies, dataport, fridge, coffeemaker, hair dryer, iron.

Holiday Inn Montréal-Midtown *(Kids)*   Not to be confused with the Holiday Inn in the Quartier Chinois (Chinatown), this midlevel entry stands among a clutch of similar hotels (including the Courtyard Marriott and Four Points hotels described immediately above) that cluster around the intersection of Sherbrooke and rue Durocher. Like them, it's among the city's best values in its class, especially for families, and does its job a little bit better than its neighbors. It is extremely efficient, has very attentive service, and provides an edge with its facilities.

420 Sherbrooke ouest (at av. du Parc), Montréal, PQ H3A 1B4. ℂ 800/387-3042 or 514/842-6111. Fax 514/842-9381. www.rosdevhotels.com. 486 units. C$119–C$220 (US$77–US$142) double. Children 19 and under stay free in parents' room. Packages available. AE, DC, DISC, MC, V. Self parking C$14 (US$9.05). Métro:

Kids Family-Friendly Hotels

Courtyard Marriott Montréal (p. 55) Parents will appreciate the self-service laundry, kids will love the indoor pool, and the whole family will enjoy the choices at the buffet breakfast.

Delta Montréal (p. 53) The Activity Centre for supervised play and crafts-making is a big draw for small kids, along with the swimming pool and (for bigger kids) an electronic-games room.

Holiday Inn Montréal-Midtown (p. 55) Two kids under 19 stay free with parents, kids under 12 eat free, and everyone gets to enjoy free in-room movies and the big swimming pool. There are special packages for families.

Hôtel Wyndham Montréal (p. 54) The glass-enclosed elevators scooting up and down the heart of this complex are fun for kids, as are the indoor pool and the easily-accessible subterranean levels of the underground city. Children stay free with their parents.

Place des Arts. **Amenities:** Restaurant (International); bar; large heated indoor pool w/ lifeguard; health club; limited room service; babysitting; coin-op washers and dryers; dry cleaning; executive floors. *In room:* A/C, TV w/pay movies, dataport, coffeemaker, hair dryer, iron.

Hôtel de la Montagne ★★ Two white lions stand sentinel at the front door, with a doorman wearing a pith helmet. The fauna fixation continues in a crowded lobby that incorporates a pair of 1.8m (6-ft.) carved elephants, two gold-colored crocodile sculptures, and a nude female figure with stained-glass butterfly wings sitting atop a splashing fountain. Clearly we are not in Kansas. Up on the mezzanine is the main dining room, Le Lutétia. Light meals are available beside the pool on the roof, 20 stories up, with dancing under the stars. Off the lobby, a cabaret lounge featuring a piano player and jazz duos (Mon–Sat) leads into Thursday's, a bar/restaurant with a spangly disco and a terrace opening onto lively rue Crescent. After all that, the relatively serene bedrooms seem downright bland. Given all these inducements, a stay here is a genuine bargain, especially in contrast to the expensive Hotel Vogue across the street.

1430 rue de la Montagne (north of Ste-Catherine), Montréal, PQ H3G 1Z5. © **800/361-6262** or 514/288-5656. Fax 514/288-9658. www.hoteldelamontagne.com. 138 units. C$178–C$190 (US$115–US$123) double. Children under 16 stay free in parents' room. Packages available. AE, MC, V. Parking C$14 (US$9.05). Métro: Peel. **Amenities:** 3 restaurants (French); 2 bars; heated outdoor pool; concierge; limited room service; laundry service; same-day dry cleaning. *In room:* A/C, TV/VCR w/pay movies, dataport, minibar, coffeemaker, hair dryer.

INEXPENSIVE

Castel St-Denis *Value* In the bohemian Latin Quarter, the Castel St-Denis is one of the more desirable budget choices. It's a little south of Sherbrooke, among the cafes of the lower reaches of the street, and 2 long blocks from the Terminus Voyageur (the city's main bus station). Most of the rooms are fairly quiet, and all are tidy and simply decorated, if hardly chic—flowered coverlets and wood room borders. The bilingual owner is a good source for guidance about nearby restaurants and attractions.

2099 rue St-Denis, Montréal, PQ H2X 3K8. © **514/842-9719**. Fax 514/843-8492. www.castelsaintdenis. qc.ca. 18 units. C$55–$75 (US$36–US$48) double. Extra person C$10 (US$6.45). MC, V. No parking available. Métro: Berri-UQAM or Sherbrooke. *In room:* A/C, TV, no phone.

Lord Berri *Value*   After a stint as a Days Inn, this economy hotel has returned to its old name and received a needed upgrading of furnishings and wallpaper. The resulting decor is as interesting as a bus schedule, but you can't argue with the economical rates, at least at the lower end. If you don't plan to spend much time in your room, then this is one of your best budget options in the city. Its central Latin Quarter location and the fact that it's a 5-minute walk from Vieux-Montréal help make up for its decor limitations.

1199 rue Berri (between bd. René-Lévesque and rue Ste-Catherine), Montréal, PQ H2L 4C6. © **888/363-0363** or 514/845-9236. Fax 514/849-9855. www.lordberri.com. 154 units. C$89–C$199 (US$57–US$128) double. AE, DC, MC, V. Limited indoor self-parking C$12 (US$8). Métro: Berri-UQAM. Pets in cages accepted. **Amenities:** Restaurant (International); bar; limited room service; same-day dry cleaning; nonsmoking floors. *In room:* A/C, TV/VCR w/pay movies, fridge, coffeemaker, hair dryer, iron.

2 Vieux-Montréal (Old Montréal)

VERY EXPENSIVE

Hôtel Inter-Continental Montréal ★★★   Only a few minutes walk from Notre-Dame Basilica and the restaurants and nightspots of Vieux-Montréal, this striking luxury hotel opened in 1991 and was instantly included in the coveted clique of "top properties" in town. The hotel's tower houses the sleek reception area and guest rooms, while the restored 1888 Nordheimer building contains a bar-bistro. (Take a look at the early-19th-century vaults below.) Guest rooms are quiet and well lit, with photographs and lithographs by local artists on the walls. The turret suites are fun, with their round bedrooms and wraparound windows. All rooms have bathrobes and two or three telephones. The lobby-level piano bar has a light menu and nightly music.

360 rue St-Antoine ouest (at rue de Bleury), Montréal, PQ H2Y 3X4. © **800/361-3600** or 514/987-9900. Fax 514/847-8550. www.montreal.interconti.com. 357 units. C$178–C$449 (US$115–US$290) double; from C$550 (US$355) suite. Packages available. AE, DC, DISC, MC, V. Valet parking C$23 ($15). Métro: Square Victoria. Small pets accepted. **Amenities:** 2 restaurants (International); 2 bars; small enclosed rooftop lap pool; health club w/ sauna and steam rooms; concierge; substantial business center; salon; 24-hr. room service; massage; laundry service; same-day dry cleaning; executive floors. *In room:* A/C, TV w/pay movies, dataport, minibar, coffeemaker, hair dryer, iron, safe.

EXPENSIVE

Auberge du Vieux-Port ★★   Housed in an 1882 building facing the port, this romantic luxury inn has an accomplished cellar restaurant, Les Remparts (p. 72). Polished hardwood floors, exposed brick walls, massive beams, and the original windows define the hideaway bedrooms. Fifteen rooms face the waterfront and 22 have whirlpool baths. CD players are standard (with a selection of disks available at the main desk). All rooms are nonsmoking. The three suite-like "lofts" have kitchenettes. Drinks and sandwiches are served on the rooftop terrace, which has unobstructed views of the Vieux-Port, a particular treat when fireworks are scheduled over the river.

97 rue de la Commune est (near rue St-Gabriel), Montréal, PQ H2Y 1J1. © **888/660-7678** or 514/876-0081. Fax 514/876-8923. www.aubergeduvieuxport.com. 27 units. C$165–C$285 (US$106–US$184) double. Extra person C$25 (US$16). Rates include full breakfast. AE, DC, DISC, MC, V. Valet parking C$15 (US$9.65). Métro: Champs-de-Mars. Pets in cages accepted. **Amenities:** Restaurant (French); concierge; limited room service; in-room massage; babysitting; laundry service; dry cleaning. *In room:* A/C, TV, dataport, kitchenette (suites), minibar, hair dryer, iron, safe.

Hôtel Le Saint-Sulpice ★   Even at the "hard opening" in July 2001, the hotel brochure still had to use architect's drawings instead of photos. A photographer will have a lot to work with: All the accommodations are suites, with TV sets in both sitting areas and bedrooms. Sony PlayStations are standard, as is high-speed Internet access. Almost 60 of the suites have wood or electric fireplaces. Most have mini-kitchens with microwave ovens, stoves, and fridges. Many have balconies. It was inspected too early to form a definitive judgment of service, but given the hotel's membership in the prestigious international Concorde chain, there's no reason to believe it won't merit at least another Frommer's star when things settle down.

414 rue St-Sulpice (behind the Notre-Dame Basilica), Montréal, PQ H2Y 2V5. © 877/785-7423 or 514/288-1000. Fax 514/288-0077. www.lesaintsulpice.com. 108 units. C$179–C$329 (US$115–US$212) double. AE, DC, MC, V. Parking C$18 (US$12). Métro: Place d'Armes. **Amenities:** Restaurant (Continental); bar; health club and spa; concierge; business center; 24-hr. room service; babysitting; laundry service; same-day dry cleaning. *In room:* A/C, TV w/pay movies, dataport, minibar, coffeemaker, hair dryer, iron, safe.

Hôtel Place d'Armes ★★ This highly desirable property is housed in a cunningly converted office building dating from the late 19th century. The elaborate architectural details of that era are in abundant evidence, especially in the ground floor lobby, with its high ceilings and richly carved capitals and moldings. An afternoon wine-and-cheese party is held around the lobby fireplace and bar in back. Room goodies include robes, down comforters, high-speed Internet access, and CD players (a collection of disks is available at the front desk). Few desires are not thought of—there's even a rooftop sundeck. Meals can be taken in the basement restaurant, which is under separate management. There are equal or better restaurant options within a few blocks.

701 Côte de la Place d'Armes, Montréal, PQ H2Y 2X6. © 888/450-1887 or 514/842-1887. Fax 514/842-6469. www.hotelplacedarmes.com. 48 units. C$170–C$275 (US$110–US$177). Extra person C$25 (US$16). Rates include breakfast. AE, DC, DISC, MC, V. Valet parking C$17 (US$11). Métro: Place d'Armes. **Amenities:** Restaurant (French/California); bar; small but efficient exercise room; concierge; secretarial services; limited room service; in-room massage; babysitting; laundry service; same-day dry cleaning. *In room:* A/C, TV, dataport, minibar, hair dryer, iron, safe.

Hôtel St-Paul ★★ Joining the laudable Vieux Montréal ranks of worthwhile old buildings converted to hotels and other contemporary uses, the St-Paul is ultra-chic in design. The exterior is of the Beaux-Arts school, but minimalism prevails inside, with simple lines, muted tones, and materials that don't deny their identity—leather, wool, rosewood, bronze, as well as fur throws here and there. Most of the guests are as trim and understated as the surroundings. An alabaster fireplace anchors one end of the long lobby and a bar is situated at the other end, next to the hotel's restaurant, Cube. Many rooms have marble tubs built for two, and extras include robes, CD players, fax machines, and high-speed Internet access.

355 rue McGill (at rue St-Paul), Montréal, PQ H2Y 2E8. © 866/380-2202 or 514/380-2222. Fax 514/380-2200. www.hotelstpaul.com. 120 units. C$200–C$240 (US$129–US$155) double; from C$285 (US$184) suite. AE, DC, MC, V. Métro: Square Victoria. **Amenities:** Restaurant (Eclectic); bar; exercise room; access to nearby health club; concierge; business center; 24-hr. room service; laundry service; same-day dry cleaning. *In room:* A/C, TV w/pay movies, dataport, minibar, coffeemaker, hair dryer, iron.

La Maison Pierre du Calvet ★ When Ben Franklin was in Montréal in 1775 during his attempt to enlist Canada in the revolt against the British, this house was already 50 years old. After a stint as a theme restaurant, the same owners made it into an atmospheric inn that attempts to transport guests to an elegant manor beside the Loire River in France. The beamed public rooms are luxuriously furnished with original antiques, not reproductions, including antique carpets on the ancient stone floors, leather sofas, gilt-framed portraits, a marquetry-topped reception desk, and ship models. A voluptuously furnished

Boutiquing in Old Montréal

The success of Vieux-Montreal's boutique hotels, coupled with the business and touristic allure of the old quarter, has encouraged other investors to cast their eyes upon the neighborhood. **Auberge Bonaparte,** the **Auberge du Vieux-Port,** and the **Hôtel Place d'Armes** (all described below) started the ball rolling. Five more hotels opened in the quarter in 2001 and 2002. The 120-room **Hôtel Saint-Paul,** 108-room **Hôtel Le Saint-Sulpice,** and **Hôtel XIXe siècle** are described in this chapter. More have opened since these and haven't been on the scene long enough for meaningful evaluation. But if you like to be on the cutting edge of the accommodations front, here are the most promising of these as-yet unproven hotels:

- A former brokerage house, the 1870 Nesbitt Thompson building has been transformed into the luxury **Hôtel Le St-James,** 355 rue St-Jacques (© **866/841-3111** or 514/841-3111). The hotel offers 61 units, most of them suites. Museum-quality antiques and art objects are part of the renovations (which were rumored to cost $11 million).
- The **Hôtel Nelligan,** 106 rue St-Paul ouest (© **888/450-1887** or 514/842-1887; www.hotelnelligan.com), got itself going in summer 2002. Occupying two adjoining 1850 buildings, it's named for a Canadian poet whose verses are excerpted on the walls of its 64 rooms and suites. Many rooms have fireplaces.
- The eagerly anticipated **Hôtel Gault,** 447–449 rue Ste-Hélène (© **866/904-1616**; www.hotelgault.com), is a transformed 19th-century warehouse It rents 30 loft-style rooms, a few with terraces.

dining room refers to no specific era but suggests a 19th-century ducal hunting lodge. Bedrooms are no less opulent, some with fireplaces and heavily carved four-poster canopied beds. TV sets would only spoil the ambience. A 50% room deposit is required.

405 rue Bonsecours (at rue St-Paul), Montréal, PQ H27 3C3. © **866/544-1725** or 514/282-1725. Fax 514/282-0456. www.pierreducalvet.ca. 9 units. C$195–C$265 (US$126–US$171); C$450 (US$290) suite. Extra person C$35 (US$23). Rates include full breakfast. AE, MC, V. Self-parking C$10 (US$6.45). Métro: Place d'Armes or Champ-de-Mars. **Amenities:** Restaurant; dry cleaning; laundry service. *In room:* A/C, dataport, hair dryer, iron on request.

MODERATE

Auberge Bonaparte ★★ The restaurant of the same name on the ground floor has long been one of Vieux-Montréal's favorites (see chapter 5). Romantic and faded in a Left Bank of Paris way, the restaurant had massive renovations done in 1999. While they were at it, the owners transformed the overhead floors into this fashionable urban inn, continuing the restaurant's romantic style, which opened in 1999. Even the smallest rooms are surprisingly spacious, and they have a variety of combinations of furniture—queen, king, and double beds—that are useful for families. Of the eight units on each floor, four have whirlpool baths with separate showers. Spring for the handsome suite on the top floor and get superb views of Notre-Dame, cloistered gardens, and cobblestone streets.

447 rue St-François-Xavier (north of St-Paul), Montréal, PQ H2Y 2T1. ⓒ **514/844-1448.** Fax 514/844-0272. www.bonaparte.com. 31 units. C$145–C$195 (US$94–US$126) double; C$325 (US$210) suite. Extra person C$15 (US$9.70). Rates include full breakfast. AE, DC, MC, V. Parking C$13 (US$8.25). Métro: Place d'Armes or Square Victoria. **Amenities:** Restaurant (French); access to nearby health club, children's programs; concierge; 24-hr. room service; in-room massage; babysitting; laundry service; same-day dry cleaning. *In room:* A/C, TV/VCR, dataport, hair dryer, iron.

Auberge Les Passants du Sans Soucy ✦   This cheery bed-and-breakfast in Vieux-Montréal is a 1723 house craftily converted into an inn by the bilingual owners. (Its seemingly misspelled name is a play on the name of one of them, Daniel Soucy.) Exposed brick, beams, and a marble floor form the entry area, which serves as the reception area, as well as an art gallery, and leads to a breakfast nook with a skylight. Each of the rooms upstairs has mortared stone walls, a buffed wood floor, a clock radio, fresh flowers, lace curtains, and a wrought-iron or brass bed. Four rooms have Jacuzzis, and gas fireplaces have been added to three others. The substantial breakfasts include chocolate croissants and café au lait.

171 rue St-Paul ouest, Montréal, PQ H2Y 1Z5. ⓒ **514/842-2634.** Fax 514/842-2912. www.lesanssoucy.com. 9 units. C$120–C$155 (US$77–US$100) double; C$190 (US$123) suite. Extra person C$15 (US$9.65). Rates include full breakfast. AE, DC, MC, V. Self-parking C$12 (US$7.40). Métro: Place d'Armes. *In room:* A/C, TV, hair dryer, iron.

Hôtel XIXe siècle   This tidy little hotel is worth seeking out for its central location and quiet demeanor. The building began life in 1870 as a bank in the Second Empire style, and the interior reflects these stately origins, with 4.5m (15-ft.) ceilings and a lobby that looks like a Victorian library. Three vaults remain from the building's original use as a bank, and one of them has been converted to a small bedroom. The other units are quite spacious, most with one queen- or king-size bed, and about half the bathrooms have whirlpool tubs. Work desks and voice mail are provided.

262 rue St-Jaques (at rue St-Jean), Montréal, PQ H2Y 1N1. ⓒ **877/553-0019** or 514/985-0019. Fax 514/ 985-0059. www.hotelxixsiecle.com. 59 units. C$140–C$195 (US$90–US$126) double; from C$245 (US$158) suite. AE, DC, MC, V. Métro: Square Victoria. **Amenities:** Bar; small exercise room; laundry service; same-day dry cleaning. *In room:* A/C, TV, dataport, hair dryer.

5

Where to Dine in Montréal

With over 5,000 dining spots, Montréal is filled to the brim with choices. Until a little over a decade ago, most of these eateries served French cuisine. A few *temples de cuisine* delivered haute standards of gastronomy, numerous accomplished bistros served up humbler ingredients in less grand settings, and folksy places featured the hearty fare of the colonial era, which employed the ingredients available in New France—game, maple syrup, and root vegetables. Everything else was "ethnic." Yes, some places offered Asian and Mediterranean cooking, but they weren't nearly as popular as they were in other North American cities. Québec was French, and that was that.

While waves of ethnic food crazes washed over Los Angeles, Chicago, Toronto, and New York in the 1980s, introducing people to Cajun, Tex-Mex, Southwestern, and fusion cuisines such as Franco-Asian, Pacific Rim, and Cal-Ital, the diners of Montréal were resolute. They stuck to their French culinary traditions. In recent years this attitude has changed dramatically. The recession of the early 1990s put many restaurateurs out of business and forced others to reexamine and streamline their operations. Immigration continued to grow, and along with it, the increased introduction of foreign cooking styles. Montréalers began sampling the exotic edibles emerging from the new storefront eateries all around them—Thai, Moroccan, Vietnamese, Portuguese, Turkish, Mexican, Indian, Creole, Szechuan, Japanese.

Innovation and intermingling of styles, ingredients, and techniques

were inevitable. The city, long one of the world's elite gastronomic centers, is now as cosmopolitan in its tastes and offerings as any city on the continent. True, some of the silliness that has attended culinary innovation elsewhere has afflicted chefs here, too. Plates arrive in towering overwrought presentations that might well incorporate spiky snow pea fans amid ponds of raspberry-beet coulis beneath wild rice and minced portobello mushrooms from which minigroves of rosemary and thyme sprout. But for most chefs, novelty is still secondary to the freshness and appropriateness of ingredients.

Deciding where to dine among the many tempting choices can be bewildering. The establishments recommended in this chapter should help you get started, because they include some of the most popular and honored restaurants in town. Getting to any of them involves passing many other worthy possibilities, for numbers of good restaurants often cluster in concentrated neighborhoods or along particular streets, such as rue Crescent, St-Denis, or St-Laurent. Nearly all of them have menus posted outside, prompting the local tradition of stopping every few yards for a little salivation-inducing reading and comparison shopping before deciding on a place for dinner.

It's a good idea, and an expected courtesy, to make a reservation to dine at one of the city's top restaurants. Unlike larger American and European cities, however, a few hours or a day in advance is usually sufficient at most

Best Dining Bets

See chapter 1 for a list of my favorite Montréal restaurants.

restaurants. A hotel concierge can make the reservation, even though nearly all restaurant hosts will switch immediately into English when they sense that a caller doesn't speak French. Dress codes are all but nonexistent, except in a handful of luxury restaurants, but adults who show up in the equivalent of T-shirts and jeans may feel uncomfortably out of place at the better establishments. Montréalers are a fashionable lot, and manage to look smart even in casual clothes. Few people want to dine in five-fork restaurants all the time. This city's moderately priced bistros, cafes, and ethnic joints often offer outstanding food, congenial surroundings, and amiable service at reasonable prices. And, speaking of value, the city's *table d'hôte* (fixed-price) meals are eye-openers. Entire two- to four-course meals, often with a beverage, can be had for little more than the price of an a la carte main course alone. Even the best restaurants offer them, so tables d'hôte present the chance to sample some excellent restaurants without breaking the bank. Having your main meal at lunch instead of dinner keeps costs down too, and is the most economical way to sample the top establishments. The delectable bottom line of dining in Montréal is that a meal here can be the equal in every dimension to the best offered in Los Angeles, Chicago, or New York—for about one-third less.

Alcohol-based beverages are heavily taxed, imported varieties even more so than domestic versions. To save a little, buy Canadian. That's not difficult when it comes to beer, for there are many breweries, micro to national, that produce highly palatable products. (The sign *"bières en fût"* tells you that a bar has brews on draft.) Wine is another matter. Wine is not largely produced in Canada due to a climate inhospitable to the essential grapes. Given the price differential with California and European pressings, though, you might want to try bottles from the Cantons-de-l'Est (east of Montréal), from British Columbia, and from the Niagara Frontier. The vineyards near the famous falls actually take advantage of the frigid winters, allowing grapes to freeze in order to make the sweet dessert "ice wines." If you drink more than one glass of wine with dinner, the half- or quarter-liter of house wine offered at many restaurants is a better deal than ordering by the glass.

Québec cheeses deserve attention, and many can only be sampled in Canada because they are often unpasteurized in the French manner, and cannot be sold in the United States. Even Quebecois themselves are coming to a new appreciation of this native product, in part due to recent interruptions in importation of European varieties. Of the many cheeses available, often as a separate course in better restaurants, you might try Mimolette Jeune (firm, fragrant, orange in color), Cru des Erables (soft, ripe, made of raw milk), Oka (semisoft, pleasantly smelly, made of cow's milk in a monastery), Le Migneron (semisoft, from goat's milk), and Le Chèvre Noire (a sharp goat variety covered in black wax).

When "cuisine" is the last thing on your mind and you want a quick meal that will do minimal damage to your credit-card balance, Montréal doesn't disappoint. Numerous places serve sandwiches and snacks for only a few dollars. Many of them go by the generic name *casse-croûte*—which means, literally, "break crust." They couldn't be simpler: often just a few stools at a counter, with a limited number of menu items that might include soup and *chien chaud* (hot dog) augmented by such homey Quebecois favorites as *tourtière* (beans and pork baked in maple syrup and served as a pie) and *poutine* (french fries doused with gravy and cheese nuggets). In addition, a number of mostly ethnic eateries serve two-course lunch specials for under C$8 (US$5.15). Look, in particular, to Thai, Chinese, and Indian restaurants for all-you-can-eat lunch buffets at that price.

For a more extended discussion of Québec dining, see "Cuisine Haute, Cuisine Bas: Smoked Meat, Fiddleheads & Caribou," in the appendix.

An insider website of irreverent reviews and observations about the local dining scene is www.montreal food.com.

PRICES The restaurants recommended below have been categorized by neighborhood and then by the cost of an average dinner for one person. Prices listed for main courses in these entries are for dinner unless otherwise indicated (luncheon prices are usually lower). Prices *do not* include wine, tip, nor the 7% federal tax and 7.5% provincial tax that are added to the restaurant bill. Food purchased in a market or grocery store is not taxed.

PARKING Because parking space is at a premium in most restaurant districts in Montréal, take the Métro or a taxi to the restaurant (most are within 1 or 2 blocks of a Métro station). Alternatively, when making a reservation, ask if valet parking is available.

SMOKING The Quebecois are no longer the heaviest smokers in Canada, that distinction having recently shifted to Nova Scotia's puffers. And even in still-addicted Montréal, new regulations require most restaurants to provide nonsmoking sections.

1 Restaurants by Cuisine

BELGIAN

L'Actuel (Downtown, $$, p. 68)
Witloof (Plateau Mont-Royal, $$, p. 79)

BREAKFAST/BRUNCH

Café Cherrier ✦ (Plateau Mont-Royal, $, p. 82)
Eggspectation (Downtown, $, p. 83)

CHINESE

La Maison Kam Fung (Downtown, $, p. 69)

DELI

Ben's (Downtown, $, p. 82)
Chez Schwartz Charcuterie Hébraïque de Montréal ✦ (Plateau Mont-Royal, $, p. 79)

FRENCH

Bonaparte ✦✦ (Vieux-Montréal, $$$, p. 70)

Le Beaver Club ✦ (Downtown, $$$$, p. 65)
Les Halles ✦ (Downtown, $$$$, p. 65)
Witloof (Plateau Mont-Royal, $$, p. 79)

FRENCH BISTRO

Boris Bistro ✦ (Downtown, $$, p. 68)
Chez l'Epicier (Vieux-Montréal, $$, p. 73)
Chez Lévêsque (Outer Districts, $$, p. 81)
La Gargote (Vieux-Montréal, $$, p. 73)
Le Bourlingueur (Vieux-Montréal, $, p. 75)
Leméac (Outer Districts, $$, p.82)
L'Express ✦✦ (Plateau Mont-Royal, $$, p. 77)
Restaurant le Paris (Downtown, $$, p. 68)

Key to Abbreviations: $$$$ = Very Expensive $$$ = Expensive $$ = Moderate $ = Inexpensive

FRENCH CONTEMPORARY

Les Remparts ★★ (Vieux-Montréal, $$$, p. 72)

Nuances ★★★ (Outer Districts, $$$$, p. 80)

Toqué! ★★★ (Plateau Mont-Royal, $$$$, p. 76)

FUSION

Area ★ (Plateau Mont-Royal, $$$, p. 76)

La Chronique ★★ (Outer Districts, $$$, p. 81)

Le Blanc ★ (Plateau Mont-Royal, $$$, p. 77)

GERMAN

Chez Better (Vieux-Montréal, $, p. 74)

GREEK

Milos ★★ (Plateau Mont-Royal, $$$$, p. 75)

INDIAN

Le Taj ★ (Downtown, $$, p. 68)

INTERNATIONAL

Mövenpick (Downtown, $, p. 70)

ITALIAN CONTEMPORARY

Buona Notte ★ (Plateau Mont-Royal, $$, p. 77)

Pavarotti (Vieux-Montréal, $$, p. 74)

JAPANESE

Katsura (Downtown, $$$, p. 65)

Na Go Ya (Vieux-Montréal, $$, p. 74)

KOREAN

Na Go Ya (Vieux-Montréal, $$, p. 74)

LIGHT FARE

Café Cherrier ★ (Plateau Mont-Royal, $, p. 82)

Eggspectation (Downtown, $, p. 83)

Kilo (Plateau Mont-Royal, $, p. 83)

La Brioche Lyonnaise (Quartier Latin, $, p. 83)

Le Jardin Nelson ★ (Vieux-Montréal, $, p. 75)

Santropol (Plateau Mont-Royal, $, p. 84)

St-Viateur Bagel & Café ★ (Plateau Mont-Royal, $, p. 83)

Titanic (Vieux-Montréal, $, p. 75)

Wilensky Light Lunch (Plateau Mont-Royal, $, p. 80)

MEDITERRANEAN

Modavie ★ (Vieux-Montréal, $$$, p. 72)

MEXICAN

Casa de Matéo (Vieux-Montréal, $$, p. 73)

PIZZA

Pizzédélic ★ (Plateau Mont-Royal, $, p. 80)

POLISH

Mazurka (Plateau Mont-Royal, $, p. 79)

SEAFOOD

Chez Delmo (Vieux-Montréal, $$$, p. 72)

Gibby's (Vieux-Montréal, $$$$, p. 70)

Maestro S.V.P. (Plateau Mont-Royal, $$, p. 78)

Magnan (Outer Districts, $$, p. 82)

Milos ★★ (Plateau Mont-Royal, $$$$, p. 75)

STEAK

Gibby's (Vieux-Montréal, $$$$, p. 70)

Magnan (Outer Districts, $$, p. 82)

THAI

Chao Phraya ★ (Outer Districts, $$, p. 81)

VEGETARIAN

Le Commensal (Downtown, $, p. 70)

Santropol (Plateau Mont-Royal, $, p. 84)

2 Downtown

VERY EXPENSIVE

Le Beaver Club ⭐ FRENCH   This restaurant takes its name from an organization of socially prominent explorers and trappers that was established in 1785. Their wilderness adventures are depicted in a stained-glass mural and carved wood panels that reveal the L-shaped room's 1950s origins and emphasize its clubby ambience. With widely spaced tables allowing a measure of privacy, it has long been a magnet for the city's power brokers (although, with about 120 seats to fill, it's hardly exclusive). Lunch is the time for the gentlest prices. The menu changes twice a year, always including the trademark roast beef, but recently expanded from the former meat-and-potatoes regimen to lighter, more fetchingly presented fish and fowl. The lobster carpaccio and morel soup with foie gras and truffles are typical. Jackets and ties are "recommended" for men. On Saturday evenings, a trio plays for dancing.

In Fairmont The Queen Elizabeth Hotel, 900 René-Lévesque ouest. © **514/861-3511.** Reservations recommended for dinner. Main courses C$33–C$39 (US$21–US$25). AE, DC, DISC, MC, V. Mon noon–3pm; Tues–Fri noon–3pm and 6–10:30pm; Sat 6–11pm (late June to Aug Tues–Sat 6–11pm only). Métro: Bonaventure.

Les Halles ⭐ FRENCH   Les Halles thrives as one of the most accomplished French restaurants in town, despite its unlikely location, squeezed into the most frenetic block of rue Crescent. Despite the prices, this isn't an "event" establishment, draped with brocade and glinting with Baccarat. Tables are close, service is correct but chummy, and animated conversations often start up between strangers—all of which promote the idea (if not the reality) of a mainstream, not fancy, establishment. Alberta beef, Québec lamb, and such game dishes as red deer and guinea hen are stars on the menu, but seafood, including sea bass and walleye, simply prepared, is also good. Ingredients are rarely exotic, yet the kitchen dresses them in unexpected ways. All of it, appetizers to desserts, comes in hefty portions. The wine cellar has more than 10,000 bottles of 450 different wines.

1450 rue Crescent (between rue Ste-Catherine and bd. de Maisonneuve). © **514/844-2328.** Reservations recommended. Dinner main courses C$21–C$38 (US$14–US$25); table d'hôte dinner C$49 (US$32). AE, DC, DISC, MC, V. Mon–Sat 6–11pm. Closed Dec 23–Jan 19. Métro: Guy-Concordia or Peel.

EXPENSIVE

Katsura JAPANESE   A tuxedoed maitre d' greets patrons at the door and leads them to one of the large convivial tables in the front room, to the smaller areas in back, or to the three-sided marble sushi bar in the middle (a refuge for those who arrive without a reservation). Whatever you choose, waitresses in kimonos move quickly and quietly to serve and, if asked, to explain the extensive menu. Katsura has been around long enough to claim credit for introducing sushi to Montréal. Although no longer a novelty, sushi and sashimi are still prepared with close attention to craft by the three able chefs working behind the bar; part of the pleasure of dining here is watching those practitioners at work. It's a common gesture, by the way, to give them a small gratuity separate from that added to the bill. Depending upon choices, a meal here can be relatively economical. Sample a lot of their creations, though, and the bill shoots into a much costlier category.

2170 rue de la Montagne (between bd. de Maisonneuve and rue Sherbrooke). © **514/849-1172.** Reservations recommended. Main courses C$13–C$29 (US$8.40–US$19); table d'hôte lunch C$15 (US$9.70), dinner C$32 (US$21). AE, DC, MC, V. Mon–Fri 11:30am–2:30pm and 5:30–10pm (Fri until 11pm); Sat 5:30–11pm; Sun 5:30–9:30pm. Métro: Peel or Guy-Concordia.

Downtown Montréal Dining

Area 23
Ben's **7**
Bleu Marin **3**
Boris Bistro **25**
Buona Notte **16**
Café Cherrier **21**
Chez Schwartz **12**
Eggspectation **4**
Katsura **5**

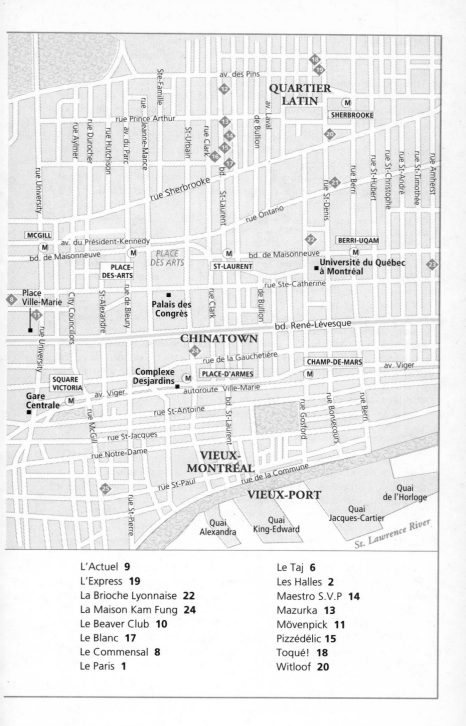

L'Actuel **9**
L'Express **19**
La Brioche Lyonnaise **22**
La Maison Kam Fung **24**
Le Beaver Club **10**
Le Blanc **17**
Le Commensal **8**
Le Paris **1**

Le Taj **6**
Les Halles **2**
Maestro S.V.P **14**
Mazurka **13**
Mövenpick **11**
Pizzédélic **15**
Toqué! **18**
Witloof **20**

MODERATE

Boris Bistro ★ *Finds* FRENCH BISTRO "Boris" is the owner's dog, depicted in the restaurant logo as a canine sophisticate in a turtleneck. Putting aside questions of Gallic relationships with their pets, this hugely popular eatery takes full advantage of the excitement of the western end of Vieux-Montréal, opposite the new Cité Multimédia. Not much work has gone into the interior, a minimalist environment with bare concrete floor and beams and exposed vents. Despite the surroundings, the staff and patrons transform it into a lighthearted space, aided in great part by very reasonable prices and such bistro classics as *blanquette de veau,* bouillabaisse, salmon *tartare,* and mussels du jour. Don't pass up the super *frites* with mayo, so good they appear as a stand-alone appetizer. If it's good weather, head straight for the courtyard and tables that seat 160 under big square patio umbrellas.

465 av. McGill (near rue des Récollets). ℂ 514/848-9575. Reservations recommended on weekend nights. Main courses C$13–C$16 (US$8.05–US$10). AE, MC, V. Daily 11:30am–11pm (may close Sun and Mon nights in winter). Closed 3 weeks at Christmas. Métro: Square Victoria.

L'Actuel BELGIAN Dine one flight up, where the most desirable of a sea of tables overlooks the square. Fittingly for a Belgian restaurant, mussels are the house specialty, in more than a dozen variations, from curried to Provençal, and in uniformly large portions averaging C$20 (US$13). They are brought to the table in the cast-iron pot in which they were cooked. Double-fried potatoes are the delectable accompaniment, and complimentary second helpings are customary. A sturdy Muscadet goes well with mussels, and there are two good ones on the list. If mollusks aren't to your liking, other options include veal cutlets and tournedos in 18 different sauces and preparations; there's also a spicy steak tartare. Although the establishment is very popular, there's almost always an available table, even on a Saturday night.

1194 rue Peel (on Square Dorchester). ℂ 514/866-1537. Main courses C$15–C$36 (US$9.35–US$23); table d'hôte lunch and dinner C$14–C$18 (US$8.70–US$12). AE, MC, V. Mon–Tues noon–10pm; Wed noon–10:30pm; Thurs–Fri noon–11pm; Sat 5–11pm. Métro: Gare Central.

Le Taj ★ NORTHERN INDIAN A large temple sculpture is prominently displayed in this dramatic setting of cream and apricot. In the glassed cubicle in the corner, a chef works diligently over a pair of tandoor ovens. His specialty is the mughlai repertoire of the northern Indian subcontinent. Seasonings of the dishes he sends forth tend more toward the tangy than the incendiary, but say you want your food spicy and you'll get it. (And watch out for the innocent-looking green coriander sauce.) Whatever the level of heat, dishes are perfumed with selections of turmeric, saffron, ginger, cumin, mango powder, and garam masala. For a rare treat, order the marinated lamb chops roasted in the tandoor; they arrive at the table sizzling and nested on braised vegetables. Vegetarians have a choice of eight dishes, the chickpea-based *channa masala* among the most complex. Main courses are huge, arriving in a boggling array of bowls, saucers, cups, and dishes, all accompanied by naan, the pillowy flat bread, and basmati rice. Evenings are quiet, and lunchtimes are busy but not hectic.

2077 rue Stanley (near rue Sherbrooke). ℂ 514/845-9015. Main courses C$7.95–C$20 (US$5.15–US$13); luncheon buffet C$9 (US$6). AE, DC, MC, V. Mon–Fri 11:30am–2:30pm and 5–10:30pm; Sat 5–11pm; Sun 5–10:30pm. Métro: Peel.

Restaurant le Paris FRENCH BISTRO If you spent your salad days at the Sorbonne 40 years ago and found yourself with a few extra francs to upgrade from your usual sparse meal, you could nip around the corner to a place much

⏴Kids⏵ Family-Friendly Restaurants

Pizzédélic (p. 80)   Pizza never fails to please the younger set, and this place caters to any taste, with toppings that stretch the imagination.

Magnan (p. 82)   Known especially for its supercheap all-you-can-eat lobster and beef extravaganzas, the menu also has lots of sandwiches and other simple foods that kids like. Parents don't have to worry about inevitable messes, especially since they'll be making big ones themselves.

McDonald's   For something familiar, but with a twist, this McDonald's, only a block from the Notre-Dame Basilica at the corner of rue Notre-Dame and boulevard St-Laurent, deserves a mention. Located in a house that was once the home of Antoine Lamet de la Mothe Cadillac, the founder of Detroit and a governor of Louisiana, it offers the usual menu, along with pizzas and the Québec favorite, *poutine* (french fries doused with gravy and cheese nuggets).

Mövenpick (p. 70)   This something-for-everyone emporium has a dozen stations selling omelets, pizzas, burgers, and just about anything a youngster might crave in a Disneyland setting with a romper room, games, and atmosphere that suggests that parents need not fear making too much of a mess.

like this. It's been open that long, and they haven't redecorated since—just some random old photos and posters. The welcome is friendly and casual, as if you were here just last night, and there's accordion music on the stereo. On the menu are such bistro staples as *foie de veau* (calf's liver) and *boudin noir* (blood sausage), but if they seem a little *too* French, wait for grain-fed roast chicken on Saturdays and steak au poivre all the time. Dishes are simple and unadorned, washed down with glasses from a selection of nine wines that go for as little as C$4.75 (US$3.05). Save room for the board of Quebecois and French cheeses.

1812 rue Ste-Catherine ouest (near rue St-Mathew). ⏴©⏵ **514/937-4898.** Main courses C$16–C$24 (US$10–US$16); table d'hôte lunch C$12–C$24 (US$7.75–US$16), dinner C$15–C$24 (US$9.70–US$16). AE, DC, MC, V. Mon–Thurs noon–3pm and 5:30–10:30pm; Fri–Sat noon–3pm and 5:30–11pm; Sun 5:30–10:30pm. Métro: Guy-Concordia

INEXPENSIVE

La Maison Kam Fung   CHINESE   Weekends are the big days, when suburban Chinese families come for a wallow in their comfort food. Although regular meals are served in the evening, the morning to mid-afternoon hours are reserved for dim sum. That's the time to go. Here's the drill: Obtain a ticket from the young woman at the podium. Wait. Once summoned to a table, be alert to the carts being trundled out of the kitchen. They are stacked with covered baskets and pots, most of which contain dumplings of one kind or another, such as balls of curried shrimp or glistening envelopes of pork nubbins or scallops, supplemented by such items as fish purée slathered on wedges of sweet pepper and, for the adventuresome, steamed chicken feet and squid. Pick these items off the cart until sated. Resist the desire to gather up the first five items that appear. Much more is on the way. You pay by the item.

1111 rue St-Urbain (near René Levésque ouest). ℂ **514/878-2888.** Main courses C$7.25–C$15 (US$4.70–US$9.70). AE, DC, MC, V. Daily 7am–3pm and 5–10:30pm. Métro: Place d'Armes.

Le Commensal VEGETARIAN   Le Commensal serves vegetarian fare buffet-style. Most of the dishes are so artfully conceived, with close attention to aroma, color, and texture that even avowed meat eaters don't feel deprived. The only likely complaint is that dishes that are supposed to be hot are too often luke-warm. Patrons circle the table helping themselves, and then pay the cashier by weight, C$1.65 (US$1.05) per 100 grams. The second-floor location affords a view, which compensates for the utilitarian decor. There is no tipping.

Le Commensal has been expanding, with nine branches scattered around the greater Montréal area and in Toronto. One of the most convenient in-town locations is at 1720 St-Denis and Sherbrooke (ℂ **514/845-2627**).

1204 av. McGill College (at rue Ste-Catherine). ℂ **514/871-1480.** Reservations not accepted. Dishes priced by weight; most meals under C$12 (US$7.75). AE, MC, V. Daily 11:30am–10pm. Métro: McGill or Bonaventure.

Mövenpick *Kids* INTERNATIONAL   The central gimmick of this outpost of the Swiss chain is its theme-park simulation of a European market. Placed around the tremendous space are more than a dozen food stations where diners line up for pizzas, crêpes, sushi, coffee, pastas, omelets, waffles, salads, rotisserie birds, grilled meats, baked goods, and seafood, including freshly opened oysters. Faux grapevines, fake flowers, and an ersatz tree are meant to evoke a Mediterranean setting. Never mind that. This is a playland cafeteria, and the food, much of it prepared to order, ranges from satisfactory to pretty good. Upon entrance, you are handed a "passport," which the servers stamp with the prices of the items ordered; you pay up when you leave. Eat a course at a time or load a tray with a complete meal and take it to the nearby tables. Children are welcome in the designated romper room, and chess and scrabble sets are available for lingerers. The bistro has table service, and two bars serve wine, beer, and spirits. Almost everything is available for takeout.

1 place Ville Marie (rue University at rue Cathcart.) ℂ **514/861-8181.** Most items under C$15 (US$9.70). MC, V. Daily 7:30am–2am. Métro: McGill or Bonaventure.

3 Vieux-Montréal (Old Montréal)

VERY EXPENSIVE

Gibby's STEAK/SEAFOOD   Given its popularity and situation in this touristy quarter, Gibby's is routinely dismissed as an overpriced snare for out-of-towners. That opinion is now closer to the truth, since they eliminated lunch and jacked up their prices a few years ago. Still, it's a handsome place, a 2-centuries-old stone-and-beam setting that's much larger than it looks from the outside. And if your taste buds cry out for a break from the novelties of fusion cookery, then this is your place. Everything comes in strapping portions, cuts of beef and lamb rearing 2 inches off the plate and slabs of fish as wide as a catcher's mitt. Grilling is usually precise and to order, and there are up to a dozen daily choices of fresh fish. In warm weather, there's a beverage-only terrace in back.

298 place d'Youville (at rue St-Pierre). ℂ **514/282-1837.** Reservations required. Main courses C$28–C$42 (US$18–US$27). AE, DC, DISC, MC, V. Free valet parking. Sun–Fri 5–10pm; Sat 4:30–11pm. Métro: Square Victoria.

EXPENSIVE

Bonaparte ★★ FRENCH   Novelty isn't pursued here, cachet isn't sought. But in a city brimming with accomplished French restaurants, this is a personal favorite.

Vieux-Montréal Dining

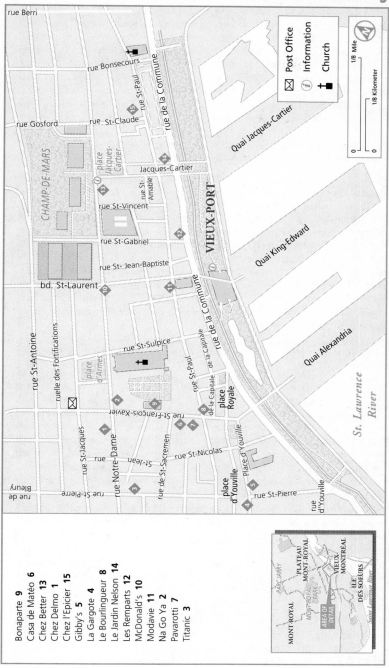

rue Berri

rue Bonsecours

rue Gosford

rue St-Claude

rue St-Paul

rue de la Commune

Quai Jacques-Cartier

CHAMP-DE-MARS

place Jacques-Cartier

Jacques-Cartier

rue St-Amable

rue St-Vincent

rue St-Gabriel

rue St-Jean-Baptiste

bd. St-Laurent

VIEUX-PORT

Quai King-Edward

Quai Alexandria

rue St-Antoine

ruelle des Fortifications

rue St-Sulpice

place d'Armes

rue St-Paul

de la Capitale

rue de la Commune

St. Lawrence River

rue St-Jacques

rue St-François-Xavier

place Royale

rue Notre-Dame

St-Jean

rue de St-Sacrement

rue St-Nicolas

Place d'Youville

place d'Youville

rue St-Pierre

rue d'Youville

rue de Bleury

rue St-Pierre

Post Office
Information
Church

1/8 Mile
1/8 Kilometer
0   0

Bonaparte **9**
Casa de Matéo **6**
Chez Better **13**
Chez Delmo **1**
Chez l'Epicier **15**
Gibby's **5**
La Gargote **4**
Le Bourlingueur **8**
Le Jardin Nelson **14**
Les Remparts **12**
McDonald's **10**
Modavie **11**
Na Go Ya **2**
Pavarotti **7**
Titanic **3**

PARC JARRY
PLATEAU MONT-ROYAL
MONT-ROYAL PARK
VIEUX MONTRÉAL
ÎLE DES SOEURS
MONT-ROYAL
AREA OF DETAIL
Saint Lawrence River

The dining rooms run through the ground floors of two old row houses, with large live trees and decorative details suggestive of namesake Nappy's era. Adroit service is by schooled pros who manage to be knowledgeable without being stuffy. If you're uncertain about appropriate wines, your waiter's suggestions will prove astute. Food portions are neither stunted nor excessive, and there is no shortage of vegetables—samplings of yellow squash, snow peas, carrots, zucchini, and red peppers encircle the swirl of linguini that comes with rare slices of wild boar. Bread is crusty and chewy, always a good sign. In the medium price range, you can't do better in Montréal.

443 St-François-Xavier (south of rue Notre-Dame). ℂ 514/844-4368. Reservations recommended. Main courses C$20–C$30 (US$13–US$19); table d'hôte C$22–C$25 (US$14–US$16). AE, DC, MC, V. Mon–Fri noon–2:30pm and 5:30–10:30pm; Sat–Sun 5:30–10:30pm. Métro: Square Victoria.

Chez Delmo SEAFOOD   This venerable fish house has resisted change for decades. But that's a good thing: It's an atmospheric retreat that evokes a time nearly lost, when the freshest available fruits of the sea were quickly broiled, poached, baked, grilled, or sautéed and presented with wisps of saucing and not a fennel slice or oven-dried tomato in sight. Enter a dim room with twin facing bars and their lines of stools, just the place for single diners in search of a lobster roll or a light lunch of opened-to-order oysters (still available only in months with an "R"). Other diners are funneled into the larger, characterless back room where full meals are served. Salmon from the Maritime Provinces, halibut, Arctic char, and real Dover sole are often featured, substantial in portion and lacking in flash, the better to lubricate the insider talk of dealmakers from nearby law offices and brokerage houses.

211 rue Notre-Dame (near rue St-François-Xavier). ℂ 514/849-4061. Reservations recommended. Main courses C$17–C$26 (US$11–US$17). AE, MC, V. Mon–Fri 11:30am–2:30pm; Tues–Sat 5:30–10pm. Métro: Square Victoria.

Les Remparts ★★ FRENCH CONTEMPORARY   There's no doubt what part of the Auberge du Vieux Port you're in, not when you're seated beneath these heavy beams and copper-painted pipes and vents. A cellar seems an unlikely setting for what has recently emerged as one of the city's most accomplished kitchens. The 20-something chef started here as an assistant and took over a few months later. He works whenever possible with products of the region, re-drawing his menu with the seasons to take full advantage of what's available. One of Canada's most desirable fish, halibut, is slow-roasted and presented with tapenade on an artichoke purée, while fork-tender venison comes with a scatter of wild mushrooms, gooseberry sauce, and braised salsify. Lunch is a particular bargain, with the top price well under US$14, but the chef's true showmanship blossoms at dinnertime, not in tortured presentations, but with more sophisticated dishes.

93 rue de la Commune est (near rue St-Gabriel). ℂ 514/392-1649. Reservations recommended on weekends. Main courses lunch C$11–C$17 (US$6.95–US$11), dinner C$31–C$37 (US$20–US$24); table d'hôte lunch C$14–C$17 (US$9.05–US$11). Mon–Fri noon–3pm and 6–10:30pm; Sat–Sun 6–11pm. Métro: Place d'Armes.

Modavie ★ MEDITERRANEAN   A highly visible location no doubt helps keep this wine bar/restaurant filled, but the management leaves little to chance. Arrayed around the handsome center bar are walls of shelves stacked with bottles of wine, single-malt scotches, and fine cigars. There are free bar snacks during the 4 to 7pm happy hours Monday through Friday. Live jazz is presented at 7pm, every night in summer, and Friday and Saturday nights in winter. Candle flames flicker in river breezes that flow in through front and side windows flung wide on summer nights. The food doesn't disappoint, either in preparation or portion. Lamb is their self-proclaimed specialty, in one version propping four double chops over a composition of sweet peppers, cauliflower, and broccoli rabe. This is one ingratiating place.

1 rue St-Paul ouest (cor rue St-Laurent). (C) 514/287-9582. Reservations recommended on weekends. Table d'hôte lunch C$14 (US$9.05), dinner C$20–C$31 (US$13–US$20); dinner main courses C$18–C$29 (US$12–US$19). Daily 11:30am–3pm and 6–11pm. Métro: Place d'Armes.

MODERATE

Casa de Matéo MEXICAN   Stepping into Casa de Matéo feels like wandering into a party in progress, especially on Friday and Saturday evenings, when mariachis come to kick the fiesta up a notch. Get in the mood with a birdbath-sized frozen margarita, which arrives with chips and salsa at the center horseshoe bar that's encased with rough terra-cotta tiles. The cheerful staff from Mexico and other Latin American countries lends authenticity. With these generous servings, appetizers can be skipped—but that would mean missing the *plato Mexicano*, a sampler of all the starters. Because the *plato Mexicano* is a meal in itself, some diners may want to stop there—but *that* would mean missing the *pescado Veracruzano:* whole red snapper quickly marinated and fried and served with a nest of crisp vegetables. The usual burritos and enchiladas, on the other hand, are easy to forget.

440 rue St-François-Xavier (near rue St-Paul). (C) 514/844-7448. Reservations recommended on weekend nights. Main courses C$15–C$25 (US$9.65–US$16); table d'hôte lunch Mon–Fri C$12 (US$7.40). AE, DC, MC, V. Daily 11:30am–10:30pm. Métro: Place d'Armes.

Chez l'Epicier FRENCH BISTRO   While it doesn't warrant a special trip, this crisp little eatery is opposite the Marché Bonsecours and on the route of the Vieux-Montréal walking tour outlined in chapter 7. And because it's also a delicatessen with an abundance of tempting prepared foods, it's a place to remember for a picnic down the hill in the Vieux Port. At lunch, choices on the blackboard emphasize soups, salads, and sandwiches; at night, offerings are heartier and more inventive, with frequent Asian touches. Foie gras poached in veal broth with shrimp, and peanut and ginger chow mein are examples. Flavorings are delicate and desserts are intriguing.

331 rue St-Paul est (at rue Gosford). (C) 514/878-2232. Main courses lunch C$12–C$16 (US$8–US$11), dinner C$19–C$39 (US$13–US$26). MC, V. Daily 11:30am–2pm and 5:30–10pm. Métro: Champ-de-Mars.

La Gargote FRENCH BISTRO   Visitors are only starting to discover this spirited little bistro. That's just as well, since it's already packed with locals, especially at lunch, when the staff is spread thin trying to deal with the crush. When patrons pay attention to their plates and not their companions, they are sure to be satisfied by such classics as duck sausage l'orange and lamb and Merguez sausage couscous, along with less familiar possibilities such as *paupiettes* of pheasant with mushrooms and currants. The surroundings are the Vieux-Montréal norm, with stone and brick walls and rough-cut rafters overhead, warmed by a fireplace in winter. Meals are also put together for takeout—meant for offices, but useful for a picnic in the nearby waterfront park. Better still is lunch at the tables set out in the plaza from May through September.

351 place d'Youville (at rue St-Pierre). (C) 514/844-1428. Reservations recommended. Main courses and lunch table d'hôte C$12–C$16 (US$7.90–US$10); table d'hôte dinner C$15–C$22 (US$9.70–US$14). MC, V. Mon–Fri 10am–2pm and 5:30–10pm; Sat–Sun 5:30–10pm. Métro: Square-Victoria.

Na Go Ya JAPANESE/KOREAN   Here's a worthy alternative for those who crave sushi but want to avoid the higher prices and hauteur of fancier purveyors in town. One lunch deal (to be taken at the bar in front) is comprised of five pieces of sushi, five maki pieces, and a handroll of rice around spicy tuna for only C$11 (US$7.05); another deal is three sashimi and four pieces of sushi for C$13 (US$8.35). (Eat the ones wrapped in seaweed first, while they're still warm—they get chewy if you save them for later.) They are put together by chatty chefs who are in sharp contrast to the stoic fellows at the posher places. For about the same prices mentioned above, you can opt for a "lunch box" of grilled beef, chicken, or salmon, each of which comes with miso soup, rice, salad, and fruits. In the dining areas in back, the food is Korean, the ethnic background of the chef and the owners, and if you haven't experienced that cuisine, you're in for a pleasant surprise.

140 rue Notre-Dame ouest (at rue St-François-Xavier). ☎ 514/845-5864. Main courses C$8.95–C$29 (US$5.75–US$19); table d'hôte lunch C$8.95–C$17 (US$5.75–US$11). AE, DC, MC, V. Daily 11am–3pm and 5–9pm (until 10pm Fri–Sun). Métro: Place d'Armes.

Pavarotti ITALIAN CONTEMPORARY   The interior of this 125-year-old stone house has a thrown-together quality, with brick walls, old photos of the port, ship models, hanging bundles of herbs, and a candle chandelier that would do justice to the lair of the Phantom of the Opera—all of which is so dimly lit that the menu is hard to make out. That's okay. Take a blind poke; you probably won't be disappointed. There isn't anything too odd, and servings are ample. The bruschetta is typical of the hearty portions, not one or two pieces of toast, but a ring of six, with a do-it-yourself heap of chopped tomato, onion, garlic, and olives in the middle. After that, plates of feathery pasta, made right there, become evening specials, like the one that comes with a tumble of clams, mussels, and shrimp. The soupy house risotto supports your choice of seafood or vegetables. By mid-evening, the place is a friendly babble, orchestrated by the always-present owner.

408 rue St-François-Xavier (north of rue St-Paul). ☎ 514/844-9656. Reservations recommended on weekends. Main courses C$12–C$18 (US$7.40–US$12); table d'hôte C$17–C$18 (US$11–US$12). AE, DC, MC, V. Mon 11am–3pm; Tues–Thurs 11am–9pm; Fri 11am–10pm; Sat 5–10pm. Métro: Square Victoria.

INEXPENSIVE

Chez Better *Value* GERMAN   They aren't making a half-hearted boast with the name of this place. This and the other five outposts of this local chain are named for the founder, a Canadian born in Germany. Presumably he grew homesick for tastes of his native land and opened his first restaurant in this 1811 building near the top of Place Jacques Cartier to assuage those cravings. Think multiple variations of chipolata, kasseler, sauerkraut, and 100 brands of beer— that gives the general outline of the menu. Forget grease and oozing globules of fat, though, for these are lighthearted sausages, brightly seasoned with herbs, curry, hot pepper, and even truffle shavings. A special lunchtime sampler of bratwurst, cevapcici, and diable comes with fries and kraut and costs just C$8.95 (US$5.75)—a terrific deal. Three jars of mustard sit on each table. While sausage plates are the stars, there are also mixed grills, chicken schnitzels, fondues, salads, and mussels nine ways. Service can be disjointed, but rarely to the point of irritation.

160 rue Notre-Dame (near place Jacques-Cartier). ☎ 514/861-2617. Main courses C$9.95–C$17 (US$6.40– US$11); table d'hôte lunch C$8.95–C$13 (US$5.75–US$8.35), dinner C$15–C$17 (US$9.50–US$11). AE, DC, MC, V. Daily 11am–10pm. Métro: Champ-de-Mars.

Le Bourlingueur *Value* FRENCH BISTRO   Although it doesn't look especially promising upon first approach, this place is a true keeper. Start with the almost unbelievably low prices they charge for several four-course meals daily. The blackboard menu changes depending on what's available at the market that day, making it possible to dine here twice a day for a week without repeating anything except the indifferent salad. Roast beef and *choucroute garnie* (sauerkraut served with meat) are likely to show up, but the specialty of the house is seafood—watch for the cold lobster with herb mayonnaise. Well short of chic, it doesn't make the most of its stone walls and old beams, but the decor hardly matters at these prices and relative quality. The crowd is diverse, with a wide range of ages, genders, and occupations.

363 St-François-Xavier (at rue St-Paul). (C) 514/845-3646. Reservations recommended on weekends. Main courses C$9.95–C$14 (US$6.40–US$9.20); table d'hôte lunch or dinner C$9.95–C$16 (US$6.40–US$10). MC, V. Daily 11:30am–9pm. Métro: Place d'Armes.

Le Jardin Nelson *R* LIGHT FARE   Near the foot of the hill, a passage leads into the tree-shaded garden court in back of a stone building dating from 1812. More a place to spend a pleasant hour or two than for serious dining, there's jazz most nights and weekend afternoons and classical chamber groups Monday to Friday during lunch hours in the good months. Food takes second place, but the kitchen does well with its pizzas and crêpes, the latter with both sweet and savory fillings (including lobster). Other choices are soups, omelets, pastas, salads, and sandwiches. There's a covered people-watching porch in front (with effective heat lamps in cold weather), and dining rooms and a bar inside.

407 place Jacques-Cartier (at rue St-Paul). (C) 514/861-5731. Main courses C$12–C$15 (US$7.60–US$9.95). MC, V. Apr–Nov Mon–Fri 11:30am–3am, Sat–Sun 10am–3am; closed Dec–Mar. Métro: Place d'Armes or Champ de Mars.

Titanic LIGHT FARE   Really good sandwiches aren't easy to find, but they come to luscious life here. Freshly baked baguettes are split and filled with such savory combos as coarse country paté with green peppercorns, or smoked ham and brie, or roast pork with chutney, or any of 26 other toothsome possibilities. Available extras to go with any of the sandwiches include cornichons (mini gherkin pickles), pickled onions, olive pesto, cukes, and capers. Stop in for a breakfast omelet, a meal-sized antipasto plate, an afternoon snack. No alcoholic beverages, but with good ol' Dad's Root Beer, who needs chablis? Two ramshackle rooms with overhead pipes contain two counters and a large communal table. Note that it closes at 4pm. Payment is on the honor system.

45 rue St-Pierre (near rue Le Moyne). (C) 514/849-0894. All items under C$10 (US$6.45). MC, V. Mon–Fri 7am–4pm. Métro: Place d'Armes.

4 Plateau Mont-Royal
VERY EXPENSIVE

Milos *RR* GREEK/SEAFOOD   Avenue du Parc used to be lined with Hellenic fish houses. That culinary population has thinned out, but the top dog remains and still holds to a standard higher than its rivals are ever likely to achieve. Inside, it is what a taverna at a picturesque Aegean fishing port would look like if it had the necessary drachmas—white plaster walls, bleached wooden floors, Greek vases, blue tiles, and refrigerated cases for the finny main events. The freshest available fish, flown in from wherever they are at peak, are the reason Milos prevails. Show the slightest interest and you'll be taken on a tour of the iced and clear-eyed denizens offered for your pleasure—Icelandic char, sushi-quality yellowfin tuna, Nova Scotia lobsters, Florida pompano, Mediterranean *loup-de-mer*. Pick your very own meal or leave it to the chefs. They'll even cook a veal chop if you absolutely insist. With drinks comes grilled bread and a dish of fragrant olive oil and freshly snipped oregano. The excellent Greek salad is the usual first course, but oh-so-lightly battered soft-shelled crabs are terrific if they're in season. The main course will be along soon, brushed with olive oil and charcoal-grilled—validation once again that the most memorable meals are often the simplest. Expect to part with over C$150 (US$97) for two plus tax, wine, and tip—it's almost worth it.

5357 av. du Parc (between rue St-Viateur and av. Fairmont). ℂ 514/272-3522. Reservations required on weekends. Main courses C$29–C$38 (US$19–US$25). AE, MC, V. Mon–Fri noon–3pm and 5–11pm; Sat–Sun 6pm–midnight. Métro: Outremont, then a 12-block walk.

Toqué! ★★★ FRENCH CONTEMPORARY Toqué! is an adornment that has single-handedly raised the gastronomic expectations of the entire city. A meal here is virtually obligatory for anyone who admires superb food dazzlingly presented. "Postnouvelle" might be an apt description of the creations of Normand Laprise and Christine Lamarche, for while presentations are eye-openers, the portions are quite sufficient and the singular combinations of ingredients are intensely flavorful. Asian and related fusion influences are more evident these days, but the chefs still work within the parameters of the contemporary French kitchen. Top-of-the-bin ingredients, some of them rarely seen in combination—for example, foie gras with milkweed buds—ensure that the menu is never set in stone. Consider just one recent dish: roasted *bas-du-fleuve* saddle of lamb joined by a lentil compote moistened with juices of the meat and served with a combination of butternut squash, cipollini onion, carrots, Jerusalem artichoke, and wilted bok choy. Duck, veal, quail, and venison are unfailingly memorable, while salmon and Arctic char are often the most desirable fish.

If you choose the tasting menu, the four or five courses are accompanied by wines selected to complement each preparation. The restaurant fills up later than most, with prosperous-looking suits and women who sparkle at throat and wrist, so while there is no stated dress code, you'll want to look your best. Service is efficient, helpful, and not a bit self-important. Allow 2 hours for dinner. Call at least 3 days ahead for reservations and confirm the night before. They open for lunch Monday through Friday during the 2 weeks before Christmas.

3842 rue St-Denis (at rue Roy). ℂ 514/499-2084. Reservations required. Menu dégustation with wine C$74 (US$48); main courses C$24–C$34 (US$16–US$22). AE, MC, V. Tues–Sat 5:30–10:30pm. Closed Dec 24–Jan 6. Métro: Sherbrooke.

EXPENSIVE

Area ★ FUSION The chef seems far too young to know as much as he obviously does about the world's cuisines. But he deftly manipulates techniques and ingredients found in a couple of dozen countries around the Pacific and Mediterranean rims, in precociously assured concoctions that challenge taste assumptions. In none of this does he neglect his homeland of Canada, nor such Canadian staples as duck and venison. Convention is disregarded, though, with dishes like the "brick" of salmon brushed with saffron oil and accompanied by Israeli couscous, and ravioli filled with ricotta and married with duck confit, mushrooms, asparagus, and oh, yes, white truffle oil. Servings are attractively put together, and, it must be said, wastefully large, as with the rack of nine prodigiously meaty ribs. The cheese list is commendable for its focus on Québec products; choose Pied-de-vent and Ciel de Charlevoix to get an idea of the possibilities. There are two seatings nightly. The seating times vary according to demand and time of the year. Call to find out when the seatings are when you're in town.

1429 rue Amherst (north of rue Ste-Catherine). ℂ 514/890-6691. Reservations recommended. Main courses C$18–C$27 (US$12–US$17); table d'hôte C$35 or C$45 (US$23 or US$29). AE, MC, V. Mon–Fri 11:30am–2:30pm and 6–11pm; Sat–Sun 6–11pm. Métro: Beaudry.

Le Blanc ⊛ FUSION   Considering that this is one of those jinxed locations that has seen three other promising restaurants crash in the last decade, some authorial trepidation accompanies this recommendation to give this latest manifestation a try. But okay—Le Blanc has lasted over 3 years, so there's hope. People in business mufti take advantage of the low fixed-price lunches, moving aside for a 20- and 30-something crowd in the evening, when jazz combos and singers provide a supper-club atmosphere, with dancing until 3am. The pleasingly Art Deco space has a few romantically secluded booths to one side. Food is of the globe-hopping sort, none of it bizarre. Bread comes with the now-clichéd dipping dish of balsamic-flavored olive oil. One special stacked four grouper filets atop a foundation of zucchini and couscous, embellished with salsa, baby asparagus, peppers, and artichoke hearts. Too much, but tasty. You might make a meal of appetizers—the smoked pepper spring roll with coconut milk sauce and the spicy strawberry and chive bowtie pasta, perhaps.

3435 bd. St-Laurent (north of Sherbrooke). ℂ 514/288-9909. Main courses C$20–C$46 (US$13–US$30); table d'hôte lunch C$15–C$18 (US$9.70–US$12), dinner C$18–C$42 (US$12–US$27). AE, DC, MC, V. Mon–Fri noon–3pm and 5:30–10:30pm (bar until 3am); Sat–Sun 5:30pm–midnight (bar until 3am). Métro: Sherbrooke.

MODERATE

Buona Notte ⊛ ITALIAN CONTEMPORARY   With its high ceiling masked by electric fans and heating ducts, Buona Notte could be in New York's SoHo. A principal component of the decor is a collection of plates painted by celebrity diners, among them Ben Kingsley, Danny DeVito, and Nicolas Cage. They are boxed (the plates, that is) and arrayed along the walls. Funk and hip-hop thump over the stereo, and the dishy waitresses look ready to depart on the next fashion shoot. They appear in black (with splashes of carefree gray), as do most of their customers, all with cellphones at the ready. Although the food takes second place to preening, it's surprisingly worthwhile. Pastas prevail, tumbled with crunchy vegetables or silky walnut sauce or any of 10 or more other combinations. The kitchen exhibits less reliance on meat than the norm. Service is stretched thin at dinner, especially on the weekends, and the noise level cranks up after 7pm. The active bar in back stays open until 3am.

If the velvet rope is up at Buona Notte, there are several other similar spots on the half block from here to Sherbrooke, including **Mediterraneo** (3500 bd. St-Laurent, ℂ **514/844-0027**), **Primadonna** (3479 bd. St-Laurent, ℂ **514/ 282-6644**), and **Globe** (3455 bd. St-Laurent, ℂ **514/284-3823**).

3518 bd. St-Laurent (near rue Sherbrooke). ℂ 514/848-0644. Reservations recommended. Pizzas and risottos C$7.50–C$17 (US$4.85–US$11); main courses C$21–C$28 (US$14–US$18); table d'hôte C$31 (US$20). AE, DC, MC, V. Mon–Sat noon–midnight; Sun 5pm–midnight (bar until 3am daily). Métro: St-Laurent.

L'Express ⊛⊛ FRENCH BISTRO   No obvious sign announces the presence of this restaurant, only its name discreetly spelled out in white tiles in the sidewalk. There's no need to call attention to itself, since *tout* Montréal knows exactly where it is. While there are no table d'hôte menus, the food is fairly priced for such an eternally busy place and costs the same at midnight as at

March of the Tongue Troopers

When the separatist Parti Quebecois took power in the province in 1976, they wasted no time in attempting to make Québec unilingual. They promptly passed Bill 101, which made French the sole official language of the government and sharply restricted the use of other languages in education and commerce. Because about 20% of the population had English as a primary language, one out of five Quebecois felt themselves declared instant second-class citizens. Francophones responded that it was about time *les Anglais,* aka *les autres* (the others), knew what that felt like and set about enforcing the new law.

The vehicle was *L'Office de la Langue Française.* Its agents fanned out across the province, scouring the landscape for linguistic insults to the state and her people. No offense was too slight for their stern attention. MERRY CHRISTMAS signs were removed from storefronts, and department stores were forced to come up with a new name for Harris Tweed. Any merchant who put up a GOING OUT OF BUSINESS poster faced the possibility of a fine to accompany his already dour situation. By fiat and threat of punishment, hamburgers became *hambourgeois,* a hot dog was rechristened *le chien chaud,* a funeral parlor was transformed into a *salon funéraire,* and Schwartz's Montréal Hebrew Delicatessen became *Chez Schwartz Charcuterie Hebraïque de Montréal.* Particular scrutiny was accorded the Eastern Townships, on the south side of the St. Lawrence River. They had been settled by United Empire Loyalists, Americans faithful to the British Crown who fled to Canada at the time of the Revolution. The region, known henceforth as Les Cantons de l'Est, had a Tea Table Island and a Molasses Lake, which became *Ile Table à Thé* and *Lac à Mélasse.*

Eventually, it might be assumed, there would be no more Anglophone words to conquer. But bureaucrats will be bureaucrats. Required definitions describe every object in the known world. One is a *petit gâteau de forme rectangulaire, aromatisé au chocolat, dont la texture se situe entre le biscuit sec et le gâteau spongieux.*

Or, in a word, a brownie.

noon. After a substantial starter like bone marrow with coarse salt or a potted chicken paté, you may opt for one of the lighter main courses, such as the ravioli *maison,* round pasta pockets flavored with a mixture of beef, pork, and veal. Larger appetites might step up to full-flavored duck breast with chewy chanterelles in a sauce with the scent of deep woods. Or simply stop by for a *croque monsieur* or a bagel with smoked salmon and cream cheese. Although reservations are usually necessary for tables, single diners can often find a seat at the zinc-topped bar, where meals are also served. Breakfast is served from 8 to 11:30am.

3927 rue St-Denis (at rue Roy). (C) **514/845-5333.** Reservations recommended. Main courses C$11–C$18 (US$7.05–US$12). AE, DC, MC, V. Mon–Fri 8am–3am; Sat 10am–3am; Sun 10am–2am. Métro: Sherbrooke.

Maestro S.V.P. SEAFOOD   You could eat well for a week on the 2 blocks of The Main north of Sherbrooke. Make this storefront bistro one of your stops.

The name of the place and the musical instruments mounted on the walls have no particular relevance to the menu, unless you count the jazz trio the owner brings in Sunday evenings at 6:30. Those are only a few of the attractions likely to get your attention; others include the several types of oysters always on hand and all-you-can-eat mussels offered every Monday. Blackboards list the recommended wines of the day, in glasses costing C$6.50 to C$12 (US$4.20–US$7.40). The "Maestro Platter" is an extravagant medley of bruschetta, clams, mussels, coconut shrimp, chicken satay, a half-lobster, *and* king crab—only C$60 (US$39) for two. Service is casual but alert, and there is valet parking Thursday through Saturday.

3615 St-Laurent (near rue Sherbrooke). ℂ 514/842-6447. Reservations recommended. Main courses C$21–C$45 (US$14–US$29); table d'hôte lunch C$9–C$19 (US$5.80–US$12), dinner C$23 (US$15). AE, DC, MC, V. Mon–Wed 11am–11pm; Thurs–Fri 11am–midnight; Sat 4pm–midnight; Sun 4–11pm. Métro: Sherbrooke.

Witloof BELGIAN/FRENCH   The name is Flemish for endive, and Witloof has long specialized in Belgian dishes. Now, with a new associate chef from the south of France, it has solidified its standing as one of the most gratifying restaurants in town. It remains at the border between casual and elegant, as exemplified by snowy linen tablecloths covered with butcher paper. Steaming casseroles of mussels in six versions, with tents of *frites* on the side, are deservedly the most popular items on the menu, but the classic Belgian fish stew, *waterzooi*, is a close second. The kitchen can fall behind on orders, but the convivial atmosphere dissuades grousing. Several Belgian beers are available, and the wine list has been expanded. Desserts range from maple crème brûlée to praline crêpes. Many diners take advantage of the early bird tables d'hôte to soak up the late-afternoon sun on the terrace.

3619 rue St-Denis (at rue Sherbrooke). ℂ **514/281-0100.** Reservations recommended. Main courses C$15–C$22 (US$9.65–US$14); table d'hôte lunch C$13–C$26 (US$8.35–US$17). AE, DC, MC, V. Mon–Fri 11:30am–3pm and 5–10pm; Sat 5–10pm. Métro: Sherbrooke.

INEXPENSIVE

Chez Schwartz Charcuterie Hébraïque de Montréal ✿ DELI   French-first language laws turned this old-line delicatessen into a linguistic mouthful, but it's still known simply as Schwartz's to its many ardent fans. They are convinced it is the only place on the continent to indulge in the guilty treat of smoked meat. Housed in a long, narrow space, it has a lunch counter and a collection of simple tables and chairs crammed impossibly close to each other. Any empty seat is up for grabs. Few mind the inconvenience or proximity to strangers, for they are soon delivered plates described either as small (meaning large) or large (meaning humongous) heaped with slices of smoked meat, along with piles of rye bread. Most people also order sides of fries and one or two mammoth garlicky pickles. There is a handful of alternative edibles, but tofu and leafy green vegetables aren't included. Expect a wait. Schwartz's has no liquor license, but it does have a nonsmoking section.

3895 bd. St-Laurent (north of rue Prince-Arthur). ℂ 514/842-4813. Most items C$4–C$13 (US$2.60–US$8.40). No credit cards. Sun–Thurs 9am–12:30am; Fri 9am–1:30am; Sat 9am–2:30am. Métro: St-Laurent.

Mazurka *Value* POLISH   Even among the low-priced ethnic eateries that line both sides of pedestrian road Prince Arthur, this old-timer (opened in 1952) is an eye-widening bargain. Do the Mazurka double take, for example, with the mixed plate of pierogies, sausage, bigos (a sauerkraut-based stew), a potato pancake, and stuffed cabbage, all for only C$11 (US$6.95). Chicken Kiev is the same, and they've been known to offer two lobsters for the same price that their competitors charge for one. Service is glum and rushed, but that doesn't deter the throngs of students, artists, frugal execs, and night people who fill the place 12 hours a day.

64 rue Prince Arthur est (near bd. St-Laurent). ✆ **514/844-3539**. Reservations accepted for 4 or more only. Main courses C$6.25–C$15 (US$4.05–US$9.50). AE, MC, V. Daily 11:30am–midnight. Métro: Sherbrooke.

Pizzédélic ★ *Kids* PIZZA   Pizza here runs the gamut from traditional to as imaginative as anyone might conceive, with toppings from feta cheese to escargots to artichokes to pesto. All arrive on thin, not-quite-crispy crusts. The difference over ordinary pizzerias is the use of fresh, not canned, ingredients, as in the antipasto plate of grilled vegetables and calamari strips. Pastas, sandwiches, and meat dishes are also available. The front opens in warm weather, and there's a terrace in back. It's a growing chain, with units all over town, but two other conveniently located Pizzédélics are at 1329 Ste-Catherine (✆ **514/526-6011**) and 370 av. Laurier ouest (✆ **514/948-6290**).

3509 bd. St-Laurent (near rue Sherbrooke). ✆ **514/282-6784**. Pizzas and pastas C$6.95–C$14 (US$4.50–US$8.85). AE, DC, MC, V. Daily 11am–midnight. Métro: St-Laurent.

Wilensky Light Lunch LIGHT FARE   Wilensky's has been a Montréal tradition since 1932, known for its grilled-meat sandwiches, low prices, curt service, and utter lack of decor. Expect to find nine stools at a counter. This is Duddy Kravitz/Mordecai Richler territory, and the ambience is Early Immigrant. The food selections are limited to a few sandwiches—not much more than bologna, salami, and mustard thrown on a bun and squashed on a grill—and hot-dog sandwiches, also squashed. They're washed down with egg creams or drinks jerked from the rank of syrups, like the old-time soda fountain it is. I'm talking tradition here, not cuisine.

34 rue Fairmount ouest (at rue Clark). ✆ **514/271-0247**. Most items under C$5 (US$3.25). No credit cards. Mon–Fri 9am–4pm. Closed 2 weeks in July, 2 weeks in Feb. Métro: Laurier; then walk about 12 blocks. Bus: 55 to St-Laurent and Fairmount; then walk a block west and then north if you're coming from the train and west if you're coming from the bus.

5 Outer Districts

VERY EXPENSIVE

Nuances ★★★ FRENCH CONTEMPORARY   Unlikely as it may seem, here is haute cuisine in a gambling casino, ensconced atop four floors of bleeping buzzers, blinking lights, and the crash of cascading jackpots. This elegant entry in Montréal's gastronomic sweepstakes quickly shouldered its way to the top of the pyramid. The designers didn't stint on the trappings, not with the mahogany paneling, soaring ceiling, Villery & Boch china, and lavish deployment of leather and linen. A maitre d' seats you, a captain explains the evening's possibilities, a waitress takes your order and serves. All of them are qualified to advise on appropriate wines from the extensive cellar. The menu is re-worked each season, so a dish that dazzled in February might not be there in August. One example of a past triumph was the wrapped round stockade of thin asparagus spears topped with greens and surmounted by the meat of a small lobster claw. Among the rhapsody of main courses are likely to be the rosy slices of lamb baked in clay and the sushi-quality tuna barely touched to flame with eggplant compote. The *plateau de fromage* has several admirable Québec-produced cheeses. Make it all the way to dessert after all that, and the waitress might suggest a dish of praline mousse and chocolate sherbet. A stiffened dress code keeps out guys attired in ripped tank tops—jackets are now required for men.

1 av. du Casino (in the Casino de Montréal, Ile Ste-Hélène). ℂ **514/392-2708.** Reservations strongly recommended. Main courses C$32–C$45. (US$21–US$29); table d'hôte C$51 (US$33) or C$75 (US$48). AE, DC, MC, V. Sun–Thurs 5:30–11pm; Fri–Sat 5:30–11:30pm. Métro: Ile Ste-Hélène.

EXPENSIVE

La Chronique ★★ FUSION   Montréal's top chefs have been recommending this modest-looking storefront restaurant near Outremont for several years now. It was feared that the resulting buzz might spoil the place, but it has only improved. Most significantly, the chef allows patrons to discover how remarkable traditional recipes can be when transformed in the hands of a master. Presentations are so impeccable you hate to disturb them, flavors so eye-rolling you want to scrape up every last smear of food. Diners who are leery of organ meats, for example, will find the veal sweetbreads a silky revelation. The menu includes Mediterranean and Southwestern touches. Originally a more humble bistro, expensive ingredients like foie gras and caviar elevate the place to a grander level. That relates to prices, too, with one tasting menu reaching C$112 (US$72) per person, with wine. A small but judicious selection of cheeses may precede or replace the tantalizing desserts, which look as if they might take flight. Menus are only in French, but the cordial waiters speak English. Smoking is entirely excluded.

99 rue Laurier ouest (at rue St-Urbain). ℂ **514/271-4770.** Reservations recommended. Main courses C$23–C$30 (US$15–US$19); table d'hôte lunch C$16–C$25 (US$10–US$16), dinner (Fri–Sat) C$55 (US$36). AE, DC, MC, V. Tues–Fri 11:30am–2:30pm and 6–10:30pm; Sat 6–10:30pm. Closed 1st 2 weeks in July. Métro: Laurier.

MODERATE

Chao Phraya ★ THAI   As the current contender for best Thai in town, this spot boasts panache a few notches above most of its rivals. It brightens its corner on increasingly fashionable Laurier Avenue with white table linens and sprays of orchids on each table. The host helps with suggestions about the most popular items on the menu. Dumplings in peanut sauce are a deservedly well-liked appetizer, as is the main event of mixed seafood, composed of squid, scallops, shrimp, crab claws, mussels, and chunks of red snapper. This food is tangy, at the least, and menu items are given one to three hot pepper symbols grading hotness. Two printed peppers are about right for most people. A cooling cucumber salad helps, and you'll want a side of sticky rice, too. Everything comes in attractive bowls and platters. There are several wines by the glass—try the semi-dry Alsatian wine.

50 av. Laurier ouest (1 block west of bd. St-Laurent). ℂ **514/272-5339.** Reservations recommended. Main courses C$8.95–C$17 (US$5.75–US$11). AE, DC, MC, V. Sun–Wed 5–10pm; Thurs–Sat 5–11pm. Métro: Laurier.

Chez Lévêsque FRENCH BISTRO   In the brasserie tradition, this place opens for breakfast and doesn't shut down until late. Drop by and stay a while. Have a coffee, write a poem, peruse *Le Monde,* dig through a full four courses. It's a place to hang out. That isn't to say it hasn't kept up with the times. There's bouillabaisse (a must), salmon tartare, and lamb Provençal on the card, but someone in charge apparently thinks fusion ideas and healthy living are important, too. That conviction shows up in Chilean sea bass laid over a comforter of mixed vegetables, and in the brace of quail infused with a peppery honey-soy marinade and set upon a nest of greens. A fireplace blazes much of the year in the upstairs room. In warm weather, the front is opened up. Service can be uneven—attentive at first, then fading into distraction.

1030 rue Laurier ouest (near rue Hutchinson, in Outremont). © 514/279-7355. Reservations recommended. Main courses C$11–C$30 (US$6.95–US$19); table d'hôte lunch C$7.80 (US$5.05), dinner C$15–C$28 (US$9.65–US$18). AE, DC, MC, V. Mon–Fri 8am–midnight; Sat–Sun 10:30am–midnight. Métro: Laurier.

Leméac FRENCH BISTRO   Named for the publishing firm that used to occupy the building, this spritely new arrival on the Laurier scene has a long tin-topped bar along one side, well-spaced tables, and, far from least, a crew of pretty, cheerful waitresses. While the bistro dishes sound conventional on the page, they are put together in freshly conceived ways. Two examples: The curried mussel soup is capped by a nicely-browned pillow of puff pastry, and the salmon pot-au-feu is a perfectly cooked filet laid over a healthful selection of small potatoes, carrots, tender Brussels sprouts, and their collective broth. Cuisine is different, not startling, and served in an atmosphere that invites lingering. Weekend brunch is popular.

1045 rue Laurier (cor rue Durocher). © 514/270-0999. Main courses C$9.50–C$29 (US$6.15–US$18); table d'hôte lunch C$17–C$19 (US$11–US$12). AE, MC, V. Mon–Wed noon–midnight; Thurs–Fri noon–1am; Sat 10:30–1am; Sun 10:30–midnight. Métro: Laurier.

Magnan *Kids* STEAK/SEAFOOD   This rough-hewn roadhouse on the south side of the Lachine Canal has a terrace next to the parking lot, a *taverne* with neon beer signs and several TV sets, and a slightly more formal dining room in the basement. So forget elegance, skip the appetizers, and go straight for the twin lobsters. They come cold and split, with potatoes or rice. Monsters of the deep they aren't, but when was the last time you had 2 pounds of lobster for under US$14? For about 40 days in May and June, they up the stakes with all-you-can-eat lobster and roast-beef nights, with all the trimmings for under US$36 per person, *including taxes and service.* (Better call now to reserve a table.) Kids are welcome in the dining room, and parents don't need to worry about the inevitable mess.

2602 rue St-Patrick, Pointe St-Charles. © 514/935-9647. Main courses C$8.25–C$22 (US$5.30–US$14). DC, MC, V. Tavern Mon–Sat 8am–midnight; Sun and holidays 9am–11pm. Restaurant Mon–Fri 11am–10pm; Sat–Sun 4–10pm. By car or taxi, drive west on rue St-Jacques, turn left on rue Atwater, following it around to the right of Atwater Marché (Market) and under the Lachine Canal; take the first exit at the sign for rue St-Patrick, turn right on St-Patrick, and go 3 blocks to the restaurant, on the right.

6 Early-Morning & Late-Night Bites

When the yen for coffee and a pastry or a sandwich strikes, you are never far from an outpost of one of the three major cafe chains: **A.L. Van Houtte, Presse Café,** or **Second Cup** (which are usually open 24 hr.). All have reasonable prices for decent food, and many have tables indoors and out for resting tired feet or plotting your next sightseeing moves.

Ben's DELI   This deli-restaurant was founded by Ben and Fanny Kravitz in 1908 and is still in the family. Autographed celebrity photos—including Burl Ives, the Ink Spots, and Ed Sullivan—attest to its heyday. The current owners persist in the claim that this is where Montréal's famous smoked meat originated. Besides the inevitable variations on that much-loved ingredient, the menu meanders through cheese blintzes, potato latkes, corned beef and cabbage, bagels and lox, and much more. They are fully licensed.

990 bd. de Maisonneuve (at rue Metcalfe). © 514/844-1000. Most items under C$12 (US$7.75). MC, V. Sun–Wed 7:30am–2am; Thurs 7:30am–3am; Fri–Sat 7:30am–4am. Métro: Peel.

Café Cherrier ★ BREAKFAST/BRUNCH/LIGHT FARE   The tables on the terrace wrapped around this corner building are filled whenever there's even a slim possibility that a heavy sweater and a bowl of café au lait will fend off frostbite. In summer, the loyalists get to stay out until way past midnight, and in winter, all the same people squeeze inside. Brunch is popular, even if the food is unexceptional, but consider this place any time a snack or a meal is in order. Portions are ample and inexpensive. An easygoing atmosphere prevails, and it's popular with musicians, actors, artists, and journalists, so contrive to look mysterious or celebrated.

3635 rue St-Denis (at rue Cherrier). ℂ 514/843-4308. Main courses C$6–C$13 (US$3.85–US$8.05); table d'hôte C$13–C$17 (US$8.05–C$11). AE, MC, V. Mon–Fri 7:30am–10pm; Sat–Sun 8:30am–11pm (to 3am in summer); brunch Sat–Sun 8:30am–3pm. Métro: Sherbrooke.

Eggspectation BREAKFAST/BRUNCH/LIGHT FARE   Let the dopey name deter you and you'll miss a meal that may constitute one of your best food memories of Montréal, at least if you're of the breakfast-is-best school of gastronomy. Prices are low and portions are huge, ensuring crowds from early morning to late afternoon. One reader lauds the thick, creamy slices of French toast spiked with Grand Marnier and joined with mounds of fresh fruits. Eggs any way are special, too, even if they are tagged with names like *eggscaliber* and *eggsileratio*. There are 10 variations on eggs Benedict. Sandwiches and pastas are also on the menu. In summer, it stays open into the evening. The ever-expanding chain has additional branches at 198 rue Laurier ouest (ℂ **514/278-6411**), near rue St-Denis, and at 213 rue St-Jacques in Vieux-Montréal (ℂ **514/282-0119**).

1313 av. bd. Maisonneuve ouest (at rue de la Montagne). ℂ 514/842-3447. Most items under C$12 (US$7.75). MC, V. Daily 6am–5pm (until 6pm Sat–Sun). Métro: Laurier.

Kilo LIGHT FARE   When dining in this neighborhood, skip the last course and make a beeline to Kilo. The mousses, cakes, and pies sold here are arrayed as enticingly as jewels in a display case. Light lunches are served, but it's the desserts, sweet and creamy or tartly piquant, that draw the crowds and pose a direct challenge to the most determined dieters among them. Strong coffee laced with cognac, amaretto, or Grand Marnier is often chosen to complement the sweets. They also have a branch at 1495 rue Ste-Catherine est (ℂ **514/596-3933**).

5206 bd. St-Laurent (between rue St-Viateur and rue Fairmount). ℂ 514/277-5039. Most items under C$8 (US$5.15). MC, V. Mon–Thurs 11am–1am; Fri 11am–1am; Sat noon–2am; Sun 1pm–midnight. Métro: Laurier.

La Brioche Lyonnaise LIGHT FARE   There are many delightful *patisseries*—pastry shops—in this French city, and this, deep in the Quartier Latin, is one of the most popular. They serve light items—quiches, salads, and sandwiches—but patrons often settle for just a sweet cake or a croissant and coffee, perhaps a bowl of café au lait. They stop in after dinner, UQAM classes, or a show at the theater across the street, or simply for a break in sightseeing. Check out what's available in the display case—from Marie Claires to mega-meringues—and then find a table in one of several seating areas. As in most patisseries, there's no pressure to move on soon.

1593 rue St-Denis (near bd. de Maisonneuve). ℂ 514/842-7017. Most items under C$12 (US$7.75). AE, MC, V. Daily 9am–midnight. Métro: Berri-UQAM.

St-Viateur Bagel & Café ✦ LIGHT FARE   The bagel wars flare as hotly as Montréal's eternal smoked-meat battles, but this, an offshoot of a beloved old bakery, is easily among the top contenders. Bagels in these parts are thinner, smaller, and crustier than the bloated, cottony monsters posing as the real thing in most parts of the republic south of the border. These are hand-rolled, twist-flipped into circles, dusted with sesame seeds or whatever, and baked in big wood-fired ovens right on premises. Try them in or out. Sandwiches come with soup or salad. Expect a short wait on weekends and not infrequently during the week.

1127 Mont-Royal est (between rues Christophe Colomb and La Roche). ℂ **514/528-6361.** Most items under C$10 (US$6.45). No credit cards. Daily 6am–midnight. Métro: Mont-Royal.

Santropol *Value* LIGHT FARE/VEGETARIAN   Mostly-vegetarian sand-wiches, salads, and potpies come in hefty flavorsome proportions at this favorite. The composition of the clientele is alluded to in the sign that reads HEY STUDENTS—BRING OUR CUTLERY BACK, but families and older folk drop by in substantial numbers, too. They dawdle at tables with chairs that don't even bear a family resemblance amid panels of stamped tin on walls and ceilings and offhanded sculptures beholden to no school. Herbal teas, coffees, and 18 differ-ent kinds of milkshakes (almond, maple, and peach-apricot are among the choices) constitute the available nonalcoholic beverages. Occupying a timeworn redbrick house, the restaurant has several dining nooks, along with a tree- and fern-filled courtyard in summer. One percent of the bill is sent to organizations that ease hunger in Québec and developing nations. Takeout is available.

3990 rue St-Urbain (at Rue Duluth). ℂ **514/842-3110.** Most items under C$10 (US$6.45). No credit cards; debit cards accepted (US cards included). Daily 11:30am–midnight. Métro: Mont-Royal; then walk through Jeanne Mance Park.

7 Picnic Fare: Where to Get It, Where to Eat It

When planning a picnic or a meal to eat back in your hotel room, consider a stop at **La Vieille Europe,** 3855 bd. St-Laurent near St-Cuthbert (ℂ **514/842-5773**), a compact storehouse of culinary sights and smells. Choose from wheels of pungent cheeses, garlands of sausages, patés, cashews, honey, fresh peanut butter, or dried fruits. Coffee beans are roasted in the back, adding to the mix-ture of maddening aromas. A stroll to the north along St-Laurent reveals other possibilities for mobile edibles.

In the rue Crescent area, **Le Faubourg Ste-Catherine,** on rue Ste-Catherine ouest between Guy and St-Mathieu, is a market and fast-food complex that was recently treated to a yearlong revitalization by its new owners. Stalls sell takeout foods as varied as sushi, enchiladas, spring rolls, tandoori, couscous, and sand-wiches, as well as breads, fresh fruits, pastries, and ice cream. There are also clothing boutiques, crafts, and a bowling alley. You'll find similar bounty under-ground at **Les Halles de la Gare,** an accumulation of food stalls, delis, and cafes beneath Le Reine Elizabeth hotel and adjacent to the main concourse of the rail-road station. Among them is an SAQ wine store. Downtown, the **Marché Mövenpick,** at the corners of Cathcart and University and Mansfield and René Lévesque, sells just about everything from its various food stalls for takeout, including sushi, panini, fruits, baked goods, cheeses, pizzas, and grills.

Better still, make the short excursion by Métro (the Lionel-Grouix stop) to **Marché Atwater,** the public market at 3025 St-Ambroise, open 7 days a week. The long shed is bordered by stalls of gleaming produce and flowers, the two-story center section given to wine purveyors, food counters, bakeries, and cheese stores. The best representatives of the last two are **La Fromagerie** (ℂ **514/932-4653**), whose highly knowledgeable attendants know every detail of production of the 450 to 550 different North American and European cheeses on offer, and the **Boulangerie Première Moison** (© 514/932-0328), which fills its space with the tantalizing aromas of baskets of breads and cases of pastries. (There is another branch of the bakery in the Gare Centrale.) From either location, it isn't far by taxi to Parc du Mont-Royal, a wonderful place to enjoy a picnic, or by bicycle to a spot along the revamped Lachine Canal.

In Vieux-Montréal, pick up supplies at the new food market in the historic **Marché Bonsecours** (© 514/872-4560) on rue de la Commune and take them to the park of the Vieux-Port, only steps away. That park can also be the picnic destination from **Olive & Gourmando** (© 514/350-1083) at 351 rue St-Paul ouest, open Tuesday through Saturday from 8am to 6pm. Primarily a bakery, it placed third in a *Gazette* reader's poll only months after it opened. That was for its baguettes, but many breads, croissants, and pastries are available. Put your sandwiches together from the cheeses and sausages in the cold case, or choose from their interesting compositions, including a grilled portobello mushroom with a purée of olives and goat cheese. A lot of the bread is out the door by mid-morning. If you want wine or beer with your lunch, there's a new *dépanneur* (convenience store), **Le Quartier** (© 514/392-1299), at 321 rue Notre-Dame est (near rue Bonsecours). There's much greater choice at the **SAQ Selection**, 440 bd. de Maisonneuve (Métro: McGill).

6

Exploring Montréal

Montréal is a feast of choices, able to satisfy the desires of both physically active and culturally curious visitors. Depending upon what interests you and how much time you have, you can hike up imposing Mont-Royal in the middle of the city, cycle beside the Lachine Canal, take in the artworks and ephemera of some 20 museums and as many historic buildings, attend a Canadiens hockey match or an Expos baseball game, party until dawn on rue Crescent and The Main, or soak up the concrete and spiritual results of some 400 years of conquest and immigration. And with riverboat rides, the fascinating Biodôme (which replicates four distinct ecosystems), a sprawling amusement park, the Vieux-Port Science Centre, puppet and magic shows, and unique Cirque du Soleil performances, few cities assure kids of as good a time as this one.

Once you've decided what you want to do, getting from hotel to museum to attraction is pretty easy: The superb Métro system, a fairly logical street grid, wide boulevards, and the vehicle-free underground city all aid in the swift, largely uncomplicated movement of people from place to place.

Montréal's 350th birthday was celebrated in 1992 with the opening or expansion of many of the attractions described in this chapter. Efforts to enhance the cultural offerings have continued since then. If you're not in town on Montréal Museums Day (p. 19), check out the **Montréal Museums Pass,** which allows entry to 25 of the city's museums and attractions and is available year-round. Good for 2 out of 3 consecutive days, the pass costs C$20 (US$13). It is sold at all participating museums, the Info-touriste Centre on Square Dorchester, and at many Montréal hotels. For further information, call ℂ **877/266-5687** from outside Montréal or 514/873-2015 within the metropolitan area.

When planning your visit, you might want to note in the listings below which museums have restaurants, so that you can plan a meal in addition to your museum visit. Most museums are closed Mondays.

SUGGESTED ITINERARIES
If You Have 1 Day

Explore the oldest part of town, called **Vieux-Montréal.** It borders the resuscitated port, with many restored buildings dating from the 18th and 19th centuries. Don't miss the **Notre-Dame Basilica** and the **Pointe-à-Callière** museum.

Then, for contrast, stroll through the downtown sections of the modern city, including its vibrant vest-pocket **Chinatown.** Visit the **Musée des Beaux Arts,** which houses an array of art, a big bookstore, and a gift shop in its neoclassical building. Enjoy a *table d'hôte* lunch or dinner in one of the city's fine downtown restaurants. *Table d'hôte* consists of a fixed-price set menu as opposed to a la carte courses.

If You Have 2 Days

Follow the itinerary above for the first day. On the second day, take the Métro to the **Olympic Complex,** which has an inclined tower and observation deck. Across the street are the carefully cultivated acres of the **Botanical Garden.** While there, see the Chinese Garden and take the informative open-air train tour. Next, visit the fascinating **Biodôme,** which replicates four distinct ecosystems, complete with live flora and fauna. In summer, make an island day of it on **Ile Ste-Hélène** by visiting the island's old fort, with its museum and changing-of-the-guard ceremony, and perhaps the new environmental exhibits at **La Biosphère.** Afterward, go to **La Ronde** amusement park, where fireworks displays are mounted many evenings in summer. Or head that night to Vieux-Montréal and take in a performance at the English-language **Centaur Theatre,** listen to jazz or folk in one of the clubs along Rue St-Paul, or, if it's in town, thrill to the magic of the acclaimed **Cirque du Soleil.**

If You Have 3 Days

On the morning of Day 3, take an exhilarating jet-boat ride through the **Lachine Rapids,** or a calmer harbor cruise aboard *Le Bateau-Mouche.* Get to know Montréal like a native by wandering along **boulevard St-Laurent,** the axis of the city's ethnic neighborhoods, to rue Prince-Arthur, then through Carré St-Louis (St. Louis Square) to the **Latin Quarter,** the center of activity for the Francophone population. In the evening, dine in one of the fine restaurants in adjacent **Plateau Mont-Royal** and cap the night with a club crawl.

If You Have 4 Days or More

On the fourth day, fit and athletic visitors might choose to climb **Mont-Royal** on rue Peel and admire the view of the city and river from the lookout, then stroll or take a picnic in the surrounding park. (If the prospect of that hike is daunting, take the Métro to the Guy station, then bus no. 165.) See chapter 7 for a walking tour of Mont-Royal. In the afternoon, take in a specialized museum, perhaps the **McCord Museum of Canadian History** or the **Canadian Centre for Architecture.**

On Day 5, visit the **Oratoire St-Joseph,** the city's most prominent shrine, which gives a glimpse into the spiritual life of devout Montréalers. If the weather's good, rent a bike and follow the **Lachine Canal** for 11km (7 miles) to Lake St-Louis. If the weather turns dicey, descend to the climate-controlled world of Montréal's **underground city,** a labyrinth of passages, subway tunnels, shops, and cinemas, all of which can be enjoyed without once stepping outdoors.

1 The Top Attractions

DOWNTOWN

Musée des Beaux-Arts ★★★ This museum ("Museum of Fine Arts" in English) is Montréal's most prominent museum and was opened in 1912 in Canada's first building designed specifically for the visual arts. The original neoclassical pavilion is on the north side of Sherbrooke. Years ago, museum administrators recognized that the collection, now totaling more than 30,000 works, had outgrown the building. That problem was solved in late 1991 with the completion of the stunning new annex, the Jean-Noël Desmarais Pavilion,

Downtown Montréal Attractions

Basilique Notre-Dame **12**
Cathédrale-Basilique
    Marie-Reine-du-Monde **6**
Centre Canadien d'Architecture **1**
Centre d'Histoire de Montréal **13**
Chapelle Notre-Dame-de-Bonsecours/
    Musée Marguerite-Bourgeoys **22**
Christ Church Cathedral **9**
Hôtel de Ville **20**

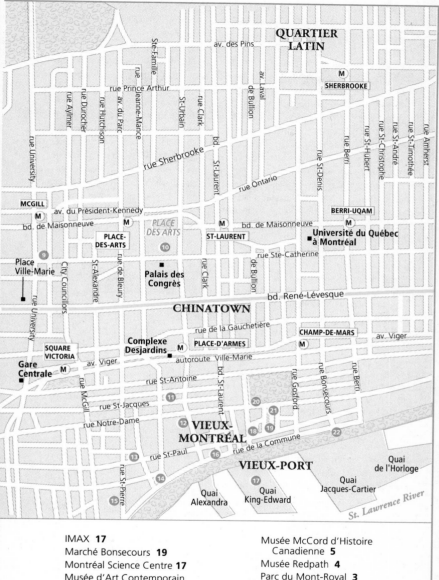

QUARTIER LATIN

av. des Pins

rue Ste-Famille
rue Prince Arthur
rue Durocher
rue Aylmer
rue Hutchison
av. du Parc
rue Jeanne-Mance
St-Urbain
rue Clark
av. Laval
de Bullion
bd. St-Laurent

M SHERBROOKE

rue Berri
rue St-Hubert
rue St-Christophe
rue St-André
rue St-Timothée
rue Amherst

rue University
rue Sherbrooke
rue St-Denis
rue Ontario

MCGILL
M
av. du Président-Kennedy

bd. de Maisonneuve
M
PLACE-DES-ARTS
PLACE DES ARTS
M ST-LAURENT
bd. de Maisonneuve
BERRI-UQAM
M

Université du Québec à Montréal

Place Ville-Marie ■
9

City Councilors
St-Alexandre
rue de Bleury
10
rue Clark
de Bullion
rue Ste-Catherine

Palais des Congrès ■

bd. René-Lévesque

CHINATOWN

rue de la Gauchetière

CHAMP-DE-MARS
M
av. Viger

rue University
SQUARE VICTORIA
M
Gare Centrale ■
av. Viger
Complexe Desjardins ■
M PLACE-D'ARMES
autoroute Ville-Marie

rue McGill
rue St-Jacques
rue St-Antoine
bd. St-Laurent
11
rue Notre-Dame

rue Gosford
rue Bonsecours
rue Berri

20
21
12 VIEUX-MONTRÉAL
18 19
22
rue St-Paul
13
rue de la Commune
16
VIEUX-PORT
Quai de l'Horloge

rue St-Pierre
14
15
Quai Alexandra
Quai King-Edward
Quai Jacques-Cartier

St. Lawrence River

directly across the street from the original building. Designed by Montréal architect Moshe Safdie, the new pavilion tripled exhibition space, adding two sub–street-level floors and underground galleries that connect the new building with the old.

For the best look at the results of the addition, enter the new annex, take the elevator to the top, and work your way down. The permanent collection is largely devoted to international contemporary art and Canadian art created after 1960, and to European paintings, sculpture, and decorative arts from the Middle Ages to the 19th century. On the upper floors are many of the gems of the collection. At the entrance to the fourth floor you'll encounter a Dalí chess set in which the pawns are thumbs. Paintings by 16th to 19th century artists Hogarth, Tintoretto, Reynolds, Brueghel, El Greco, Ribera, and portraitist George Romney make up the bulk of the fourth floor offerings. On subsequent levels, view examples—representative, if not world-class—of more recent artists, including Renoir, Monet, Picasso, Matisse, Cézanne, Léger, and Rodin. On the subterranean floors are works by 20th-century modernists, primarily those who rose to prominence after World War II, including the Abstract Expressionists and their successors

From the lowest level of the new pavilion, follow the under-street corridor, taking in primitive artworks from Oceania and Africa along the way, and then take the elevator into the original building, with its displays of pre-Columbian ceramics, Inuit carvings, and Amerindian crafts. The rest of that building is used primarily for traveling exhibitions assembled by some of the world's great museums. Throughout, works are nearly always dramatically mounted, carefully lit, and diligently explained in both French and English. Across the street you'll find a street-level store with an impressive selection of quality books, games, and folk art, and a good cafe.

1379–1380 rue Sherbrooke ouest (at rue Crescent). ✆ 514/285-2000. www.mmfa.qc.ca. Permanent collection free (but donations are welcome); temporary exhibitions C$12 (US$7.75) adults, C$6 (US$3.85) seniors and students, C$3 (US$1.95) children 12 and under; half-price Wed 5:30–9pm. AE, MC, V. Tues and Thurs–Sun 11am–6pm; Wed 11am–9pm. Métro: Peel or Guy-Corcordia.

Musée McCord d'Histoire Canadienne   Associated with McGill University, the McCord Museum of Canadian History showcases the eclectic—and not infrequently eccentric—collections of scores of 19th- and 20th-century benefactors. Over 29,000 costumes, numerous artifacts, and 750,000 historical photographs are rotated in and out of storage to be displayed. In general, expect to view furniture, clothing, china, silver, paintings, photographs, and folk art that reveal rural and urban life as it was lived by English-speaking immigrants of the past 3 centuries. The First Nations room displays portions of the museum's extensive collection of objects from Canada's Native population, including jewelry and meticulous beadwork. Exhibits are intelligently mounted, with texts in English and French, although the upstairs rooms are of narrower interest. There's a popular cafe near the front entrance.

690 rue Sherbrooke ouest (at rue Victoria). ✆ 514/398-7100. www.mccord-museum.qc.ca. Admission C$7 (US$4.50) adults, C$5 (US$3.25) seniors, C$4 (US$2.60) students, C$1.50 (US$1) ages 7–11, free for children under 7, C$14 (US$9.05) families; free admission Sat 10am–noon. Tues–Fri 10am–6pm; Sat–Sun 10am–5pm (summer daily from 9am). Métro: McGill. Bus: 24.

Parc du Mont-Royal   Montréal is named for the 232m (761-ft.) hill that rises at its heart—the "Royal Mountain." Joggers, cyclists, dog walkers, skaters, and others use it throughout the year. On Sundays, hundreds congregate around the statue of George-Etienne Cartier to listen and sometimes dance to impromptu music. In summer, Lac des Castors (Beaver Lake) is surrounded by sunbathers and picnickers (no swimming allowed, however). In wintertime, cross-country skiers follow the miles of paths and snowshoers tramp along trails laid out for their use. The large, refurbished Chalet Lookout near the crest of the hill provides a sweeping view of the city from its terrace and the opportunity for a snack. Up the hill behind the chalet is the spot where, tradition says, de Maisonneuve erected his wooden cross to establish the first colony here in 1642. Today the cross is a 30m (100-ft.) high steel structure visible from all over the city, illuminated at night.

℗ **514/844-4928** (general information) or 514/872-6559 (special events). Daily 6am–midnight. Métro: Mont-Royal. Bus: No. 11; hop off at Lac des Castors.

VIEUX-MONTREAL (OLD MONTREAL)

For further information about this quarter, log on to **www.vieux.montreal. qc.ca**, and try the walking tour in chapter 7.

Basilique Notre-Dame ★★★ Big enough to hold 4,000 worshipers, and breathtaking in the richness of its interior furnishings, this magnificent structure was designed in 1824 by James O'Donnell, an Irish-American Protestant architect from New York. So profoundly was he moved by the experience that O'Donnell converted to Catholicism after the basilica was completed. The impact is understandable. Of the hundreds of churches on the island of Montréal, Notre-Dame's interior is the most stunning, with its wealth of exquisite detail, most of it carved from rare woods that have been delicately gilded and painted. O'Donnell, one of the proponents of the Gothic Revival style in the early decades of the 19th century, is the only person honored by burial in the crypt.

The main altar was carved from linden wood, the work of Victor Bourgeau. Behind it is the Chapelle Sacré-Coeur (Sacred Heart Chapel), much of it destroyed by a deranged arsonist in 1978 but rebuilt and rededicated in 1982. The altar was cast in bronze by Charles Daudelin of Montréal, with 32 panels representing birth, life, and death. A 10-bell carillon resides in the east tower, while the west tower contains a single massive bell. Nicknamed "Le Gros Bourdon," it weighs more than 12 tons and has a low, resonant rumble that vibrates right up through your feet. It is tolled only on special occasions.

Although you can go through on your own, there are guided tours in English at various times through the day, beginning with one at 9am. Sound-and-light shows were initiated recently, with two performances nightly Tuesday through Saturday (see below for times).

110 rue Notre-Dame ouest (on place d'Armes). ℗ **514/842-2925.** Basilica C$2 (US$1.30) adults, C$1 (US65¢) students, free for praying. Light show C$10 (US$6.45) adults, C$9 (US$5.80) seniors, C$5 (US$3.25) ages 7–17, free for children age 6 and under. MC, V. Basilica daily 8am–5pm; tours daily 9am–4pm. Light shows Tues–Fri 6:30 and 8:30pm, Sat 7–8:30pm. Métro: Place d'Armes.

Montréal Science Centre This ambitious $49-million complex occupies a new steel-and-glass building running the length of King Edward Pier. Focusing on science and technology, it employs a variety of interactive displays and a cinema, as well as a popular IMAX theater, to enlighten visitors about the life sciences, energy conservation, and 21st-century communications. With its extensive use of computers and electronic visual displays, it is no surprise that youngsters usually take to the exhibits more readily than their elders. Admission fees vary according to combinations of exhibits and attractions.

King Edward Pier, Vieux-Port. ☎ **514/496-4724.** www.montrealsciencecentre.com. C$9.95–C$22 (US$6.40–US$14) adults, C$8.95–C$19 (US$5.75–US$12) ages 13–17 and 60 and over, C$7.95–C$17 (US$5.15–US$11) ages 4–12, free for children under 4. Summer Sun–Wed 10am–6pm, Thurs–Sat 10am–9pm; rest of year Sun–Thurs 10am–6pm, Fri–Sat 10am–9pm (hours subject to change). Métro: Square Victoria, Place d'Armes, or Champ-de-Mars.

Place Jacques-Cartier Across the street from the Hôtel de Ville (City Hall), this plaza is the focus of summer activity in Vieux-Montréal. The area has two recently repaved streets bracketing a center promenade that slopes down to the port past venerable stone buildings from the 1700s. Outdoor cafes, street per-formers, flower sellers, and the horse-drawn carriages that gather at the plaza's base recall a Montréal of a century ago. Montréalers insist they would never go to a place so overrun by tourists—which makes one wonder why so many of them do, in fact, congregate here. They take the sun and sip sangria on the bor-dering terraces on warm days, enjoying the unfolding pageant just as much as visitors do.

Between rue Notre-Dame and rue de la Commune. Métro: Place d'Armes.

Pointe-à-Callière (Montréal Museum of Archaeology and History) ★★★

A first visit to Montréal might best begin here. Built on the very site where the original colony was established in 1642 (Pointe-à-Callière), the modern Museum of Archaeology and History engages visitors in rare, beguiling ways. The striking new building echoes the triangular Royal Insurance building (1861) that stood here for many years. Go first to the 16-minute multimedia show in an auditorium that actually stands above exposed ruins of the earlier city. The show is accompanied by music and a playful bilingual narration that keeps the history slick and painless (if a little too chamber-of-commerce upbeat).

Pointe-à-Callière was the point where the St-Pierre River merged with the St. Lawrence. Evidence of the many inhabitants of this spot—from Amerindians to French trappers to Scottish merchants—were unearthed during archaeological digs that took more than a decade. Artifacts are on view in display cases set among the ancient building foundations and burial grounds below street level. Wind your way on the self-guided tour through the subterranean complex until you find yourself in the former Custom House, where there are more exhibits and a well-stocked gift shop. Allow at least an hour for a visit.

New expansion has incorporated the Youville Pumping Station, across from the main building. Dating from 1915, it has been restored to serve as an inter-pretation center. The main building contains L'Arrivage cafe and affords a fine view of Vieux-Montréal and the Vieux-Port.

350 place Royale (at rue de la Commune). ☎ **514/872-9150.** www.musee-pointe-a-calliere.qc.ca. Admission C$9.50 (US$6.15) adults, C$7 (US$4.50) seniors, C$5.50 (US$3.55) students, C$3 (US$1.95) children 6–12, free for children under 6, C$19 (US$12) families. AE, MC, V. July–Aug Mon–Fri 10am–6pm, Sat–Sun 11am–6pm; rest of year Tues–Fri 10am–5pm, Sat–Sun 11am–5pm. Métro: Place d'Armes.

Vieux-Port ★★

Montréal's Old Port, a once-dreary commercial wharf area, was transformed in 1992 into a 2km- (1¼-mile-) long, 53 hectare (133-acre) promenade and park with public spaces, bicycle paths, tram rides, exhibition halls, and a variety of family activities. Harbor cruises also leave from here. To get an idea of all there is to see and do, hop aboard the small, free Balade tram that travels throughout the port. At the far eastern end of the port is a 1922 clock tower, La Tour de l'Horloge, with 192 steps leading past the exposed clockworks to observation decks at three different levels (admission is free).

Most cruises, entertainment, and special events take place from mid-May to October. Information booths with bilingual attendants assist visitors during that period. The Vieux-Port stretches along the waterfront from rue McGill to rue Berri. Quadricycles, bicycles, and in-line skates are available for rent.

333 rue de la Commune ouest (at rue McGill). © 514/496-7678. www.oldportofmontreal.com. Free admission to port and interpretation center. Interpretation Center mid-May to early Sept daily 10am–9pm; hours for specific attractions vary. Métro: Champ-de-Mars, Place d'Armes, or Square-Victoria.

ELSEWHERE IN THE CITY

Biodôme de Montréal ★★★   Near Montréal's Botanical Garden and next to the Olympic Stadium, you'll discover the engrossing Biodôme, possibly the only institution of its kind. Originally built as the velodrome for the 1976 Olympics, it has been refitted to house replications of four distinct ecosystems— a Laurentian forest, the St. Lawrence marine system, a tropical rain forest, and a polar environment—complete with appropriate temperatures, flora, fauna, and changing seasons. All four re-creations are allowed a measure of freedom to grow and shift, so the exhibits are never static. With more than 6,000 creatures of 210 species and 4,000 trees and plants, the Biodôme incorporates exhibits gathered from the old aquarium and the modest zoos at the Angrignon and LaFontaine parks. Among the fauna are specimens of certain threatened and endangered species, including macaws, marmosets, and tamarins. The Polar World contains puffins and four kinds of penguins. Biodôme also has a game room for kids called Naturalia, a shop, a restaurant, and a cafeteria.

4777 av. Pierre-de-Coubertin (next to Olympic Stadium). © 514/868-3000. www.biodome.qc.ca. Admission C$10 (US$6.45) adults, C$7.50 (US$4.85) seniors and students over 17, C$5 (US$3.25) children 5–17, free for children under 5. AE, MC, V. Daily 9am–5pm (until 7pm in summer). Métro: Viau.

Jardin Botanique ★★   Across the street from the former Olympic sports complex, the Botanical Garden is spread across 72 hectares (180 acres). Begun in 1931, it has grown to include 21,000 varieties of plants in 31 specialized seg- ments, ensuring something beautiful and fragrant for visitors year-round. Ten large conservatory greenhouses shelter tropical and desert plants, plus bonsai and penjing (Chinese bonsai), from the Canadian winter. Roses bloom here from mid-June to the first frost, May is the month for lilacs, and June is for the flowering hawthorn trees. Inaugurated in summer 1991, the 2.5-hectare (6-acre) Chinese Garden, a joint project of Montréal and Shanghai, is the largest Chi- nese garden ever built outside Asia. Meant to evoke the 14th to 17th century era of the Ming Dynasty, it incorporates pavilions, inner courtyards, ponds, and myriad plants indigenous to China. The serene Japanese Garden fills 6 hectares (15 acres) and contains a cultural pavilion with an art gallery, a tearoom where ancient tea ceremonies are performed, a stunning bonsai collection, and a Zen garden. The grounds are also home to the Insectarium, displaying some of the world's most beautiful insects, not to mention some of its sinister ones (see "Especially for Kids," later in this chapter). The Insectarium is home to the award-winning "Insect Tasting," in November and December, featuring gour- met snacks made with insects. Birders should bring along binoculars on summer visits to spot some of the more than 130 species of birds that spend at least part of the year in the garden. In summer, an outdoor aviary is filled with butterflies. Year-round, a free shuttle bus links the Botanical Garden and nearby Olympic Park. A small train runs regularly through the gardens and is worth the small fee charged to ride it.

4101 rue Sherbrooke est (opposite Olympic Stadium). $\mathcal{C}$ **514/872-1400.** www.ville.montreal.qc.ca/jardin. Admission to outside gardens, greenhouses, and insectarium May–Oct C$10 (US$6.45) adults, C$7.50 (US$4.85) seniors and students, C$4.75 (US$3.05) children 5–17; Nov–Apr C$7.25 (US$4.70) adults, C$5.75 (US$3.70) seniors and students, C$3.75 (US$2.40) children 5–17. Tickets for Botanical Garden, Insectarium, and Biodôme (good for 30 days) C$16 (US$10) adults, C$12 (US$7.75) seniors, C$8 (US$5.15) children. MC, V. Daily 9am–5pm (until 7pm in summer). Métro: Pie-IX, then walk up the hill to the gardens; or, take the shuttle bus from Olympic Park (Métro: Viau).

Stade Olympique Centerpiece of the 1976 Olympic Games, Montréal's controversial Olympic Stadium and its associated facilities provide considerable opportunities for both active and passive diversion. The complex incorporates a natatorium with six different pools, including one with competition dimensions and an adjustable bottom, and a 15m (50-ft.) deep pool for scuba diving. The stadium seats 60,000 to 80,000 spectators, who come here to see the Expos, rock concerts, and trade shows.

The roof doesn't retract anymore, and never did perform that action well. That's only one reason that what was first known as "The Big O" was scorned as "The Big Owe" after cost overruns led to heavy increases in taxes. Plans for its future have run from total demolition to adding thousands of seats.

The 188m (626-ft.) inclined tower, which leans at a 45° angle, also does duty as an observation deck, with a funicular that whisks 90 passengers to the top in 95 seconds. On a clear day, the deck bestows a 56km (35-mile) view over Montréal and into the neighboring Laurentides. A free shuttle bus links the Olympic Park and the Botanical Garden.

4141 av. Pierre-de-Coubertin (bd. Pie IX). $\mathcal{C}$ **514/252-8687.** www.rio.gouv.qc.ca. Funicular ride C$9 (US$6) adults, C$5.50 (US$3.65) students and children. Guided tours of the stadium are available. Public swim periods are scheduled daily, with low admission rates. Funicular open mid-June to early Sept Mon noon–6pm, Tues–Thurs 10am–9pm, Fri–Sat 10am–11pm; early Sept to mid-Jan and mid-Feb to mid-June daily noon–6pm. Closed mid-Jan to mid-Feb. Métro: Pie-IX or Viau (choose the Viau station to meet up with the guided tour).

2 More Attractions

DOWNTOWN

Christ Church Cathedral This Anglican cathedral, which is reflected in the shiny exterior of the postmodernist Maison des Coopérants office tower, stands in glorious Gothic contrast to the city's glassy downtown skyscrapers. Sometimes called the "floating cathedral" because of the many tiers of malls and corridors in the underground city beneath it, the building was completed in 1859. The original steeple, too heavy for the structure, was replaced by a lighter aluminum version in 1940. Christ Church Cathedral hosts concerts throughout the year, most frequently from mid-January through August on Wednesdays at 12:30pm.

635 rue Ste-Catherine (at rue University). $\mathcal{C}$ **514/843-6577** ext. 369 (recorded information about concerts). www.montreal.anglican.org/cathedral. Free admission; donations accepted. Daily 8am–6pm; services Sun 8am, 10am, and 4pm. Métro: McGill.

Cathédrale-Basilique Marie-Reine-du-Monde No one who has seen both will confuse Montréal's "Mary Queen of the World" Cathedral with St. Peter's Basilica in Rome, but a scaled-down homage was the intention of Bishop Ignace Bourget, who oversaw its construction after the first Catholic cathedral burned to the ground in 1852. Construction lasted from 1875 to 1894, its start delayed by the Bishop's desire to place it not in Francophone east Montréal but in the heart of the Protestant Anglophone west. The resulting structure covers less than a quarter of the area of its Roman inspiration. Most impressive is the 76m (252-ft.) high dome, about a third of the size of the original. A local touch is provided by the statues standing on the roofline, representing patron saints of the region. The interior is less rewarding visually than the exterior, but the high altar is worth the visit.

Bd. René-Lévesque (at rue Mansfield). © **514/866-1661.** Free admission; donations accepted. Mon–Fri 7am–7:30pm; Sat 7:30am–8:30pm; Sun 8:30am–7:30pm. Métro: Bonaventure.

Musée d'Art Contemporain de Montréal ★   Montréal's Museum of Contemporary Art, the only museum in Canada devoted exclusively to contemporary art, moved into this new facility at the Place des Arts in 1992. "Contemporary" is defined here as art produced since 1939. About 60% of the permanent collection of some 6,000 works is composed of the work of Quebecois artists, but it also includes examples of such international painters as Jean Dubuffet, Max Ernst, Jean Arp, Larry Poons, and Antoni Tàpies, as well as photographers Robert Mapplethorpe and Ansel Adams. A few larger pieces are seen on the ground floor, but most are one flight up, with space for temporary exhibitions to the left and selections from the permanent collection on the right. No single style prevails, so expect to see installations; video displays; and examples of Pop, Op, and Abstract Expressionism. That the works often arouse strong opinions signifies a museum that is doing something right. The museum's restaurant, La Rotonde, has a summer dining terrace.

185 rue Ste-Catherine ouest. © **514/847-6226.** www.macm.org. Admission C$6 (US$3.85) adults, C$4 (US$2.60) seniors, C$3 (US$1.95) students, free for children under 12, C$12 (US$7.75) families; free to all Wed 6–9pm. Tues–Sun 11am–6pm (until 9pm Wed). Métro: Place des Arts.

VIEUX-MONTREAL (OLD MONTREAL)

Hôtel de Ville   City Hall, finished in 1878, is relatively young by Vieux-Montréal standards. The French Second Empire design makes it look as though it was imported stone by stone from the mother country. Balconies, turrets, and mansard roofs detail the exterior, seen particularly well when illuminated at night. It was from the balcony above the awning that an ill-mannered Charles de Gaulle proclaimed, "Vive le Québec Libre!" in 1967, thereby pleasing his immediate audience but straining relations with the Canadian government for years. Fifteen-minute guided tours are given throughout the day on weekdays May through October. The Hall of Honour is made of green marble from Campagna, Italy, and houses Art Deco lamps from Paris and a bronze-and-glass chandelier, also from France, that weighs a metric ton. The chamber has a hand-carved ceiling and five stained-glass windows representing religion, the port, industry and commerce, finance, and transportation. The mayor's office is on that floor.

275 rue Notre-Dame (at the corner of rue Gosford). © **514/872-3355.** Free admission. Daily 8:30am–4:30pm. Métro: Champ-de-Mars.

Chapelle Notre-Dame-de-Bon-Secours/Musée Marguerite-Bourgeoys
Just to the east of Marché Bonsecours, Notre Dame de Bonsecours Chapel is called the Sailors' Church because of the special attachment that fishermen and other mariners have to the church. That devotion is manifest in the several ship models hanging inside. A revered 16th-century 6-inch-high carving of the Madonna is once again on display. There's an excellent view of the harbor and the old quarter from the church's tower.

The first church building, which no longer stands, was the project of an energetic teacher named Marguerite Bourgeoys, and was built in 1678. She arrived with de Maisonneuve to undertake the education of the children of Montréal in the latter half of the 17th century. Later on, she and several other teachers founded a nuns' order called the Congregation of Notre-Dame, Canada's first. The pioneering Bourgeoys was recognized as a saint in 1982.

The present church, which dates from 1773, incorporates a new museum and a restored 18th-century crypt, an archaeological site that has unearthed ruins and materials from the earliest days of the colony as well as a firepit dated to 400 B.C. A collection of dolls and miniature furnishings is arranged in 58 scenes depicting life in Québec from the earliest days of European settlement.

400 rue St-Paul est (at the foot of rue Bonsecours). ℂ 514/282-8670. www.marguerite-bourgeoys.com. Free admission to chapel. Museum C$6 (US$3.85) adults, C$4 (US$2.60) seniors and students, C$3 (US$1.95) ages 6–12, free for children under 6; archeological site and museum C$8 (US$5.15). May–Oct Tues–Sun 10am–5pm; Nov–Jan 15 and Mar–Apr Tues–Sun 11am–3:30pm. Closed Jan 15–Feb 28. Métro: Champ-de-Mars.

Marché Bonsecours   Bonsecours Market, an imposing neoclassical building with a long facade, a colonnaded portico, and a silvery dome, was built in the mid-1800s and first used as Montréal's City Hall, then for many years after 1878 as the central market. Its uses have never been decided with finality since then. Essentially abandoned for much of the 20th century, it was restored in 1964 to house city government offices, and in 1992 became the information and exhibition center for the celebration of the city's 350th birthday. It continues to be used as an exhibition space, with shopping stalls and three restaurants with terraces. The architecture alone makes a brief visit worthwhile.

350 rue St-Paul est (at the foot of rue St-Claude). ℂ 514/872-7730. www.marchebonsecours.qc.ca. Free admission. June 24–Sept 2 Mon–Sat 10am–9pm, Sun 10am–6pm; rest of year daily 10am–6pm (until 9pm Thurs and Fri). Métro: Champ-de-Mars.

Musée du Château Ramezay ⍟   Claude de Ramezay, the 11th governor of the colony, built his residence at this site in 1705. The château was the home of the city's royal French governors for almost 4 decades, but in 1745, Ramezay's heirs sold it to a trading company, who left parts of the original structure but altered it considerably. Fifteen years later, it was taken over by the British conquerors. In 1775, an army of American revolutionaries invaded and held Montréal, using the château as their headquarters. Benjamin Franklin, sent to persuade the Quebecois to rise with the American colonists against British rule, stayed in the château for a time, but failed to persuade the city's people to join his cause. After the American interlude, the house was used as a courthouse, a government office building, a teachers' college, and headquarters for Laval University, before being converted into a museum in 1895. Old coins and prints, portraits, furnishings, tools, a loom, Amerindian artifacts, and other memorabilia related to the economic and social activities of the 18th and first half of the 19th centuries fill the main floor. In the cellar are the vaults of the original house. Descriptive placards appear in both French and English. It was closed recently for 6 months and has reopened with new exhibitions.

280 rue Notre-Dame (east of Place Jacques-Cartier). ℂ 514/861-3708. www.chateauramezay.qc.ca. Admission C$6 (US$3.85) adults, C$5 (US$3.25) seniors, C$4 (US$2.60) students, C$3 (US$1.95) ages 5–17, free for children under 4, C$12 (US$7.75) families. MC, V. June–Sept daily 10am–6pm; Oct–May Tues–Sun 10am–4:30pm. Métro: Champ-de-Mars.

PLATEAU MONT-ROYAL

For further information about this area, log on to **www.tpmr.qc.ca**, and try the walking tour in chapter 7.

Oratoire St-Joseph ✮   This huge basilica with a giant copper dome was built by Québec's Catholics to honor St. Joseph, patron saint of Canada. Dominating the north slope of Mont-Royal, its imposing dimensions are seen by some as inspiring, by others as forbidding. It came into being through the efforts of Brother André, a lay brother in the Holy Cross order who enjoyed a reputation as a healer. By the time he had built a small wooden chapel in 1904 near the site of the basilica, he was said to have performed hundreds of cures. His powers attracted supplicants from great distances, and Brother André performed his work until his death in 1937. His dream of building this shrine to his patron saint became a completed reality in 1967, years after his death. He is buried in the basilica and was beatified by the Pope in 1982, a status one step below saint-hood. The basilica is largely Italian Renaissance in style, its dome recalling the shape of the Duomo in Florence, but of much greater size and less grace. Inside is a museum where a central exhibit is the heart of Brother André. Outside, a Way of the Cross lined with sculptures was the setting of scenes for the film *Jesus of Montréal*. Brother André's wooden chapel, with his tiny bedroom, is on the grounds and open to the public. Pilgrims, some ill, come to seek intercession from St. Joseph and Brother André and often climb the middle set of 100 steps on their knees. At 263m (862 ft.), the shrine is the highest point in Montréal. A cafeteria and snack bar are on the premises. Ninety-minute guided tours are offered in several languages at 10am and 2pm daily in summer and on weekends in September and October; call for times. There is no fee for the walks, but a donation is requested.

3800 Chemin Queen Mary (on the north slope of Mont-Royal). ✆ **514/733-8211.** Free admission, but donations are requested. Daily 6am–9:30pm; museum daily 9am–5pm; tours 10am and 2pm in summer and weekends Sept–Oct. 56-bell carillon plays Wed–Fri noon–3pm; Sat–Sun noon–2:30pm. Métro: Côtes-des-Neiges. Bus: 165.

Parc Lafontaine   The European-style park in Plateau Mont-Royal is one of the city's oldest. Illustrating the dual identities of the city's populace, half the park is landscaped in the formal French manner, the other in the more casual English style. Among its several bodies of water is a lake used for paddle boat-ing in summer and ice-skating in winter. Snowshoeing and cross-country trails wind through the trees. An open amphitheater, the **Théâtre de Verdure,** is the setting for free outdoor theater and movies in summer.

Rue Sherbrooke and av. Parc Lafontaine. ✆ **514/872-2644.** Free admission; small fee for use of tennis courts. Park daily 24 hr. Tennis courts summer daily 9am–10pm. Métro: Sherbrooke.

ILE STE-HELENE

La Biosphère   Not to be confused with the Biodôme at Olympic Park, this facility is located in the geodesic dome designed by Buckminster Fuller to serve as the American Pavilion for Expo '67. A fire destroyed the acrylic skin of the sphere in 1976, and it served no purpose other than as a harbor landmark until 1995. The motivation behind the Biosphère is unabashedly environmental, with four exhibition areas, a water theater, and an amphitheater, all devoted to pro-moting awareness of the St. Lawrence–Great Lakes ecosystem. Multimedia shows and hands-on displays invite the active participation of visitors, and there is an exhibition related to the activities of the ocean explorer Jacques-Yves Cousteau. In the highest point of Visions Hall is an observation level with an unobstructed view of the river. Connections Hall offers a "Call to Action" pres-entation employing six giant screens and three stages. There is a preaching-to-the-choir quality to all this that slips over the edge into zealous philosophizing.

But the various displays and exhibits are put together thoughtfully and will engage and enlighten most visitors, at least for a while. Don't make a special trip, but if you're on the island for something else, stop by.

160 Chemin Tour-de-l'Isle (Ile Ste-Hélène). ✆ 514/283-5000. http://biosphere.ec.qc.ca. Admission C$8.50 adults (US$5.50), C$6.50 (US$4.20) seniors and students, C$5 (US$3.25) ages 7–17, free for children under 7, C$19 (US$12.25) families. June 24 to Labour Day daily 10am–6pm; Sept–May Tues–Sun 10am–5pm. Métro: Parc Jean-Drapeau, then a short walk. Just follow the signs to the park.

Musée David M. Stewart ⍟   After the War of 1812, the British prepared for a possible future American invasion by building this moated fortress, which now houses the David M. Stewart Museum. The duke of Wellington ordered its construction as another link in the chain of defenses along the St. Lawrence. Completed in 1824, it was never involved in armed conflict. The British garrison left in 1870, after confederation of the former Canadian colonies. Today the low stone barracks and blockhouses contain the museum, which displays maps and scientific instruments that helped Europeans explore the New World, as well as military and naval artifacts, weaponry, uniforms, housewares, and related paraphernalia from the time of Jacques Cartier (1535) through 1763, the end of the colonial period. Useful labels appear in both French and English.

From late June through late August, the fort comes to life with reenactments of military parades and retreats by La Compagnie Franche de la Marine and the 78th Fraser Highlanders, at 11am, 3pm, and 4:30pm. The presence of the French unit is an unhistorical bow to Francophone sensibilities, because New France had become English Canada almost 65 years before the fort was erected. If you absolutely must be photographed in stocks, they are provided on the parade grounds.

Vieux Fort, Ile Ste-Hélène. ✆ 514/861-6701. www.stewart-museum.org. Admission C$7 (US$4.50) adults, C$5 (US$3.25) seniors and students, free for children under 7, C$14 (US$9.05) families. May–Sept daily 10am–6pm; Sept–May Wed–Mon 10am–5pm. Métro: Parc Jean-Drapeau, then a 15-min. walk. By car: Take the Jacques-Cartier Bridge to the Parc Jean-Drapeau exit, then follow signs to Vieux Fort.

3 Especially for Kids

IMAX Theatre   The images and special effects are larger than life, always visually dazzling and often vertiginous, thrown on a five-story screen in the renovated theater of the Montréal Science Centre. Recent films made the most of charging elephants, underwater scenes in Yucatán cenotes once used for Mayan sacrifices, and cameras swooping low over glaciers and through the Grand Canyon. Running time is usually under an hour. Arrive for shows at least 10 minutes before starting time, earlier on weekends and evenings. Tickets can be ordered online.

Vieux-Port, Quai King Edward (end of bd. St-Laurent). ✆ 800/349-4629 or 514/496-4629 (information and tickets). www.montrealsciencecentre.com. Admission C$9.95 (US$6.40) adults, C$8.95 (US$5.75) seniors and students 13–17, C$7.95 (US$5.15) ages 4–11. Open daily. Call for current schedule of shows in English. Métro: Place d'Armes.

Insectarium de Montréal ⍟   A relatively young addition to the Botanical Garden, this two-level structure near the Sherbrooke gate exhibits the collections of two avid entomologists: Georges Brossard (whose brainchild this place is) and Father Firmia Liberté. More than 3,000 mounted butterflies, scarabs, maggots, locusts, beetles, tarantulas, and giraffe weevils are displayed, and live exhibits feature scorpions, tarantulas, crickets, cockroaches, and praying mantises. Needless to say, kids are delighted by the creepy critters and glistening mounted butterflies.

During the summer beautiful live specimens flutter among the nectar-bearing plants in the Butterfly House. In November and early December, check out the award-winning "Insect Tasting" (Croque-insectes), an event which features expertly cooked, spiced and sauced insects for your eating enjoyment!

Botanical Garden, 4581 rue Sherbrooke est. © 514/872-1400. www.ville.montreal.qc.ca/insectarium. May–Oct C$10 (US$6.45) adults, C$7.50 (US$4.85) seniors, C$5 (US$3.25) children 6–17, free for children under 6; Nov–Apr C$7.25 (US$4.70) adults, C$5.75 (US$3.70) seniors, C$3.75 (US$2.40) children 6–17, free for children under 6. MC, V. Summer daily 9am–7pm; rest of year daily 9am–5pm. Métro: Pie-IX or Viau.

La Ronde Amusement Park   Montréal's amusement park was run for most of its 35 years by the city. Lately, that arrangement clearly wasn't working, with the facility sliding into massive disrepair. Now, though, it has been sold to the American-owned Six Flags theme park empire, which plans to invest $90 million in renovations. At first, La Ronde under the new management seemed pretty much as it had been, minus the threat of insolvency. Now, it has introduced the first of several promised new rides, Le Vampire. It's a suspended coaster, where willing riders experience five loops at over 80 kilometers per hour, meaning that they are upside down much of the time.

The park fills the northern reaches of the Ile Ste-Hélène with a sailing lagoon, an "Enchanted Forest" with costumed storytellers, and a Western town with a saloon. There are also Ferris wheels, carousels, roller coasters, carnival booths, and plenty of places to eat and drink. Thrill-seekers will love rides like Le Boomerang, Le Monstre, and Le Cobra, a stand-up roller coaster that incorporates a 360° loop and reaches speeds in excess of 97km (60 miles) per hour. While many of the 35 rides test adult nerves and stomachs, there are ample attractions for youngsters, such as the Tchou Tchou Train and the Super Volcanozor, which combines 3-D images of dinosaurs with swooping, twirling transport among them.

A big attraction every year is the International Fireworks Competition, held once a week in June and July (postponed in bad weather). The pyromusical displays are launched at 10pm and last at least 30 minutes. (Many Montréalers choose to watch them from the Jacques Cartier Bridge, which is closed to traffic during the display. Take along a Walkman to listen to the accompanying music, which is broadcast.)

Parc des Iles, Ile Ste-Hélène. © 800/797-4537 or 514/872-4537. www.laronde.com. Ground admission C$20 (US$13); rides admission C$28 (US$18) ages 12 and over, C$17 (US$11) ages 3–11. Parking C$8.70 (US$5.60). Last week in May Sat–Sun only; June–Aug and Labour Day weekend daily 10am–9pm. Métro: Papineau and bus no. 169, or Parc Jean-Drapeau and bus no. 167.

Planétarium de Montréal   A window on the night sky, with mythical monsters and magical heroes, Montréal's planetarium is right downtown, only 3 blocks south of Centre Molsen. Changing shows under the 20m (65-ft.) dome dazzle and inform kids at the same time. Shows change with the seasons, exploring time and space travel and collisions of celestial bodies. The special Christmas show, "Star of the Magi," which can be seen in December and early January, is based on recent investigations of historians and astronomers into the mysterious light that guided the Magi. Shows in English alternate with those in French.

1000 rue St-Jacques (at Peel). © 514/872-4530. www.planetarium.montreal.qc.ca. Admission C$6 (US$3.85) adults, $4.50 (US$2.90) seniors and students, C$3 (US$1.95) children 6–17. MC, V. Show schedule changes frequently, so call ahead. Métro: Bonaventure (Cathédrale exit).

4 Special-Interest Sightseeing

Centre Canadien d'Architecture (CCA)   The understated but handsome Canadian Center of Architecture building occupies a city block, with lawns, joining a contemporary structure with an older building, the 1875 Shaughnessy House. The CCA functions as both a study center and a museum, with changing exhibits devoted to the art of architecture and its history, including architects' sketchbooks, elevation drawings, and photography. The collection is international in scope and encompasses architecture, urban planning, and landscape design. Texts are in French and English. Opened in 1989, the museum has received rave notices from scholars, critics, and serious architecture buffs. That said, it is only fair to note that the average visitor is likely to find it somewhat less enthralling. The bookstore has a special section on Canadian architecture with emphasis on Montréal and Québec City. The sculpture garden across the Ville-Marie autoroute is part of the CCA, designed by artist/architect Melvin Charney.

1920 rue Baile (at rue du Fort). © **514/939-7026.** www.cca.qc.ca. Admission C$6 (US$3.85) adults, C$4 (US$2.60) seniors, C$3 (US$1.95) students, free for children under 12. June–Sept Tues–Sun 11am–6pm (until 9pm Thurs); rest of year Wed–Fri 11am–6pm (until 8pm Thurs), Sat–Sun 11am–5pm. Guided tours available on request. Métro: Atwater or Guy-Concordia.

Centre d'Histoire de Montréal   Built in 1903 as Montréal's Central Fire Station, this redbrick and sandstone building is now the Montréal History Center, which traces the development of the city from its first residents, the Amerindians, to the European settlers who arrived in 1642, to the present day. Throughout its 14 rooms, carefully conceived presentations chart the contributions of the city fathers and mothers and subsequent generations. The development of the railroad, Métro, and related infrastructure are recalled, as is that of domestic and public architecture, in imaginative exhibits, videos, and slide shows. On the second floor, reached by a spiral staircase, is memorabilia from the early 20th century.

335 place d'Youville (at St-Pierre). © **514/872-3207.** www.ville.montreal.qc.ca/chm. Admission C$4.50 (US$2.90) adults; C$3 (US$1.95) seniors, students, and children 6–17; free for children under 6. May–Sept daily 10am–5pm; Sept–Dec 30 and Jan 15–Apr 30 Tues–Sun 10am–5pm. Métro: Square-Victoria.

Musée de la Banque de Montréal   Facing Place d'Armes is Montréal's oldest bank building, with a classic facade beneath a graceful dome, a carved pediment, and six Corinthian columns. The outside dimensions and appearance remain largely unchanged since the building's completion in 1847. The interior was renovated from 1901 through 1905 by the famed U.S. firm McKim, Mead, and White, who added Ionic and Corinthian columns of Vermont granite, walls of pink marble from Tennessee, and a counter of Levanto marble. The bank contains a small museum with a replica of its first office (and its 1st bank teller, Henry Stone from Boston), gold nuggets from the Yukon, a $3 bill (one of only two known), and a collection of 100-year-old mechanical banks.

119 and 129 rue St-Jacques (at place d'Armes). © **514/877-6810.** Free admission. Museum Mon–Fri 10am–4pm. Métro: Place d'Armes.

Musée Marc-Aurèle Fortin   This is Montréal's only museum dedicated to the work of a single French-Canadian artist. Landscape watercolorist Marc-Aurèle Fortin (1888–1970) interpreted the beauty of the Québec countryside, especially the Laurentians and Charlevoix. His paintings are on the ground floor, while temporary exhibits—varied in style, but typically representative rather than nonobjective or abstract—usually feature the work of other Quebecois painters.

118 rue St-Pierre (at rue d'Youville). ℭ **514/845-6108.** Admission C$4 (US$2.60) adults, C$2 (US$1.30) seniors and students, free for children under 12. Tues–Sun 11am–5pm. Métro: Square Victoria.

Musée Redpath　If the unusual name seems slightly familiar, think of the wrappings on sugar cubes in many Canadian restaurants. John Redpath was a 19th-century industrialist who built Canada's first sugar refinery and later distributed much of his fortune in philanthropy. This modest museum housed in an 1882 building is on the McGill University campus. The main draw is its collection of Egyptian antiquities, the second largest in Canada, but also on view are fossils and geological fragments.

859 rue Sherbrooke ouest (rue University). ℭ **514/398-4086.** Free admission. Sept–June Mon–Fri 9am–5pm, Sun 1–5pm; July–Aug Mon–Thurs 9am–5pm, Sun 1–5pm (closed holiday weekends). Métro: McGill. Bus: 24.

5 Organized Tours

A generalized guided tour is often the most desirable—or, at least efficient—way to begin explorations of a new city. Even a mediocre tour with a guide who imagines her or himself a wit can provide a timesaving sense of the topography of the city, its history, and which attractions are most likely to reward an in-depth return visit.

For a complete listing of tours and tour operators, check under "Guided Tours" in the annually revised *Montréal Tourist Guide,* or at **Infotouriste** (ℭ **877/266-5687** or 514/873-2015; www.bonjourquebec.com). Most of the land tours leave from downtown at Square Dorchester, near the Infotouriste office. Boat tours depart from the port bordering Vieux-Montréal. Parking is free at the dock, or take the Métro to the Champ-de-Mars or Square-Victoria station and walk 6 blocks.

BOAT TOURS

Among numerous opportunities for experiencing Montréal and environs by water, a few of the more popular include the following:

Le Bateau-Mouche (ℭ **800/361-9952** or 514/849-9952; www.bateau-mouche.com) is an air-conditioned, glass-enclosed vessel reminiscent of those on the Seine in Paris. It plies the St. Lawrence River from mid-May to mid-October. Cruises depart for 90-minute excursions at 10am, noon, 2pm, and 4pm, and for a 3½-hour dinner cruise at 7pm (boarding at 6:30pm). The shallow-draft boat takes up to 158 passengers on a route inaccessible by traditional vessels. It passes under seven bridges and provides sweeping views of the city, Mont-Royal, the St. Lawrence, and its islands. Daytime snacks are available on board, and dinners are prepared by the kitchens of Le Reine Elizabeth hotel. Families get a discount on the first trip of the day, at 10am. Day tours cost C$20 (US$13) adults, C$17 (US$11) students and seniors, C$9 (US$5.80) children ages 5 to 12, children under 5 free, C$40 (US$26) families; dinner cruises C$65 to C$113 (US$42–US$73). *Le Bateau-Mouche* departs from the Jacques Cartier Pier, opposite Place Jacques-Cartier.

Croisières du Port de Montréal (AML Cruises; ℭ **800/667-3131** or 514/842-3871; www.croisieresaml.com) also travels the harbor and the St. Lawrence. The boats depart up to four times a day from May to October from the Clock Tower Pier at the foot of rue Berri in Vieux-Montréal, for tours, dinner and dancing, or extended sightseeing for 1 to 9 hours. Fares are C$15 to C$35 (US$9.70–US$26) adults, C$13 to C$33 (US$8.40–US$21) students

and seniors, C$7 to C$25 (US$4.50–US$16) children 12 and under, C$35 to
C$65 (US$23–US$42) families of 2 adults and 2 children. The higher prices
above are for dinner cruises. AML also offers cruises down the St. Lawrence to
Québec City, Charlevoix, for whale watching, and up the Saguenay River.

For an exciting—and wet—experience, consider a ride with **Saute Moutons**
(© **514/284-9607;** www.jetboatingmontreal.com). Their wave-jumper power-
boats take on the roiling Lachine Rapids of the St. Lawrence River. The stream-
lined hydrojet makes the 1-hour trip from May to mid-October daily, with
departures every 2 hours from 10am to 6pm. It takes half an hour to get to and
from the rapids, which leaves 30 minutes for storming up the river. Arrive 45
minutes early to obtain and don rain gear and life jacket. Wearing a sweater and
bringing a change of clothes are good ideas, because you almost certainly will get
splashed or even soaked through. Fares are C$17 to C$46 (US$11–US$30)
adults, C$14 to C$37 (US$8.95–US$24) ages 13 to 18, C$12 to C$29
(US$7.85–US$19) ages 6 to 12, kids under 6 free. Boats depart from the Clock
Tower Pier.

A much milder water voyage, with great views, is the **ferry** (© **514/
281-8000**) from Jacques-Cartier Pier in Vieux-Montréal to Ile Ste-Hélène, a
good way to begin and end a picnic outing or visits to the old fort or La Ronde
amusement park. It operates from mid-May to mid-October. Rates change frequently, so call or visit for details.

LAND TOURS

Commercial guided tours in air-conditioned buses are offered two to eight times
daily year-round by **Gray Line de Montréal/Autocar Connaisseur** (© **514/
934-1222;** www.coachcanada-montreal.com). The basic city tour takes 3 hours;
the deluxe half-day version includes long stops at the Botanical Garden and the
Biodôme. Other tours take you to the Ile Ste-Hélène, the St. Lawrence Seaway,
the Laurentians, and Québec City. Tours depart from Dorchester Square. The
basic city tour costs C$33 (US$21) ages 13 and up, C$20 (US$13) ages 12 and
under. Similar tours, but fewer in number, are provided by **Autocar Imperial**
(© **514/871-4733**). The 3-hour city tour costs C$29 (US$19) for adults, C$26
(US$17) seniors and students, C$14 (US$9.05) ages 5 to 12.

Now for something a little different: **Amphi-Bus** (© **514/849-5181**) tours
Vieux-Montréal much like any other bus, until it waddles into the waters of the
harbor for a dramatic finish. It has a few variations, including a basic 1-hour day
tour and an evening cruise followed by dinner at a nearby restaurant. Daily
hours are 10am to midnight in the warmer months and noon, 2pm, and 4pm
off-season. Reservations required. Departures are from Quai King Edward in
Vieux-Montréal. The short tour costs C$16 (US$11) adults, C$15 (US$10)
seniors and ages 4 to 16; C$45 (US$30) per person for the dinner cruise.

Montréal's romantic *calèches* (© **514/934-6105**) are horse-drawn open carriages whose drivers serve as guides. These carriages operate year-round. In winter the steeds are also hitched to old-fashioned sleighs for a ride around the top
of Mont-Royal, the horses puffing steam clouds in the cold air, the passengers
bundled in lap rugs. Prices run about C$45 (US$29) for an hour's tour in the
carriage or sleigh, which can seat four comfortably, five if one sits with the
driver. In addition to Mont-Royal, calèches depart from Square Dorchester and
in Vieux-Montréal from Place Jacques-Cartier and rue de la Commune, and
Place d'Armes opposite Notre-Dame Basilica. The carriages run year-round, but
the schedules vary in the off-season, so call first.

Rollin' Down the River

River cruises are a wholly different experience from that provided by the ships that sail the Caribbean and the Mediterranean. The vessels plying North America's rivers are far smaller than the monsters calling at Barcelona and San Juan, with shallower drafts to glide over closer bottoms and to negotiate channels their big brothers can't enter. Typically, riverboats have only one dining room, requiring separate sittings and kitchens and crews too small to prepare six meals from morning to midnight. Staterooms are, at best, compact, with few extras beyond hair dryers, two-channel radios, and bathrooms of telephone booth dimensions.

In compensation, schedules are less frantic, social directors more subdued, and the urge to flaunt status all but absent. Informality and casual conversation reign. Characteristic are the cruises offered by the **St. Lawrence Cruise Lines Inc.,** 253 Ontario St., Kingston, Ontario K7L 2Z4, © **800/267-7868** or 613/549-8091, fax 613/549-8410; www. stlawrencecruiselines.com. The company lays out itineraries of varying lengths and port connections. A 5-night version runs from Kingston, Ontario through the Thousand Islands to Montréal, and then up the Ottawa River to the national capital. Stops along the way include Boldt Castle, a millionaire's unfinished monument to the love of his life; Upper Canada Village, a museum settlement of restored early-19th-century buildings; several locks in the Seaway; and a wildlife park in Québec. An especially popular 6-night cruise goes from Kingston all the way downriver to Québec City. The food served is adequate, the onboard staff friendly and eager to please, the nightly entertainment missable (take books).

Best of all (compared to the big guys) are the fares, ranging from a low of US$1,171 per person, double occupancy, in shoulder season to a high of US$1,883 in peak season in the best stateroom on the longest trip, all meals and attractions included.

WALKING & CYCLING TOURS

Walking tours of Vieux-Montréal, the underground city, or any other section that piques interest are available through **Guidatour** (© **514/844-4021;** www.guidatour.qc.ca) or **Visites de Montréal** (© **514/933-6674**). Cycling tours in French or English are available through **Vélo Montréal** (© **514/ 236-8356;** www.velomontreal.com), located at 55 rue de la Commune ouest and 3880 rue Rachel est. If you're interested primarily in the city's architecture, landscaping, and urban planning, **Heritage Montréal** (© **514/286-2662;** www.heritagemontreal.qc.ca) conducts most of its "Architectours" on foot or on bicycles, and in French and English (just ask when you call). Each has a theme and a different neighborhood to traverse, from the Golden Square Mile to Square St-Louis to Little Italy. Heritage Montreal's summer schedule begins in mid-June and proceeds until late September, rain or shine.

6 Spectator Sports

Montréalers are as devoted to ice hockey as are other Canadians, with plenty of enthusiasm left over for baseball, football, and soccer. There are several prominent annual sporting events of other kinds, such as the Grand Prix Air Canada (p. 19; call ℭ **514/350-0000** for information) in June, The Player's Ltd. International men's tennis championship in late July, and the Montréal Marathon in September.

BASEBALL

Despite periodic successful seasons amidst mostly losing seasons, the **Montréal Expos** will almost certainly have either moved to another city or ceased to exist by the time you read this. In the unlikely event the team survives in place, you should be able to make ticket reservations by telephone, with a credit card. Call ℭ **514/790-1245** for information or log on to www.montrealexpos.com. Métro: Pie-IX.

FOOTBALL

Canadian professional football returned to Montréal after an experimental 3-year league with U.S. teams. The team that was briefly the Baltimore Colts is now in its second incarnation as the **Montréal Alouettes,** and has enjoyed considerable success since its return, frequently appearing in the Grey Cup, the CFL's Super Bowl. The Alouettes (French for "larks") play at McGill University's Molson Stadium on a schedule that runs from June into October. Tickets start at C$10 (US$6.45). Call ℭ **514/790-1245** or visit www.alouettes.net for information, www.admission.com for tickets.

 The Great American Pastime Goes North

U.S. broadcast networks and the team owners of Major League Baseball suffer night sweats over a worst-case scenario of labor strife, misbehaving superstars, and laws banning the sale of beer in their stadiums. The terrifying scenario that truly keeps them up at night is that of a World Series featuring either the Toronto Blue Jays or the Montréal Expos (or—*quelle calamité!*—both). Ratings plummet whenever a playoff game takes place in either of those cities, as happened with Toronto in the early 1990s. When colorless teams from undesirably small TV markets in the Midwest match up, network executives shrug their shoulders and comfort themselves with a resigned, "Well, at least they ain't Canadians."

This is an unfortunate analysis, for Canadians are as enthusiastic about the American game as anyone—at least after their national secular religion, hockey, is taken into account. Even though there is the ever-present possibility of early- and late-season games being called off on account of snow, professional baseball has been a fixture in Montréal—on and off—since the last century.

HARNESS RACING

Popularly known as Blue Bonnets Racetrack, the **Hippodrome de Montréal** at 7440 bd. Décarie, in Jean-Talon (© **514/739-2741**), is the host facility for international harness-racing events, including the Coupe des Elevers (Breeders Cup). Restaurants, bars, a snack bar, and pari–mutuel betting can make for a satisfying evening or Sunday-afternoon outing. There are no races on Tuesday and Thursday. General admission is free, C$5 (US$3.25) for the VIP section. Races begin at 7:30pm on Monday, Wednesday, Friday, and Saturday; on Sunday at 1:30pm. Métro: Namur, and then take the shuttle bus.

HOCKEY

The NHL's **Montréal Canadiens** play at the Centre Bell (formerly Molson Centre), which opened in 1996 at 1260 rue de la Gauchetière, replacing the beloved old Forum. The team has won 24 Stanley Cup championships since 1929. The season runs from October into April, with playoffs continuing to mid-June. Tickets range from about C$16 to C$95 (US$10–US$61). Ticket and schedule information can be obtained by phone at © **514/932-2582** (CLUB). Métro: Bonaventure.

7 Outdoor Activities

BICYCLING

Cycling is hugely popular in Montréal, and the city enjoys an expanding network of 349km (217 miles) of cycling paths. Heavily used routes include the nearly flat 11km (7-mile) *piste cyclable* (bicycle path) along the Lachine Canal that leads to Lac St-Louis, the 16km (10-mile) path west from the St-Lambert Lock (see "Special-Interest Sightseeing," earlier in this chapter) to the city of Côte Ste-Catherine, and Angrignon Park with its 6.4km (4-mile) biking path and inviting picnic areas (take the Métro, which accepts bikes in the last two doors of the last car, to Angrignon station). Bikes can be rented at the Vieux-Port (at the end of bd. St-Laurent) for C$8 to C$10 (US$5.15–US$6.45) an hour or C$20 to C$25 (US$13–US$16) a day. **Velo Montréal** at 3880 rue Rachel est and 55 rue de la Commune ouest (© **514/236-8356;** www.velomontreal.com) is another principal bike rental source. Bikes, along with the popular four-wheel "Q Cycles," may also be rented at the Place Jacques-Cartier entrance to the Vieux-Port. The Q Cycles, for use in the Vieux-Port only, cost C$4.75 (US$2.05) per half-hour for adults and C$3.50 (US$2.25) per half-hour for children. Another source for bikes is **Caroule,** which also rents in-line skates (see below).

A useful booklet, *Pédaler Montréal,* is available at the Infotourist office on Square Dominion. For additional information, log on to **www.velo.qc.ca**.

CROSS-COUNTRY SKIING

Parc Mont-Royal has a 2.1km (1½-mile) cross-country course called the *parcours de la croix.* The Botanical Garden has an ecology trail used by cross-country skiers during the winter. The problem with both is that skiers have to supply their own equipment. Just an hour from the city, in the Laurentides, are almost 20 ski centers, all offering cross-country as well as downhill skiing. See chapter 10.

HIKING

The most popular—and obvious—hike is up to the top of Mont-Royal. Start downtown on rue Peel, which leads north to a stairway, which in turn leads to an 800m (half-mile) path of switchbacks called Le Serpent. Or opt for the 200 steps that lead up to the Chalet Lookout, with the reward of a panoramic view of the city. Figure about 2km (1¼ miles) one-way.

ICE-SKATING

One of the most agreeable venues for ice-skating is the Atrium Le 1000 de la Gauchertière in the downtown skyscraper at that address. For one thing, it's indoors and warm. For another, it's surrounded by cafes and places to relax after a twirl around the big rink. It's open all year Sunday and Tuesday through Friday from 11:30am to 6pm, Saturday from 10am to 11am for children and their families, from 11:30am to 7pm for all, from 7pm to 10pm for "DJ Nights." Skates are available for rent for C$4.50 (US$2.90). Admission is C$5 (US$3.25) for adults 16 and up, C$3 (US$1.95) for seniors and children. Call ℂ **514/395-0555** or log on to www.le1000.com for information.

IN-LINE SKATING

More than 230 pairs of in-line skates and all the requisite protective gear can be rented from **Caroule/Montréal on Wheels** (ℂ **514/866-0633;** www.caroule montreal.com) at 27 rue de la Commune est, bordering the Vieux-Port. The cost is C$7.50 (US$4.85) weekdays or C$9 (US$5.80) weekends for the first hour, up to a maximum of C$20 (US$13) for a full day. Protective gear is included, and a deposit is required. Lessons on skates are available for C$25 (US$16) for 2 hours.

JOGGING

There are many possibilities for running. One is to follow rue Peel north to the Le Serpent switchback path on Mont-Royal, continuing uphill on it for 800km (half-mile) until it peters out. Turn right and continue 2km (1 mile) to the monument of George-Etienne Cartier, one of Canada's fathers of confederation. From here, either take a bus back downtown or run back down the same route or along avenue du Parc and avenue des Pins (turn right when you get to it). It's also fun to jog along the Lachine Canal.

7

Montréal Strolls

Cities best reveal themselves on foot, and Montréal is one of the most pedestrian-friendly cities in North America. There's much to see in the concentrated districts—the Old Town, the center city, around rue Crescent, the Latin Quarter, and on "The Mountain"—and the city's layout is fairly straightforward and easily navigated.

WALKING TOUR 1   VIEUX-MONTREAL

Start: Place d' Armes, opposite the Notre-Dame Basilica
Finish: Vieux-Port
Time: 2 to 3 hours
Best Times: Almost any day the weather is decent. Vieux-Montréal is lively and safe day or night. Note, however, that most of the museums in the area are closed on Monday. On warm weekends and holidays, Montréalers turn out in full force, enjoying the plazas, the 18th- and 19th-century architecture, and the ambience of the most picturesque part of their city.
Worst Times: Evenings, when museums and historic places are closed and rue St-Paul can get a little rowdy with young barhoppers.

Take the Métro to the Place d'Armes station (actually beside the Palais des Congrès convention center) and follow the signs up the short hill 2 blocks to Vieux-Montréal (Old Montréal) and the place d'Armes.

Turn right on rue St-Jacques. On your immediate right is the domed, colonnaded:

❶ Banque de Montréal

Montréal's oldest bank building dates from 1847. Besides being impressively proportioned and lavishly appointed inside and out, it houses a small banking museum that illustrates its early operations (go in the front door, turn left, then left again). Admission is free. From 1901 to 1905, American architect Stanford White was in charge of extending the original building beyond Ruelle des Fortifications to what is now rue St-Antoine. In this enlarged space he created a vast chamber with high, green-marble columns topped with golden capitals. The public is welcome to stop in for a look.

Exiting the bank, cross the street to the:

❷ Place d'Armes

The centerpiece of this square is a monument to city founder Paul de Chomedey, sieur de Maisonneuve (1612–76). It marks the spot where the settlers defeated Iroquois warriors in bloody hand-to-hand fighting, with de Maisonneuve himself locked in combat with the Iroquois chief. De Maisonneuve won and lived here another 23 years. The inscription on the monument reads: YOU ARE THE BUCKWHEAT SEED WHICH WILL GROW AND MULTIPLY AND SPREAD THROUGHOUT THE COUNTRY. The sculptures at the base of the monument represent three prominent citizens of early Montréal: Charles Lemoyne (1626–85), a farmer; Jeanne Mance, the woman who founded the first hospital in Montréal; and Raphael-Lambert Closse, a soldier and the mayor of Ville-Marie. The fourth sculpture represents an Iroquois brave. Closse is depicted with his dog, Pilote, whose bark once warned the early settlers of an impending Iroquois attack.

Facing the Notre-Dame Basilica from the square, look over to the left. At the corner of St-Jacques is the:

❸ Edifice New York Life

This Romanesque red-stone Richardson building, with a striking wrought-iron door and clock tower, is located at 511 place d'Armes. At all of eight stories, this was Montréal's first skyscraper back in 1888, and it was equipped with a technological marvel—an elevator.

Next to it, on the right, stands the 23-story Art Deco:

❹ Edifice Aldred

If the building looks somehow familiar, there's a reason: Built in 1931, it clearly resembles the Empire State Building in New York, also completed that year. The building's original tenant was Aldred and Co. Ltd., a New York–based multinational finance company with offices in New York, London, and Paris.

From the square, cross rue Notre-Dame, bearing right of the Basilica to the:

❺ Vieux Séminaire de St-Sulpice

In the city's oldest building, surrounded by equally ancient stone walls, this seminary was erected by the Sulpician priests who arrived in Ville-Marie in 1657, 15 years after the colony was founded. (The Sulpicians are part of an order founded in Paris by Jean-Jacques Olier in 1641.) The clock on the facade dates from 1701 and has gears made almost entirely of wood. Unfortunately, the seminary is not open to the public.

After a look through the iron gate, head east on rue Notre-Dame to the magnificent Gothic Revival:

❻ Basilique Notre-Dame (1829)

This brilliantly crafted church was designed by James O'Donnell, a Protestant Irish architect living in New York. Transformed by his experience in building the basilica, he later converted to Roman Catholicism and is the only layman buried here. The main altar is made from a hand-carved linden tree. Behind the altar is the Chapel of the Sacred Heart (1982), a perennially popular choice for weddings. The chapel's altar, 32 bronze panels by Montréal artist Charles Daudelin, represents birth, life, and death. The church can seat 4,000 people, and its bell, one of the largest in North America, weighs 12 tons. There's a small museum beside the chapel.

Exiting the basilica, turn right (east) on rue Notre-Dame, crossing rue St-Sulpice. In 4 blocks, on the left, is the:

❼ Vieux Palais de Justice (Old Court House)

Most of the structure was built in 1856. The third floor and dome were added in 1891, as can be easily discerned with a close look. You can explore the Court House although there are no organized tours. The city's civil cases were tried here until a new courthouse, the Palais de Justice, was built next door in 1978. Civic departments for the city of Montréal are housed here now. The statue beside the Old Court House, called *Homage to Marguerite Bourgeoys* (a teacher and nun), is by sculptor Jules LaSalle.

Next, on the right, is:

❽ Place Vauquelin

This small public square, with a splashing fountain and a view of the Champ-de-Mars park (which lies behind and beneath the city hall), was created in 1858. The statue is of Jean Vauquelin, commander of the French

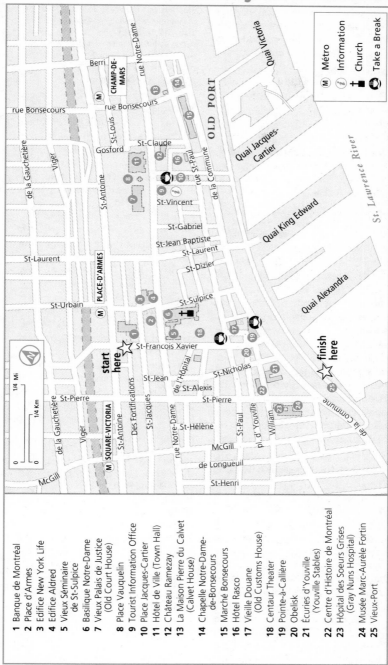

1 Banque de Montréal
2 Place d'Armes
3 Edifice New York Life
4 Edifice Aldred
5 Vieux Séminaire
   de St-Sulpice
6 Basilique Notre-Dame
7 Vieux Palais de Justice
   (Old Court House)
8 Place Vauquelin
9 Tourist Information Office
10 Place Jacques-Cartier
11 Hôtel de Ville (Town Hall)
12 Château Ramezay
13 La Maison Pierre du Calvet
   (Calvet House)
14 Chapelle Notre-Dame-
   de-Bonsecours
15 Marché Bonsecours
16 Hôtel Rasco
17 Vieille Douane
   (Old Customs House)
18 Centaur Theater
19 Pointe-à-Callière
20 Obelisk
21 Écuries d'Youville
   (Youville Stables)
22 Centre d'Histoire de Montréal
23 Hôpital des Soeurs Grises
   (Gray Nuns Hospital)
24 Musée Marc-Aurèle Fortin
25 Vieux-Port

fleet in New France. It stares across rue Notre-Dame at his counterpart, the English Nelson. The two statues are symbols of Montréal's duality.

On the opposite corner is a small but helpful:

⑨ Tourist information office

A bilingual staff is ready to answer questions and hand out many useful brochures and maps (only Thurs–Sun in winter). On this site once stood the famed Silver Dollar Saloon, long since torn down. The tavern was named for 350 silver dollars embedded in its floor.

Around the corner, on the right, is a focus of activity in Vieux-Montréal, a magnet for both citizens and visitors year-round, the:

⑩ Place Jacques-Cartier

Opened as a marketplace in 1804, this is the most appealing of the Old Town's squares, despite its obviously touristy aspects. Its cobbled cross-streets, gentle downhill slope, and ancient buildings set the mood, while outdoor cafes, street entertainers, itinerant artists, and fruit and flower vendors invite lingering, at least in warm weather. Calèches (horse-drawn carriages) depart from both the lower and upper ends of the square for tours of Vieux-Montréal. Save a lingering visit to the plaza for a little later in the walk.

Rising on the other side of rue Notre-Dame, opposite the top of the square is the impressive:

⑪ Hôtel de Ville (Town Hall)

Built between 1872 and 1878 in the florid French Second Empire style, the edifice houses the city's administrative offices. In 1922, it barely survived a disastrous fire. Only the exterior walls remained, and after substantial rebuilding and the addition of another floor, it reopened in 1926.

Take a minute to look inside at the generous use of Italian marble, the Art Deco lamps, and the bronze-and-glass chandelier. The sculptures at the entry are *Woman with a Pail* and *The Sower,* both by Alfred Laliberté.

Cross rue Notre-Dame once again. After passing the recently completed terraced park, with its orderly ranks of trees and a statue honoring the controversial long-time mayor of Montréal, Jean Drapeau, enter the circular drive to:

⑫ Château Ramezay

Built by Claude de Ramezay between 1705 and 1706 in the French Regime style of the period, this was the home of the city's French governors for 4 decades, starting with de Ramezay, before being taken over and used for the same purpose by the British.

In 1775 an army of American rebels invaded and held Montréal, using the château as their headquarters. Benjamin Franklin was sent to persuade Montréalers to join the American revolt against British rule. He stayed in the château but failed to sway Québec's leaders to join his cause.

The house has had other uses over the years. It was a courthouse, government office building, teachers' college, and headquarters for Laval University before becoming a museum in 1895. Inside are furnishings, tools, oil paintings, costumes, and other objects related to the economic and social activities of the 18th century and the first half of the 19th century.

Continue in the same direction (east) along rue Notre-Dame to the corner of rue Bonsecours. Turn right. Near the bottom, at no. 401 on the left, is a house that offers a look at what life was like in Montréal in the late 18th century, the:

⑬ La Maison Pierre du Calvet (Calvet House)

Built in the 18th century and restored between 1964 and 1966, this appears to be a modest dwelling. In the early days, though, such a house would have been inhabited by a fairly well-to-do family. Pierre du Calvet, believed to be the original owner, was a French Huguenot who supported the American Revolution. Calvet met with Benjamin Franklin here in 1775 and was imprisoned from 1780 to 1783 for supplying money to the

Americans. The house, with its characteristic sloped roof meant to discourage snow buildup and raised end walls that serve as firebreaks, is constructed of Montréal graystone. It is now part of an inn, with an entrance at no. 405.

The next street, rue St-Paul, is the oldest thoroughfare in Montréal, dating from 1672. Across the way is the small:

⑭ Notre-Dame-de-Bonsecours Chapel (1673)

This chapel, called the Sailors' Church because so many seamen come to worship here, was founded by Marguerite Bourgeoys, a nun and teacher who was made a saint in 1982. Although recent excavations in the basement have unearthed foundations of her original 1675 church, the building has been much altered, and the present facade was built in the late 19th century. A museum (entrance on the left) tells the story of Bourgeoys' life and incorporates a newly opened archaeological site, with discoveries dated to 400 B.C. Historically, sailors saved at sea have made pilgrimages to the church to give thanks. Climb up to the tower for a view of the port and the Old Town.

Just beyond the Sailor's Church, heading west down rue St-Paul, is an imposing building with a colonnaded facade and silvery dome, the limestone:

⑮ Marché Bonsecours (Bonsecours Market)

Completed in 1847, this building was briefly used, in order, as the Parliament of United Canada, the City Hall, the central market, a music recital hall, and the home of the municipality's housing and planning offices. The building was restored in 1992 to serve as a center for temporary exhibitions and musical performances during the city's 350th-birthday celebration. It continues to be used for exhibitions, celebrations, and the like. There are retail stalls inside and three sidewalk cafes near the entrance.

When the Bonsecours Market was first built, the dome could be seen from everywhere in the city. The Doric columns of the portico were cast of iron in England, and the prominent dome has long served as a landmark for seafarers steaming into the harbor.

Continue down rue St-Paul. At no. 281 is the former:

⑯ Hôtel Rasco

Built in 1836 for Francisco Rasco, an Italian who came to Canada to manage a hotel for the Molson family and later became successful with Hôtel Rasco, his own hotel. The 150-room Rasco was the Ritz of its day in Montréal, hosting, among other honored guests, Charles Dickens and his wife in 1842, when the author was directing some of his plays at the theater that used to stand across the street. The hotel lives on in legend if not in fact, devoid of much of its original architectural detail. Rasco left in 1844, and the hotel slipped into decline. Between 1960 and 1981 it stood empty, but the city took it over and restored it in 1982. At the moment, it has a successful restaurant on the ground floor, but city officials can't seem to decide what to do with the rest of the building.

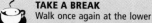

TAKE A BREAK
Walk once again at the lower end of place Jacques-Cartier. Most of the old buildings in and around the inclined plaza harbor restaurants and cafes. For a drink or a light meal, try to find a seat in Le Jardin Nelson (no. 407), at the southeast corner, near the bottom of the hill. Sit in the courtyard in back when the weather is good—there often is live music—or on the terrace overlooking the activity of the square.

After your break, walk slowly uphill, taking in the old buildings that bracket the plaza. Plaques in French and English describe some of them: the **Vandelac House** (no. 433), the **del Vecchio House** (nos. 404–410), and the **Cartier House** (no. 407). All these houses were well suited to the rigors of life in the raw young settlement. Their steeply pitched roofs shed the heavy winter snows rather than collapsing under the burden, and small windows with double casements let in light while keeping out wintry breezes. When shuttered, the windows were almost as effective as the heavy stone walls in deflecting hostile arrows or the antics of trappers fresh from raucous evenings in nearby taverns.

At the upper (northern) end of the plaza stands a monument to Horatio Nelson, hero of Trafalgar, erected in 1809. This monument preceded the much larger version in London by several years. However, after years of being subjected to vandalism, presumably by Québec separatists, the original statue was replaced by the one currently occupying the crown of the column.

At the top of the plaza, turn left and descend on the other side back down to rue St-Paul. Turn right. The next few short blocks are given to art galleries and loud souvenir shops, but at 150 rue St-Paul is the neoclassical:

⑰ Vieille Douane (Old Customs House)

Erected from 1836 to 1838, the building was doubled in size to its present proportions when an extension to the south was added in 1882; walk around to the other side of the building for a look at the extension. The extended end of the building faces place Royale, the first public square in the early settlement of Ville-Marie. Europeans and Amerindians used to come here to trade.

Continue down rue St-Paul to rue St-François-Xavier. Turn right on a short detour up rue St-François-Xavier. At rue de l'Hôpital, to the right, is the stately:

⑱ Centaur Theater

The home of Montréal's principal English-language theater is a former stock-exchange building. The beaux arts architecture is interesting in that the two entrances are on either side rather than in the center of the facade. American architect George Post, who was also responsible for the New York Stock Exchange, designed the building, erected in 1903. It served in its original function until 1965, when it was redesigned as a theater with two stages.

Return back down rue St-François-Xavier, crossing St-Paul. Up ahead, the dramatic wedge-shaped building is the:

⑲ Pointe-à-Callière

Housing the Museum of Archaeology and History, with artifacts unearthed here during more than 10 years of excavation, this site was where Ville-Marie (Montréal) was founded in 1642. The museum also incorporates, via an underground connection, the Old Customs House you just passed.

A fort stood on this spot in 1645 as did, 30 years later, the château of a monsieur de Callière, from whom the building and triangular square take their names. At that time, the St. Pierre River separated this piece of land from the mainland. It was made a canal in the 19th century and later filled in.

>
> **TAKE A BREAK**
> One possibility for lunch or an afternoon pick-me-up is the casual, second-floor **L'Arrivage Café** at the museum. Another is the moderately priced **Stash**, 200 rue St-Paul ouest at rue St-François-Xavier, which specializes in Polish fare and is open from 11am until late in the evening.

Proceeding west from Pointe-à-Callière, near rue St-François-Xavier, stands an:

⑳ Obelisk

It commemorates the founding of Ville-Marie on May 18, 1642. The obelisk was erected here in 1893 by the Montréal Historical Society and bears the names of the city's early pioneers, including de Maisonneuve and Jeanne Mance.

Continuing west from the obelisk 2 blocks, look for the:

㉑ Ecuries d'Youville (Youville Stables)

It's on the left at 296–316 place d'Youville. Despite the name, the rooms in the iron-gated compound, built in 1825 on land owned by the Gray Nuns, were used mainly as warehouses, rather than to stable horses. Like much of the waterfront area, the U-shaped Youville building (the actual stables, next door, were made of wood and disappeared long ago) was rundown and forgotten until the 1960s, when a group of enterprising businesspeople decided to buy and renovate the property. Today the compound contains offices and a popular restaurant, **Gibbys.** Go inside the courtyard and take a look if the gates are open, as they usually are.

Continue another block west to 335 rue St-Pierre and the:

㉒ Centre d'Histoire de Montréal (Montréal History Center)

Built in 1903 as Montréal's Central Fire Station, this building now houses exhibits, including many audiovisual ones, about the city's past and present. Visitors will learn about the early routes of exploration, the fur trade, architecture, public squares, the railroad, and life in Montréal from 1920 to 1950.

Less than a block away, on the left at 138 rue St-Pierre, pass the former:

㉓ Hôpital des Soeurs Grises (Gray Nuns Hospital)

The hospital was in operation from 1693 to 1851 and served as a novitiate for future nuns. The order, founded

by the widow Marguerite d'Youville in 1737, is officially known as the Sisters of Charity of Montréal. The present building incorporates several additions and was part of the city's General Hospital, run by the Charon Brothers but administered by d'Youville, who died here in 1771. The wing in which she died was restored in 1980. The wall of the original chapel remains. Visits inside must be arranged in advance. Call ⓒ **514/842-9411** to schedule a visit.

From here, look down rue St-Pierre for the brown awning at no. 118 that marks the entrance to the:

㉔ Musée Marc-Aurèle Fortin

This museum is devoted to Canadian artist Fortin, who died in 1972. He was known for his watercolors of the Québec countryside, including Charlevoix and the Laurentian Mountains. His depictions of Dutch elms give a glimpse of the time when these giant trees lined rues Sherbrooke and St-Joseph in Montréal, before blight decimated them.

Continue past the museum and cross rue de la Commune and the railroad tracks to enter the:

㉕ Vieux-Port (Old Port)

Montréal's historic commercial wharves have been reborn as a waterfront park frequented by cyclists, in-line skaters, joggers, walkers, strollers, lovers, and picnickers, in good weather. This is the entry to **Parc des Écluses (Locks Park),** where the first locks on the St. Lawrence River are located.

From there, walk back north along rue McGill to reach **Square Victoria** and its Métro station. Or pick up the beginning of the path along the **Lachine Canal** at Parc des Ecluses and follow it for an hour or less to arrive at Montréal's colorful indoor/outdoor Atwater Market.

WALKING TOUR 2	DOWNTOWN

Start:	Bonaventure Métro stop
Finish:	Musée McCord
Time:	1½ hours
Best Times:	Weekdays in the morning or after 2pm, when the streets hum with big-city vibrancy but aren't too crowded.
Worst Times:	Weekdays from noon to 2pm, when the streets, stores, and restaurants are crowded with businesspeople on lunch-break errands; Monday, when museums are closed; and Sunday, when most stores are closed and the area is virtually deserted (museums, however, are open).

After a tour of Vieux-Montréal, a look around the heart of the new 20th-century city will highlight the ample contrast between these two areas. To see the city at its contemporary best, take the Métro to the Bonaventure stop.

Emerging from that station, the dramatic skyscraper immediately to the west is:

① 1000 rue de la Gauchetière

This recent contribution to the already memorable skyline is easily identified by its copper-and-blue pyramidal top, which rises to the maximum height permitted by the municipal building code. Inside, past an atrium planted with live trees, is a huge indoor skating rink bordered by cafes with seating for more than 1,500 spectators.

Walk west on rue de la Gauchetière. In 1 block, on the left, is:

② Le Marriott Château Champlain

The hotel's distinctive facade of half-moon windows inspired its nickname: the "cheese grater."

Turn right on rue Peel, walking north. In another block, you'll arrive at:

③ Square Dorchester

The square's tall old trees and benches invite lunchtime brown-baggers. This used to be called Dominion Square, but it was renamed for Baron Dorchester, an early English governor, when the adjacent street, once named for him, was changed to boulevard René-Lévesque. Along the east side of the square is the **Sun Life Insurance building,** built in three stages between 1914 and 1931, and the tallest building in Québec from 1931 until the

skyscraper boom of the post–World War II era. This is a gathering point for tour buses and calèches (horse-drawn carriages). In winter, the calèche drivers replace their carriages with sleighs and give rides around the top of Mont-Royal.

At the northeast corner of the square is the main office of:

④ Infotouriste

Many useful maps and brochures are in stock here, most of them free for the taking. Visitors can ask questions of bilingual attendants, purchase tour tickets, change money, make hotel reservations, connect with the Internet, and rent a car.

From that office, go back to the other end of the square and turn left (east) on:

⑤ Boulevard René-Lévesque

Formerly Dorchester Boulevard, this road was renamed in 1988 following the death of René-Lévesque, the Parti Quebecois leader who led the movement in favor of Québec independence and the use of the French language. Boulevard René-Lévesque is the city's broadest downtown thoroughfare, and the one with the fastest traffic.

On the right is the:

⑥ Cathédrale Marie-Reine-du-Monde (Mary Queen of the World Cathedral)

Built between 1875 and 1894 as the headquarters for Montréal's Roman Catholic bishop, the cathedral is a copy of St. Peter's Basilica in Rome, built to roughly one-quarter scale. The statue in front of the cathedral is of Bishop Ignace Bourget (1799–1885), the force behind the construction of the basilica. It was sculpted in 1903 by Louis-Philippe Hébert, who is also responsible for the statue of de Maisonneuve in the Place d'Armes in Vieux-Montréal.

Continue past the cathedral and cross rue Mansfield, and you will see:

⑦ Fairmont The Queen Elizabeth (Le Reine Elizabeth)

Opened in 1958, Montréal's largest hotel stands above **Gare Centrale,** the main railroad station, making it most convenient for people arriving by train. It also has direct access to the underground city, and buses leave for Dorval and Mirabel airports from here.

Across boulevard René-Lévesque from Fairmont Le Reine Elizabeth hotel is:

⑧ Place Ville-Marie

Known as PVM to Montréalers, this massive structure was the keystone of the postwar urban redevelopment efforts in Montréal. The skyscraper, with its cross-shaped floor plan, was designed by I. M. Pei. It is meant to recall Cartier's cross, planted on Mount Royal to claim the island for France, and de Maisonneuve's first little settlement, Ville-Marie. The complex, completed in 1962, has a fountain in its plaza called *Feminine Landscape* (1972), executed by Toronto artist Gerald Gladstone.

At the end of the hotel, turn left along rue Université, crossing boulevard René-Lévesque and walking 2 blocks to rue Ste-Catherine. On the right is:

⑨ Carré Phillips

This plaza contains a statue of Edward VII and, during much of the year, a farm stand selling Québec maple products.

Over to the left, across rue Ste-Catherine, is:

⑩ Cathédrale Christ Church

Built from 1856 to 1859, this neo-Gothic building is the seat of the Anglican bishop of Montréal. The church garden is modeled on a medieval European cloister. The cathedral donated the land on which place de la Cathédrale and the shopping complex underneath it, Promenades de la Cathédrale, were built, in return for eventual ownership of the skyscraper and the underground complex. All those subterranean corridors and levels have caused some to dub it the "floating" or "flying" church.

Turn left on:

⑪ Rue Ste-Catherine

Head west through the center of Montréal's shopping district. Most of the remaining department stores are along here, including, to the right of the church, La Baie (or "The Bay," short for Hudson's Bay Company, successor to the famous fur-trapping firm). Movie houses, cafes, and shops line rue Ste-Catherine for several blocks.

At the corner of rue de la Montagne is:

⑫ Ogilvy

This is the most vibrant of a classy breed of department store that appears to be fading from the scene. Founded in 1866, it strives to maintain its upmarket stature by blending tradition with tasteful marketing strategies. Its Christmas windows are eagerly awaited each year, and a bagpiper announces openings, closings, and high noon.

Continue 1 more block to:

⑬ Rue Crescent

This and nearby streets are the locus of the center-city social and dining district, largely yuppie Anglo in character, if not necessarily in strict demographics. Pricey boutiques, inexpensive pizza joints, upscale restaurants, and dozens of bars and dance clubs draw enthusiastic, stylish consumers looking to spend money, find

Walking Tour: Downtown Montréal

1 1000 rue de la Gauchetière
2 Le Marriott Château Champlain
3 Square Dorchester
4 Infotouriste
5 Boulevard René-Lévesque
6 Cathédral Marie-Reine-du-Monde
7 Le Reine Elisabeth/ Queen Elizabeth Hotel
8 Place Ville-Marie
9 Carré Phillips
10 Christ Church Cathedral
11 Rue Ste-Catherine
12 Ogilvy
13 Rue Crescent

14 Musée des Beaux-Arts
   (Museum of Fine Arts)
15 Maison Alcan
16 McGill University
17 Musée Redpath
18 *The Illuminated Crowd*
19 Musée McCord

love or undemanding lust and party the night away. This center of gilded youth and glamour was once a run-down slum area slated for demolition. Luckily, buyers with a good aesthetic sense saw the possibilities of these late-19th-century row houses and brought them back to life.

Turn right on rue Crescent and:

TAKE A BREAK
Lively spots for coffee or snacks are abundant along rue Crescent. **Thursdays** (no. 1449) is one, if you can find a seat on the balcony, or walk a little farther up rue Crescent and get a sidewalk table at **Sir Winston Churchill Pub** (no. 1459).

Continue up rue Crescent, past boulevard de Maisonneuve, to the corner of rues Crescent and Sherbrooke. On this left corner, and on the opposite side of Sherbrooke, is the:

⓮ Musée des Beaux-Arts (Museum of Fine Arts)
This is Canada's oldest and Montréal's most prominent museum. The modern annex was added in 1991 and is connected to the original stately beaux arts building (1912) across the way by an underground tunnel that doubles as a gallery. Both buildings are made of Vermont marble.

Turn right on rue Sherbrooke, passing, at the next corner, the Holt Renfrew department store, identified on its marquee only as HOLTS. Continue on rue Sherbrooke, passing, on the right, the:

⓯ Maison Alcan
This structure has been frequently lauded for its incorporation of 19th-century houses into its late-20th-century facade. Step inside the lobby to see the results, especially over to the right.

Walk 4 more blocks in the same direction. On the opposite side of rue Sherbrooke is the entrance to:

⓰ McGill University
The gate is usually open to this, Canada's most prestigious university. Step inside and see, just to the left, a large stone that marks the site of the native Horchelaga settlement that existed here before the arrival of the Europeans.

Also on the campus is the:

⓱ Musée Redpath
Housed in a building dating from 1882, this museum's main draw is the Egyptian antiquities collection, the second largest of its kind in Canada.

Opposite the university, and just half a block south of rue Sherbrooke, on the left, is a now cream-colored resin sculpture called:

⓲ *The Illuminated Crowd* (1979)
Raymond Mason's sculpture is frequently photographed and widely admired for its evocation of the human condition, although its detractors find it sentimental and obvious. Circle it at leisure and then return to rue Sherbrooke, turning right.

One block east is the:

⓳ Musée McCord
This private museum of Canadian history first opened in 1921 and was substantially renovated and expanded in 1992. Named for its founder, David Ross McCord (1844–1930), the McCord has an eclectic and often eccentric collection of 80,000 artifacts. Furniture, clothing, china, silver, paintings, photographs, and folk art reveal elements of city and rural life from the 18th to the 20th century. Amerindians are represented in the First Nations room.

WALKING TOUR 3   PLATEAU MONT-ROYAL

Start:	The corner of avenue du Mont-Royal and rue St-Denis
Finish:	Square St-Louis
Time:	At least 2 hours, but allow more time to explore this intriguing neighborhood
Best Times:	Monday through Saturday during the day, when the shops are open. Boulevard St-Laurent is at its liveliest on Saturday. For barhopping, evenings should work well.
Worst Times:	Sunday, when most stores are closed, if shopping is important to you.

This is essentially a window-shopping, browsing, and grazing tour, designed to give you a sampling of the sea of ethnicities that make up Plateau Mont-Royal, north of downtown Montréal and due east of Mont-Royal Park. The neighborhood, which in recent years has seen an explosion of restaurants, cafes, clubs, and shops, is bounded on the south by rue Sherbrooke, on the north by boulevard St-Joseph, on the east by avenue Papineau, and on the west by rue St-Dominique. Monuments and obligatory sights are few along these commercial avenues, and the residential side streets are filled with row houses that are home to students, young professionals, and immigrants old and new. This walk is a glance into the lives of both established and freshly-minted Montréalers and the way they spend their leisure time. To begin, take the Métro to the Mont-Royal station. Be aware that stores and bistros open and close with considerable frequency in this neighborhood, so some of the highlights listed below may not exist when you visit.

There's a fruit stand in front of the Métro station. Turn left, walking west on avenue du Mont-Royal to St-Denis. Turn left. In the coming blocks, there's much to discover. On the left side of the street, at 4481 rue St-Denis, is:

① Quai des Brumes

This popular gathering spot for jazz, blues, and beer offers live music most evenings, and even some afternoons. Its name means "Foggy Dock."

Go back to the corner and cross the street to 4430 St-Denis:

② Requin Chagrin

Check out this retro shop with a good selection of secondhand clothing.

Walk farther along at St-Denis to no. 4380:

③ Champigny

A large bookstore with mostly French stock, it also carries travel guides and literature in English, as well as CDs, magazines, and newspapers in many languages from all over the world.

Most of the books are upstairs. There's a greatly expanded children's section. It's open daily until midnight.

Continue down the right side of St-Denis to no. 4338:

④ Côté Sud

Here you'll find shelves of distinctive glassware, plus cooking and dining implements, including chef's knives, flatware, china, and related items, such as aluminum canisters and candles. They fill two floors of connecting buildings.

Keep walking down St-Denis and:

TAKE A BREAK
At 4325 rue St-Denis, **Fonduementale** specializes in (guess what?) fondue—fondues as appetizers, as main courses, as desserts. Excess is not without its virtues. The turn-of-the-century house has a terrace in front and a garden.

Walking Tour: Plateau Mont-Royal

1 Quai des Brumes
2 Requin Chagrin
3 Champigny
4 Côte Sud
5 Départ en Mer
6 Zone
7 Antiques Puces-Libre
8 Fruits & Passion
9 Artefact
10 Kaliyana
11 Senteurs de Provence
12 Rue Duluth
13 Boulevard St-Laurent
14 Schwartz's
15 La Vieille Europe
16 Le Swimming
17 Rue Prince-Arthur
18 Square St-Louis

Not far down the street at no. 4306 is:

⑤ Départ en Mer

A nautical theme prevails at this store, with brass navigation instruments, bells, fisherman shirts, and a variety of ship models ranging in price from a handful of loonies to several hundred dollars. Most of the merchandise is produced in France.

Continue down rue St-Denis to no. 4246:

⑥ Zone

This shop purveys contemporary housewares, most of them sleekly monochromatic, some brightly hued.

Next door, at 4240 rue St-Denis, is the wonderfully cluttered:

⑦ Antiques Puces-Libre

This store offers three floors of 19th-century French-Canadian country collectibles—pine and oak furniture, lamps, clocks, vases, and much more.

Continue to rue Rachel, cross to the left side of the street and continue south to 4159A rue St-Denis, where you'll find:

⑧ Fruits & Passion

This company uses "natural extracts" to fabricate their undeniably appealing soaps, aromatherapy, sunscreens, moisturizers . . . and, in the back, olive oils, balsamic vinegars, chutneys, and honey.

Just down the street, at 4117 rue St-Denis, is:

⑨ Artefact

Quebecois designers and artists display (and sell) clothing and paintings at this shop.

After that, look for no. 4107:

⑩ Kaliyana

Loose and comfortable clothing for women is created by a Czech-born designer who uses hand-printed fabrics.

Next, at 4077 rue St-Denis, you'll come upon:

⑪ Senteurs de Provence

One of a small chain, this store displays hand-painted pottery and printed linens, as well as bath soaps, shower gels, and lotions of high order, all from France.

At the corner of St-Denis and rue Duluth, cross over and walk west along:

⑫ Rue Duluth

This street is dotted with ever-changing Greek, Portuguese, Italian, North African, Malaysian, and Vietnamese eateries, as well as several small antique shops.

Continue along rue Duluth until it arrives at the Boulevard St-Laurent, a north–south thoroughfare that's so prominent in the cultural history of the city that it's known to Anglophones, Francophones, and Allophones alike simply as "The Main."

Turn left on:

⑬ Boulevard St-Laurent

Traditionally a beachhead for immigrants to Montréal, St-Laurent has increasingly become a street of chic bistros and clubs. The late-night section runs for several miles, roughly from rue Laurier all the way down to rue Sherbrooke. This bistro and club boom was fueled by low rents and the large number of industrial lofts in this area, a legacy of St-Laurent's heyday as a garment-manufacturing center. Today these cavernous spaces have been converted into restaurants and clubs, many of which have the life spans of fireflies, but some of which pound on for years.

At 3895 bd. St-Laurent you'll find:

⑭ Schwartz's

The language police insisted on the exterior sign with the French mouthful CHEZ SCHWARZ CHARCUTERIE HEBRAÏQUE DE MONTREAL, but everyone just calls it Schwartz's. This narrow, no-frills deli serves smoked meat against which all other smoked meats must be measured. Vegetarians and those who require some distance from their neighbors' elbows will hate it.

Next, a few steps along at no. 3855, is:

⑮ La Vieille Europe

The "Old Europe" delicatessen sells aromatic coffee beans from many nations, plus sausages and meats, cheeses, and cooking utensils.

At no. 3643 you'll find:

⑯ Le Swimming

Here, you'll find a bar downstairs and an upstairs hall with a dozen pool tables.

Continue down boulevard St-Laurent and turn left (east) into:

⑰ Rue Prince-Arthur

Named after Queen Victoria's third son, who was governor-general of Canada from 1911 to 1916, this is a pedestrian street filled with bars and restaurants, most of which add more to the liveliness of the street than to the gastronomic reputation of the city. The older establishments go by such names as La Caverne Grecque, La Gourmet Grec, Cabane Grecque—no doubt you will discern an emerging theme—but are being challenged by Latino and Asian newcomers. Their owners vie constantly with gimmicks to haul in passersby, including two-drinks-for-the-price-of-one specials

and dueling table d'hôte prices that plummet to C$7 (US$4.50) or lower for three courses. Beer and sangria are the popular drinks at the white resin tables and chairs set out along the sides of the street. Mimes, vendors, street performers, and caricaturists also compete for the tourist dollar.

Five blocks along, rue Prince-Arthur ends at:

⑱ Square St-Louis

This public garden plaza is framed by attractive row houses erected for well-to-do Francophones in the late 19th and early 20th centuries. People stretch out on the grass to take the sun or sit bundled on benches willing March away. Among them are usually a few harmless derelicts and street people. On occasional summer days, there are impromptu concerts. The square ends at rue St-Denis.

From here, bear left onto rue Cherrier to catch the Métro at the Sherbrooke station, less than half a block away.

WALKING TOUR 4   MONT-ROYAL

Start:	At the corner of rue Peel and avenue des Pins
Finish:	At the cross on top of the mountain
Time:	Two hours, allowing for some dawdling. If you're pressed for time, it's possible to get to the lookout in a little more than half an hour and back down the mountain in 15 minutes.
Best Times:	Spring, summer, and autumn mornings.
Worst Times:	Winter, when snow and slush make a sleigh ride to the top of the mountain much more enticing than a hike.

Assuming a reasonable measure of physical fitness, an enjoyable way to explore Parc Mont-Royal is simply to hike up from downtown. Joggers, cyclists, in-line skaters, and anyone in search of a little greenery and space head here in warm weather. In winter, cross-country skiers follow the miles of paths within the park, and snowshoers tramp along trails laid out especially for them. The 200-hectare (494-acre) park was created in 1876 to a plan by American landscape architect Frederick Law Olmsted, who designed Central Park in New York City and Prospect Park in Brooklyn, as well as parks in Philadelphia, Boston, and Chicago.

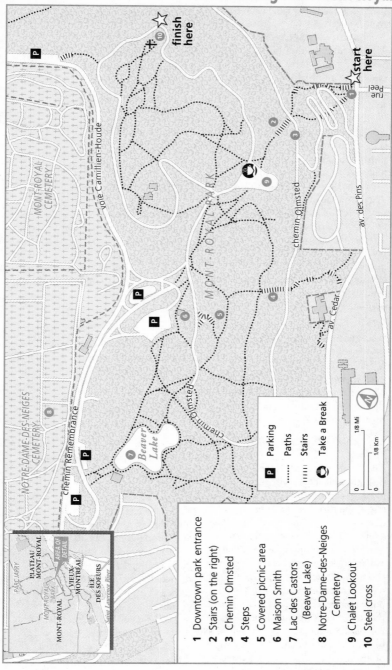

Walking Tour: Mont-Royal

1 Downtown park entrance
2 Stairs (on the right)
3 Chemin Olmsted
4 Steps
5 Covered picnic area
6 Maison Smith
7 Lac des Castors (Beaver Lake)
8 Notre-Dame-des-Neiges Cemetery
9 Chalet Lookout
10 Steel cross

Start this tour at the corner of rue Peel and avenue des Pins, at the:

❶ Downtown park entrance

A handy map at the site helps to set bearings. From here, it's possible to ascend the mountain by several routes. Hearty souls can choose the quickest and most strenuous approach—scaling the steep slope directly to the lookout at the top. Those who prefer to take their time and gain altitude slowly can take one short set of stairs followed by a switchback bridle path (turn left onto it) leading to the top. The approach outlined here falls somewhere in between but points out the other alternatives as they arrive.

Take the gravel path to the right (facing the map of the park). It has intervals of four to six steps, and parallels the wall that separates the park from the outside world. When the path dead-ends, turn left (away from the steep steps seen beside a small lookout).

Those who have chosen the athletic route can take the next:

❷ Stairs on the right

Fair warning: There are more than 250 steps in all, and the last 100 go almost straight up. For a less taxing route, stay on the wide:

❸ Chemin Olmsted (Olmsted Road)

The road was named for the park's designer, and it's actually the only part of his design that became a reality (the rest of the park wasn't completed to his design). Following this road will bypass a few of this tour's stops and get to the next stop (no. 6) in about 45 minutes.

Frederick Law Olmsted designed the road at such a gradual grade not only for pedestrians, but also for horse-drawn carriages. Horses could pull their loads up the hill at a steady pace, and on the way down would not be pushed from behind by the weight of the carriage. Chemin Olmsted is closed to automobiles. Early on, it passes some beautiful stone houses off

Redpath Circle, to the left. A couple of paths lead up the mountain to the right. They get walkers to their destination more quickly but aren't as strenuous as the steps recently bypassed. So if the road begins to seem a little too slow, take the:

❹ Steps

The steps eventually appear on the right. They lead to an old pump station, to the right. From here, continue in an uphill direction until you arrive at a:

❺ Covered picnic area

At this open-air stone-and-wood structure with a copper roof—take a snack break, if you wish—walk around behind the shelter and take the stairway behind it down the hill, which descends again to Chemin Olmsted, minus a couple of big loops edited out of the walk. Up ahead is the back of the:

❻ Maison Smith

Regardless of which route you choose at the beginning of the tour, you will end up here. Built in 1858, this structure has been used as a park rangers' station and park police headquarters. From 1983 to 1992 it served as a small nature museum. Nearby is the 90m (300-ft.) high Radio Canada Tower.

From the house, walk through the field of sculptures, away from the radio tower, until you reach:

❼ Lac des Castors (Beaver Lake)

The name refers to the once-profitable fur industry, not to the actual presence of the long-gone animals. In summer it's surrounded by sunbathers and picnickers and filled with boaters. In the cold winter months before the snow sets in, it becomes an ice-skater's paradise.

There's a small concession stand in the recently renovated pavilion here, but if you're planning to have something to eat or drink on the mountain, wait for the snack bar at the chalet at the nearby lookout. Both the chalet and the pavilion have restrooms and telephones.

Walk across the road, called Chemin de la Remembrance (Remembrance Rd.), behind the pavilion, to enter:

⑧ Notre-Dame-des-Neiges Cemetery

From this, the city's predominantly Catholic cemetery, you can visit the adjacent Protestant Mount Royal graveyard and then behind it (to the north), if you're up for a time-consuming walk, see the small adjoining Jewish and Spanish-Portuguese cemetery. Notre-Dame-des-Neiges Cemetery reveals much of the ethnic mix in Montréal. There are headstones, some with likenesses in photos or tiles, for Montréalers with surnames as diverse as Zagorska, Skwyrska, De Ciccio, Sen, Lavoie, Barrett, O'Neill, Hammerschmid, Fernandez, Müller, Giordano, Haddad, and Boudreault.

After wandering through this part of the cemetery, return to Chemin Remembrance, pass the Maison Smith again, and continue along the road for a few minutes until you arrive at a water spigot embedded in a granite slab. Take the narrow blacktop path below it through the trees. Along the way, look for a tree trunk carved by artist Jacques Morin in 1986; part of the inscription reads: an "old, sick tree, sculpted and transformed, neither male nor female."

This path leads to the:

⑨ Chalet Lookout

The chalet was constructed from 1931 to 1932 at a cost of $230,000 and has been used over the years for receptions, concerts, and various other events. Inside the chalet, note the 17 paintings hanging just below the ceiling, starting to the right of the door

that leads into the snack bar. They tell of the history of the region and of the French explorations of North America. The front terrace offers a panoramic view of the city and the river. In winter, there's a warming room for skiers here.

TAKE A BREAK
The concession stand in the chalet, usually open daily from 9am to 5pm, sells sandwiches, muffins, apples, ice cream, milk, juice, tea, and coffee. Heed the signs that ask patrons to refrain from feeding the squirrels seen begging so adorably.

Facing the chalet from the terrace, locate the path running off to the right. Follow it for about 8 minutes to a giant:

⑩ Steel cross

Legend has it that de Maisonneuve erected a wooden cross here in 1642. The present incarnation, erected in 1924, is lighted at night, making it visible from all over the city. Beside the cross is a plaque marking the spot where a time capsule was placed in August 1992, during Montréal's 350th-birthday celebration. Some 12,000 children ages 6 to 12 filled the capsule with messages and drawings depicting their visions for the city in the year 2142, when Montréal will be 500 years old and the capsule will be opened.

To return to downtown Montréal, go back along the path to the chalet terrace. On the left, just before the terrace, is another path. It leads to the 250 or so steps that descend to where this tour began, at the entrance to the park. Or catch bus no. 11 at Beaver Lake, hop off at Chemin de la Remembrance and Côte-des-Neiges, and pick up bus no. 165, which goes to the Guy Métro station.

8

Montréal Shopping

You can shop in Montréal until your feet swell and your eyes cross. Whether you view shopping as a focus of your travels or just a diversion, you won't be disappointed. It ranks right up there with dining out as a prime activity among the natives. Most Montréalers are of French ancestry, after all, and seem to believe that impeccable taste bubbles through the Gallic gene pool. The city has produced a thriving fashion industry, from couture to ready-to-wear, with a history that reaches back to the earliest trade in furs and leather. In any event, it is unlikely that any reasonable consumer need—and even outlandish fantasies—cannot be met here. There are more than 1,500 shops in the underground city alone, and many more than that at street level and above.

1 The Shopping Scene

American visitors have the advantage of a markdown on all prices encountered in Montréal shops due to the contrast in exchange rates between the Canadian and U.S. dollars. When traveling with U.S. dollars, go to a bank to exchange cash or traveler's checks for Canadian currency—or, better yet, withdraw Canadian dollars from a local ATM with either a credit card or debit card. While stores typically accept U.S. currency (in both dollars and traveler's checks), the exchange is likely to be less favorable than that obtained in a bank. There are exceptions, however, as some stores, in an attempt to attract customers carrying U.S. funds, put out signs offering better exchange rates.

Note that when you're making purchases with a credit card, the charges are automatically converted at the going bank rate before appearing on the following monthly statement. In most cases, this is the best deal of all for visitors. Visa and MasterCard are the most popular bank cards in this part of Canada, while Discover is less frequently accepted by shops, and American Express is only accepted reluctantly and sometimes not at all.

THE BEST BUYS

Most items are priced at approximately the same costs as in their countries of origin, including such big international names as Burberry and Ralph Lauren.

Exceptions are British products, including **tweeds, porcelain,** and **glassware,** which tend to cost less. While not cheap, **Inuit sculptures** and 19th- to early-20th-century **country furniture** are handsome and authentic. Less expensive crafts than the intensely collected Inuit works are also available, including quilts, drawings, and carvings by Amerindian and other folk artists. While demand has diminished somewhat, superbly constructed furs and leather goods are high-ticket items for which you can retrieve the high sales taxes. In addition, Québec's daring clothing designers produce some appealing fashions at prices that are often reasonable.

THE BEST SHOPPING AREAS

Rue Sherbrooke is a major shopping street for international and domestic designers, luxury items such as furs and jewelry, art galleries, and the Holts department store. **Rue Crescent** has a number of scattered upscale boutiques and numerous cafes for a break from shopping. **Boulevard St-Laurent** covers everything from budget practicalities to off-the-wall handmade fashions. Look along **avenue Laurier** between St-Laurent and de l'Epée for French boutiques, home accessories shops, and young Quebecois designers. **Rue St-Paul** in Vieux-Montréal has a growing number of art galleries, a few jewelry shops, souvenir stands, and a shop that sells kites.

Antiques can be found along rue Sherbrooke near the Musée des Beaux-Arts and on the little side streets near the museum. More antiques and collectibles, in more than 50 tempting shops one after another, can be found along the lengthening "Antiques Alley" of **rue Notre-Dame,** especially concentrated between Guy and Atwater. Artists display and sell their largely undistinguished but nevertheless competent works along compact **rue St-Amable,** just off place Jacques-Cartier. From there, meander into a walkway called **Le Jardin Amable** to find a courtyard filled with kiosks stocked with eye-catching costume jewelry and items crafted in silver and gold. **Rue St-Denis** north of Sherbrooke has strings of shops filled with fun, funky items.

Some of the best shops in Montréal are found in city museums. Tops among them are shops in **Pointe-à-Callière,** the Montréal Museum of Archaeology and History in Vieux-Montréal; the **Musée des Beaux-Arts** and the **Musée McCord,** both on rue Sherbrooke in the center city; and the **Musée d'Art Contemporain** in the Place-des-Arts.

Rue Ste-Catherine is home to the city's four top department stores and myriad satellite shops, while **rue Peel** is known for its men's fashions. **Avenue Greene** in Anglophone Westmount has some decidedly English stores. Most of Montréal's big department stores were founded when Scottish, Irish, and English families dominated the city's mercantile class, and most of their names are identifiably English, albeit shorn of their apostrophes. The principal exception is La Baie, French for "The Bay," itself a shortened reference to an earlier name, the Hudson's Bay Company. Montréal's long history as a center for the fur trade buttresses the many wholesale and retail furriers, with outlets downtown and in Plateau Mont-Royal, but nowhere more concentrated than on the "fur row" of **rue Mayor,** between rue de Bleury and rue City Councillors.

Those who delight in the hunt for bargains—and possess the tenacity to plunge into barely managed chaos to find them—won't want to miss **rue Chabanel.** It's a long trek north from downtown (nearest Métro station: Crémazie), a street that runs west of boulevard St-Laurent and is lined with factory buildings and warehouses. On Saturday mornings from 8:30am to 1pm—very roughly—the clothing manufacturers and importers use ground and mezzanine level showrooms and suites to put out all manner

> **Tips Taxes & Refunds**
>
> Visitors can obtain refunds of taxes incurred for lodgings and shop purchases. See "Fast Facts: Montreal," in chapter 3, for details.

of men's, women's, and children's clothing for sale for those few hours a week (usually not in Jan or July). Coats, leather goods, sportswear, suits, sweaters—all are on offer at deeply discounted prices, and diligence and a willingness to bargain are rewarded. Prowl the 8 blocks numbered 99 to 555; the higher the number, the better the quality, or at least so goes the commonly held conviction.

SHOPPING COMPLEXES

A unique facet of Montréal is the **underground city,** a warren of passageways connecting more than 1,500 shops in 10 shopping complexes that have levels both above and below street level. **Complexe Desjardins** is bounded by rues Jeanne-Mance, Ste-Catherine, St-Urbain, and boulevard René-Lévesque (© **514/281-1870**). It has waterfalls and fountains, trees and hanging vines, music, lanes of shops going off in every direction, and elevators whisking people up to one of the four tall office towers or into the Wyndham hotel (formerly Le Meridien). **Les Cours Mont-Royal,** 1455 rue Peel at boulevard de Maisonneuve (© **514/842-7777**), is a recycling of the old Mount Royal Hotel, lately adding a huge Harry Rosen fashion emporium. The venerable Eaton department store is in limbo, but it spawned **Le Centre Eaton,** 705 rue Ste-Catherine ouest (© **514/288-3708**), with over 175 shops, cinemas, and eating places on five floors. **Place Bonaventure,** at rues de la Gauchetière and University (© **514/397-2325**), has some 125 boutiques beneath the Bonaventure Hilton. **Place Montréal Trust,** at 1500 rue McGill at rue Ste-Catherine (© **514/843-8000**), is a 5-story shopping complex, and **Place Ville-Marie,** opposite Le Reine Elizabeth hotel, between boulevard René-Lévêsque and Cathcart (© **514/861-9393**), was Montréal's first major postwar shopping complex, known locally simply as "PVM." **Les Promenades de la Cathédrale,** at the corner of rue University and rue Ste-Catherine (© **514/849-9925**), has more than 70 shops on the levels below the Cathédrale Christ Church. The new **Ruelle des Fortifications,** on rue St-Pierre between St-Antoine and St-Jacques (© **514/982-9888**), is in the Centre Mondial du Commerce (World Trade Center), at the edge of Vieux-Montréal. There are more than 80 upscale boutiques, centered around two fountains, one modern and one traditional. **Westmount Square,** at rue Wood and rue Ste-Catherine (© **514/932-0211**), combines a shopping center, an office complex, and a condominium complex designed by the famed Mies van der Rohe.

2 Shopping from A to Z

Most **stores** are open from 9 or 10am to 6pm Monday through Wednesday, 9am to 9pm on Thursday and Friday, and 9am to 5pm on Saturday. Many stores are now also open on Sunday from noon to 5pm.

ANTIQUES

The best place to find antiques and collectibles is in the more than 50 storefronts along Rue Notre-Dame between rues Guy and Atwater.

Antiques Puces-Libres   Three fascinatingly cluttered floors are packed with pine and oak furniture, lamps, clocks, vases, and more, most of it 19th- and early-20th-century French-Canadian Art Nouveau. 4240 rue St-Denis (near rue Rachel). © **514/842-5931**.

ARTS & CRAFTS

Boutique Canadiana Worn Doorstep   The ongoing development of the Bonsecours Market has altered focus from temporary exhibitions to shops and food stalls. This one concentrates on crafts, children's storybooks, maps, small furniture, and packaged foods, all with a Canadian connection. 350 St-Paul est, Vieux-Montréal. ℂ **514/397-0666.**

Guilde Canadienne des Métier d'Art Québec   A small but choice collection of craft items is displayed in a meticulously arranged gallery setting. Among the objects are blown glass, paintings on silk, pewter, tapestries, and ceramics. The stock is particularly strong in avant-garde jewelry and Inuit sculpture. A small carving might be had for C$100 to C$200 (US$67–US$133), but the larger, more important pieces go for hundreds, even thousands, more. 1460 rue Sherbrooke ouest (near rue Mackay). ℂ **514/849-6091.**

La Guilde Graphique   More than 200 contemporary artists are represented here, working in a variety of media and techniques but producing primarily works on paper, including drawings, serigraphs, etchings, lithographs, and woodcuts. Some of the artists can often be seen working in the upstairs studio. 9 rue St-Paul ouest, Vieux-Montréal. ℂ **514/844-3438.**

L'Empreinte   This is a *coopérative artisane* (a craftspersons' collective), 1 block off place Jacques-Cartier at the corner of rue du Marché Bonsecours. The ceramics, textiles, glassware, and other items on sale often occupy that vaguely defined territory between art and craft. Quality is uneven but usually tips toward the high end. 272 rue St-Paul est, Vieux-Montréal. ℂ **514/861-4427.**

BOOKS

Canadian Centre for Architecture Bookstore   This bookstore may be the Centre's most engrossing department. It features a comprehensive selection of books on architecture, with emphasis on Montréal in particular and Canada in general. Volumes are also available on landscape and garden history, photography, preservation, conservation, design, and city planning. 1920 rue Baile (rue du Fort). ℂ **514/939-7020.**

Champigny   For those who know the language or want to brush up, this two-level bookstore with a primarily French-language stock is a valuable resource. It also sells tapes, CDs, and newspapers and magazines from all over the world. Most English-language books are on the upper floor. There's an expanded children's section. 4380 rue St-Denis (at rue Marie-Anne). ℂ **514/844-2587.**

Chapters   This is the flagship store of a chain with many branches, the result of a merger between the Smithbooks and Coles booksellers. (The Indigo bookstores also merged with Chapters recently, but retain their own identity.) Thousands of titles are available in French and English on both general and specialized subjects. 1171 rue Ste-Catherine ouest (at rue Stanley). ℂ **514/849-8825.**

Indigo   A very complete store with music, books, magazines, gifts, and a cafe upstairs, this occupies a street-level space in the Place Montréal Trust. 1500 rue McGill College (rue St-Catherine). ℂ **514/281-5549.**

Paragraphe   Prowl the rows of shelves in this long storefront, then take your purchases to the adjoining Second Cup cafe, popular with students from the McGill campus, a block away. The store hosts frequent autograph parties, author readings, and occasional musical performances. 2220 av. McGill College (south of rue Sherbrooke). ℂ **514/845-5811.**

Ulysse   Traveler needs are served by this good stock of guidebooks, many in English, as well as accessories, including maps, day packs, money pouches, electrical adapters, sewing kits, coffeemakers, and pill cases. 4176 rue St-Denis. ℂ **514/ 843-9447.** Also at 560 av. du Président-Kennedy (at Alymer). ℂ **514/843-7222.**

CLOTHING

FOR MEN

Brisson & Brisson   Expensive apparel of the nipped-and-trim British and European variety fills three floors, from makers as diverse as Burberry, Brioni, and Valentino. 1472 rue Sherbrooke ouest (near rue Mackay). ℂ **514/937-7456.**

Club Monsieur   Hugo Boss styles prevail, for those with the fit frames to carry them and the required discretionary income. 1407 rue Crescent (near bd. de Maisonneuve). ℂ **514/843-5476.**

Eccetera & Co.   Favoring ready-to-wear from such higher-end manufacturers as Hugo Boss and Canali, this store lays out the goods in a soothing setting with personalized service. 2021 rue Peel. ℂ **514/845-9181.**

L'Uomo   This store largely purveys Italian menswear by such forward-thinking designers as Cerruti, Missoni, Ungaro, Versace, Armani, and Dolce & Gabbana. 1452 rue Peel (near rue Ste-Catherine). ℂ **514/844-1008.** A branch of the store, Via Uomo, can be found down the street at 1478 rue Peel (ℂ 514/284-0104).

FOR WOMEN

Ambre   Sonia Kozma is the star designer here, of fashionable suits, cocktail dresses, and dinner and casual wear made of linen, rayon, and cotton. And to go with the clothes, there are bold but complementary accessories. 201 rue St-Paul ouest (at place Jacques-Cartier). ℂ **514/982-0325.**

Artéfact Montréal   Browse here among articles of clothing and paintings by up-and-coming Quebecois designers and artists. Moderate to expensive. 4117 rue St-Denis (near rue Rachel). ℂ **514/842-2780.**

Kyoze   The eye-catching creations of Quebecois and other Canadian designers are featured, including jewelry and accessories. This store is also moderate to expensive. There's a downtown outlet at 1455 rue Peel in Les Cours Mont-Royal. ℂ **514/849-6552.** There's also a store at Centre Mondial du Commerce, 393 rue St-Jacques ouest, 2nd floor (ℂ 514/847-7572).

UNISEX

Aritmetik   This fun shop features sportswear by young, forward-looking Toronto and California designers of a sort you don't see everywhere. 2011 rue St-Denis. ℂ **514/847-8965.** There are also branches in the Cours Mont-Royal mall downtown (ℂ 514/286-0565), and at 3688 bd. St-Laurent (north of Sherbrooke; ℂ 514/985-4130).

Club Monaco   Awareness of this expanding Canadian-owned international chain is growing, as is appreciation of its minimalist, largely monochromatic garments for men and women, along with silver jewelry, eyewear, and cosmetics. Think Prada but affordable, with a helpful young staff. 1455 rue Peel (north of rue Ste-Catherine). ℂ **514/499-0959.**

EnrgXchange   If you're young and sleek, male or female, the stretchy garments purveyed here shouldn't put you off, nor will the substantial discounts on items from terminated lines by Dolce & Gabbana, Moschino, Helmut Lang, and the like. 1455 rue Peel (in Les Cours Mont-Royal). ℂ **514/282-0912.**

Les Cuirs Danier   This coast-to-coast national chain got that way with quality leather garments, belts, bags, and such—mostly for women, but men aren't ignored. Place Ville Marie. ℂ **514/874-0472.** Also at 730 rue Ste-Catherine ouest (near av. McGill College; ℂ 514/392-0936).

Polo Ralph Lauren   As he has elsewhere, the international designer has set up shop in a townhouse in the poshest part of town, near the Ritz-Carlton. Apparel for the well-heeled family, plus house accessories. 1290 rue Sherbrooke (near rue de la Montagne). © **514/288-3988.**

Roots   The company whose berets and uniforms made such a hit at the 2002 Winter Olympics has a three-floor store here, among many locations throughout Canada. They also display table settings, furniture, perfume, books, and CDs. 1035 rue Ste-Catherine ouest (at rue Peel). © **514/845-7995.**

Terra Firma   The sign reads "T. Firma," but everyone knows it by the full name, which is the only way you'll get directions in Le Centre Eaton (it's toward the back on the ground floor). Shoes are the products, men's and women's, with labels that include Ecco, Stonefly, Rockport, Bostonian, Hush Puppies, Cole Haan, and pricey Mephisto. 705 rue Ste-Catherine ouest. © **514/288-3708.** There's another outlet in Les Cours Mont-Royal (© 514/845-3007).

Terra Nostra   An exclusively Québec chain, this spiffy new store features mostly casual ware for men and women in deceptively simple shapes—sort of an upscale Gap. 900 rue Ste-Catherine. © **514/861-6315.**

COFFEES & TEAS

Brulerie St-Denis   This enticingly aromatic shop has an international selection of coffees from more than two dozen countries, whole or ground to order. There are tables at which to try a cup of the selections, and some desserts to go with it. 3965 rue St-Denis (at Duluth). © **514/286-9158.** There are several branches, including one in the Maison Alcan, at 2100 rue Stanley (© 514/985-9159).

DEPARTMENT STORES

Montréal's major shopping emporia stretch along rue Ste-Catherine (except for Holt Renfrew), from rue Guy eastward to Carré Phillips at Aylmer. An excursion along this 12-block stretch can keep a diligent shopper busy for hours, even days. Most of the stores mentioned below have branches elsewhere, including the underground city.

Henry Birks et Fils   Across from Christ Church Cathedral stands Henry Birks et Fils, a highly regarded jeweler since 1879. This beautiful old store, with its dark-wood display cases, stone pillars, and marble floors, is a living part of Montréal's Victorian heritage. Valuable products on display go well beyond jewelry to encompass pens and desk accessories, watches, ties, leather goods, belts and other personal accessories, glassware, and china. 1240 Carré Phillips (at av. Union). © **514/397-2511.**

Holt Renfrew   Begun as a furrier in 1837, this showcase for International Style focuses on fashion for men and women. Such prestigious names as Giorgio Armani, Prada, Gucci, and Chanel are displayed with a tastefulness bordering on solemnity. The marquee outside reads only HOLTS. An actual human operates the elevator. 1300 rue Sherbrooke ouest (at rue de la Montagne). © **514/842-5111.**

La Baie   No retailer has an older or more celebrated name than that of the Hudson's Bay Company, a name shortened in recent years to "The Bay," then transformed into "La Baie" by the language laws. The company has done business in Canada for the better part of 300 years. Its main store emphasizes clothing, but also offers crystal, china, and Inuit carvings. Its Canadiana Boutique features historical souvenir items and wool merchandise, including their

famous Hudson's Bay blankets. 585 rue Ste-Catherine ouest (near rue Aylmer). ℂ 514/
281-4422.

La Maison Simons This is the first foray out of its home area for Québec City's long-established family-owned department store. Most Montréalers had never heard of it, but that changed fast as attention was quickly captured by the fashions that fill the refurbished first three floors of a building that once housed the old Simpson's. One guidebook describes it as "swanky," but the actuality is closer to the "softer side of Sears," with good prices. 977 rue Ste-Catherine ouest (at rue Mansfield). ℂ 514/282-1840.

Ogilvy Established in 1866, Ogilvy has been at this location since 1912. Besides having a reputation for quality merchandise, the store is known for its eagerly awaited Christmas windows. Once thought of as hidebound with tradition—a bagpiper still announces the noon hour and special events—it now contains over 50 boutiques, including such high-profile purveyors as Guy Laroche, Escada, Anne Klein, Aquascutum, and Rodier Paris. Wide aisles and glowing chandeliers enhance the experience. 1307 rue Ste-Catherine ouest (at rue de la Montagne). ℂ 514/842-7711.

GIFTS

Collection Méli Mélo Quality shops continue to challenge Vieux-Montréal's purveyors of mock moccasins, trashy T-shirts, and related doodads. Here's one, a pleasure to poke about with its mix of exotica originating in the band of nations reaching from Morocco to Pakistan. You'll find carpets, jewelry, carved chests, mirrors, and objects of polished camel bone. With essences of sandalwood and drifting incense, it even smells good. 205 St-Paul ouest (at rue St-François-Xavier). ℂ 514/285-5585.

Ex Voto After a bagel brunch at the St-Viateur Café down the street, drop in here for a look among the many varieties of candles, aromatic soaps, decorative and functional Moroccan oil lamps and, for some reason, watering cans and hand puppets. 1254 rue Mont-Royal est. ℂ 514/525-1012.

Franc Jeu Expectant parents (and new grandparents) will want to make a detour to browse through the expansive collections of Corolle dolls and the clothes, jewelry, and accessories with which to dress them. 4152 rue St-Denis (near rue Rachel). ℂ 514/849-9253.

La Cerf-Volanterie This corner shop in Vieux-Montréal is filled with sturdy, dazzling cloth kites created by the owner, who is often seen at his workbench in back. He has flown or hung kites in many of the city's public places, including Eaton Center. 224 rue St-Paul ouest (at rue St-Pierre). ℂ 514/845-7613.

Les Artisans du Meuble Québécois A mix of crafts, jewelry, and other objects—some noteworthy, others mediocre—make this an intriguing stop in Vieux-Montréal. Among the possibilities are clothing and accessories for women, greeting cards, woven goods, items for the home, and handmade quilts. 88 rue St-Paul est (near Place Jacques-Cartier). ℂ 514/866-1836.

Musée des Beaux-Arts Boutique Next to the annex of the Museum of Fine Arts, this unusually large and impressive shop sells everything from folk art to furniture. The expected art-related postcards and prints are at hand, along with ties, jewelry, watches, scarves, address books, toys, games, clocks, and even designer napkins and paper plates. The boutique is to the right of the entrance, a large bookstore to the left. 380 rue Sherbrooke ouest (at rue Bishop). ℂ 514/285-1600.

Musée McCord Shop   Part of the newly expanded museum that tells the history of the province, this shop has a small, carefully chosen selection of cards, books with an emphasis on history, coloring books, jewelry, and handcrafts. 690 rue Sherbrooke ouest (at rue Victoria). ℂ 514/398-3142.

Pointe-à-Callière Gift Shop   Located in the Old Customs House at the end of the underground tour of the Museum of Archaeology and History, this boutique sells collectibles for the home, gift items, paper products, souvenirs, toys, and books (in French). Some are worthwhile, some not. 150 rue St-Paul ouest (at place Royale). ℂ 514/872-9150.

Senteurs de Provence   The sunny south of France is evoked in pottery hand-painted in the creamy-bright colors of Provence, complemented by cunning collections of bath soaps and gels, printed linens, and lightly perfumed lotions and creams. 4077 rue St-Denis. ℂ 514/845-6867. There are also branches at 4859 rue Sherbrooke (ℂ 514/369-7888) and 363 rue St-Paul est, Vieux-Montréal (ℂ 514/395-8686).

Urban Outfitters   Impossible to categorize, this outpost of the sizeable North American chain is more hoot than harbinger, with an unpredictable stock that ranges from women's tops and skirts to off-kilter lamps and glassware to such life essentials as the *Star Wars Cookbook* and a nun doll that walks and spits fire. 1246 rue Ste-Catherine ouest (near rue de la Montagne). ℂ 514/874-0063.

HOUSEWARES

Caban   While it doesn't slide easily into a pigeonhole, think of this as a place that sells "life . . . with style." It's a newborn sibling to the Club Monaco chain, whose classy minimalist standards are applied to an eclectic stock that includes lawn furniture, glassware, flowerpots, deck chairs, and simple summery clothing. It's one of only three outlets, the others in Toronto and Vancouver—to date, at least. 777 rue Ste-Catherine ouest. ℂ 514/844-9300.

MUSIC

Archambault Musique   French-Canadian singers are gaining fans across the border—Céline Dion only the most popular among them—and their music can be found here, along with recordings by the Montréal Symphony Orchestra, Ensemble I Musici, and others, some of which may be hard to find outside of Québec. Open daily. 500 rue Ste-Catherine est. (across the park from the Voyageur bus terminal). ℂ 514/849-6201. A new outlet is located at Place des Arts (ℂ 514/281-0367).

Inbeat   Decor is storefront plain, but the stock includes CDs and vinyl that just isn't available anywhere else. They describe the offering as "deep house, progressive, tribal, techno, trance, old skool, Afro-Latin nu jazz, US & UK garage," and there are things that don't even fit *those* categories. 3814 bd. St-Laurent. ℂ 514/499-2063.

WINES & SPIRITS

Although wine and beer are sold in supermarkets and convenience stores, liquor and other spirits can be sold only in shops operated by the provincial Société des Alcools du Québec (SAQ). Though it was once as bureaucratic as most state-run agencies, successful efforts have made the stores more inviting. Some serve particular needs, others strive to be comprehensive. One of the largest is the **SAQ Selection** at 440 bd. de Maisonneuve ouest at rue City Councillors (ℂ 514/873-2274), a virtual supermarket of wines and liquors, with more than 3,000 labels from some 55 countries. Prices run from C$10 (US$6.65) to C$1,000

(US$666) for some Bordeaux vintages. **SAQ Signature** at 998 bd. de Maisonneuve ouest at rue Metcalf (© **514/282-9445**) specializes in single-malt scotches, whiskeys, brandies, and liqueurs, and has a bar for tastings. Smaller and less fancy, the **SAQ Express** at 1108 Ste-Catherine ouest is meant for quick in-and-out purchases; it's open daily and later, 11am to 10pm.

In addition, the food markets described at the end of chapter 5 in "Picnic Fare: Where to Get It, Where to Eat It," shouldn't be overlooked. They carry abundant assortments of cheeses, wines, and packaged food products that can serve as gifts or delicious reminders of your visit when you get home.

9

Montréal After Dark

Montréal's reputation for effervescent nightlife reaches back to the Roaring Twenties, specifically to the 13-year experiment with Prohibition in the United States. Canadian distillers and brewers made fortunes—few of them with meticulous regard for legalistic niceties—and Americans streamed into Montréal for temporary relief from alcohol deprivation. The city already enjoyed a sophisticated and slightly naughty reputation as the Paris of North America, which added to the allure. Nightclubbing and barhopping remain popular activities, with nightspots keeping much later hours in Montréal than in archrival Toronto, still in thrall to Calvinist notions of propriety and early bedtimes.

Montréalers' nocturnal pursuits are often as cultural as they are social. The city boasts its own outstanding symphony, French- and English-speaking theater companies, and the incomparable avant-garde performance company Cirque du Soleil. It's also on the standard concert circuit that includes Chicago, Boston, and New York, so internationally known entertainers, rock bands, orchestra conductors and classical virtuosos, and ballet and modern-dance companies pass through frequently. A decidedly French enthusiasm for film, as well as the city's increasing reputation as a movie-production center, ensures support for cinemas showcasing experimental, offbeat, and foreign films, as well as the usual Hollywood blockbusters.

And in summer, the city becomes even livelier than usual with several enticing events: the Festival de Théâtre des Amériques, the flashy Montréal International Fireworks Competition, the renowned Festival International de Jazz, the humor-packed Juste pour Rire/Just for Laughs Festival, the Festival International Nuits d'Afrique, and the Festival International de Nouvelle Danse, which attracts modern-dance troupes and choreographers from around the world. To this bursting roster, the city has added the Montréal Highlights Festival/Festival Montréal en Lumière, held for 2 weeks in February and dedicated to the arts, which, by this gastronomic city's measure, includes chefs the caliber of Paul Bocuse; and Les Franco Folíes de Montréal, presenting artists and musicians from French-speaking nations during 10 days in July and August.

Concentrations of pubs and discos underscore the city's linguistic dichotomy. While there's a great deal of crossover mingling, the parallel blocks of **rue Crescent,** rue Bishop, and rue de la Montagne north of rue Ste-Catherine have a pronounced Anglophone character, while Francophones dominate the **Latin Quarter,** with college-age patrons most evident along the lower reaches of rue St-Denis and their yuppie elders gravitating to the nightspots of the slightly more uptown blocks of the same street. **Vieux-Montréal (Old Montréal),** especially along rue St-Paul, has a more universal quality, and many of the bars and clubs there feature live jazz, blues, and folk music. In the **Plateau Mont-Royal** area,

---

⌐ Tips **Finding Out What's On**

For details on performances or special events that are on when you're in town, pick up a free copy of **Montréal Scope,** a weekly ads-and-events booklet usually available at hotel reception desks, or the free weekly newspapers **Mirror** and **Hour** (in English) or **Voir** and **Ici** (in French). The self-described "bilingual queer newspaper" **Village** provides news and views of gay and lesbian events, clubs, restaurants, and activities. For extensive listings of largely mainstream cultural and entertainment events, log on to **www.montrealonline.com**. A similar service is provided by **Hour** at **www.afterhour.com**. Also try the official website of Tourisme Montréal: **www.tourisme-montreal.org**.

---

boulevard St-Laurent, parallel to St-Denis and known locally as "The Main," has become a miles-long haven of hip restaurants and clubs, roughly from rue Laurier to rue Sherbrooke. Boulevard St-Laurent is a good place to wind up in the wee hours, as there's always some place with the welcome mat still out.

1 The Performing Arts

THEATER

The **Festival de Théâtre des Amériques** (✆ 866/533-7848), held every spring from late May to mid-June, presents innovative dramatic and musical stage productions that are international in scope, not simply North American as the name suggests. There have been works from Vietnam and China as well as from Canada, the United States, and Mexico. As many as 20 plays are performed in their original languages, with simultaneous translations in French and/or English when appropriate. Ticket packages are available, including lodging, from C$169 to C$209 (US$113–US$139) for two people. Call for information.

Centaur Theatre   A former stock-exchange building (1903) is home to Montréal's principal English-language theater. A mix of classics, foreign adaptations, and works by Canadian playwrights is presented. A sampling of past productions includes *Driving Miss Daisy, Oliver!,* and *Cabaret,* as well as such new works as *The Cripple of Inishmaan.* Off-season, the recently refurbished theater is rented out to other groups. Performances are held October to June. Box office hours are noon to 5pm. 453 rue St-François-Xavier (near rue Notre-Dame). ✆ 514/288-3161. www.centaurtheatre.com. Tickets C$20–C$36 (US$13–US$23). Métro: Place d'Armes.

Saidye Bronfman Centre for the Arts   Montréal's Yiddish Theatre, founded in 1937, is housed in the Saidye Bronfman Centre for the Arts, not far from St. Joseph's Oratory. It stages plays in both Yiddish and English, usually running 3 to 4 weeks in June and October. At other times during the year, the 300-seat theater hosts dance and music recitals, a bilingual puppet festival, occasional lectures, and three English-language plays. There's also an art gallery on the premises, with exhibits that change almost monthly. Across the street, in the Edifice Cummings House, is a small Holocaust museum and the Jewish Public Library. The center takes its name from late philanthropist Saidye Bronfman, widow of Samuel Bronfman, founder of the Seagram Company. The box office is usually open Monday through Thursday 11am to 8pm and Sunday noon to

THE PERFORMING ARTS **137**

7pm. Call ahead. 5170 Côte-Ste-Catherine (near bd. Décarie). ℂ **514/739-7944.** www.the
saidye.org. Tickets C$15–C$35 (US$9.70–US$23). Métro: Côte-Ste-Catherine. Bus: no. 129 ouest.

DANCE

Frequent appearances by notable dancers and troupes from other parts of
Canada and the world—among them Paul Taylor, the Feld Ballet, and Le Ballet
National du Canada—augment the accomplished resident companies. During
the summer, Les Grands Ballets Canadiens often perform at the outdoor Théâtre
de Verdure in Parc Lafontaine. In winter, they're scheduled at various venues
around the city, but especially in the several halls at the Place des Arts. The fall
season is kicked off by the always-provocative **Festival International de Nouvelle Danse,** in late September and early October.

Les Grands Ballets Canadiens   This prestigious company, performing both
a classical and a modern repertoire, has developed a following far beyond
national borders over its 35 years. In the process, it has brought prominence to
many gifted Canadian choreographers and composers. It tours internationally
and was the first Canadian ballet company to be invited to the People's Republic of China. The troupe's production of *The Nutcracker* during the last couple
of weeks in December is always a big event in Montréal. The box office is open
Monday to Saturday noon to 8pm. Performances are held late October to early
May. Place des Arts, 175 Ste-Catherine ouest. ℂ **514/842-2112.** www.grandsballets.qc.ca. Tickets C$25–C$69 (US$16–US$45). Métro: Place des Arts.

Tangente   A September-to-June season of contemporary dance and often out-
there performance art is laid out by this nonprofit organization. Housed in a
new building devoted exclusively to dance, its approximately 90 performances
per year give priority to Québec artists, but also include appearances by other
Canadian and international artists and troupes. Agora de la Danse, 840 rue Cherrier.
ℂ **514/525-5584.** www.tangente.qc.ca. Tickets C$13–C$15 (US$8.40–US$9.70). Metro:
Sherbrooke.

CLASSICAL MUSIC & OPERA

L'Opéra de Montréal   Founded in 1980, this outstanding opera company
mounts six productions a year in Montréal, with artists from Québec and abroad
participating in such shows as *La Traviata, Carmen, Aida, Otello,* and *Mefistofele.*
Video translations are provided from the original languages into French and
English. The box office is open Monday to Friday 9am to 5pm. Performances
are held from September to June in three theaters at Place des Arts and occasionally at other venues. Salle Wilfrid-Pelletier, Place des Arts, 260 bd. de Maisonneuve ouest.
ℂ **514/985-2258.** www.operademontreal.qc.ca. Tickets C$39–C$110 (US$25–US$71). Métro:
Place des Arts.

L'Orchestre Symphonique de Montréal (OSM)   This world-famous
orchestra performs at Place des Arts and the Notre-Dame Basilica, as well as
around the world, and may be heard on numerous recordings. For many years,
it was under the baton of Swiss conductor Charles Dutoit, but a well-publicized
flap involving charges of his autocratic rule brought about his resignation in
2002. His replacement (or return) is uncertain at this writing, but it can be
assumed that the orchestra's balanced repertoire will continue to run from Elgar
to Rabaud to Saint-Saëns, in addition to Beethoven and Mozart. The box office
is open Monday to Saturday noon to 8pm. The full season runs September to
May, supplemented by Mozart concerts in Notre-Dame Basilica on six evenings

A Circus Extraordinaire

Through the exposure generated by its frequent tours across North America, Europe, and Australia, the **Cirque du Soleil**, 8400 2e Av., St-Michel (✆ **800/361-4595** or 514/722-2324; www.cirquedusoleil.com), is enjoying an ever-widening following. One reason is the absence of animals in the troupe, which means no one need be troubled by the possibility of mistreated lions and elephants. Linear descriptions and even photographs can't begin to do justice to what is presented during a Cirque du Soleil performance. The experience is nothing less than magical, a celebration of pure skill and theater. There are plenty of acrobats, clowns, trapeze artists, tightrope walkers, and contortionists, but there is dance, too, and people costumed to look like creatures not of this world—iguanas crossed with goblins, say, or peacocks born of trolls. There are even storylines, of a sort. This is truly for children of all ages. Since 1984, more than 15 million people in over 120 cities have seen the Cirque du Soleil in action. The troupe is so much in demand it's difficult to track from year to year how long it will alight in its hometown, although most recently it has stayed from mid-April to early June every 2 years. Check ahead to discover its current plans. Ticket prices range unpredictably, but at a recent production of the show called "Varekai" in the tent in Montréal's Vieux Port, the top price was C$76 (US$49). It was really worth it.

in June and July, interspersed with free performances at three parks in the metropolitan region. People under 25 can purchase tickets for only C$10 (US$6.45) on the day of a concert. Salle Wilfrid-Pelletier, Place des Arts, 260 bd. de Maisonneuve ouest. ✆ **514/842-9951** (for tickets, Mon–Fri 9am–5pm). www.osm.ca. Tickets C$16–C$90 (US$10–US$58). Métro: Place des Arts.

Orchestre Métropolitain de Montréal   This orchestra has a regular season at Place des Arts, where it works with L'Opera de Montréal, but it also performs concerts in the St-Jean-Baptiste Church and tours regionally. The box office is open Monday to Saturday noon to 8pm. Performances are held mid-October to early April and outdoors in Parc Lafontaine in August. Maisonneuve Theatre, Place des Arts, 260 bd. de Maisonneuve ouest. ✆ **514/598-0870.** Tickets C$13–C$40 (US$8.40–US$26). Métro: Place des Arts.

CONCERT HALLS & AUDITORIUMS

Montréal has a score of venues, so check the papers upon arrival to see who's playing where during your stay. Big-name rock bands and pop stars that used to play at the Forum now show up at the new downtown arena, Centre Bell (below), which is also the home of the Montréal Canadiens hockey team.

Centre Bell   Initially called the Centre Molson, this remains the home of the Montréal Canadiens and hosts big international pop stars on the order of Ricky Martin and Alanis Morissette, as well as such dissimilar attractions as Disney's World On Ice. These stars used to be booked into the old Forum but are now diverted to this sparkling facility, which opened in 1996. Most people agree that it's vastly superior to the old Forum on all but the nostalgia scale, and the location is better. Over 21,000 can be seated. The box office is open Monday through Friday 10am to 6pm (or to 9pm on days of events). Ticket prices vary greatly, depending on the attraction. 1260 rue de la Gauchetière ouest. ℂ **514/932-2582.** www.centre-molson.com. Métro: Bonaventure.

Place des Arts   Founded in 1963 and in its striking present home in the heart of Montréal since 1992, Place des Arts mounts performances of musical concerts, opera, dance, and theater in five halls: **Salle Wilfrid-Pelletier** (2,982 seats), where the Orchestre Symphonique de Montréal often performs; the **Théâtre Maisonneuve** (1,460 seats), where the Orchestre Métropolitan de Montréal and the McGill Chamber Orchestra perform; the **Théâtre Jean-Duceppe** (755 seats); the **Cinquième Salle** (350 seats); and the small **Studio-Théâtre Stella Artois** (138 seats). Traveling productions of Broadway classics have limited runs at the center, and portions of the city's arts festivals are staged here. The box office is open Monday through Saturday noon to 8pm. Ticket prices vary according to hall and the group performing. 175 rue Ste-Catherine ouest. ℂ **514/285-4200** for information, 514/842-2112 for tickets, or www.pdarts.com for tickets online. Métro: Place des Arts.

Pollack Concert Hall   In a landmark building dating from 1899 and fronted by a statue of Queen Victoria, this hall is in nearly constant use, especially during the university year. Among the attractions are concerts and recitals by McGill students or professionals from McGill's music faculty. Recordings of some of the more memorable concerts are available on the university's own label, McGill Records. Box office hours are Monday to Friday noon to 6pm. Concerts are also given in the campus's smaller **Redpath Hall,** 3461 rue McTavish (ℂ **514/398-4547**). Performances are often free, but tickets for some events can cost up to C$22 (US$14). On the McGill University campus, 555 rue Sherbrooke ouest. ℂ **514/398-4547.** www.music.mcgill.ca. Métro: McGill.

Spectrum de Montréal   A broad range of Canadian and international performers, usually modest celebrities unlikely to fill the larger Centre Bell, use this converted movie theater. Rock groups on the order of Grimskunk and Phish are among the higher-profile acts, comedians are sometimes booked, and the space also hosts segments of the city's annual jazz festival. Seats are available on a first-come, first-served basis. The box office is open Monday through Friday noon to 9pm and Saturday and Sunday noon to 5pm. Tickets are priced according to attraction. 318 rue Ste-Catherine ouest (at rue de Bleury). ℂ **800/361-4595** or 514/861-5851. www.admission.com for tickets. Métro: Place des Arts; then take the Bleury exit.

Théâtre de Verdure   Nestled in a popular park in Plateau Mont-Royal, this open-air theater presents free music and dance concerts and theater, often with well-known artists and performers. Sometimes they show outdoor movies. Many in the audience pack picnics. Performances are held from June to August; call for days and times. In Lafontaine Park. ℂ **514/872-2644.** Métro: Sherbrooke.

Théâtre St-Denis   Recently refurbished, this theater in the heart of the Latin Quarter hosts a variety of shows, including pop singers, rock groups, and comedians, as well as segments of the Juste pour Rire/Just for Laughs Festival in late July. It's actually two theaters, one seating more than 2,000, the other almost 1,000. The box office is open daily noon to 9pm. 1594 rue St-Denis (at Emery). ℂ **514/790-1111.** Métro: Berri-UQAM.

2 The Club & Music Scene

COMEDY

The once-enthusiastic market for comedy clubs across North America has long since cooled, but Montréal still has a couple of laugh spots, mostly because it's the home to the highly-regarded **Juste pour Rire/Just for Laughs Festival** held every summer (for information, call 📞 **514/845-2322**). Those who have so far eluded the comedy-club experience should know that profanity, bathroom humor, and assorted ethnic slurs are common fodder for performers. If patrons wish to avoid becoming objects of the comedians' barbs, it's wise to sit well back from the stage. Performances are in French or English (about 50/50, it seems) or both.

Comedyworks There's a full card of comedy at this long-running club, up the stairs from Jimbo's Pub on a jumping block of rue Bishop south of rue Ste-Catherine. Monday is usually open-mike night, while on Tuesday and Wednesday, improvisational groups work off of the audience's suggestions. Headliners—usually from Montréal, Toronto, New York, or Boston—take the stage Thursday through Sunday. No food is served, just drinks. Reservations are recommended, especially on Friday, when early arrival may be necessary to secure a seat. Shows are nightly at 9pm, and also at 11:15pm on Fridays and Saturdays. Most drinks cost C$5 to C$8 (US$3.25–US$5.15). 1238 rue Bishop (at rue Ste-Catherine). 📞 **514/398-9661**. Cover up to C$15 (US$9.70). Métro: Guy-Concordia.

Comedy Zone Mostly local talent is showcased at this club in the Nouvel Hotel, but among the comics who stopped off here on their way up were Howie Mandel, Norm MacDonald, and superstar Jim Carrey. Shows are held Wednesday through Sunday at 8:30pm, with added shows on Friday and Saturday at 11:30pm. Drinks cost C$5 to C$8 (US$3.25–US$5.15). 1740 bd. René-Lévesque (at rue Guy). 📞 **514/937-3888**. www.comedynest.com. Cover C$10 (US$6.45). Métro: Guy-Concordia.

FOLK, ROCK & POP

Scores of bars, cafes, theaters, clubs, and even churches present live music on at least an occasional basis, even if only at Sunday brunch. The performers, local or touring, traffic in every idiom, from metal to funk to reggae to grunge and unvarnished Vegas. Here are a few places that focus their energies on music.

Café Campus When anyone over 25 shows up inside this bleak club on touristy Prince-Arthur, he or she is probably a parent of one of the musicians. Alternative rock prevails, but blues and retro-rock bands also make appearances. Groups such as Liquid Soul, Come, and Carapace have hit the stage here. Disco parties are often scheduled Wednesday nights, and a smaller room, Petit Café Campus, usually has deejayed hip-hop—no cover. 57 rue Prince-Arthur est (near bd. St-Laurent). 📞 **514/844-1010**. Cover usually C$5–C$12 (US$3.25–US$7.75). Métro: Sherbrooke.

Club Soda This long-established club's new quarters are even larger than their old location on avenue du Parc. It remains one of the prime destinations for attractions below the megastar level and is a principal venue for the "Just for Laughs" festival. Performers are given a stage in a hall that seats several hundred fans. Five bars pump audience enthusiasm. Musical choices hop all over the charts—folk, rock, blues, country, Afro-Cuban, heavy metal—you name it. Acts for the annual jazz festival are booked here, too. 1225 bd. St-Laurent (at Ste-Catherine). 📞 **514/286-1010**. www.clubsoda.ca. Cover up to C$25 (US$16). Métro: St-Laurent.

Hard Rock Cafe No surprises here, not with clones around the world. The hamburgers are good enough and not overly expensive. The formula still works, and it gets crowded at lunch and on weekend evenings. There's a terrace seating about 30 patrons. Open Sunday to Thursday from 11:30am to midnight, Friday to Saturday from 11:30am to 3am; the disco is up and going from 11:30pm to 1am. Drinks cost C$4 to C$8 (US$2.60–US$5.15). 1458 rue Crescent (near bd. de Maisonneuve). ☎ 514/987-1420. No cover. Métro: Guy-Concordia.

Hurley's Irish Pub The Irish have been one of the largest immigrant groups in Montréal since the famine of the 1840s, and their musical tradition thrives here. Celtic instrumentalists and dancers perform every night of the week, often both on the ground floor and upstairs, usually starting around 9:30pm. Guinness and other drinks go for C$3 to C$8 (US$1.95–US$5.15). 1225 rue Crescent (south of rue Ste-Catherine). ☎ 514/861-4111. No cover. Métro: Peel or Guy-Concordia.

Le Pierrot/Aux Deux Pierrots Perhaps the best known of Montréal's *boîtes-à-chansons*—song clubs—Le Pierrot is an intimate French-style cabaret. The singers interact animatedly with the crowd, often bilingually. Le Pierrot is open daily from early June to late September, Thursday through Sunday the other months, with music into the wee hours. Its sister club next door, the larger Les Deux Pierrots, features live bands playing rock Friday and Saturday nights year-round, with vocals half in French and half in English. It is open at other times according to the management's whims. The terrace joining the two clubs is open on Friday and Saturday nights in summer. Shooters cost C$3 (US$1.95), other drinks to C$8 (US$5.15). 114 and 104 rue St-Paul est (west of place Jacques-Cartier). ☎ 514/861-1270. www.lespierrots.com. Cover: Le Pierrot C$3 (US$1.95) Fri–Sat, free other nights; Aux Deux Pierrots C$5 (US$3.25). Métro: Place d'Armes.

Le P'tit Bar One of many cramped, packed, smoky, and entertaining boîtes-à-chansons featuring the kinds of French pop and folk songs made known by Charles Azvanour and Jacques Brel, this bar is near the east end of Square St-Louis. In between sets from the singers who occupy the postage-stamp-sized stage near the front door, express your views of Sartre and Camus. 3451 rue St-Denis ☎ 514/281-9124. No cover. Métro: Sherbrooke.

Le Swimming A nondescript entry and a stairway that smells of stale beer lead to a trendy pool hall that attracts an equal number of drinkers/socializers and pool players (*le swimming*, get it?). Many Montréal bars have a pool table, but this one has 13, along with 9 TVs and a terrace. Most nights of the week they have bands churning out ska, funk, reggae, or jazz. Open daily 1pm to 3am; pool is free until 5pm. 3643 bd. St-Laurent (north of rue Sherbrooke). ☎ 514/282-7665. www.leswimming.com. Cover C$5 (US$3.15) Thurs–Sat (when live bands are booked). Métro: Sherbrooke.

O'Donnell's Replacing a rock/blues club called Déjà Vu, this casual family-owned room feeds a local enthusiasm for Gaelic music and libations. It's a fun, friendly place, relatively inexpensive, with a couple of dance floors and live Irish music every weekend. 1224 rue Bishop (near rue Ste-Catherine). ☎ 514/877-3128. www.bar-resto.com/odonnell. No cover. Métro: Guy-Concordia.

JAZZ & BLUES

The respected and heavily attended **Festival International de Jazz,** held every summer in the city, caters to the public's interest in the most original American art form. During the 9 days of the event, more than 2,500 musicians perform on 16 stages for an average total audience of 1.7 million. (For information, call

℃ **888/515-0515** or 514/871-1881, or visit www.montrealjazzfest.com.) Scores of events are scheduled, indoors and out, most of them free. "Jazz" is broadly interpreted to include everything from Dixieland to reggae, world beat, and the unclassifiable experimental. In 2001, for example, The Artist Once Again Known As Prince was featured. Performers more closely associated with jazz have included George Benson, Pat Metheny, Gil Evans, Dave Brubeck, and B.B. King. Piano legend Oscar Peterson grew up here and sometimes returns to perform in his hometown.

There are many more clubs featuring jazz and related forms than the sampling that follows. Pick up a copy of *Mirror* or *Hour,* distributed free everywhere, or buy the Friday or Saturday editions of the *Gazette* for the entertainment section. These publications have full listings of the bands and stars appearing during the week.

Unhappily, **L'Air du Temps,** a Montréal tradition since 1976, has closed. An ardent jazz emporium of the old school, seedy and without gimmicks, it will be missed. There are faint rumors it will re-open, but they are probably wishful thinking.

Biddle's   Right downtown, where there's little after-dark action, this stalwart is a club-restaurant with hanging plants and faux Art Nouveau glass. It fills up early with lovers of barbecued ribs and jazz. The live music starts around 6:30pm (at 7pm Sun and Mon) and continues until closing time. Charlie Biddle plays bass when he doesn't have a gig elsewhere. He and his stand-ins favor jazz of the swinging mainstream variety, with occasional digressions into more esoteric forms. It's open Sunday 6pm to 1am, Monday through Wednesday 11:30am to 1am, Thursday and Friday 11:30am to 3am, Saturday 6pm to 3am. Drinks cost C$5 to C$8 (US$3.15–US$5.15), and there's a mandatory paid coat check. 2060 rue Aylmer (south of rue Sherbrooke). ℃ **514/842-8656.** No cover, but a drink minimum Fri–Sat. Métro: McGill.

Le Quai des Brumes   Loosely translated, the name means "foggy dock," a reference of elusive significance. But it's an atmospheric place in which to listen to jazz, blues, and rock. Upstairs, the Bar Central attracts its share of Plateau notables and has a small dance floor. The crowd has been described as "a fairly uniform group of post-sixties Francophone smokers." A short menu of nibbles is available in each place. Open daily 2pm to 3am. Drinks cost C$3 to C$8 (US$1.95–US$5.15). 4481 and 4479 rue St-Denis (at av. du Mont-Royal). ℃ **514/499-0467.** No cover. Métro: Mont-Royal.

Maestro S.V.P.   Good eats and live music aren't strangers in Montréal. Although this bistro is best known for seafood, especially its oyster bar (see chapter 5), the owner brings in a jazz trio on Sunday nights at 6:30. That justifies the name and the musical instruments that constitute most of the decor. 3615 bd. St-Laurent (north of Sherbrooke). ℃ **514/842-6447.** No cover. Metro: Sherbrooke.

Moldavie   In winter, set aside Friday or Saturday night for dinner with jazz at this popular Vieux-Montréal bistro-bar-lounge (see chapter 5); or set aside any night at 7pm in summer. Bar snacks are free during happy hour and single-malt scotches and cigars are at the ready. Music is usually mainstream jazz, by trios. It's a friendly place, and the food is good too. 1 rue St-Paul ouest (corner of rue St-Laurent) ℃ **514/287-9582.** No cover. Métro: Place d'Armes.

DANCE CLUBS

As elsewhere, Montréal's dance clubs change in tenor and popularity in mere eye blinks, and new ones sprout like toadstools after a heavy rain; they also wither as quickly. For the latest feverish spots, quiz concierges, guides, waiters—all those who look as if they might follow the scene. Here are a few that appear more likely to survive the whims of night owls and landlords. At some, you'll encounter steroid abusers with funny haircuts guarding the doors. Usually they'll let you inside; the admittance game is neither as strict nor as arbitrary as the "hipper than thou" criteria encountered at some New York and Los Angeles clubs.

Club Balattou   An infectious, sensual tropical beat issues from this club-with-a-difference on The Main, a hot, happy variation from the prevailing grunge and murk that seeps out of what might be described as mainstream clubs. Although most of the patrons revel in their ancestral origins in the Caribbean and Africa (which are the sources of the live and recorded music), everyone is welcome. Admittedly, the hip-waggling expertise of the dancers might be intimidating to the rhythmically challenged. Things get going about 10pm every night but Monday. The cover charge includes one beer or glass of wine; additional drinks are C$4 to C$8 (US$2.60–US$5.15). 4372 bd. St-Laurent (at rue Marie-Anne). ℂ 514/845-5447. Cover C$8 (US$5.35). Métro: Mont-Royal.

FunkyTown   For most of the vivacious crowd that swirls through this downtown disco, the Seventies were the old days when they were still in rompers. Much of the music is of that era, with supporting decor. Think mirrored balls, floors lit from below, and a setting resembling that in which John Travolta committed The Hustle in his ice cream suit. Go too late and you'll most likely encounter a line and a wait. Most drinks are in the C$4 to C$9 range (US$2.60–US$5.80). It opens at 10pm, Thursday through Saturday. 1454 rue Peel. ℂ 514/282-8387. www.clubsmontreal.com. Cover C$5 (US$3.35) Fri–Sat; no cover Thurs. Metro: Guy-Concordia.

Les Foufounes Electriques   On the scene for more than a decade, this multilevel disco–rock club has mellowed somewhat from its outlaw days, although it still features hardcore rock and industrial bands. An occasional one-hit wonder puts in an appearance—Vanilla Ice, anyone? With three dance floors and a couple of beer gardens in back, there's plenty to keep you busy, starting with the C$1.50 (US95¢) beers during the 4 to 6pm happy hour and shooters for C$1.25 to C$2.50 (US80¢–US$1.60). The higher prices are applied at the weekend. Look for the rocket ship over the door. 87 Ste-Catherine est (near St-Denis). ℂ 514/844-5539. www.foufounes.qc.ca. Cover C$8–C$12 (US$5.15–US$7.75). Métro: Berri-UQAM.

Newtown   Huge fanfare, generated both through marketing and rabid word-of-mouth, trumpeted the summer 2001 opening of this tri-level club in the white-hot center of rue Crescent nightlife. One of the owners is Formula One racecar driver and local hero Jacques Villeneuve, whose last name can be translated as "New Town." Adjoining town houses were scooped out to make one big trendy nightspot at a reported cost of C$7.5 million, with a disco in the basement, big barroom on the main floor, and restaurant up top. Reservations are usually required for the restaurant, but admission to the bar and dance floor shouldn't be a problem. At this writing, there is still no cover and no minimum. 1476 rue Crescent (at de Maisonneuve). ℂ 514/284-6555. No cover. Métro: Peel.

Salsathèque   It's been on the scene for years, so they're obviously doing something right. The big upstairs room is all glittery, bouncing, mirrored light, the better to get the dancers moving to mambo, merengue, and other tropical beats. Open Wednesday through Sunday 9pm to 3am, it rarely kicks into high gear before midnight. The house band comes on at 11pm or thereabouts, and they bring in other acts. The main source of entertainment, though, is the patrons themselves, a highly proficient lot on the dance floor. Drinks run about C$4 to C$8 (US$2.60–US$5.15). 1220 rue Peel (at Ste-Catherine). © **514/875-0016.** Cover C$5 (US$3.25) Fri–Sat. Métro: Peel.

Wax Lounge　A jovial, thoroughly mixed crowd ankles over to this second-floor club after dinner at one of the half-dozen scene restaurants clustered around this busy south end of The Main. The velvet-rope policy is more in the interest of crowd control than exclusivity. When the live band (usually soul/rock with rap undertones) takes a break, the DJ pumps the house music right up through the soles of your shoes. Good brands of booze are poured, most from C$4 to C$8 (US$2.60–US$5.15) per drink. 3481 bd. St-Laurent (north of rue Sherbrooke). © **514/282-0919.** Cover C$5 (US$3.25) Mon–Thurs, C$7 (US$4.50) Fri–Sat. Metro: Sherbrooke.

3 The Bar & Cafe Scene

An abundance of restaurants, bars, and cafes line the streets near the downtown commercial district, from rue Stanley to rue Guy between rue Ste-Catherine and boulevard de Maisonneuve. **Rue Crescent,** in particular, hums with activity from late afternoon until far into the evening, especially after 10pm on cool summer weekend nights, when the street swarms with people careening from bar to restaurant to club. **Boulevard St-Laurent,** or "The Main," as it's known, is another nightlife hub, abounding in bars and clubs, most with a distinctive European—particularly French—personality, as opposed to the Anglo flavor of the rue Crescent area. Increasingly active **rue St-Paul,** west of place Jacques-Cartier in Vieux-Montréal, falls somewhere in the middle on the Anglophone-Francophone spectrum. It's also a little more likely to get rowdy on late weekend nights. In all cases, bars tend to open around 11:30am and go late. Many of them have *heures joyeuses*—happy hours—from as early as 3pm to as late as 9pm, but usually for a shorter period within those hours. At those times, two-for-one drinks are the rule. Last call for orders is 3am, but patrons are often allowed to dawdle over those drinks until 4am.

DOWNTOWN/RUE CRESCENT

Le Tour de Ville　Memorable. Breathtaking. The view, that is, from Montréal's only revolving restaurant and bar (the bar doesn't revolve, but you still get a great view). The best time to go is when the sun is setting and the city lights are beginning to blink on. In the bar, one floor down from the restaurant, the same wonderful vistas are augmented by a dance floor, with a band Thursday through Saturday 9pm to 1 or 2am. There's no cover, but drinks range from C$6 to C$9 (US$3.85–US$5.80). In the Delta Centre-Ville Hôtel, 777 rue University. © **514/879-1370.** Métro: Square Victoria.

Lutetia Bar　Within sight of the trademark lobby fountain with its nude bronze sprite sporting stained-glass wings, this appealing bar draws a standing-room–only crowd of youngish to middle-aged professionals after 5:30pm. Later on, there's often music by jazz duos. In summer the hotel opens the terrace bar on the roof by the pool. In L'Hôtel de la Montagne, 1430 rue de la Montagne (north of rue Ste-Catherine). © **514/288-5656.** Métro: Guy-Concordia.

Ritz Bar　A mature, prosperous crowd seeks out the quiet Ritz Bar in the Ritz-Carlton, adjacent to its semi-legendary Café de Paris restaurant. Anyone can take advantage of the tranquil room and the professionalism of its staff, but because the atmosphere is rather formal, most men will be more at ease with a jacket. Piano music flutters softly around conversation during cocktail hour Monday through Friday 5 to 8pm and at dinnertime (5–11pm) from September to mid-May. The bar is just off the hotel lobby, to the right. In the Ritz-Carlton Hôtel, 1228 rue Sherbrooke ouest (at rue Drummond). ✆ 514/842-4212. Métro: Peel.

Sir Winston Churchill Pub   The three levels of bars and cafes incorporated in the Sir Winston Churchill Pub are rue Crescent landmarks. One reason is the sidewalk terrace, open in summer, enclosed in winter, and a vantage point for checking out the pedestrian traffic at all times. Inside and down the stairs, the pub, with English ales on tap, attempts to imitate a British public house. The burgers and such have to look up to reach mediocrity. A mixed crowd of questing young professionals mills around a total of 17 bars and 2 dance floors. Winnie, on the second floor, is a restaurant with a terrace of its own. Open daily noon to 2am. During the 5 to 8pm happy hour, drinks are two-for-one. 1459 rue Crescent (near rue Ste-Catherine). ✆ 514/288-0623. Métro: Guy-Concordia.

Thursday's   A prime watering hole for Montréal's young professional set— those who are ever alert for possibilities of companionship. The pubby bar spills out onto a terrace that hangs over the street, and there's a glittery disco in back, both in the Hôtel de la Montagne. Thursday's presumably takes its name from the Montréal custom of prowling nightspots on Thursday evening in search of the perfect date for Friday. 1441–1449 rue Crescent (near rue Ste-Catherine). ✆ 514/288-5656. Métro: Guy-Concordia.

Ziggy's   Maybe they get away with that Francophobic apostrophe because this place looks so bloody Brit. Steps down from a shelf of outdoor tables, the long, low-ceilinged pub has two bars with hockey sticks and ports and celeb photos (Alan Thicke) on the walls. A mixed crowd partakes of the eight brews on draft, hanging around until 3am. Drinks range from C$2.50 to C$7 (US$1.60–US$4.50). 1470 rue Crescent (near rue Ste-Catherine). ✆ 514/285-8855. Metro: Guy-Concordia.

PLATEAU MONT-ROYAL

Bleu Est Noir   Wear anything better than a tank top and jeans or the January equivalent thereof and you'll feel conspicuously overdressed. Grungy and beery it is, with a battered sheet-metal bar, a pool table, and a beat-up fireplace—all the better to receive neighborhood regulars from 3pm to dinnertime, and clogs of students from then until the third wee hour. A DJ works the turntables most nights, with live bands appearing many Sundays. When there's a cover charge, it's usually C$5 to C$7 (US$3.25–US$4.40). 812 rue Rachel est (near St-Hubert). ✆ 514/524-4809. Metro: Mont-Royal.

Blizzarts   Remnants of Fifties modern, much of it mismatched, fill the space around the small dance floor. Most nights, heavy-beat dance music is designed to get the 20ish crowd up and moving. Next to the DJ booth is a full bar with an espresso machine. On weekends, there's usually a band. Last we saw, the bartender on duty poured with a generous tilt of the bottle. His efforts go for about C$3 to C$7 (US$2–C$4.65). 3956a bd. St-Laurent (near rue Duluth). ✆ 514/843-4860. Cover up to C$5 (US$3.25). Metro: Mont-Royal.

C@fé Internet   Keep in touch, word-process, play games, or just surf the Web on any of 16 computers with big 21-inch monitors. Time at the keyboard costs

C$3.50 (US$2.25) per half-hour, plus tax. There's no booze, just coffee and soft drinks. It's open Monday to Friday 10am to 11pm, Saturday 11am to 11pm, Sunday 11:30am to 11pm. 3672 bd. Saint-Laurent (north of rue Prince Arthur). ☎ 514/842-1726. Metro: Sherbrooke.

Champs   Montréalers are no less enthusiastic about sports, especially hockey, than other Canadians, and fans both avid and casual drop by this three-story sports emporium to catch up with their teams and hoist a few. Games from around the world are fed to 35 TV monitors through 20 satellites, so they don't miss a goal, run, or TD. Food is what you expect—burgers, steaks, and such. 3956 bd. St-Laurent (near rue Duluth). ☎ 514/987-6444. Metro: Mont-Royal.

Laïka   Amidst the plethora of St-Laurent watering stops, this bright little boîte stands out for its open front in summer and the fresh flowers on the bar and some of the tables. Tasty sandwiches and tapas are served, and the Sunday brunch is popular. The DJ spins house, funk, and the mirrored ball from 8pm to 3am for the mostly 18- to 35-year-old crowd. Drinks range from C$3 to C$7 (US$1.95–US$4.50). 4040 bd. St-Laurent. (near rue Duluth). ☎ 514/842-8088. Metro: Mont-Royal.

Shed Café   This bar/restaurant, in a lively stretch of The Main near rue Sherbrooke, used to look as if the ceiling was caving in. Now it's been transformed to a Gothic dungeon look, and it's not a whit less frenetically popular. There are local beers on tap, as well as good fries and oversize portions of cake. The crowd skews young, but with enough diversity to make an hour or two interesting. 3515 bd. St-Laurent (north of rue Sherbrooke). ☎ 514/842-0220. Métro: Sherbrooke.

Whisky Café   Those who enjoy scotch, particularly single-malts like Laphraoig and Glenfiddich, will find 30 different labels to sample here. Trouble is, the Québec government applies stiff taxes for the privilege, so most of the patrons (suits to students) seem to stick to beer. The decor is sophisticated, with exposed beams and vents, handmade tiled tables, and large wood-enclosed columns, but the real decorative triumph is the men's urinal, with a waterfall acting as the *pissoir.* Women are welcome to have a look. The bar opens at 5pm most evenings. 5800 bd. St-Laurent (at rue Bernard). ☎ 514/278-2646. Métro: Outremont.

QUARTIER LATIN

Jello Bar   Lava lamps and other fixtures make it look like the rumpus room of a suburban ranch house in the 1960s, but central to the rep of this goofy throwback is the menu of more than 30 kinds of martinis. Most are flavored excuses for people who don't really like liquor, but the classic gin and vodka versions are stalwarts to be savored. Live music, usually Tuesday, Wednesday, Friday, and Saturday, helps fuel the rollicking good mood. Other times, there's DJ and a dance floor. Martinis are only C$5 (US$3.35). 151 rue Ontario est (near bd. St-Laurent). ☎ 514/285-2621. www.jello-bar.com. Metro: St-Laurent or Berri-UQAM.

Le Sainte-Elisabeth   Aided by Guinness "on draught," this place comes closer to resembling an Irish pub than most of the many efforts in town. Past the Queen Anne Victorian facade is a copper-topped bar near the fireplace with a smattering of heavily used sofas, and beyond all that is a boxy, tree-shaded, vine-covered open courtyard, known as a *terrasse* in these parts. University and grad students predominate but don't overwhelm. Blues and jazz are on the stereo and sometimes live blues and jazz acts perform (usually on Tues). 1412 rue Ste-Elizabeth (north of rue Ste-Catherine). ☎ 514/286-4302. Metro: Berri-UQAM.

Le Saint-Sulpice   Adjoining four-story buildings still can't absorb the youthful crowds, both straight and gay, longing to be a part of the scene here. Expect lines up to six people deep and a block long on any night of even slightly tolerable weather. The club has a crowded terrace, a DJ most nights and live music on some, and dance floors and bars always. Beer is the favored quaff, with drinks going for C$3 to C$8 (US$2–US$5.35). 1680 rue St-Denis (near rue St-Catherine). ✆ 514/844-9458. Metro: Berri-UQUAM.

4 The Gay & Lesbian Scene

The city's lively **Quartier Gai/Gay Village** comprises a stretch of rue Ste-Catherine from rue St-Hubert to rue Papineau. One of the largest gay and lesbian communities in North America, it is action central for both natives and visitors, especially during such annual events as the 10 days celebrating sexual diversity known as Divers/Cité in early August (www.diverscite.org). Much excitement has attended the announcement that Montréal will host the Gay Games in 2006 (www.montreal2006.org). Of several targeted local publications, the most useful magazine is *Fugues*, describing current and future events as well as listing gay-friendly lodgings, clubs, saunas, and other resources. Get a copy at the tourist office (✆ 514/522-1885) opposite the Beaudry Métro station, or check www.fugues.com.

Club Chez Mado   Very new on the Village scene, this determinedly trendy place lays on both cabaret performances and dancing to DJ tracks. Every night of the week has a different theme, from Monday karaoke to Wednesday variety shows to drag shows Fridays and Saturdays. At least those were the plans when it opened in 2002. Check ahead to see what's on. Cover is free most nights, from C$2 to C$5 (US$1.30–US$3.25) on weekends. 1115 rue Ste-Catherine est (near rue Amherst). ✆ 514/525-7566. Métro: Beaudry.

Complexe Bourbon   Stop first in this block-long, block-wide compound billed as "the largest gay complex in the world" and you might never get to the Village's other attractions. Open 24 hours, it incorporates a 37-room hotel, a sauna, the Club Back Track and Le Zone discos, a theater, a wedding chapel, an ice cream parlor, and several bars and restaurants. One of the latter is the 24-hour Le Club Sandwich, a hyperventilating take on a 1950s diner with lots of neon and glass block. The signature edibles are huge, with slabs of bread as thick as a couple of fingers and ingredients to match. The large terrace is a prominent Village gathering place. Rooms in the Hôtel Bourbon cost from C$75 to C$230 (US$48–US$148), depending on the season. 1574 rue Ste-Catherine est (at Plessis). ✆ 514/523-4679. Metro: Papineau.

Magnolia   One of the Village's brightest new lesbian bars is known for its singers of blues, rock, house, and salsa. The shows follow the 6 to 9pm happy hour on Tuesdays and at 7pm Sundays. Gay men show up those nights. Drinks are in the C$3 to C$8 (US$1.95–US$5.15) range. 1329 rue Ste-Catherine est (near rue St-Hubert). ✆ 514/526-6011. Métro: Berri-QQAM.

Sisters   It comes and goes, but this dance club above the Saloon restaurant (a good choice for dinner) is thriving once again. Lesbian and bi women constitute most of the celebrants and contribute to the high energy level. Men, straight or gay, will almost certainly find more congenial surroundings elsewhere, but they are allowed entrance Sunday afternoons. 1313 rue Ste-Catherine est (near rue St-Hubert). ✆ 514/523-0292. No cover. Métro: Berri-UQAM.

Sky Club & Pub   Thought by many to be the city's best gay club, Sky continues to thrive after its recent renovations. Spiffy decor and thumping (usually house) music in the upstairs disco contribute to the popularity. Up to six transvestite performers present a cabaret show Friday and Saturday nights. Also on the second floor is a male strip club called Nirvana. In addition to the restaurant, which serves dinner Monday through Saturday and brunch on weekends, there's an outdoor terrace and frequent two-for-one beer hours. 1474 rue Ste-Catherine est (near rue Amherst). ℭ 514/529-6969. No cover. Métro: Beaudry.

Stéréo   One of a growing number of after-hours clubs, this hyper-hip disco doesn't crank up the jaw-dropping sound system until 2am. If you remember Richard Nixon, you'll feel like grandpa in this crowd, which stays on until dawn and beyond. 858 rue Ste-Catherine est (near rue Berri). No phone. Métro: Berri-UQAM.

5 More Entertainment

CINEMA

In Montréal, English-language films are usually presented with subtitles in French. However, when the initials "VF" (for *version française*) follow the title of a non-Francophone movie, it means that the movie has been dubbed into French. Policies vary on English subtitles on non–English-language films—the best idea is to ask at the box office. Besides the many first-run movie houses that advertise in the daily newspapers, Montréal is rich in "ciné-clubs," which tend to be slightly older and show second-run, foreign, and art films at reduced prices.

In first-run movie houses, admission is usually C$9.50 (US$6.15) for adults in the evening, C$5 to C$7 (US$3.25–US$4.50) for adults on some afternoons (usually Tues and Wed), and C$4.50 (US$2.90) for seniors and children all the time. The **Centre Eaton,** 705 rue Ste-Catherine ouest, near the corner of rue McGill, has a multiplex cinema with six modern theaters. Foreign-language and independent films are the menu at **Ex-Centris,** 3536 bd. St-Laurent (ℭ 514/847-2206; www.ex-centris.com), and the architectural surroundings are at least as interesting—sort of a post–machine age spaceship. A hip bar-cafe is included. The films are in English about half the time. Call and ask.

Similar fare, without the jazzy setting, is presented at the repertory **Cinéma du Parc,** 3575 av. du Parc (ℭ 514/281-1900; www.cinemaduparc.com). The **National Film Board of Canada** (Cinema ONF), 1564 rue St-Denis (ℭ 514/496-6887), shows Canadian and international films, primarily in English and French, particularly classics. Shows are Tuesday through Sunday; call for times.

Imposing, sometimes visually disorienting images confront viewers of the seven-story screen in the **IMAX theater** in the new Interactive Science Centre in the Vieux-Port (Old Port; ℭ 514/496-4629), and at **Imax Paramount Montréal,** 977 rue Ste-Catherine (ℭ 514/842-5828). Available productions are limited, so efforts are made to create films suitable for the entire family. See "Especially for Kids," in chapter 6, for more details.

GAMBLING

The **Casino de Montréal** (ℭ 800/665-2274 or 514/392-2746; www.casinosquebec.com), Québec's first, is on Ile Notre-Dame in the former French Pavilion, which was left over from the 1967 Expo World's Fair. Its several floors contain 118 game tables, including roulette, craps, blackjack, and baccarat, and more than 3,000 slot machines. Its four restaurants get good notices, especially **Nuances** (see chapter 5). There are also four bars and live shows. No alcoholic beverages are served in the gambling areas. Patrons must be 18 or over. The casino is open around the clock. Tickets to the cabaret can be purchased at the casino or on the Internet at **www.admission.com**. They are priced from C$39 (US$25) for the show alone, or from C$65 (US$42) for the show and dinner. The originally strict dress code has been relaxed somewhat, but the following items of clothing are still prohibited: "cut-off sweaters and shirts, tank tops, jogging outfits, cut-off shorts and bike shorts, beachwear, work or motorcycle boots, and clothing associated with violence or with an organization known to be violent." To get to the casino, take the Métro to the Ile Ste-Hélène stop, which is adjacent to Ile Notre-Dame, and walk or take the shuttle bus from there.

10

Side Trips from Montréal

For respite from urban stresses and demands, Montréalers need only drive 30 minutes or so to the north or east of the city to find themselves in the hearts of the resort regions of the Laurentides or the Cantons-de-l'Est. The lakes and mountains of both areas have invited development of year-round vacation retreats and ski centers. The pearl of the Laurentides is Mont-Tremblant, the highest peak in eastern Canada, but the region has 18 other ski centers with scores of trails at every level of difficulty, many of them less than an hour from Montréal.

The bucolic Cantons-de-l'Est, known as the Eastern Townships when it was a haven for English Loyalists and their descendants, is blessed with a trio of memorable country inns on beautiful Lake Massawippi. The region promotes four seasons of outdoor diversions. It has fewer ski centers than the Laurentides, and the resort hotels that serve them are generally smaller and less extensive in their facilities, but its many lakes and gentle pastimes give it the edge for warm-weather vacations. Because the people of both regions rely heavily on tourism for their livelihoods, knowledge of at least rudimentary English is widespread, even outside such obvious places as hotels and ski resorts.

In the Cantons-de-l'Est, many of the same trails and settings developed for winter sports are used for parallel activities in summer. Bromont, for example, has 100km (62 miles) of marked trails for mountain biking, and Mont-Orford Park is the focal point for another 160km (99 miles) of hiking trails linking six regional parks. Rock climbing, white-water kayaking, sailing, and fishing are additional options. Appropriate equipment is readily available for rent on-site, wilderness shelters and trail cabins are at hand, and even meals can be catered in the woods.

1 North into the Laurentians (Laurentides)

55–129km (34–80 miles) N of Montréal

Don't expect spiked peaks or high ragged ridges. The rolling hills and rounded mountains of the Laurentian Shield are among the oldest in the world, worn down by wind and water over eons. They average between 300m and 520m (980 ft.–1,700 ft.) in height, with the highest being Mont-Tremblant, at 968m (3,175 ft.). In the lower precincts, nearer Montréal, the terrain resembles a rumpled quilt, its folds and hollows cupping a multitude of lakes large and small. Farther north the summits are higher and craggier, with patches of snow persisting well into spring, but these are still not the Alps or the Rockies. They're welcoming and embracing rather than awe-inspiring.

Half a century ago the first ski schools, rope tows, and trails began to appear; today there are 19 ski centers within a 40-mile radius, and cross-country skiing has as enthusiastic a following as downhill. (The best cross-country trails are at Far Hills in Val-Morin, L'Esterel in Ville d'Esterel, and on the grounds of

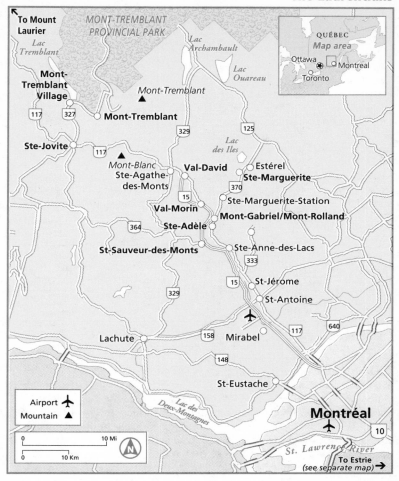

a monastery called Domaine du St-Bernard near Villa Bellevue in Mont-Tremblant.) Sprawling resorts and modest lodges and inns are packed each winter with skiers, some of them through April. Trails for advanced skiers typically have short pitches and challenging moguls, with broad, hard-packed avenues for beginners and the less experienced.

But skiing is only half the story. As transportation improved, people took advantage of the obvious opportunities for watersports, golf (courses in the area now number 30), tennis, mountain biking, hiking, and every other kind of summer sport. Before long the region had gained an often-deserved reputation for fine dining and a convivial atmosphere that survives to this day. Bird-watchers of both intense and casual bent are fully occupied. Loon lovers, in particular, know that the lakes of Québec province's mountains are home to an estimated 16,000 of the native waterfowl that gives its name to the dollar coin. Excellent divers and swimmers, the birds are unable to walk on land, which makes nesting a trial.

They're identified by a distinctive call that might be described as an extended mournful giggle.

Winter or summer, a visit to any of the villages and resorts in the Laurentians is likely to yield pleasant memories. The busiest times are in February and March, in July and August, and during the Christmas to New Year holiday period. Other times of the year, reservations are easier to get, prices of virtually everything are lower, and crowds are less dense. May and September are often characterized by warm days, cool nights, and just enough people that the streets don't seem deserted. In May and June, it must be said, the indigenous black flies and mosquitoes can seem as big and as ill-tempered as buzzards, so be prepared for them. Some of the resorts, inns, and lodges close down for a couple of weeks in the spring and the fall; a handful are open only for a few winter months.

March and April are the months when the maple trees are tapped, and *cabanes à sucre* ("sugar shacks") open up everywhere, some selling only maple candies and syrup, others serving full meals featuring the principal product and even staging entertainment.

July and August bring glorious summer days to the Laurentians, and during the last 2 weeks in September the leaves put on a stunning show of autumnal color. Skiers can usually expect reliable snow from early December to mid-April.

As for prices, they can be difficult to pin down: The large resorts have so many types of rooms, suites, cottages, meal plans, discounts, and packages that you may need a travel agent to pick through the thicket of options. In planning, remember that Montréalers fill the highways when they "go up north" on weekends, particularly during the top skiing months of February and March, so plan ahead when making reservations. An unfortunate note for pet owners: Few Laurentian resorts accept animals.

ESSENTIALS
GETTING THERE
BY CAR The fast and scenic Autoroute des Laurentides, also known as Autoroute 15, goes straight from Montréal to the Laurentian mountains. Just follow the signs to St-Jérôme. The exit numbers are actually the distance in kilometers that the village is from Montréal. One likely early stop, for instance, is La Maison du Tourisme (Tourism House) at Exit 39 in St-Jérôme, and St-Jérôme is 39km (24 miles) from Montréal. Although the pace of development is quickening, crowding the highway with water parks, condos, and chain restaurants, this is still a comely drive, once you're out of the clutches of the tangle of expressways surrounding Montréal. The Autoroute des Laurentides gives a sweeping, panoramic introduction to the area, from the rolling hills and forests of the lower Laurentians to the mountain drama of the upper Laurentians.

Those with the time to meander can exit at St-Jérôme and pick up the older, parallel Route 117, which plays tag with the autoroute all the way to Ste-Agathe-des-Monts, where the highway ends. Most of the region's more appealing towns are strung along or near Route 117. Approaching each town, signs direct drivers to the local tourism information office, where attendants provide helpful tips on lodging, restaurants, and things to do. North of Ste-Agathe, the Autoroute ends and Route 117 becomes the major artery for the region, continuing deep into Québec's north country and finally ending at the Ontario border hundreds of miles from Montréal.

Québec's equivalent of the Highway Patrol maintains a presence along the stretch of Autoroute 15 between St-Faustin and Ste-Adèle. While enforcement of speed limits is loose, if you are pulled over, remember that radar detectors are illegal in the province (even if they're not turned on) and can be confiscated.

BY BUS   Limocar Laurentides buses depart Montréal's **Terminus Voyageur,** 505 bd. de Maisonneuve est, stopping in the larger Laurentian towns, including Ste-Agathe, Ste-Adèle, St-Jovite, and Mont-Tremblant; call © **514/842-2281** or 450/435-6767 or check www.limocar.ca for schedules. An express bus can make the run to St-Jovite and Mont-Tremblant in less than 2 hours, while a local bus, making all the stops, takes almost 3 hours. From Montréal to Ste-Adèle takes about 1½ hours, 15 minutes more to Val-Morin and Val-David. Some of the major resorts provide their own bus service at an additional charge.

BY LIMOUSINE   Taxis and limousines await arrivals at Dorval Airport in Montréal, where all domestic and international commercial flights arrive, and will take you to any Laurentian hideaway—for a price. While the fare for the 1-hour trip by limo from Dorval is steep, four or five people can share the cost and lessen the pain. Ask for the standard fare to your inn or lodge when calling to make accommodation reservations. The inn will usually take responsibility for seeing that a taxi or limo is waiting at the airport and may even help to find other guests arriving at the same time to share the cost.

VISITOR INFORMATION

For an orientation to the entire region, stop at **La Maison du Tourisme des Laurentides,** 14142 rue de la Chapelle, St-Jérôme, PQ J7J 2CB (© **450/436-8532**), a regional tourist information office located at Exit 39 off the Autoroute 15. In addition to its racks of helpful brochures, the staff can make reservations for lodging throughout the Laurentides, and the service is free. The red-roofed stone cottage is off the highway to the east; follow the signs. It's open daily June 24 to Labour Day from 8:30am to 8:30pm; the rest of the year 9am to 5pm. For information about the entire region, log on to **www.laurentides.com**.

ST-SAUVEUR & ST-SAUVEUR-DES-MONTS

Only 60km (37 miles) north of Montréal, the adjacent villages of St-Sauveur and St-Sauveur-des-Monts (pop. 5,864) can easily be visited on a day trip. The village square is dominated by a handsome church, and the streets around it bustle with activity much of the year, so be prepared to have difficulty finding a parking place in season (try the large lot behind the church). Dining and snacking on everything from crêpes to hot dogs are big activities here, evidenced by the many beckoning cafes. In season, there's a tourist kiosk on the square.

The area is well known for its night skiing—23 well-lit trails, only 3 fewer than those available during the day. The mountain is wide, with a 700-foot vertical drop and a variety of well-groomed trails, making it a good choice for families. In summer, the **Parc Aquatique du Mont St-Sauveur,** 350 rue St-Denis (© **800/363-2426** or 450/227-4671; www.montsaintsauveur.com), Canada's largest water park, features rafting, a wave pool, a "tidal wave" river, and a mountain slide where you go up in chairlifts and come down in tubes. The last week of July and first week in August are given to the annual **Festival des Arts** (© **450/227-0427**; www.artssaintsauveur.com), with an emphasis on music and dance, including jazz and chamber concerts and ballet troupes as celebrated as the Kirov Ballet and the José Greco Flamenco Group.

The **tourist information office** serving the area is located at Exit 60 of Autoroute 15, at 605 Chemin des Frênes, Piedmont, PQ J0R 1K0 (© **450/229-3729**; www.sdeph.org), and is open year-round daily from 9am to 5pm, with longer hours in summer. There is also a seasonal booth (© **450/227-2564**) in St-Sauveur in the park in front of the church.

WHERE TO STAY

Le Relais St-Denis Set back from the road, the cream-colored U-shaped building is surrounded by birch and evergreens and extensive flower gardens. The Relais resembles a country club, complete with a heated outdoor pool and nearby golf. Rooms are of good size, with fireplaces and large bathrooms. Those in the new wing are larger and more polished, with Jacuzzi baths. Note that the one-bedroom suites are only C$25 (US$16) more than the regular rooms, a deal worth considering. Ski and golf packages are available, as are therapeutic massages. Reception is inside the building with the green awning. Pets are allowed, unusual in these hills.

61 rue St-Denis, St-Sauveur-des-Monts, PQ J0R 1R4. © **888/997-4766** or 450/227-4766. Fax 450/227-8504. www.relaisst-denis.com. 41 units. C$180–C$200 (US$116–US$129) double; C$225 (US$145) suite. Packages available. AE, DC, MC, V. **Amenities:** 2 restaurants (Continental); bar; indoor and outdoor pools; golf nearby; babysitting; dry cleaning. *In room:* A/C, TV, minibar, coffeemaker, hair dryer.

Manoir Saint-Sauveur ★ This is one of the region's several large resort hotels, with a monster outdoor pool and a comprehensive roster of four-season activities. Racquetball, squash, and in-house movies are among the extras. Rooms are roomy and comfortable, blandly modern with light wood furnishings that hint vaguely of 19th-century Gallic inspirations. Units in the condo section have kitchenettes. The main building is easily spotted from the road, with its green roof and many dormers. The front desk adjusts room prices up or down according to season, demand, and the occupancy rate on any given night, so keep asking if they have anything cheaper. The hotel cuts 10% off the rack rates if you book online.

246 Chemin du Lac-Millette, St-Sauveur-des-Monts, PQ J0R 1R3. © **800/361-0505** or 450/227-1811. Fax 450/227-8512. www.manoir-saint-sauveur.com. 300 units. Mid-June to mid-Oct C$159–C$229 (US$103–US$148) double, from C$279 (US$180) suite; mid-Oct to mid-June C$129–C$229 (US$83–US$148) double, from C$229 (US$148) suite. Extra person C$20 (US$13). Children 17 and under stay free in parents' room. Packages available. AE, DC, MC, V. Take Exit 60 off Autoroute 15. **Amenities:** Restaurant (Continental); bar; large indoor and outdoor pools; golf nearby; tennis courts (2 lit for night play); substantial health club w/ Jacuzzi and sauna; limited room service; massage; babysitting; laundry service; same-day dry cleaning. *In room:* A/C, TV, dataport, minibar, coffeemaker, hair dryer.

WHERE TO DINE

Les Oliviers COUNTRY FRENCH There are many restaurants in St-Sauveur, both in the center and out by the highway. None of them are distinguished, but this is representative of those that provide food more elevated than crêpes and pizza. Certainly the proprietors endeavor to be accessible to all budgets and most tastes. Try to overlook the clumsy decor of fake vines and rough stucco walls with amateurish paintings of windows. The kitchen can be slow, but can be forgiven when six tender steaming escargots arrive with garlicky melted butter. Main courses run to beef, duck, and salmon, accompanied by rice or potato, a vegetable mélange, and uncomplicated but flavorful sauces you'll want to sop up with bread.

239 rue Principale. © **450/227-2110**. 2-course menu du jour C$6.95–C$12 (US$4.50–US$7.70); table d'hôte lunch C$14–C$30 (US$9–US$19); menu dégustation for 2 C$70 (US$45). AE, MC, V. Daily 11:30am–3pm and 5:30–11pm.

MONT-GABRIEL

Mont-Gabriel is only 4km (2½ miles) from St-Sauveur. To get there, follow Autoroute 15 to Exit 64 and turn right at the stop sign. Although popular in summer, Mont-Gabriel comes into its own each winter when guests schuss down its 21 trails and slopes and then slide back up again on the 7 T-bar lifts, the triple-chair, or the quadruple-chair lift. Eight trails are lit for night skiing. Cross-country trails girdle the mountain and range through the surrounding countryside. For lodgings, see "Mont-Gabriel Resort" under Ste-Adèle, below.

STE-ADELE

Route 117 swings directly into Ste-Adèle to become its main street, boulevard Ste-Adèle; if you're on Autoroute 15 North take Exit 67. The village (pop. 8,720), only 67km (42 miles) north of Montréal, is a near-metropolis compared to the other Laurentian villages that line the upper reaches of Route 117. What makes it seem big are its services: police, doctors, ambulances, a shopping center, cinema, art galleries, and a larger collection of places to stay and dine than is found elsewhere in the Laurentians. As rue Morin mounts the hill to Lac Rond, Ste-Adèle's resort lake, it's easily seen why the town is divided into a lower part *(en bas)* and an upper part *(en haut).*

EXPLORING STE-ADELE

The main street of Ste-Adèle, **rue Valiquette,** is a busy one-way thoroughfare lined with cafes, galleries, and bakeries. But **Lac Rond** is the center of activities during the Ste-Adèle summer. Canoes, sailboats, and *pédalos* (pedal-powered watercraft), rented from several docks, glide over the placid surface, while swimmers splash and play near shore-side beaches.

In winter the surrounding green hills are swathed in white, and the **ski trails** descend to the shores of the frozen lake. Downhill ski equipment can be rented and lessons obtained at **Le Chantecler** resort (see below), which has 22 trails served by 6 chair lifts and 2 T-bars. Some of the trails end right by the main hotel. At the town's **Centre Municipal,** Côtes 40/80, 1400 rue Rolland (© **450/229-2921**), the trails are good for beginners: three T-bar lifts carry skiers up the slopes for the run down five different trails.

Ste-Adèle has a **cinema** showing first-run English-language movies all year.

WHERE TO STAY & DINE

L'Eau à la Bouche ★★★   L'Eau à la Bouche started as a roadside restaurant, with the separate hotel added later. The owners leave no doubt where their priorities lie. While the hotel is entirely satisfactory, the restaurant is their beloved baby, and it has the glowing reviews to prove its prowess. (Those stars up there are for dining.) False modesty isn't a factor—*l'eau à la bouche* means "mouthwatering"— and the kitchen delivers. Native ingredients and ample portions are meshed with *nouvelle* presentations, and the menu changes often. Full advantage is taken of seasonal products, as with the springtime starter of trout roe layered atop a lobster timbale with fiddleheads and baby asparagus heads; game dishes arrive in fall. Desserts are impressive, but the cheese plate—pungent nubbins of Québec varieties delivered with warm baguette slices—is truly special. A meal here might well be the most memorable (and pricey) dining experience of a Laurentian visit.

The bedrooms have reproductions of Québec country furniture and six have fireplaces and balconies or patios. There are no elevators and no porters, but help with luggage can be obtained if necessary. The hotel faces Mont-Chantecler and its ski trails.

3003 bd. Ste-Adèle (Rte. 117), Ste-Adèle, PQ J8B 2N6. © **450/229-2991.** Fax 514/229-7573. www.relais chateaux.fr/eaubouche. 25 units. From C$150–C$245 (US$97–US$158) double; C$255–C$330 (US$165–US$213) suite. Packages and meal plans available. AE, DC, MC, V. **Amenities:** Restaurant (Contemporary

French); bar; heated outdoor pool; golf nearby; limited room service; babysitting; laundry service; dry cleaning. *In room:* A/C, TV, dataport, hair dryer, iron, safe.

WHERE TO STAY

Hôtel Alpine *Value* This collection of rustic log structures, begun in 1924, contains several types of accommodations. The four cabins have two-bedroom suites with fireplaces, and kitchenettes with microwave ovens. Sleeping up to eight people, they are meant for families. At the other end of the spectrum are *les suites romantiques,* with king-size beds, sofas in front of fireplaces, double Jacuzzis, and VCRs—meant for *making* families. Meals are served at two communal tables. A large new lounge has been added next to the dining room; drinks are served.

1440 Chemin Pierre-Péladeau, Ste-Adèle, PQ J8B 1Z4. © **877/257-4630** or 450/229-1545. Fax 450/229-1544. www.hotelalpineinn.com. 17 units. C$95–C$165 (US$61–US$106) double. Rates include breakfast. Packages available. AE, MC, V. From the south, take Exit 69, then Rte. 370 east 3km (2 miles) to the hotel. **Amenities:** Restaurant (Quebecois); heated outdoor pool; adjacent 9-hole golf course; tennis court. *In room:* A/C, TV, no phone.

Le Chantecler ★ Sprawled across steep slopes cupping Lac à la Truite, this resort is composed of several stone buildings of varying heights, its roofs bristling with steeples and dormers. It has 23 runs (13 lit at night) on 4 mountains for all levels of skiers, including a 622-foot vertical drop, plus a ski school. Cross-country skiing and ice-skating are available. A chalet up top has a cafeteria and bar. There's a disco in the main lodge in winter and a summer-stock theater. Warm weather brings the possibilities of windsurfing and boating on the lake. The rooms are filled with pine furniture; most have air-conditioning. Many of the suites have fireplaces, and most have Jacuzzi baths. A bountiful buffet breakfast is served in the glass-enclosed dining room, which overlooks the slopes and the lake with its small beach. Recent upgrading has covered most of the dings and dents that routinely afflict family resorts, and new rooms were added each of the last 3 years.

1474 Chemin Chantecler, Ste-Adèle, PQ J8B 1A2. © **800/363-2420** or 450/229-3555. Fax 450/229-1098. www.lechantecler.com. 200 units. C$99–C$179 (US$64–C$115) double. Rates include breakfast. Children 17 and under stay free in parents' room. Packages and meal plans available. AE, DC, DISC, MC, V. Take Exit 67 off Autoroute 15, turn left at the 4th traffic light onto rue Morin, then turn right at the top of the hill onto Chemin Chantecler. **Amenities:** Restaurant (Regional); bar; indoor pool; lake beach; 18-hole and lit 9-hole golf courses; 6 lit tennis courts; health club w/ squash, racquetball, and badminton; watersports equipment; bike rental; children's programs; massage; babysitting; coin-op washers and dryers; dry cleaning. *In room:* TV, dataport.

L'Excelsior *Value* More distinctive architecturally and larger than most roadside resorts in the Laurentians, L'Excelsior benefits from management that maintains high standards of housekeeping. Many rooms have balconies. Elaborate spa treatments are available, including hydrotherapy, mineral and algae wraps, massages, and salt baths. Various packages include combinations of these with lodging and meals. Volleyball, squash, basketball, and badminton supplement the spa and tennis.

3655 bd. Ste-Adèle (Rte. 117), Ste-Adèle, PQ J8B 2N8. © **800/363-2483** or 450/229-7676. Fax 450/229-9991. www.spaexcelsior.com. 52 units. C$80–C$110 (US$52–US$71) double; C$160–C$227 (US$103–US$146) suite. Rates include breakfast. Packages available. AE, MC, V. Coming from Montréal, take Exit 67 off the autoroute. **Amenities:** Restaurant (Eclectic); bar; large indoor and outdoor pools; tennis court; health club and spa; massage. *In room:* A/C, TV.

Mont-Gabriel Resort ★ Perched high above highways and the valley and looking like the rambling log "cottages" of the turn-of-the-century wealthy, this desirable, kid-friendly hotel is only 20 miles from Montréal's Dorval Airport. Set on a 480-hectare (1,200-acre) forest estate, the resort complex features golf and tennis programs in summer and ski packages in winter. The spacious rooms in the Tyrol section are the most desirable, many with views of the surrounding hills, while those in what they call the Old Lodge are more rustic, but a $7 million renovation in 1998 upgraded most of these. With the Club Package come three meals and unlimited access to all sports facilities, and prices include tax and service charge. Rates drop for stays of 2 to 5 nights. Meals are served poolside as well as in the resort's dining rooms.

1699 Chemin Montée Gabriel, PQ J8B 1A5. 🄯 450/229-3547, 514/861-2852 in Montréal, or 800/668-5253 in Canada. Fax 450/229-7034. www.montgabriel.com. 129 units. C$116–C$153 (US$75–US$99) double. Rates include full breakfast. Meal plans and packages available. AE, DC, MC, V. Take Exit 64 from Autoroute 15. **Amenities:** Restaurant (Continental); bar; heated indoor and outdoor pools; 18-hole golf course; 6 night-lit clay tennis courts; exercise room; spa; Jacuzzi; sauna; children's programs; small business center; massage; babysitting. *In room:* A/C, TV, dataport, coffeemaker, hair dryer.

WHERE TO DINE

La Vanoise 🄯 FRENCH BISTRO   Diners look out on a lake from the deck or through the wide windows of this converted frame house. Uncomplicated bistro standards include pea soup, slivers of duck confit on salad, pork with honey and thyme, and sole meunière. The menu is brightened by the presence of such excellent specials as gazpacho and the ravioli, which changes daily with fillings as diverse as lobster and caribou. Little of this is truly out-of-the-ordinary, but all is quite well done, and at very reasonable prices. Top it all with the apple tart with vanilla ice cream. It's more popular with locals than tourists, and families appreciate the child's menu at C$6.95 (US$4.65).

1261 Chemin du Chantecler, Ste-Adèle. 🄯 450/229-4396. Main courses C$18–C$36 (US$12–US$24); table d'hôte lunch C$7.95–C$14 (US$5.15–US$9), dinner C$21–C$33 (US$14–US$21). MC, V. May–Oct Tues–Sun 11:30am–10pm; Nov–Apr Tues–Sun noon–9pm.

STE-MARGUERITE & ESTEREL

To get to Ste-Marguerite (pop. 2,250) or the less populous Estérel, only 3km (2 miles) apart, follow Autoroute 15 north to Exit 69. Or if driving from Ste-Adèle, look for a street heading northeast named Chemin Ste-Marguerite (Rte. 370). It becomes a narrow road that crosses the Laurentian Autoroute (at Exit 69), bridges the Rivière du Nord, and leads into an area of many lakes bordered by upscale vacation properties.

Ste-Marguerite and Estérel are 85km (53 miles) and 88km (55 miles) north of Montréal, respectively. In summer, information about the area is available from Pavillon du Parc, 74 Chemin Masson, in Ste-Marguerite-du-Lac-Masson (🄯 **514/228-3525**).

WHERE TO STAY IN ESTEREL

L'Estérel 🄯🄯   One of the more prominent Laurentian resorts lies a few miles past Ste-Marguerite in the hamlet of Estérel. This year-round complex is capable of accommodating 300 guests on its 2,000-hectare (5,000-acre) estate with three linked lakes. Occupying an expanse of otherwise vacant lakeshore, L'Estérel offers conventionally furnished rooms, many with balconies. Those with a view of the lake are more expensive. For a special winter experience, inquire about the dogsled trips through the woods and over the frozen lake. There are 85km (53 miles) of cross-country trails, nearby downhill skiing, and ice-skating on a rink; in summer, horseback riding, sailing, parasailing, and water-skiing are options. In summer, there is a dining terrace with a barbeque menu.

Bd. Fridolin-Simard (C.P. 38), Ville d'Estérel, PQ J0T 1E0. ℂ **888/378-3735** or 450/228-2571. Fax 450/228-4977. www.esterel.com. 124 units. C$198–C$278 (US$128–US$179) double, including full breakfast and dinner and use of most facilities. Lower rates Dec–May. Discounts for stays of 3 or more nights. Packages available. AE, DC, MC, V. Take the Limocar bus from Montréal into Ste-Adèle; the hotel picks up guests there. **Amenities:** Restaurant (Eclectic); coffee shop; bar; heated indoor pool; golf; 7 tennis courts; spa; Jacuzzi; sauna; watersports equipment; bike rental; children's programs (summer); concierge; small business center; limited room service; babysitting; laundry service. *In room:* A/C, TV w/pay movies, coffeemaker.

WHERE TO DINE IN STE-MARGUERITE

Le Bistro à Champlain ★★ FRENCH   On the shore of Lac Masson is one of the most honored restaurants in the Laurentians. Its 1864 building used to be a general store, and it retains the original rough-hewn board walls, exposed beams, and cash register. Gastronomy, not hardware, is now the motivation for customers who routinely motor up from Montréal for dinner. The 35,000-bottle cellar is also a big reason for these pilgrimages, its very reputation making it the target of thieves a few years ago. The devastated owner, a practicing radiologist, carried on after the robbery and an unusually large number of wines can still be sampled by the glass. The food matches the wines, both flavorful and attractively presented. For those still caught up in the fading fad, there is a cigar lounge with dozens of single-malt scotches available.

75 Chemin Masson. ℂ **450/228-4988.** Reservations recommended. Main courses C$24–C$30 (US$16–US$19); table d'hôte C$39 (US$25); dégustation menu C$69 (US$45). AE, DC, MC, V. Summer Tues–Sat 6–10pm, Sun noon–10pm; rest of year Thurs–Sat 6–10pm.

VAL-DAVID

Follow Route 117 north to Exit 76 or 80, respectively, to reach Val-David. To those who know it, the faintly bohemian enclave (pop. 3,800), 80km (50 miles) north of Montréal, conjures up images of cabin hideaways set among hills rearing above ponds and lakes, and laced with creeks tumbling through fragrant forests. The village celebrated its 75th anniversary in 1996.

The **tourist office** is on the main street at 2501 rue de l'Eglise (ℂ **888/322-7030** or 819/322-2900). It's open June 20 to Labour Day daily 9am to 7pm; September 5 to June 19 daily 10am to 4pm. Another possibility for assistance is **La Maison du Village,** a cultural center that mounts art exhibits in a two-story wooden building at 2495 rue de l'Eglise (ℂ **819/322-2900,** ext. 237). Note that this far north into the Laurentians, the telephone area code changes to 819.

EXPLORING VAL-DAVID

Val-David is small, so park anywhere and meander at leisure. Visiting the studios of local artists is a possible activity, and the village sponsors an annual **art festival** in the first 2 weeks of August, when painters, sculptors, ceramicists, jewelers, pewter smiths, and other craftspeople display their work. There are concerts and other outdoor activities.

Val-David sits astride a 200km (124-mile) parkway called the **Parc Linéaire le P'Tit Train du Nord,** a former railroad right-of-way. It is now a trail that runs from St-Jérôme to Mont-Laurier, heavily used for cycling in summer and for cross-country skiing and snowmobiling in winter. Have a picnic beside the North River in the **Parc des Amoureax,** which is 4km (2½ miles) from the main road through town. It has plenty of benches, and some parking spaces on the approach to the park. Watch for the sign SITE PITTORESQUE and turn at Chemin de la Rivière.

WHERE TO STAY & DINE IN VAL-DAVID

Edelweiss ⟨★⟩   Business is good at this intimate hostelry hidden in the woods east of town, enough to underwrite a new building next to the original Tyrolean structure. That makes a total of 14 bedrooms that stay full of admirers of the inn's kitchen. Despite the Austro-Germanic appearance of the place, the Belgian chef and co-owner (his wife, who is also the manager, is from Québec) draws from the French repertoire. His graceful touch is drawing more and more notice from serious eaters. Don't miss his foie gras terrine. Table d'hôte meals run from C$15 to C$325 (US$9.65–US$21). Note that room rates include breakfast and dinner for two, making for a true bargain.

Twelve of the rooms have gas fireplaces, eight have Jacuzzi baths. Deer are kept in a pen behind the inn.

3050 chemin Doncaster, Val-David, J0T 2N0. ✆ **819/322-7800.** Fax 819/322-1550. www.ar-edelweiss.com. 14 units. C$156–C$196 (US$101–US$126). Rates include breakfast and dinner. AE, MC, V. Drive through downtown and watch for the sign on the left, about 2.8km (1³/₄ miles). **Amenities:** Restaurant (French); heated outdoor pool with Jacuzzi; golf nearby. *In room:* TV, hairdryer.

Hôtel La Sapinière ⟨★⟩   This sedate lakeside inn celebrated its 65th anniversary with a thorough renovation and paint job. It remains a tranquil lakeside retreat, upper-middle-class in tone, with a largely 40-plus clientele who are in search of a sedate, relaxing vacation. They return faithfully year after year. Demanding diners, they are treated to five-course meals that are changed daily and embellished with wines from a 10,000-bottle cellar. The lake is private, with motorized boats banned. Shuffleboard, croquet, and the putting green are predictably popular with guests, but a driving range and hiking and cross-country trails are available to more active guests. Saturday nights have live music in the bar for dancing.

1244 Chemin de la Sapinière, Val-David, PQ J0T 2N0. ✆ **800/567-6635** or 819/322-2020. Fax 819/322-6510. www.sapiniere.com. 70 units. C$270 (US$174) double; C$335 (US$216) suite. Rates include full breakfast and dinner. AE, DC, MC, V. Drive through downtown and pick up the road with the sign to the inn on the right. **Amenities:** Restaurant (French/Continental); bar; heated outdoor pool; golf nearby; 2 tennis courts; Jacuzzi; watersports equipment; limited room service. *In room:* A/C, TV, dataport, coffeemaker, hair dryer.

WHERE TO DINE IN VAL-DAVID

Le Grand Pa ITALIAN/CANADIAN   In the middle of the town, near the tourist information office, an open deck reaches out to the sidewalk. It's crowded with white resin chairs and tables under big umbrellas, where locals dig into a dozen varieties of pizzas, baked in the brick oven inside. With their puffy crusts and fresh ingredients, in two sizes, they're the star attractions, often eaten with pitchers of beer or sangria. They come with a spicy olive oil deceptively contained in a baby bottle with nipple. Full meals are also available, with mostly limited choices of veal, chicken, and seafood. On Friday and Saturday nights there's live music.

2481 rue de l'Eglise. ✆ **819/322-3104.** Pizzas and pastas C$6.95–C$17 (US$4.50–US$11); main courses C$18–C$26 (US$12–US$17); table d'hôte C$15–C$20 (US$9.65–US$13). MC, V. Daily 11:30am–2pm and 5–8pm (bar until midnight). Closed Apr.

STE-AGATHE-DES-MONTS

With a population approaching 10,000, Ste-Agathe-des-Monts, 85km (53 miles) north of Montréal, is the largest town in the Laurentians and marks the end of Autoroute 15. Follow the Autoroute north to Exit 83 or 86.

Early settlers and vacationers flocked here in search of land fronting on Lac des Sables, and entrepreneurs followed the crowds. Ste-Agathe's main street, **rue**

Principale, is the closest you'll get to citification in these mountains, but it's only a touch of urbanity. Follow rue Principale from the highway through town and end up at the town dock on the lake. Watch out for four-way stops along the way.

The dock and surrounding **waterfront park** make Ste-Agathe a good place to pause for a few hours. One possibility is renting a bicycle from **Jacques Champoux Sports,** 74 rue St-Vincent (© **819/326-3480;** www.jacque-champoux. com), for the 5km (3-mile) ride around the lake. Lake cruises, beaches, and watercraft rentals seduce many visitors into lingering for days.

The **Bureau Touristique de Ste-Agathe-des-Monts,** 24 rue St-Paul (© **819/ 326-0457**), is open daily 9am to 8:30pm in summer, 9am to 5pm the rest of the year.

Croisières Alouette (© **819/326-3656;** www.canada-laurentides.com) provides cruises on the lake that depart the dock at the foot of rue Principale from mid-May to late October. It's a 50-minute, 19km (12-mile) voyage on a boat equipped with a bar. There is a running commentary on the sights that you'll observe, and a discussion of the water-ski competitions and windsurfing that Ste-Agathe and the Lac des Sables are famous for. The cost for the Alouette cruise is C$12 (US$7.75) adults, C$10 (US$6.45) seniors, and C$5 (US$3.25) for children 5 to 15. Children under 5 are free. There are regular departures from mid-May to late June 11:30am to 3:30pm, with additional departures until 7:30pm late June to late August.

WHERE TO STAY & DINE

For a night or two, the motels near town on Route 117 are sufficient, but for longer stays consider a lakeside lodge.

Auberge Chez Girard   Head toward the town dock, and near the end of rue Principale, on the left, is a Québec-style house with a crimson roof. That's Chez Girard. In good weather, diners can sit on the terrace overlooking the lake. The summer menu emphasizes lighter pasta and seafood dishes, an example being tortellini with razor clams, langoustines, and scallops in a goat cheese sauce. Ostrich and bison steak show up when the weather gets cooler. The kitchen prides itself on using the freshest ingredients, and on the absence of a deep fryer. Dinner table d'hôtes are C$19 to C$30 (US$12–US$19); lunch (served only in summer) is about 50% less.

The inn also has eight serviceable rooms and suites in a separate building behind the restaurant. Most units have fireplaces, Jacuzzi baths, and TV; suites have serving pantries stocked with breakfast fixings. Bikes are available, and guests have access to a private beach.

18 rue Principale ouest, St-Agathe-des-Monts, PQ J8C 1A3. © **800/663-0922** or 819/326-0922. www.poly inter.com/girard. 8 units. C$80–C$100 (US$52–US$65) double. Rates include breakfast. Meal plans available. AE, MC, V. Restaurant closed Mon; inn closed Apr and Nov. **Amenities:** Restaurant (French); bikes. *In room:* TV, no phone.

Auberge du Lac des Sables   All the rooms in this small lakefront inn have Jacuzzi baths, their chief distinguishing feature. Some have fireplaces and/or kitchenettes. Those with double Jacuzzis and a view of the lake are slightly more expensive. There's a small terrace overlooking the lake, a good vantage for watching the sunset. Downstairs is a game room with a pool table and pinball machine. The inn is about 2.5km (1½ miles) from the village center and within walking distance of the beach and boating. Because of the many levels and stairs (no elevator), this isn't the best choice for the elderly or travelers with disabilities.

230 rue St-Venant, Ste-Agathe-des-Monts, PQ J8C 2Z7. ② **800/567-8329** or 819/326-3994. Fax 819/326-9159. www.aubergedulac.com. 23 units. C$80–C$112 (US$52–US$75) double; C$118–C$128 (US$76–US$83) suite. Rates include breakfast (except for suites). Packages available. AE, MC, V. **Amenities:** Outdoor Jacuzzi; game room. *In room:* A/C, TV, no phone.

Auberge La Sauvagine   For something a little different, check this out—an 1890s inn housed in a deconsecrated chapel. (An order of nuns added the chapel when they ran the property as a retirement home.) Antiques and near-antiques are scattered throughout, with an impressive armoire in the elegant dining room. Chef-owner René Kissler gathered many culinary awards in his native Belgium and is accumulating them here. His table d'hôte menu is C$37 (US$24). Only two of the rooms upstairs share a bathroom; five have TVs. From June 15 to October 15, the restaurant is open nightly 6 to 9pm for dinner; in winter it's open nightly Wednesday to Sunday. If his rooms are full, ask about the inn Kissler has bought on a nearby lake.

1592 Rte. 329 nord, Ste-Agathe, PQ J8C 2Z8. ② **888/787-7172** or 819/326-7673. Fax 819/326-9351. www.lasauvagine.com. 9 units, 7 with bathroom. C$96–C$126 (US$62–US$81) double. Rates include breakfast. Packages available. AE, MC, V. The inn is 2km (1¼ miles) north of Ste-Agathe, on the road to St-Donat. **Amenities:** Restaurant (Contemporary French); heated outdoor pool. *In room:* A/C, TV, hair dryer.

ST-JOVITE & MONT-TREMBLANT

Follow Route 117 about 37km (23 miles) north from Ste-Agathe to the St-Jovite exit. It's 122km (76 miles) north of Montréal. To get to Mont-Tremblant, turn right on Route 327 just before the church in St-Jovite. Most vacationers make their base at one of the resorts or lodges scattered along Route 327. Mont-Tremblant is 45km (28 miles) north of Ste-Agathe and 130km (80 miles) north of Montréal.

A few words of clarification about the use of the name Tremblant, a subject of considerable confusion to first-time visitors. First, there is Mont-Tremblant, the mountain. On its slope is Tremblant, the growing resort village described below. Its most important hotels are the Fairmont Château Mont Tremblant and the new Westin Tremblant. At the base of the mountain is Lac (Lake) Tremblant, and on the opposite shore is Club Tremblant, also described below, an independently owned resort that has no connection to Tremblant resort (although its guests ski the mountain). And, finally, there is the organic village of Mont-Tremblant, about 5km (3 miles) west, with its own market, post office, restaurants, and inns that have no specific affiliation with any of the aforementioned properties and geographical features.

Mont-Tremblant, at 650m (2,135 ft.), is the highest peak in the Laurentians. In 1894 the provincial government set aside almost 386 sq. km (1,000 sq. miles) of wilderness as **Parc Mont-Tremblant,** and the foresight of this early conservation effort has yielded outdoor enjoyment to skiers and four-season vacationers ever since. The mountain's name comes from a legend of the area's first inhabitants. Amerindians named the peak after the god Manitou. When humans disturbed nature in any way, Manitou became enraged and made the great mountain tremble—*montagne tremblante.*

St-Jovite (pop. 4,118), about 12km (7½ miles) south of Mont-Tremblant, is the commercial center for this most famous and popular of Laurentian districts. A pleasant community, it provides all the expected services. The main street, **rue Ouimet,** is lined with cafes and shops, including **Le Coq Rouge,** which sells folk art and country antiques.

Tourist information, including maps of local ski trails, is available at the **Bureau Touristique de Mont-Tremblant,** rue du Couvent at Mont-Tremblant

(© 819/425-2434), open daily 8:30am to 6pm (until 7pm Fri and Sat) in summer and 9am to 5pm the rest of the year; and from the **Bureau Touristique de Saint-Jovite/Mont-Tremblant,** 305 chemin Brébeuf in St-Jovite (© 819/425-3300), open daily in summer 9am to 8pm, the rest of the year daily 9am to 5pm. You can also log on to www.tremblant.com.

SKIING, WATERSPORTS & MORE

Watersports in summer are almost as popular as the ski slopes and trails in winter, because the base of Mont-Tremblant is surrounded by no fewer than 10 lakes: Lac Tremblant, a gorgeous stretch of water 16km (10 miles) long, and also Lac Ouimet, Lac Mercier, Lac Gelinas, Lac Desmarais, and five smaller bodies of water, not to mention rivers and streams. From June to October, **Croisières Mont-Tremblant,** 2810 Chemin Principale, in Mont-Tremblant (© 819/425-1045), offers a 70-minute narrated tour of Lac Tremblant, focusing on its history, nature, and legends. Fares are C$12 (US$7.75) adults, C$10 (US$6.45) seniors, C$5 (US$3.25) children ages 6 to 15, free for children under 6. Twilight cruises are given Tuesday through Thursday, June 24 to August 20.

Mont-Tremblant, which has a vertical drop of 650m (2,131 ft.), draws the biggest downhill ski crowds in the Laurentians. Founded in 1939 by the Philadelphia millionaire Joe Ryan, Mont-Tremblant is one of the oldest ski areas in North America, the first to create trails on both sides of a mountain and the second in the world to install a chair lift. There are higher mountains with longer runs and steeper pitches, but something about Mont-Tremblant compels people to return time and again.

Today Mont-Tremblant has the snowmaking capability to cover 131 hectares (328 acres), making skiing possible from early November to late May, and keeping at least 30 of the trails open at Christmastime (as opposed to 9 in 1992). There are now a total of 92 downhill runs and trails, including the recently opened Dynamite and Verige trails, with 245m (810-ft.) and 225m (745-ft.) drops, respectively, and the Edge, a peak with two gladed trails. The 13 lifts are mostly gondolas (one of which is heated) and quad chairs, no T-bars. There is plenty of cross-country action on 90km (56 miles) of maintained trails. And in summer, choose from golf, tennis, horseback riding, boating, swimming, biking, and hiking—for starters.

WHERE TO STAY & DINE

Auberge La Porte Rouge *Value* This unusual motel is in the middle of everything, across the road from the Hôtel de Ville (Town Hall). Wake to a view of Lake Mercier through the picture window or from the little balcony. Some rooms have both fireplaces and Jacuzzis. Later in the day, take lunch on the terrace facing the lake or wind down in the cocktail lounge. Deluxe rooms with a kitchen and fireplace accommodate 3 to 10 people. The dining room serves all three meals, including a four-course table d'hôte. Rowboats and paddleboats are available, and the motel is directly on the regional bike path.

1874 Chemin Principale, Mont-Tremblant, PQ J0T 1Z0. © **800/665-3505** or 819/425-3505. Fax 819/425-6700. www.aubergelaporterouge.com. 26 units. C$132–C$168 (US$85–US$108) double. Rates include breakfast and dinner. Packages available. MC, V. **Amenities:** Restaurant (Canadian); bar; heated outdoor pool; golf nearby; tennis nearby; watersports equipment rentals; bike rental. *In room:* A/C, TV.

Auberge Mountain View *Value* Just over a mile from the center of St-Jovite is this conventional motel. The building is perpendicular to the highway, minimizing traffic noise. Some rooms have fireplaces and refrigerators, and two have kitchenettes. In the slack periods, when many other Laurentian lodgings are closed, its rates are lowered by 20% to 40%. Snowmobiles are available for rent.

1177 rue Labelle (Rte. 327), St-Jovite, PQ J8E 2W5. ℂ **800/561-5122** or 819/425-3429. Fax 819/425-9109. www.aubergemountainviewinn.com. 44 units. C$69–C$95 (US$45–US$61) double. Rates include breakfast. Extra person C$20 (US$13). Meal plan and packages available. AE, MC, V. **Amenities:** Restaurant (Regional); small heated outdoor pool; golf nearby; coin-op laundry. *In room:* A/C, TV.

Club Intrawest ⧸★★ Not directly on the main resort property, but at the nearby intersection of chemin Principal and Montée Ryan, this luxury facility has the look of an exclusive golf club, confirmed by the 18-hole course around which it is positioned. Accommodations are generously proportioned, with impressively tasteful appointments. One- to three-bedroom suites (the highest price quoted below) have full kitchens, deep two-person Jacuzzi baths, gas fireplaces, and stereos. Great views, too, but no restaurant.

Mont-Tremblant, PQ, J0T 1Z0. ℂ **800/799-3258.** www.clubintrawesthotels.com. 42 units. C$299–C$349 (US$193–US$225) double; C$388–C$1,099 (US$250–US$709) suite. AE, DC, MC, V. **Amenities:** Lounge with bar; heated outdoor pool; golf on premises; 2 tennis courts; exercise room; outdoor and indoor Jacuzzis; children's center; game room; concierge; babysitting. *In room:* A/C, TV/VCR, dataport, kitchen, coffeemaker, hair dryer, iron.

Fairmont Mont Tremblant ⧸★★ This 1996 luxury lodging commands a crest above the village, as befits its stature among the Tremblant hostelries. The enlarged lobby area has a north woods look, with a monster fireplace. Guests use the outdoor pool right through the winter, and they can ski-out and ski-in this close to the bottom of the chairlift.

3045 rue Principale, Mont-Tremblant, PQ J0T 1Z0. ℂ **800/441-1414** or 819/681-7000. Fax 819/681-7099. www.fairmont.com. 316 units. C$169–C$429 (US$109–US$277) double. Packages available. AE, DC, DISC, MC, V. **Amenities:** Restaurant (International); cafe; bar; indoor lap pool and heated outdoor pools; golf nearby; tennis nearby; health club and spa; watersports equipment; bike rental; children's programs; concierge; business center; shopping arcade; limited room service; in-room massage; babysitting; laundry service; same-day dry cleaning. *In room:* A/C, TV w/pay movies, dataport, unstocked fridge, coffeemaker, hair dryer, iron.

Gray Rocks The area's dowager resort has been under new management since 1993, and its ministrations are evident. The accommodations—rooms and condos—are in a huge rambling main building, in the cozier Le Château lodge, or in one of the resort's four-person cottages. (Ask for a room in the redecorated Center or Pavilion wings of the main building.) Condos have full kitchens and washers and dryers. The family-friendly resort covers most of the recreational bases, including, for summer, two 18-hole golf courses, junior and adult tennis schools, horseback riding, and boating. In winter, it has its own mountain, Sugar Hill, with 22 trails, 4 lifts, and a ski school. Guests also have access to 90km (56 miles) of cross-country trails. And there is not only a private airport for guests who fly in, but also a seaplane base for joyrides over Lac Ouimet. There's a playground complete with attendants to provide child care, as well as a program of free swimming lessons. The bar has piano and other music for dancing.

525 Chemin Principal, Mont-Tremblant, PQ J0T 1Z0. ℂ **800/567-6767** or 819/425-2771. Fax 819/425-9156. www.grayrocks.com. 277 units, including 62 condos. C$260–C$344 (US$168–US$222) double; C$216–C$555 (US$139–US$358) condo (4–8 persons). Rates include breakfast and dinner in hotel, but not in condos. Discounts for children sharing parents' room. Meals optional in condos. Ski-school packages available. AE, DISC, MC, V. **Amenities:** Restaurant (Continental); bar; large indoor pool; 36 holes of golf; 22 tennis courts; health club; sauna; watersports equipment; bike rental; business center; babysitting; same-day dry cleaning and laundry; self-service laundry. *In room:* A/C, TV, coffeemaker, hair dryer, iron.

Hôtel Club Tremblant ★★   Terraced into a hillside sloping steeply to the shore of Lac Tremblant, this attractive property consists of several lodges in blessedly muted alpine style. Essentially a concentration of privately owned condominium apartments operated by a single management, the accommodations represent excellent value and that greatest of luxuries: space. Most of the rental units are suites of one to three bedrooms, for the price of a single room at many other resorts in the region. A typical suite has a fireplace, balcony, sitting room with cable TV and dining table, full kitchen with cookware and dishwasher, one or two bathrooms with Jacuzzi, and clothes washer and dryer. Nearly all have views of the lake and Mont-Tremblant, which rises from the opposite shore. This is a family resort, so expect childish yips and squeals in the dining rooms in peak months—July, August, February, and March. A drawback on the hottest days of summer is the lack of air-conditioning in the suites, but they'll deliver a portable fan on request. There's usually piano music Thursday through Saturday nights in the bar. During ski season, a 22-passenger bus shuttles between the lodge and the slopes.

Rue Cuttle, Mont-Tremblant, PQ J0T 1Z0. ☎ 800/567-8341 or 819/425-2731. Fax 819/425-5617. www.club tremblant.com. 100 units. C$230–C$330 (US$148–US$212) suite. Rates include full breakfast and dinner. Rates are lower for stays of 2 days or more. Children 6–12 C$115 (US$79). Packages available. AE, DC, MC, V. Turn left off Montée Ryan, then right on Lac Tremblant North and follow signs for less than a mile. **Amenities:** 2 restaurants in summer (French/Continental), 1 in winter; 2 bars in summer, 1 in winter; heated indoor and outdoor pools; 6 golf courses nearby; 4 tennis courts; exercise room; spa w/ therapeutic baths; Jacuzzi; watersports equipment rental; children's programs; massage; babysitting. *In room:* TV, kitchen, unstocked fridge, coffeemaker, hair dryer, iron.

Le Grand Lodge ★★   Replacing the old Villa Bellevue on the bank of Lake Ouimet is this handsome all-suites hotel built with the palatial log construction of the north country. The atmosphere here is adult and sophisticated. The suites leave little to be desired—all come with full kitchens, fireplaces, and balconies—and, because it's new, the furniture is fresh, without the battering of many ski seasons. Canoeing and kayaking on the lake, float-plane tours, dog-sledding, horseback riding, snowshoeing, and snowmobiling flesh out the more obvious skiing and golfing pursuits. But as comfortable as the suites are, you might pass much of the time with a bottle of wine in front of the fire. This is a highly desirable addition to Mont Tremblant's housing stock and at a quiet distance from the frequent clamor of the main resort.

845 chemin Principale, Mont-Tremblant, PQ J0T 1Z0. ☎ 800/567-6763 or 819/425-2734. Fax 819/425-9360. www.legrandlodge.com. 112 units. C$99–C$559 (US$64–US$361) suite. Children under 14 stay free in parents' room. Packages available. AE, DC, MC, V. Small pets accepted ($25 a night). **Amenities:** Restaurant (International); bar; golf nearby; 4 tennis courts; large heated indoor pool; exercise room; spa; watersports equipment rental; children's programs; concierge; activities desk; limited room service; in-room massage; babysitting; coin-op laundry; same-day dry cleaning. *In room:* A/C, TV w/pay movies, dataport, kitchen, unstocked fridge, coffeemaker, hair dryer, iron.

Le Westin Resort Tremblant ★★★   Easily one of the most attractive hotels in the ever-expanding resort, this year 2000 entry competes for king of the hill. Restrained corporate decor prevails, applied to rooms that have every convenience you might expect and some you don't. In the latter category are gas fireplaces, wet bars, Nintendo PlayStations, and Internet access through the TV with wireless keyboards. All units have at least small kitchenettes with microwaves, toasters, fridges, and enough plates and flatware for four. Many have balconies, and while you can easily spend more, most units are under US$200.

Lodging at Tremblant Resort

Not merely a hotel with a pool, Tremblant is a complete and growing resort village stretching from the mountain's skirts to the shores of 16km- (10-mile) long Lac Tremblant. It'll be a pretty nice place if they ever finish it, but this is the kind of enterprise that always has another "phase" to go. It has the prefabricated look of a theme park, but at least they used the Quebecois architectural style of pitched or mansard roofs in bright colors, not ersatz Tyrolean or Bavarian Alpine flourishes. At recent count, there were several hotels and condo complexes, an 18-hole golf course (with another on the way), and 14 shops, including a liquor store, as well as over 30 eating places and bars. When the snow is deep, skiers here like to follow the sun around the mountain, making the run down slopes with an eastern exposure in the morning and down the western-facing ones in the afternoon.

To get to the village, drive 5km (3 miles) north of St-Jovite on Route 117; then take Montée Ryan and follow the blue signs for about 10km (6 miles). The Limocar bus from Montréal stops at the entrance, and there's door-to-door shuttle service from Dorval Airport; reservations are required (© **800/471-1155**).

Reservations for lodgings at the resort can be made through the central number (© **800/567-6760** or **888/289-8888**), on www.tremblant. com, or by contacting the establishments directly. Although you can follow signs directly to your hotel, if you don't have reservations you can stop in the building labeled *Les Cèdres* near the entrance, announced by a large brown sign with gold lettering reading RECEPTION—take the right turn just before the old church. The more prominent hotels, most of which incorporate privately owned condominium units, are described in this section.

Several of the less expensive lodgings have only limited facilities. Pools and health clubs are provided at centers located around the resort. Supervision is provided for children ages 1 to 12 in the Kidz Club with excursions, crafts, games, and activities. They and their older siblings can also get blissfully waterlogged at the AquaClub, with indoor and outdoor pools and Jacuzzi baths. The facility also has a well-equipped fitness area.

In summer, extensive possible diversions include lake swimming, boat cruises, chairlift rides to the top of Mont-Tremblant, playing on 1 of the 11 lighted Har-Tru tennis courts, minigolfing, and biking and in-line skating (rentals are readily available). In winter, in addition to the chair and gondola lifts, shops rent and repair ski equipment and provide information about access to the cross-country trails.

Mont-Tremblant, PQ J0T 1Z0. © **877/873-6252** or 819/681-8000. Fax 819/681-8001. www.tremblant.ca. 126 units. C$230–C$500 (US$153–US$333) double. Packages available. AE, DC, MC, V. **Amenities:** 2 restaurants (Asian, International); bar; heated outdoor saltwater pool with Jacuzzi; golf nearby; tennis; health club and spa; watersports equipment rental; children's programs; concierge; business center; shopping arcade; 24-hr. room service; massage; babysitting; laundry service; same-day dry cleaning; executive floors. *In room:* A/C, TV w/pay movies, dataport, kitchen or kitchenette, fridge, coffeemaker, hair dryer, iron, safe.

Dining at Tremblant Resort

In addition to the bars and restaurants of the hotels of the Tremblant resort village described above, there are over 30 freestanding places at which to get a meal or a snack in the pedestrian areas of the resort. That isn't to say they are especially satisfying, for few restaurants in the village rise above mediocrity. A notable exception is Aux Truffes, reviewed below. Otherwise, my recommendation is to do the ski and après-ski thing, sport about, have cocktails, and hear some music in the resort, but take serious meals off the premises.

That said, there are plenty of eating options for the exhausted or car-less. Serving a variety of kinds of food implicit in their names are La Pizzateria, Coco Pazzo (Italian), Créperie Catherine, La Savoie (fondues), and Mexicali Rosa's. Popular Les Artistes, in the village center, has four loud levels and a menu that scrupulously avoids challenges to convention. On the summit of the mountain is Le Rendezvous Café, with a circular fireplace, and the 1,000-seat Le Grand Manitou restaurant complex, with a dining room called La Légende, plus a bistro and cafeteria. On the food-with-entertainment front, Le Shack opens for breakfast at 7am and doesn't close the bar until 3am. La Diable pours craft beers to accompany live jazz on weekends, and Le P'tit Caribou brings in pop performers weekly.

Les Suites Tremblant A collection of several buildings scattered around the complex, each with slightly different profiles of decor and amenities, there are choices here for families, couples traveling together, or those who require economical accommodation. The least expensive two-bedroom units can accommodate up to six people, bringing the cost down to US$18 per person. The bedroom units also have kitchenettes, for greater savings (cook your own meals), and many have fireplaces and/or washing machines.

3005 rue Principale, Mont-Tremblant, PQ, J0T 1Z0. © **800/461-8711** or 819/681-2000. Fax 819/681-5990. www.tremblant.ca. 900 units. C$129–C$325 (US$83–US$210) double; C$139–C$575 (US$90–US$371) 1-bedroom condo, C$159–C$795 (US$103–US$513) 2-bedroom condo. AE, DC, DISC, MC, V. **Amenities:** Golf nearby; access to nearby health club and spa; babysitting; coin-op laundry. *In room:* A/C, TV, kitchenette, fridge, coffeemaker, hair dryer, iron.

Marriott Residence Inn Near the terminus of the lower chairlift, which runs through the central part of the village, this mid-level hotel has ready access to the slopes, the lake, and the resort's Aquaclub (a large indoor pool). The higher-priced suites have two bedrooms and fireplaces.

Mont-Tremblant, PQ J0T 1Z0. © **888/272-4000** or 819/681-4000. Fax 819/681-4099. www.marriott-tremblant.com. 127 units. C$125–C$145 (US$81–US$94) double; C$145–C$299 (US$94–US$193) suite. Rates include breakfast. Packages available. AE, DC, MC, V. **Amenities:** Restaurant (International); bar; heated outdoor pool; golf nearby; 13 tennis courts; exercise room; children's center; concierge; dry cleaning. *In room:* A/C, TV, hair dryer.

WHERE TO DINE

Although most Laurentian inns and resorts have their own dining facilities and often require that guests use them (especially in winter), Mont-Tremblant and places in the vicinity have several decent independent dining options for casual lunches or the odd night out. Note that restaurants in the area open and close with irritating unpredictability, so call ahead before setting out. Those recommended below are among the more reliable.

Antipasto ITALIAN   Housed in an old train station moved to this site, there is the expected railroad memorabilia on the walls, but the owners have resisted the temptation to play up the theme aspect to excess. Captain's chairs are drawn up to big tables with green Formica tops. Almost everyone orders the César salad (their spelling), which is dense and strongly flavored—the half portion is more than enough as a first course. Individual pizzas emerge from the brick ovens in more than 50 versions, on a choice of regular or whole-wheat crust. Pastas are available in even greater variety; those with shellfish are among the winners. The sauces are savory, if a bit thin. There are outdoor tables in summer.

855 rue Ouimet, St-Jovite. ✆ **819/425-7580.** Main courses C$11–C$28 (US$7.05–US$18). MC, V. Daily 11am–11pm.

Auberge Sauvignon GRILLS   This roadside inn, a block from Lac Tremblant, packs happy patrons into two rooms, with the spillover perching on stools at the bar in back. Even a short staff is able to handle the crowds, because service is very casual and preps and cooking are simple. Most of the main courses, which run from about C$16 to C$28 (US$11–US$19), are grills—salmon, lamb, rib steak, *entrecôte au poivre*. A trip to the substantial salad bar is included, so you may want to skip an appetizer, or, if you're vegetarian, fill up with salad alone for C$11 (US$7.30). There are frequent off-menu specials, but you may have to ask. Reservations are suggested. Dress is casual.

Upstairs are seven cozy rooms, all with bathrooms and air-conditioning, two with TV, one with a sitting area and Jacuzzi. Smoking is not permitted in guest rooms.

2723 chemin Principal, Mont-Tremblant. ✆ **819/425-5466.** www.aubergesauvignon.com. Main courses C$16–C$29 (US$10–US$19). AE, DC, MC, V. Daily noon–3pm and 6–10pm (bar until midnight).

Aux Truffes ✦ CONTEMPORARY FRENCH   Small hurricane lamps flicker on each table, which are set with tablecloths and silver. That includes those out on the terrace, but anytime but deepest summer is likely to be chilly out there. The management and kitchen are more ambitious than just about any on the mountain, evidenced by a wine cellar that sails through Canadian, Californian, Chilean, Australian, Spanish, and many admirable French bottlings to a Château Latour '90 for $1,200. Put yourself in the hands of the knowledgeable wine steward. The meal proceeds from a heartier-than-usual *amuse-bouche* to very good salad to such imaginative mains as a succulent slab of bison filet on black rice shot with cashews and capped by slices of duck foie gras. If you are among the growing number of Americans intrigued by fine cheeses, you will want to try the *plateau* of four raw milk Québec varieties.

3035 chemin Principale, Mont-Tremblant. ✆ **819/681-4544.** Main courses C$18–C$32 (US$12–US$21). AE, MC, V. Daily 6–11pm.

Le Bistro Brunch Café INTERNATIONAL   While the menu lists many sandwiches, salads, pastas, and pizzas (30 of them), the most satisfying choices are among the sausages picked from a list of six designer varieties, served with sauerkraut, mustard, and pan fries. They have complementary *bières en fût* (beer on tap), plus an interesting selection of regional microbrews and imports. The cafe is located downtown, not far from Antipasto, which is under the same management. There are umbrellas over the tables facing the main street, close tables inside. Live music is offered most summer weekends.

816 rue Ouimet, St-Jovite. ⓒ **819/425-8233**. Main courses C$8–C$21 (US$5.15–US$14); table d'hôte C$9–C$16 (US$5.80–US$10). MC, V. Apr–Oct daily 8am–10pm; Nov–Mar daily 8am–4pm.

La Table Enchantée QUEBECOIS   The lace-covered tables in this tidy little restaurant support some of the most carefully prepared dishes in the region. The kitchen does riffs on the traditional Québec repertoire—the rare loin of caribou in rich gravy with wild rice and three vegetable garnishes, for instance. Clam chowder is a favored starter, then perhaps the paté called *cretons,* followed by Quebecois *cipaille,* a potpie layered with pheasant, guinea hen, rabbit, veal, and pork. Dessert might be *grand-pères au sirop d'érable* (dumplings in maple syrup). Or, substitute the cheese course, which comes with a glass of port, for an extra C$10 (US$6.60).

600 Rte. 117 nord, Lac Duhamel. ⓒ **819/425-7113**. Reservations usually required. Main courses C$15–C$29 (US$9.70–US$19); table d'hôte C$20 (US$13). AE, MC, V. Mid-May to early Oct Tues–Sun 5–10pm; late Nov to Apr weekends only 5–9pm. Closed mid-Oct to mid-Nov and 2 weeks in May.

2 East into Montérégie & the Cantons-de-l'Est

24–77km (15–48 miles) SE of Montréal

The tourist region designated as Montérégie occupies the south bank of the St. Lawrence opposite the island of Montréal, much of it within sight of the downtown skyline. Despite that proximity and the crossings of massive power lines, it has a largely rural, small-town aspect, with miles of orchards and truck farms that have encouraged the authorities to dub it the "Garden of Québec." Given its relative tranquility and easy commuting distance, many Montréalers keep weekend houses here, especially along the region's principal topographical feature, the Richelieu River Valley. The river runs north and south, leaving the St. Lawrence near Sorel and flowing south 130km (80 miles) into Lake Champlain in New York State. It supports several provincial parks along the way and, primarily in its southern reaches, is the site of fortifications built during the French and Indian Wars.

The Cantons-de-l'Est, until recently called Estrie or the Eastern Townships, borders Montérégie to the east, and also serves as breadbasket to Montréal and the province. It is a largely pastoral region marked by billowing hills and the 792m (2,600-ft.) peak of Mont-Orford, centerpiece of a provincial park and the district's premier downhill ski area. A short distance from Mont-Orford is Sherbrooke, the industrial and commercial capital of the region, and throughout the Mont-Orford–Sherbrooke area are serene glacial lakes that attract summer fishing enthusiasts, sailors, and swimmers from all over. In terms of tourism, the Cantons are one of Québec's best-kept secrets, for it's mostly Quebecois who occupy rental houses to ski, fish, cycle, or launch their boats.

Follow their lead: Once out of Montréal, drive east along arrow-straight Autoroute 10 past silos and fields, clusters of cows, and meadows strewn with wildflowers. Clumps of mountains rise with improbable suddenness from the rolling terrain that flattens as it approaches the St. Lawrence. Cresting the hill at km 100, there's an especially beguiling view of countryside stretching toward New England, not far over the horizon.

Unlike the Laurentides, which virtually close down in "mud time," when spring warmth thaws the ground, the Cantons-de-l'Est kick into gear as crews penetrate every "sugar bush" (stand of sugar maples) to tap the sap and "sugar

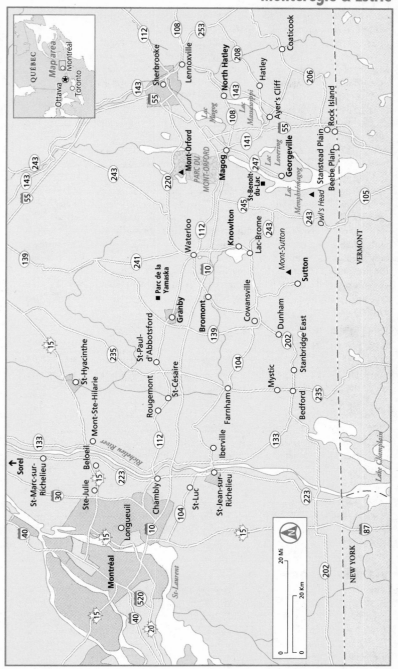

off." The result? Maple festivals and farms hosting "sugaring parties"—guests wolfing down prodigious country repasts capped by traditional maple-syrup desserts. For one popular example, hot maple syrup is poured on the fast-melting winter snow and cooled instantly to produce a kind of maple-sugar taffy. Montréal newspapers and local tourist offices and chambers of commerce keep up-to-date lists of what's happening where and when.

Autumn has its special attractions, too, for in addition to the glorious fall foliage (usually best in the weeks on either side of the 3rd weekend in Sept), the orchards of Cantons-de-l'Est sag under the weight of apples of every variety, and cider mills hum day and night to produce what has been described as Québec's "wine." Visitors are invited to help with the harvest, paying a low price for the baskets of fruit they gather themselves. Cider mills open their doors for tours and tastings.

English town names such as Granby, Waterloo, and Sherbrooke are vestiges of the time when Americans loyal to the Crown migrated here during and shortly after the Revolutionary War. The region was long known as the Eastern Townships. Now, however, the Cantons-de-l'Est are about 90% French-speaking, with a name to reflect that demographic. A few words of French and a little sign language are sometimes necessary outside hotels and other tourist facilities, since the area draws fewer Anglophone visitors than do the Laurentides.

For extended stays in the region, consider making your base in one of the several inns along the shores of Lac Massawippi, especially in and around **North Hatley,** and take day trips from there.

ESSENTIALS
GETTING THERE
BY CAR   For Montérégie, leave the island of Montréal on Route 20, taking the Sortie (Exit) 112 on the other side in the vicinity of Ste-Julie and heading north on Route 223 in the direction of Sorel. Several bridges across the Richelieu River connect Route 223 to Route 133, which skirts the east bank.

For the Cantons-de-l'Est, leave Montréal by the Champlain Bridge, which funnels into Autoroute 10, in the direction of Sherbrooke, the grungy metropolis of the region. People in a hurry can remain on Autoroute 10—and plenty of express buses do this, too—but to get to know the countryside, turn off the autoroute at Exit 37 and go north the short distance to join Route 112 east.

BY BUS   Local buses leave Montréal to follow Route 112 more than a dozen times a day, arriving in Sherbrooke, 160km (100 miles) away, 3¼ hours later. Express buses use Autoroute 10, making a stop in Magog and arriving in Sherbrooke in 2 hours and 10 minutes (2½ hrs. from Québec City). Call © **450/ 842-2281** at the Terminus Voyageur in Montréal for information. There is no bus service to the Montérégie region.

VISITOR INFORMATION
There are 8 permanent **tourist offices in Montérégie** and 19 that operate only in summer. Two of the most conveniently situated are the seasonal offices in Chambly at 1900 av. Bourgogne, Route 112 (© **450/658-0321**), and in Beloeil at 35 bd. Laurier (© **450/536-2921**); they are open daily mid-June to Labour Day 9am to 5pm. On the opposite side of the river from Beloeil is a permanent information office in Mont-Ste-Hilaire, at 1080 Chemin des Patriotes nord (© **450/536-0395;** www.vallee-du-richelieu.ca). It's open Monday to Friday 9am to 5pm.

La Maison du Tourisme (Tourism House) for the **Cantons-de-l'Est,** at Exit 68 off Autoroute 10 (© **800/263-1068** or 450/375-8774, fax 450/375-3530; www.granby-bromont.com), is open Monday through Thursday 8:30am to 5pm, Friday 8:30 to 8pm, Saturday 8:30 to 6pm, Sunday 8:30 to 5pm (shorter hours in winter). Or contact **Tourisme Cantons-de-l'Est,** 20 rue Don Bosco sud, Sherbrooke, PQ J1L 1W4 (© **800/355-5755;** fax 819/566-4445; www. tourisme-cantons.qc.ca), for more information. The Sherbrooke tourist information bureau is at 3010 rue King ouest (© **819/821-1919**), open daily late June to Labour Day 8:30am to 7:30pm, and the rest of the year 9am to 5pm.

The **telephone area codes** are 450 or 819, depending on the part of the region called (towns with a 450 area code are closer to Montréal).

EXPLORING MONTEREGIE
CHAMBLY
This largely residential suburb of 19,700 residents stands beside a wide basin of the Richelieu River. Today it is the site of marinas for recreational boating and windsurfing, but its history began as a frontier outpost of French Canada. In 1665, a Captain Chambly was commissioned to erect a wooden fort as defense against the Iroquois, who repeatedly attacked the colony of Ville-Marie, later to become Montréal. In 1711, the wooden fort was replaced by a stone fortress, this time for service in the several French and Indian Wars with the British. The restored **Fort Chambly National Historic Site** at 2 rue de Richelieu (© **450/ 658-1585;** www.parcscanada.gc.ca/fortchambly) now serves as an interpretation center, with a small museum. It's open mid-March to April 2 Saturday and Sunday 10am to 5pm, April 3 to May 17 and September 3 to November 24 Wednesday to Sunday 10am to 5pm; May 18 to Labour Day daily 10am to 5pm (until 6pm in July and Aug). The site is closed December to mid-March. Admission is C$5 (US$3.25) adults, C$4 (US$2.60) seniors, C$3 (US$1.95) ages 6 to 16, free for children 5 and under.

ST-MARC-SUR-RICHELIEU
About 10km (6 miles) north of Autoroute 20 on Route 223, past farms, orchards, and a few small wineries, this residential and resort hamlet is strung along the west bank of the Richelieu. Among tidy houses and modest bed-and-breakfast inns stands one of the most honored hotels in all of Québec, one of only four Relais & Châteaux properties in the entire province.

Where to Stay & Dine
Hostellerie Les Trois Tilleuls ★★★ Looming beside the road, this inn doesn't look especially impressive, at least until you realize that the very new structure to the right is part of the complex. That's the $4 million Givenchy Spa, opened in 2001. The backs of both buildings face the river, bestowing water views on every room. Bedrooms have balconies to take in the view, over room-service breakfast if you wish. While the accommodations in the original inn aren't grand, except for the jaw-dropping Royal Suite, the spa has 17 spacious deluxe suites with walkabout showers and Jacuzzis. Those are in addition to a dozen treatment rooms, a dining room with a special menu, and a substantial health club.

Ah, but the food in the old inn! Stop first in the atmospheric bar for the house cocktail of champagne and raspberry liqueur touched with Armagnac. Then, enjoy your dinner by the fireplace or out on the terrace. The event begins with a plate of nibbles—quail paté, perhaps, with a taste of lobster tartar or smoked ostrich and scampi. The kitchen emphasizes regional products, so main courses might involve sweetbreads with maple vinegar or foie gras harvested in nearby Granby. The head waiter knows every bottle in the 16,000-bottle cellar. At C$22 (US$14), the luncheon table d'hôte is a special low-cost treat.

290 rue Richelieu, St-Marc-sur-Richelieu, PQ J0L 2E0. ✆ 800/263-2230 outside the greater Montréal area, or 450/856-7787. Fax 450/584-3146. www.lestroistilleuls.com. 24 units. C$125–C$275 (US$81–US$177) double; C$250–C$450 (US$161–US$290) suite. Meal plans and packages available. AE, DC, MC, V. **Amenities:** 2 restaurants (Creative French, Spa); bar; golf nearby; tennis; health club and spa. *In room:* A/C, TV, hair dryer.

EXPLORING ESTRIE
GRANBY
North of the Autoroute at Exit 68, this not-especially-beguiling city (pop. 45,440) does have a couple of surprises.

First is the **Zoo de Granby,** 525 rue St-Hubert (✆ **877/472-6290;** www. moijezoo.com). Take Exit 68 or 74 off Autoroute 10 and follow the signs. The zoo's 28 wooded hectares (70 acres) harbor more than 1,000 mammals, exotic birds, reptiles, and amphibians of 225 species from around the world. Founded in 1953, the zoo has an educational program for children and presents shows every day in summer, including demonstrations of and explanations about raptors—birds of prey. Among the newer exhibits are a nocturnal cave, a display of robotic whales, and the "Afrika" pavilion, notable for its group of gorillas. There are restaurants, picnic areas, gift shops, free rides, and a water park with what is said to be the largest pool in Québec. The zoo is open weekends in May and September, daily June through August. Open times vary but are usually 10am to 6pm in high season, until 5pm in shoulder periods. Admission is C$20 (US$13) for ages 13 and older, C$14 (US$8.85) for seniors and children ages 5 to 12, and C$8.95 (US$5.75) for children 2 to 4. Parking is C$4 (US$2.60). The visitor entrance is on boulevard David-Bouchard nord.

Granby also has **Parc de la Yamaska** (✆ **450/776-7182;** www.sepaq.com) with swimming on the longest beach in the area, a 3km (2-mile) hiking trail, 40km (25 miles) of cross-country ski trails, and 22km (13½ miles) of cycling trails along an old railroad track between Granby and the towns of Bromont and Waterloo.

Tourisme Granby is located at 650 rue Principale, Granby, PQ J2G 8L4 (✆ **800/567-7273** or 450/372-7273; fax 450/372-7782; www.granby-bromont.com). It's open in summer daily 10am to 6pm, the rest of the year Monday to Friday 9am to 5pm.

BROMONT
Take Exit 78 off Autoroute 10.

Founded in 1964 primarily to accommodate an industrial park and other commercial enterprises, this town of 4,000 is now a popular destination for day and night skiing, mountain biking (rent bikes at the entrance to the town opposite the tourist office), golf, hiking, and horseback riding. Shoppers have two of the largest **factory outlets** in Canada—Versants de Bromont and Les Manufacturiers de Bromont—and the area's largest **flea market,** with over 350 stalls set up in the local drive-in from 9am to 5pm the first Sunday in May to the last Sunday in October.

Where to Stay & Dine
Hôtel Château Bromont ✿ All the rooms at the château have rocking chairs, Internet connections and Nintendo games; half have fireplaces. A landscaped

terrace looks up at the ski mountain across the way, a most attractive setting. The interior decor gets a trifle gaudy here and there, but not jarring. The staff is young and bilingual. In addition to squash and racquetball courts, there's a European spa featuring mud and algae baths (use of the spa facilities costs extra).

90 rue Stanstead, Bromont, PQ J2L 1K6. ℭ **800/304-3433** or 450/534-3433. Fax 450/534-0514. www. chateaubromont.qc.ca. 152 units. C$200–C$220 (US$129–US$142) double; C$330 (US$221) suite. Rates include breakfast. Free for children under 12 in parents' room. Packages available. AE, DC, DISC, MC, V. **Amenities:** 2 restaurants (French, Continental); bar; heated indoor and outdoor pools; 4 golf courses nearby; exercise room; spa; Jacuzzi; sauna; massage; babysitting. *In room:* A/C, TV w/pay movies, minibar, coffee-maker, iron, safe.

KNOWLTON

Those who shop for amusement, not mere necessity, will want to make this a destination. Knowlton is compact, but its two main shopping streets have a number of clothing and antique stores that reveal a creeping chic influenced by refugees and day-trippers from Montréal. Ralph Lauren is here, and a shop that replaced a Liz Claiborne outlet sells outdoor gear and clothing and whimsically refers to itself as *L.L. Brome.* The main shopping streets are **Lakeside Street** and **Knowlton Road.**

Knowlton is at the southeast corner of Brome Lake and is part of the seven-village municipality known as **Lac Brome** (pop. 5,073). It is one of the last towns in the region where a majority of the residents have English as their mother tongue. The first settler here was Paul Holland Knowlton, a Loyalist from Vermont. He arrived in 1815 and established a farm where the golf course stands today. By 1834, he had added a sawmill, a blacksmith shop, a gristmill, and a store. He also founded the first high school.

The **tourist information office** is at 696 rue Lakeside (ℭ **450/242-2870;** www.cclacbrome.qc.ca). The major local sight is the **Musée Historique du Comté de Brome** (Brome County Historical Museum) at 130 rue Lakeside (Rte. 243), ℭ **450/243-6782.** It occupies five historic buildings, including the town's first school, established by Paul Holland Knowlton. Exhibits focus on the various aspects of town life, with re-creations of a schoolroom, bedroom, parlor, and kitchen. The Martin Annex (1921) is dominated by a 1917 Fokker single-seat biplane, the foremost German aircraft in World War I. Also on premises are collections of old radios and 18th- to early-20th-century weapons. The museum sells books about the area. Admission is C$3.50 (US$2.25) adults, C$2 (US$1.30) seniors, and C$1.50 (US95¢) ages 16 and under. It's open mid-May to mid-September Monday to Saturday 10am to 4:30pm, Sunday 11am to 4:30pm, and closed the rest of the year.

Where to Stay & Dine

Auberge Lakeview   The core structure of this Victorian inn dates from 1874, and a 19th-century flavor has been sustained through many renovations. Leather chairs are arranged around the fireplace in the lobby, tin ceilings prevail, and Spencer's, the brass and mahogany pub that is a replica of the London original, is a nice place to settle in for an evening. On weekends, there's dancing to live music. The bedrooms come in four categories of relative comfort—go for the best ones and get two robes, a sitting area, access to the veranda, and a heart-shaped Jacuzzi. Much of the furniture is crafted in Quebecois country style. Rooms in the least expensive category lack TVs, but the rest have cable. Make sure to try the duck wings served as a bar snack.

Cantons-de-l'Est: Wine Country?

Canada is known more for its beers and ales than its wines, and rightly so. But that hasn't stopped a few stouthearted agriculturists from attempting to plant vines and transform the fruit into approximations of drinkable clarets, Chardonnays, and Sauternes. So far, the most successful efforts have blossomed along the Niagara Frontier in southern Ontario and in the relatively warmer precincts of British Columbia. The Cantons-de-l'Est enjoy the mildest microclimates in Québec; where apples grow, as they do in abundance in these parts, so will other fruits, including grapes. Inevitably, a few hardy entrepreneurial sorts decided to give winemaking a go.

Most of their efforts are concentrated around **Dunham,** a farming village about 29km (18 miles) west of Sutton, with several nearby vineyards along Route 202. They've been at it for only about 20 years, so their vines and the end product are still maturing. No winemaker in the valleys of Napa or the Gironde is feeling the hot breath of competition from the vintages of the Cantons-de-l'Est. Still, a stop for a snack or a tour of vineyard facilities makes for an agreeable break from driving, and those demonstrating such daring deserve to be encouraged.

One possibility is the family-owned and -run **Les Blancs Coteaux,** at 1046 Route 202 (© **450/295-3503**), which opened in 1990. They serve picnic baskets and give tours in summer, but they welcome visitors all year, daily 9am to 5pm. The vineyard's shop sells its Seyval Blanc and Vendange de Bacchus white wines, hard cider, apple liqueur and syrup, strawberry vinegar, relish, cider jelly, and dried wreaths and wildflower arrangements. The area's oldest vineyard, **l'Orpailleur,** 1086 Route 202 (© **450/295-2763**), opened in 1982. Look, too, for **Domaine des Côtes d'Ardoise,** at 879 Route 202 (© **450/295-2020**), and **Les Trois Clochers,** at 341 Route 202 (© **450/295-2034**). L'Orpailleur serves meals and all three vineyards have picnic tables, offer wine tastings, and conduct tours; call ahead to determine schedules and hours, which vary by the season.

So far, though, the most credible bottlings in the region come out of **Le Cep d'Argent,** outside Magog, at 1257 Chemin de la Rivière (© **819/864-4441**). They produce eight different wines, their prizewinners being the Le Cep d'Argent dry white made from the Seyval varietal, the aperitif Mistral, and the L'Archer, a port-like fortified wine blended from red wine, brandy, and maple syrup, which sounds weird but tastes good. The cheerful owners pour samples and run a snack shop with terrace tables. They're open all year and offer frequent guided tours daily May to August, weekends only the rest of the year. Tours cost C$4 (US$2.60) for visitors over age 14.

50 rue Victoria, Knowlton (Lac Brome), PQ J0E 1V0. © **800/661-6183** or 450/243-6183. Fax 450/243-0602. www.quebecweb.com/lakeview. 28 units. C$196–C$310 (US$126–US$200) double. Rates include breakfast and dinner. Packages available. AE, MC, V. 1 block south of the town hall. **Amenities:** Restaurant (Continental); bar; heated outdoor pool. *In room:* A/C, TV in most units.

SUTTON

A pleasant outing from Knowlton, or anywhere in the vicinity, Sutton (pop. 3,360) is a town with a number of promising cafes and the best bookstore in the region. This excellent bookstore, **The Book Nook,** at 14 rue Principale sud (© **450/538-2207**), is open 7 days a week. Nearby **Mont-Sutton** is known in summer for its 54km (33 miles) of hiking trails that link up with the Appalachian Trail, and in winter for its glade skiing. The surrounding country roads are popular with bikers. For more information, drop by the **Tourist Office of Sutton,** 11B rue Principale sud (© **800/565-8455** or 450/538-8455; www. sutton-info.qc.ca), opposite the bookstore.

MONT-ORFORD

Exit 115 north off the Autoroute leads into one of Québec's most popular provincial parks. From mid-September to mid-October, **Parc du Mont-Orford** blazes with autumn color. Visitors come to try the 18-hole golf course in summer; in winter, they visit for the more than 40km (25 miles) of ski trails and slopes, with a vertical drop of more than 488m (1,600 ft.), or for the extensive network of cross-country ski and snowshoe trails.

Mont-Orford is a veteran ski area compared to Bromont (see above) and has long provided slopes of choice for the moneyed families of the Cantons-de-l'Est and Montréal. It is composed of contiguous Mont Giroux, Mont Desrochers, and Mont Orford itself, the highest peak. Children enjoy special treatment with "Kinderski," where some 100 instructors conduct a ski and snowboard school and supervise a tube slide. Aprés-ski drinks, dinner, and entertainment are provided by the Slalom Pub.

The area's other ski resorts—Owl's Head and Mont-Sutton—are more family-oriented and less glitzy than Mont-Orford. They have banded together to offer a "multi-day ski" program enabling skiers to purchase all-inclusive 2- to 7-day tickets good at all three areas anytime. Prices range from C$68 to C$217 (US$44–US$140) for adults, C$53 to C$182 (US$34–US$117) for ages 14 to 23, C$40 to C$147 (US$26–US$95) for seniors and ages 6 to 13. Rental equipment is available.

Orford has another claim to fame in the **Centre d'Arts Orford,** 3165 chemin du Parc (© **800/567-6155** or 819/843-3981), set on a 89-hectare (222-acre) estate within the park and providing music classes for talented young musicians every summer. From early July to the middle of August, a series of more than 30 classical and chamber music concerts is given in connection with **Festival Orford.** Prices usually are C$12 to C$25 (US$7.75–US$16) for professional concerts, free for student performances. Concerts are held Thursday to Sunday. A complete luncheon is served outside following the Saturday concert. Visual-arts exhibitions at the center are open to the public, and walking trails connect it to a nearby campground.

Where to Stay

Manoir des Sables ★★   This attractive, thoroughly contemporary facility is one of the most complete resort hotels in the region, serving business groups, couples, families, golfers, skiers, skaters, fitness enthusiasts, tennis players, and kayakers. And, as the pitchmen say, that's not all! Add snowshoeing trails, snow-mobiling, toboggan rides, tube slides, fishing in the hotel's lake, and Saturday-night horse-drawn sleigh rides to the list of activities. Bedrooms have all the big-city gadgets and niceties, which is to be expected since the hotel began life

Doing a Sugar Shack Near Mont-Orford

For a purely Québec experience that shouldn't be missed, take Exit 106 off Autoroute 10. Turn right, then right again. In about 1km (⅔ mile), watch for the "Camping Normand" sign. Make a left turn on rue Georges Bonnallie. In about 5km (3 miles), there is a sign for **La Sucrerie des Normand,** 426 Georges Bonnallie, Easton (*Ⓒ* **450/297-2659**). Turn into the parking lot next to the long angled log-and-plank-sided building. This is a classic sugar shack, as that institution has evolved from the time when it was merely a place that processed the gathered sap from maple trees.

As you enter, the rendering room is to your right. Here the sap gathered from taps in more than 13,000 maple trees is boiled in a trough called the evaporator, then cooked further on a stove. Temperatures must be precise—216°F (102°C)—if the emerging syrup is too cold it might ferment and explode in the can; too hot, and crystals form. Lastly, the syrup is filtered and poured into cans. One popular sales device is to set up a long narrow tray of snow and pour a wriggly stream of syrup down the middle. This forms a sort of maple taffy, which is then rolled up on Popsicle sticks and eaten.

Over to your left is what happened when the producers realized that they drew audiences who wanted a wider experience. There is a full bar to one side and wooden tables next to a fireplace, the walls crowded with vintage radios, a sewing machine, apple corers, oxbows, snowshoes, and a moose head. Beyond that is a larger room with a dance floor and a stage for musicians, and finally a still-larger dining room with long plank tables.

as a Sheraton. All rooms have either one queen or two double beds and sitting areas. About half have fireplaces. The new Château section contains 24 upscale suites and its own lounge.

90 av. des Jardins, Orford, PQ J1X 6M6. *Ⓒ* **800/567-3514** or 819/847-4747. Fax 819/847-3519. www.hotel. manoirdessables.com. 141 units. C$150–C$325 (US$97–US$210) double. AE, DC, MC, V. Meal plans and other packages available. Take Exit 118 from Autoroute 10 and follow Rte. 141 north to the hotel, on the right. **Amenities:** 2 restaurants (International); bar; indoor and outdoor pools; golf course on property; 4 lit tennis courts; health club and spa; bike rental; children's programs; game room; secretarial services; limited room service; massage; babysitting; laundry service; dry cleaning. *In room:* A/C, TV, dataport, coffeemaker, hair dryer, iron.

MAGOG & LAC MEMPHREMAGOG

Orford is where people visit, but Magog (pop. 14,500) is where people live. As with countless other North American place names, Magog came by its handle through corruption of a Native Canadian word. The Abenaki name *Memrobagak* (Great Expanse of Water) somehow became Memphrémagog, which was eventually shortened to Magog (pronounced *May*-gog). The town is positioned at the northernmost end of Lac Memphrémagog (pronounced Mem-*phree*-maygog), *not* on Lac Magog, which is about 13km (8 miles) north of Magog. The lake spills across the U.S.-Canadian border into Vermont.

The proprietor speaks fluent English, although that isn't really necessary. There is no menu. Sit down at a table, and she just starts bringing food: crudités with a mustard/mayo dip, a bowl of thick pea soup, a towering loaf of fragrant bread, a plate with an omelet supported by sausage and ham slices, a bowl of home fries, pork rinds, baked beans, cole slaw, and a stack of pancakes topped with samples of four maple desserts. At the ready are preserves, pickles, and all the maple syrup you can ingest. You won't be considered a bad person if you can't finish it all; few diners can. The lineup is the same for lunch or dinner. It costs all of C$18 (US$11) per person, *including* tips and taxes. If you can't move afterward, they have four basic bedrooms for rent.

Meals are served February through April, and reservations are required. Sleigh rides can be arranged, they have a campground, and, when there's snow, mountain tube-sliding is on the docket. The basic products are available in several sizes and forms, primarily syrup and candy. Keep in mind that the best syrup is from the first run of sap and is clear and light in color. It gets darker as the weeks of the season proceed.

Sugar shacks usually call themselves *cabane à sucre* or *érablière*. Québéc Province has more than 400. While most restrict meal service to the sugaring season (spring), some provide food through the summer for tourists. Small directional signs are often positioned at roadside. A website concerned with sugar shacks is **www.erabliere.com**.

The helpful **Bureau d'Information Touristique Memphrémagog,** at 55 rue Cabana (via Rte. 112), Magog, PQ J1X 2C4 (② **800/267-2744** or 819/843-2744; fax 819/847-4036; www.tourisme-memphremagog.com), is open daily in summer 8:30am to 7:30pm, and in winter 10:30am to 6pm.

OUTDOOR ACTIVITIES & GREGORIAN CHANTS

Magog has a fully used waterfront, and in July each year the **Lac Memphrémagog International Swimming Marathon** (② **818/843-5000;** www.traversee-memphremagog.com) creates a big splash. Participants start out in Newport, Vermont, at 6am and swim 24 miles to Magog, arriving in mid-afternoon around 3:30 or 4pm. To experience the lake without such soggy exertion, take a 1¾-hour **lake cruise** aboard the *Aventure I* or *Aventure II* (② **819/843-8068;** www.croisiere-memphremagog.com). The cost is C$15 (US$9.70) for adults, C$7 (US$4.50) for children 11 and under; a daylong cruise is C$55 (US$36). The boats leave from Point Merry Park, the focal point for many of the town's outdoor activities. Cruises off-season depend upon demand, so call ahead.

Several firms rent sailboats, motorboats, kayaks, and windsurfers, among them **Boutique Nautique 30°,** 201 rue Merry sud (② **819/843-2102;** www.30degres.com); **Marina Le Merry Club,** 201 rue Merry sud (② **819/843-2728**); and **Voile Memphrémagog,** Plage des Cantons (② **819/847-3181**). And while you're on the water, scan the ripples for Memphre, the lake's own legendary sea creature, which supposedly surfaced for the first time in 1798. It will come as no surprise that other sightings have been claimed since then.

An 18.5km (11-mile) bike path links the lake with Mont-Orford; in winter it is transformed into a **cross-country ski trail,** and a 2.5km- (1½-mile-) long **skating rink** is created on the shores of the lake. Snowmobiling trails crisscross the region.

Other popular activities in the area include golf, tennis, and horseback riding. A **Grape Harvest Festival** is held over 4 days at the end of August and start of September.

Abbaye de Saint-Benoît-du-Lac   There's no mistaking the abbey, with its granite steeple that thrusts into the sky above the lake and with Owl's Head Mountain in the background. Although Saint-Benoît-du-Lac dates only from 1912, the serenity of the site is timeless. Some 40 monks help keep the art of Gregorian chant alive in their liturgy, which can be attended by outsiders. For the 45-minute service, walk to the rear of the abbey and down the stairs; follow signs for the *oratoire* and sit in back to avoid a lot of otherwise obligatory standing up and then sitting down. The abbey receives 7,000 pilgrims a year, most of them between the ages of 16 and 25. It maintains separate hostels for men (© **819/843-4080**) and women (© **819/843-2340**). You can find out more at www.st-benoit-du-lac.com. Make room reservations in advance, figuring about C$35 (US$23) per person.

A blue cheese known as L'Ermite, among Québec's most famous, is produced at the monastery, along with a creamy version and Swiss and cheddar types. They are on sale in the little shop, which also sells chocolate from Oka, honey, a nonalcoholic cider, and tapes of religious chants. Peek into the tiny stone chapel to the left at the entrance to the property, opposite the small cemetery. Visitors during the last 2 weeks of September or the first 2 weeks of October may want to help pick apples in the orchard.

Chemin Fisher. © **819/843-4080.** Free admission; donations accepted. Daily 5am–9pm; mass with Gregorian chant daily at 11am, vespers with Gregorian chant at 5pm (7pm Thurs). No vespers Tues July–Aug. Shop June–Oct Mon–Sat 9–10:45am and 11:45am–4:30pm; Nov–May Mon–Fri 9–10:45am and 1:30–4:30pm, Sat 9–10:45am and 11:45am–4:30pm. Driving west from Magog on Rte. 112, watch for the 1st road on the left on the far side of the lake; take Chemin Bolton est 19km (12 miles) south to the turnoff to the abbey.

Where to Stay

Lodging choices in Magog aren't beguiling. However, if you must spend the night here, there are a number of modest B&Bs, and three of them are conveniently located along the blocks of rue Merry nord, immediately north of its intersection with the main street, rue Principale. Otherwise, the recommendation here is to look for accommodations in one of the nearby towns described in this section.

GEORGEVILLE

Established in 1797 on the eastern shore of Lac Memphrémagog, this peaceful settlement was once a stop along the stagecoach route from Montréal to Brome, which was a 5-day trip at that time. Development has been scant. Today, the town has just enough buildings to shelter 988 residents, a general store, a little Anglican church, and a 9-hole golf course with views of the lake. It also contains actor Donald Sutherland's summer home.

The 22km (14-mile) drive along Route 247 south from Georgeville to Beebe Plain (see below) is pleasant rather than stunning. Owl's Head is the name of the prominent mountain off to the right.

Where to Stay & Dine

Auberge Georgeville 1889 ⍟   The owners continue to reinvigorate this 1889 inn, buffing its culinary image while perking up the six upstairs bedrooms and four suites with antiques and Laura Ashley designs. Suites have TV/VCRs. Plans are in the works for a new wing (scheduled to be finished at the end of 2002), expected to have 10 one-bedroom suites, a spa, and a 100-seat dining room.

All the sprucing up is secondary to the attention devoted to gastronomy. The five-course table d'hôte dinner varies according to seasonal availability and the chef-owner's whim, but he comes up with such innovative fare as an *amuse-bouche* smoked Arctic char and caribou mousse, and the flavors of subsequent dishes explode like little firecrackers on a string. His head-grazing cellar is stocked primarily with top French and California labels. Reservations are essential on weekends. The exterior paint job retains the house's traditional pink-and-white scheme, and there's a fancy new sign out front, so the inn is hard to miss. No smoking, and no jeans are allowed in the dining rooms. Lunch is served only to houseguests on request. A new wing scheduled for the end of 2002 will contain the dining room, a spa, and 10 more suites.

71 Chemin Channel, Georgeville, PQ J0B 1T0 (Rte. 247). ℂ **888/843-8686** or 819/843-8683. Fax 819/843-5045. www.fortune1000.ca/georgeville. 11 units. C$220–C$335 (US$142–US$216) double. Rates include full breakfast, afternoon tea, and dinner. AE, MC, V. Meal plans available. Take Rte. 247 16km (10 miles) south from Magog. **Amenities:** Restaurant (Contemporary French); golf nearby; free use of bikes; limited room service, massage; babysitting. *In room:* A/C.

LAKE MASSAWIPPI

Southeast of Magog, reachable by Routes 141 or 108, east of Autoroute 55, is Lake Massawippi, easily the most desirable resort area in the Cantons-de-l'Est. Set among rolling hills and fertile farm country, the 19km- (12-mile-) long lake, with its scalloped shoreline, was discovered in the early years of this century by people of wealth and power, many of whom were American Southerners trying to escape the sultry summers of Virginia and Georgia. (They came up by train and are said to have pulled down their window shades while they crossed through Yankee territory.) They built grand "cottages" on slopes in prime locations along the lakeshore, with enough bedrooms to house their extended families and friends for months at a time. Several of these have now been converted to inns. Boating, fishing, golf, and cross-country skiing are all readily available. For a few days' escape from work or intensive travel, it's difficult to do better than Lake Massawippi.

The jewel of Lake Massawippi is the town of **North Hatley** (pop. 704). Only half an hour from the United States border and 138km (85½ miles) from Montréal, the town has a river meandering through it that empties into the lake. Old photographs show flocks of people coursing along the one main village street. Apart from impressive sunsets over the lake, the town has a variety of lodgings and restaurants, shops, golf, a marina, and an unlabeled laundromat between the general store and the post office. Horse lovers will want to know about **Equitation Jacques Robidas** at 32 Chemin McFarland (ℂ **819/563-0166**). Guides lead trail rides through forest and meadow beside the Massawippi in summer, with rates from C$20 to C$25 (US$13–US$16) per hour. Buggy and winter sleigh rides are possibilities, and packages that include longer rides, meals, and vineyard visits are also available.

An English-language theater, the **Piggery,** on Route 108, a country road outside town (ℂ **819/842-2431**), presents plays of an often-experimental nature

Dragonwatch: 4bdrm, eat-in kit, frpl, lake vu

Rare is the frequent traveler who has alighted in yet another vivacious city or sensual island or serene mountaintop who has never uttered the words, "I could live here." It's the highest compliment, really.

People have been saying that about Lake Massawippi for at least a century or three, and not a few start checking the real estate listings hours after arrival. Pickings are slim, but those who want to test the waters, for a month or a summer, say, can ferret out a few rental properties. Here's one:

"Dragonwatch" is a three-story house on the property of Stephen J. Stafford, owner of Manoir Hovey, and it is the "only lakeside cottage for rent by the week" in the area, he says. Think Aunt Emma's farmhouse, permeated with old-shoe comforts like rag rugs on wood floors, and rustic sociability. It sleeps eight, two of them in a four-poster queen. The oversized, fully-outfitted kitchen is more than large enough for cooking and dining, and there's a cable TV with VCR to slow down the kids.

The facilities of the inn are available to renters, including the tennis court, and the hill pitches down from the deck to a boathouse with kayaks and canoes and a private sandy beach. The water hits 85° (29°C) in summer. Price?

Not bad at all—from C$2,500 to C$3,700 a week (US$1,600–US$2,390), from shoulder to high season.

You could live there.

during the summer. For 10 Sundays from mid-April to mid-June, **Le Festival du Lac Massawippi** (© 819/823-7810) brings recitals by soloists and groups playing jazz, ethnic, and new music to North Hatley at the Ste-Elisabeth Church on Chemin Capelton.

Where to Stay

Le Tricorne   While the core of the main house is 125 years old, it looks as if it were erected only a few years ago. The exterior is shocking pink and white, the interior decked out in perfect *Good Housekeeping* manner, with lots of duck decoys and tartans. That decorative scheme is quite different from the one that informs the brand-new structure 50 yards up the hill. The five bedrooms there are much larger and have a more sophisticated corporate style. Eight rooms have fireplaces, 10 have Jacuzzis. No phones or TVs, but those are available in common rooms. There are spectacular views of Lake Massawippi from the property.

50 Chemin Gosselin, North Hatley, PQ J0B 2C0. © **819/842-4522.** Fax 819/842-2692. www.manoirletricorne.com. 17 units. C$125–C$260 (US$81–US$167) double. Rates include full breakfast. AE, MC, V. Take Rte. 108 west out of North Hatley and follow the signs. Children over 8 years are welcome. **Amenities:** Heated outdoor pool; golf nearby. *In room:* A/C, no phone.

Where to Stay & Dine

Auberge Hatley ✦✦✦   This acclaimed gastronomic resort occupies a hillside above the lake. It exudes a sense of well-being, felt as soon as you enter the front door. More than half the rooms have Jacuzzis and/or fireplaces. Abundant antiques, many of them sizeable Quebecois country pieces, are joined by attractive reproductions. But there's no uncertainty where owners Liliane and Robert Gagnon place their priorities: the pleasures of the table. Reserve one—set with Rosenthal china, thin-stemmed glasses, fresh flowers, and candles—overlooking the lake. It's a soothing environment, since dinner can easily extend over 3 hours. Updated but essentially classical French techniques are applied to such ingredients as salmon, red deer, halibut, partridge, bison, and wild boar. Most herbs, edible flowers, and some vegetables come from the Gagnons' hydroponic farm; the ducks and pheasants from their 40-hectare (100-acre) game island. A particular treat is the meal-ending selection of cheeses, half French, half Quebecois, served with the waiter's careful description and not a little ceremony. They've built a new wine cellar and expanded their already prodigious wine holdings to more than 10,000 bottles, still providing interesting wines by the glass and enough half bottles to satisfy lighter imbibers. Table d'hôte menus start at C$55 (US$35) and top out with the gastronomic spectacular at C$105 (US$68), and are worth every last loonie. This dining room is second to none in all Québec, and its equals can be counted on one hand.

325 rue Virgin (P.O. Box 330), North Hatley, PQ J0B 2C0. (C) **819/842-2451**. Fax 819/842-2907. www.north hatley.com. 25 units. C$276–C$540 (US$178–US$348) double. Rates include breakfast, dinner, and gratuities. Packages available. AE, MC, V. Closed 2 weeks in Jan. Take Exit 29 from Autoroute 55 and follow Rte. 108 east, watching for signs. **Amenities:** Restaurant (Contemporary French); bar; heated outdoor pool; golf nearby; in-room massage. *In room:* A/C, TV, hair dryer.

Auberge Ripplecove ★★   A warm welcome is extended by the staff of this handsome inn, and impeccable housekeeping standards are observed throughout. The core structure dates from 1945, but subsequent expansions have added rooms, suites, and cottages. About half the rooms have gas fireplaces, balconies, and Jacuzzis, and the suites add kitchenettes and stocked minibars to the list of amenities. Check out the elegant lobby lounge and its ornate 4.2m- (14-ft.-) high breakfront built in 1880. The 4.8-hectare (12-acre) property beside Lake Massawippi has a private beach, and instruction and equipment are available for sailing, sailboarding, water-skiing, canoeing, kayaking, and cross-country skiing. The inn's award-winning lakeside restaurant fills up most nights in season with diners drawn to the kitchen's reputation for creativity. "Caribou perfumed with essence of black spruce" or "seafood navarin nesting in lemongrass, garnished with caramelized endives," anyone? Innkeeper Jeffrey Stafford is the brother of the owner of Manoir Hovey in North Hatley. Taste and energy run in the family.

700 chemin Ripplecove (P.O. Box 26), Ayer's Cliff, PQ J0B 1C0. (C) **800/668-4296** or 819/838-4296. Fax 819/838-5541. www.ripplecove.com. 25 units. C$270–C$430 (US$174–US$310) double; C$440–C$650 (US$284–US$420) suite and cottage for 2. Rates include breakfast and dinner, gratuities, and the use of most recreational facilities. AE, MC, V. Take Rte. 55 to Exit 21; follow Rte. 141 east, watching for signs. **Amenities:** Restaurant (Contemporary French); pub; heated outdoor pool; golf nearby; tennis court; free watersports equipment; free bikes; chidren's programs; concierge; secretarial services; limited room service; in-room massage; babysitting; laundry service; dry cleaning. *In room:* A/C, TV, dataport, coffeemaker, hair dryer, iron.

Manoir Hovey ★★★   Named for Capt. Ebenezer Hovey, a Connecticut Yankee who came upon Lake Massawippi in 1793, this columned manor was built in 1899. Encompassing 8 hectares (20 acres) and 488m (1,600 ft.) of lakefront property, it's one of eastern Canada's most complete resort inns. If Auberge Hatley (above) has the edge in wine and cuisine, Manoir Hovey trumps with its sumptuously appointed rooms, especially in the 25 that were accorded extensive renovations in recent months and the two lavishly rustic suites in a separate building above the main inn. All have been rendered even more desirable than before—ravishingly luxurious, in some cases—with fireplaces, balconies, and Jacuzzi baths. The library lounge is as beckoning a room as can be found, with floor-to-ceiling bookshelves, deep chairs and sofas, and a stone fireplace, chess sets and the daily newspapers laid out. Free touring bikes, two beaches, and the use of canoes, kayaks, and rowboats add to the appeal. Water-skiing is available at extra charge. In winter, they push a heated cabin out onto the lake for ice fishing. The menu in the paneled dining room features fresh herbs, vegetables, and edible flowers from the kitchen garden. Dishes are fragrant and full-bodied, in attractive presentations. Take brandy in the atmospheric pub. Steve and Kathy Stafford are the gracious hosts.

Chemin Hovey (P.O. Box 60), North Hatley, PQ J0B 2C0. ✆ **800/661-2421** or 819/842-2421. Fax 819/842-2248. www.manoirhovey.com. 40 units. C$200–C$570 (US$129–US$368) double. Rates include full breakfast, dinner, tax, gratuities, and use of most recreational facilities. Packages available. AE, DC, MC, V. Take Exit 29 off Autoroute 55 and follow Rte. 108 east, watching for signs. **Amenities:** Restaurant (Contemporary French); bar; heated outdoor pool; golf nearby; lighted tennis court; exercise room; concierge; limited room service; massage; dry cleaning. *In room:* A/C, TV, coffeemaker, hair dryer.

Where to Dine

Pilsen INTERNATIONAL   For food less grand and less expensive than that at the three inns listed above, all drives through North Hatley pass this pub and restaurant in the center of town. There's a terrace in front and a narrow deck overhanging the river that feeds the lake. The place fills up quickly on warm days, the better to watch boats setting out or returning. Patrons snaffle up renditions of nachos and burgers, pastas, and lobster bisque. Vegetarian plates are available. There's an extensive choice of beers, including local microbrews Massawippi Blonde and Townships Pale Ale. Park behind the restaurant.

55 rue Principale. ✆ **819/842-2971.** Reservations recommended on weekends. Main courses C$7–C$23 (US$4.50–US$15). AE, MC, V. Daily 11:30am–10:30pm (closed Mon–Tues late Oct to late Apr). The bar stays open until 3am Fri–Sat.

STANSTEAD PLAIN, ROCK ISLAND & BEEBE PLAIN

For a modestly diverting half-day trip from North Hatley, follow Route 143 as far south as possible without actually crossing into the United States, and turn west to explore the three border villages that comprise the town of Stanstead. If you cross the border accidentally, which is easy to do, just report to the inspectors and come back across. There may not even be anyone on duty.

Stanstead (pop. 3,160) is some 49km (30 miles) south of North Hatley and only 15km (9 miles) north of Newport, Vermont. With a modest reputation for distinctive architecture, Stanstead offers the **Centenary United Church,** with a clock face that bears the name of the person who donated the granite to build the church; the **Victorian Butler House** (1866), at 10 rue Dufferin; and the 1859 **Musée Colby-Curtis,** 35 rue Dufferin (✆ **819/876-7322**), a house museum furnished accurately to the period, with two rooms for changing exhibits of such collections as antique dolls, glassware, and 19th-century tools and furnishings. Tours are given by bilingual guides. It's open mid-June to mid-September Tuesday through Sunday 10am to 5pm; the rest of the year Tuesday through Friday 10am to noon and 1 to 5pm, Saturday and Sunday 12:30 to 4:30pm. Admission is C$4 (US$2.60) for adults, C$2 (US$1.30) for seniors and students, free for kids under age six.

In 1995, Stanstead incorporated the village of **Rock Island,** which is the commercial center of the area. Collectors of geographical oddities will love the **Haskell Opera House.** Dating from 1904, it's literally and logistically half

Canadian and half American: the stage and performers are in Canada, and the audience is in the United States.

Also gathered into the township was **Beebe Plain,** west of Rock Island, a center for quarrying granite. What makes this town notable is 1km- (½-mile-) long **Canusa Street.** The north side is in Canada, the south side in the United States—thus its name, CAN-USA. Check the car license plates on either side. Here, it's long distance to call a neighbor across the street, and while they're free to walk across the street for a visit, they are expected, at least technically, to report to the authorities if they decide to drive.

11

Getting to Know Québec City

Québec City is the soul of New France. It was the first significant settlement in Canada, and today it is the capital of politically prickly Québec, a province larger than Alaska. The old city, a tumble of slate-roofed granite houses clustered around the dominating Château Frontenac, is a haunting evocation of a coastal town in the motherland, as romantic as any on the continent. The St. Lawrence makes a majestic sweep beneath the palisades on which the capital stands, as gray as gunmetal under dark skies, but silvered by sunlight when the clouds pass. Because of its history, beauty, and unique stature as the only walled city north of Mexico, the historic district of Québec was named a UNESCO World Heritage site in 1985—the only area so designated in North America.

Québec City is almost entirely French in feeling, in spirit, and in language; 95% of the population is Francophone. But many of its 167,000 citizens speak some English, especially those who work in hotels, restaurants, and shops where they deal with Anglophones every day. Québec City and adjoining Sainte-Foy are also college towns, and thousands of resident young people study English as a second language. So although it is often more difficult in Québec City than in Montréal to understand and be understood, the average Quebecois goes out of his or her way to communicate—in halting English, sign language, simplified French, or a combination of all three. Most of the Quebecois are an uncommonly gracious lot, and it is a pleasure to spend time in their company and in their city.

In the following chapters are tips on where to stay, where to dine, and what to do in the city itself. After exploring Québec City, consider such excursions as a day trip around the Ile d'Orléans, an agricultural and resort island within sight of the Château Frontenac, extended, perhaps, by a drive along the northern coast past the shrine of Ste-Anne-de-Beaupré to the provincial park and ski resort at Mont Ste-Anne, and on to Charlevoix and the dramatic Saguenay River, where whales come to play.

1 Orientation

Almost all of a visit to Québec can be spent in the old city, because many hotels and lodging places, restaurants, and tourist-oriented services are based there. The colonial city was first built right down by the St. Lawrence at the foot of rearing Cap Diamant (Cape Diamond). It was here that the earliest merchants, traders, and boatmen earned their livelihoods; but due to unfriendly fire from the British and Amerindians in the 1700s, this Basse-Ville (Lower Town) became primarily a wharf and warehouse area after residents moved to safer houses atop the steep cliffs that form the rim of Cap Diamant. That trend is being reversed of late, with several new *auberges* (inns), small hotels, and many attractive bistros and shops bringing new life to the area.

Haute-Ville, or Upper Town, the Quebecois later discovered, was not immune to cannon fire either, as the British General Wolfe was to prove. Nevertheless, the division into Upper and Lower Towns persisted for obvious topographical reasons. The Upper Town remains enclosed by fortification walls, and several ramp-like streets and a cliff-side elevator *(funiculaire)* connect it to the Lower Town.

ARRIVING

BY PLANE   **Jean-Lesage International Airport** (✆ **418/640-2700;** www. aeroportdequebec.com) is small, despite the grand name. Bus service is no longer available between the airport and the city. A taxi to downtown Québec City is a fixed-rate C$25 (US$16).

BY TRAIN   The train station in Québec City, **Gare du Palais,** 450 rue de la Gare-du-Palais (✆ **418/692-3940**), was designed by Bruce Price, who was also responsible for the fabled Château Frontenac. Handsome though it is, the Lower Town location isn't central. Plan on a moderately strenuous uphill hike or a C$6 to C$8 (US$3.85–US$5.15) cab ride to the Upper Town. That's per trip, incidentally, not per passenger, as an occasional cabbie may pretend.

BY BUS   The bus station, **Gare d'Autobus de la Vieille Capitale,** at 320 rue Abraham-Martin (✆ **418/525-3000**), is near the train station. As from the train station, it is an uphill climb or quick cab ride to Château Frontenac and the Upper Town. A taxi should cost about the same as from the train station.

BY CAR   From New York City, follow I-87 to Autoroute 15 to Montréal, picking up Autoroute 20 to Québec City. Take 73 nord across the Pont Pierre-Laporte and exit onto boulevard Champlain immediately after crossing the bridge. This skirts the city at river level. Turn left at Parc des Champs-de-Bataille (Battlefields Park) and right onto the Grande-Allée. Alternatively, take Autoroute 40 from Montréal, which follows the north shore of the St. Lawrence. That trip takes about 2½ hours.

From Boston, take I-89 to I-93 to I-91 in Montpelier, Vermont, which connects with Autoroute 55 in Québec to link up with Autoroute 20. Or follow I-90 up the Atlantic coast, through Portland, Maine, to Route 201 west of Bangor, then Autoroute 173 to Lévis. A car-ferry there, **Traverse Québec-Lévis** (✆ **418/644-3704**), provides a 10-minute ride across the St. Lawrence River. Although the schedule varies substantially according to time of day, week, and season, the ferry leaves at least every hour (more often during rush hours) from 6am to 2am. One way, it costs C$5.10 or C$5.60 (US$3.30 or US$3.60) for the car, C$8.50 or $C9.85 (US$5.50 or US$6.35) for up to six passengers. Passengers without vehicles pay C$2 or $C2.50 (US$1.30 or US$1.60) for ages 12 to 64, C$1.40 or C$1.75 (US90¢ or US$1.15) for ages 5 to 11, C$1.80 or C$2.25 (US$1.15 or US$1.45) for each passenger over 65.

VISITOR INFORMATION

The Greater Québec Area Tourism and Convention Bureau operates two useful provincial information centers in and near the city. One has moved from its former location on rue d'Auteuil to the larger Discovery Pavilion at 835 av. Wilfrid-Laurier (✆ **418/649-2608**), bordering the Plaines d'Abraham, and the other is in suburban Ste-Foy, at 3300 av. des Hôtels (✆ **418/651-2882**). They have rack after rack of brochures and attendants who can answer questions and make hotel reservations. Both offices are open daily 8:30am to 7pm from June 24 to Thanksgiving Day, the rest of the year 9am to 5pm Monday through Saturday, 10am to 4pm Sunday.

The Québec Government's tourism department operates an **Infotouriste de Québec** office on place d'Armes, down the hill from the Château Frontenac, at 12 rue Ste-Anne (© **514/873-2015,** or 800/363-7777 from other parts of Québec, Canada, and the U.S.). It's open from 9:30am to 5pm late June to early September, and from 10am to 5pm the rest of the year. The office has many brochures, information about cruise and bus tour operators, a souvenir shop, a 24-hour ATM *(guichet automatique),* a currency-exchange office, and a free lodging reservation service.

Parks Canada operates an information kiosk in front of the Château Frontenac; it's open daily 9am to noon and 1 to 5pm. From June to August, bilingual university students on motorbikes are paid to station themselves near tourist sites in the Upper and Lower Towns to answer the questions of visitors. Spot them by the flags on the backs of their bikes. For additional information, log on to **www.quebecregion.com**.

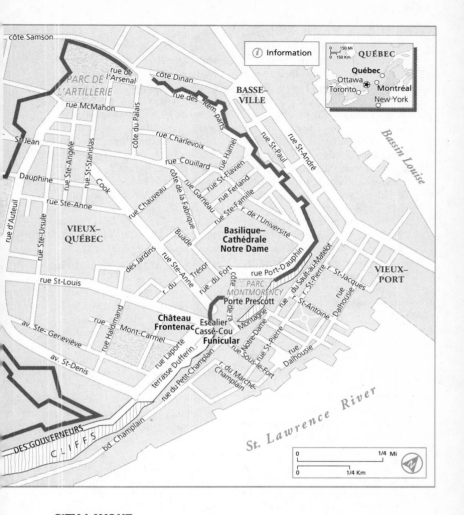

CITY LAYOUT

MAIN AVENUES & STREETS Within the walls of the **Haute-Ville** (Upper Town), the principal streets are rues St-Louis (which becomes the Grande-Allée outside the city walls), Ste-Anne, and St-Jean, and the pedestrians-only Terrasse Dufferin, which overlooks the river in front of the Château Frontenac. In the **Basse-Ville** (Lower Town), major streets are St-Pierre, Dalhousie, St-Paul, and, parallel to St-Paul, St-André. There are good maps of the Upper and Lower Towns and the metropolitan area available at any tourist office.

FINDING AN ADDRESS If it were larger, the historic district, with its winding and plunging streets, might be confusing to negotiate. However, it's very compact, so most visitors have little difficulty finding their way around. Most streets are only a few blocks long, so when the name of the street is known, it is fairly easy to find a specific address.

THE NEIGHBORHOODS IN BRIEF

HAUTE-VILLE The Upper Town, surrounded by thick ramparts, occupies the crest of Cap Diamant and overlooks the Fleuve Saint-Laurent (St. Lawrence River). It includes many of the sites for which the city is famous, among them the Château Frontenac, Place d'Armes, Basilica of Notre-Dame, Québec Seminary and Museum, and the Terrasse Dufferin. At a higher elevation, to the south of the Château, is the Citadel, a partially star-shaped fortress begun by the French in the 18th century and augmented often by the English well into the 19th century. Since most buildings are at least 100 years old, made of granite in similar styles, the Haute-Ville is visually harmonious, with few jarring modern intrusions. When they added a new wing to the château a few years ago, they modeled it after the original—standing policy here. The Terrasse Dufferin is a pedestrian promenade that attracts crowds in all seasons for its magnificent views of the river and the land to the south, ferries gliding back and forth, cruise ships, and Great Lakes freighters putting in at the harbor below.

BASSE-VILLE The Lower Town encompasses the restored Quartier du Petit-Champlain, including pedestrian-only rue du Petit-Champlain; Place Royale and the small Notre-Dame-des-Victoires church; and, nearby, the impressive Museum of Civilization, a highlight of any visit. Basse is linked to Haute by the funicular on Terrasse Dufferin and by several streets and stairways, including one near the entrance to the funicular. Petit-Champlain is undeniably touristy, but not unpleasantly so: T-shirt vendors have been held in check, though hardly banned. It contains several agreeable cafes and shops. Restored Place Royale is perhaps the most attractive of the city's many squares, upper or lower.

GRANDE-ALLEE This boulevard is the western extension of rue St-Louis, from the St-Louis Gate in the fortified walls to avenue Taché. It passes the stately Parliament building, in front of which the Winter Carnival takes place every year (the ice sculptures are installed across the street), as well as the numerous terraced bars and restaurants that line both sides from rue de la Chevrotière to rue de Claire-Fontaine. Later, it skirts the Musée des Beaux-Arts and the Plains of Abraham, where one of the most important battles in the history of North America took place between the French and the British for control of the city. The city's large contemporary hotels are also on or near the Grande-Allée.

2 Getting Around

Once you're within or near the walls of the Haute-Ville, virtually no place of interest, hotel, or restaurant is beyond walking distance. In bad weather, or when you're traversing between opposite ends of Lower and Upper Towns, a taxi might be necessary, but in general, walking is the best way to explore the city.

BY BUS

Local buses run quite often and charge C$2.25 (US$1.45) in exact change; tickets purchased in a *dépanneur* (convenience store) cost C$1.90 (US$1.25). Discounts are available for seniors and students. Bus no. 7 travels up and down rue St-Jean; no. 11 shuttles along Grande-Allée/rue St-Louis and, along with nos. 7

and 8, also goes well into suburban Ste-Foy, for those who want to visit the shopping centers there.

BY FUNICULAR

Although there are streets and stairs between the Château Frontenac on the top of the cliff and Place Royale in the Lower Town, there is also a funicular, which has long operated along an inclined 63m (210-ft.) track between the Terrasse Dufferin and the Quartier du Petit-Champlain. It was closed for a couple of years due to a fatal accident in 1996. Repaired now—although subject to occasional stoppages—the **upper station** is near the front of the Château Frontenac and Place d'Armes, while the **lower station** is actually inside the Maison Louis-Jolliet, on rue du Petit-Champlain. It runs year-round daily from early morning until 11:30pm. Wheelchairs are accommodated. The one-way fare is C$1.50 (US95¢).

BY TAXI

Taxis are everywhere, cruising and parked in front of the big hotels and in some of the larger squares of the Upper Town. In theory, they can be hailed, but they are best obtained by locating one of their stands, as in the Place d'Armes or in front of the Hôtel-de-Ville (City Hall). Restaurant managers and hotel bell captains will also summon them. Fares are the same as in Montréal, meaning they're somewhat expensive, given the short distances of most rides. The starting rate is C$2.50 (US$1.60), each kilometer costs C$1.20 (US80¢), and each minute when stopped costs another C45¢ (US30¢). Tip about 10% to 15%. A taxi from the train station to one of the big hotels is about C$6 to C$8 (US$3.85–US$5.15) plus tip. To call a cab, try **Taxi Coop** (© 418/525-5191) or **Taxi Québec** (© 418/525-8123).

BY CAR

See "By Car" under "Getting Around," in chapter 3, for information on gasoline and driving rules in Canada.

RENTALS   Car-rental companies include **Avis,** at the airport (© 800/879-2847 or 418/872-2861) and in the city (© 418/523-1075); **Budget,** at the airport (© 800/268-8900 or 418/872-9885) and in the city (© 418/687-4220); **Hertz Canada,** at the airport (© 800/654-3131 or 418/871-1571) and in the city (© 418/697-4949); **Thrifty,** at the airport (© 800/367-2277 or 418/877-2870) and in the city (© 418/648-7766); and **Tilden National,** at the airport (© 418/871-1224) and in the city (© 418/692-1727).

PARKING   On-street parking is very difficult in the cramped quarters of old Québec City. When you find a rare space on the street, be sure to check the signs for the hours when parking is permissible. When meters are in place, the charge is C25¢ (US15¢) per 15 minutes up to 120 minutes. Metered spots are free on Sundays, before 9am and after 6pm Monday through Wednesday and on Saturday, and before 9am and after 9pm Thursday and Friday.

Many of the smaller hotels have special arrangements with local garages, resulting in discounts for their guests of three or four dollars less per day than the usual C$10 (US$6.45) a day or more. Check at the hotel first before parking in a lot or garage.

If a particular hotel or auberge doesn't have access to a garage or lot, plenty are available, clearly marked on the foldout city map available at tourist offices. Several convenient ones include the one next to the Hôtel-de-Ville (City Hall), where parking is free in the evening and on weekends; Complexe G, off the Grande-Allée on rue St-Cyrille, with twice-daily in-and-out privileges at no extra charge; and in the Lower Town across the street from the Musée de la Civilisation, on rue Dalhousie, where discounts are often offered on weekends.

BY BICYCLE

Given the hilly topography of the Upper Town, cycling isn't a particularly attractive option for most. But pedal and motorized bicycles are available at a shop in the flatter Lower Town. Bikes are about C$10 (US$6.45) an hour or C$20 (US$13) for 12 hours. The shop, **Cyclo Services,** 160 quai Saint-André (© **418/692-4052;** www.cyclo.services.qc.ca), also rents tandems, child trailers, and in-line skates, and it's open daily throughout the year. Up in the Haute-Ville, near rue St-Jean, is **Vélo Passe-Sport Plein Air,** at 22 côte du Palais (© **418/692-3643;** www.velopasse-sport.com). They rent bikes and scooters in summer, skis and snowshoes in winter. Prices are similar.

 FAST FACTS: **Québec City**

American Express There is no office right in town, but for lost traveler's checks or credit cards, call © **418/692-0997.** American Express keeps a customer-service desk in two shopping centers in Ste-Foy, a bus or taxi ride away: Les Galeries de la Capitale, 5401 bd. des Galeries (© **418/627-2580);** and Place Laurier, 2740 bd. Laurier (© **418/658-8820).**

Babysitters Check at the hotel concierge or front desk.

Business Hours Banks are open from 10am to 3pm, with most also having hours on Thursday and Friday evenings. Several banks have Saturday hours, but the ones that do are mostly located outside of the Old Town. Most stores are open Monday through Wednesday from 9 or 10am to 6pm, Thursday and/or Friday from 9am to 9pm, and Saturday from 9am to 5pm. Many stores are now also open on Sunday from noon to 5pm.

Consulate The U.S. Consulate is near the Château Frontenac, facing Jardin des Gouverneurs at 2 place Terrasse-Dufferin (© **418/692-2095).**

Currency Exchange Conveniently located near the Château Frontenac, the Bureau de Change at 19 rue Ste-Anne and rue des Jardins is open Monday, Tuesday, and Friday from 10am to 3pm, and Wednesday and Thursday from 10am to 6pm. On weekends, it's possible to change money in hotels and shops, but you'll get an equal or better rate at an ATM, such as the one at the corner of rues Ste-Anne and des Jardins.

Dentists Call © **418/653-5412** any day or © **418/524-2444** Monday through Saturday. Both numbers are hot lines that refer callers to available dentists.

Doctors For emergency treatment, call **Info-Santé** (© **418/648-2626)** 24 hours a day, or the **Hôtel-Dieu de Québec** hospital emergency room (© **418/691-5042).** Call © **911** for an ambulance.

Drugstores **Caron & Bernier,** in the Upper Town, 38 Côte du Palais (at rue Charlevoix; © **418/692-4252),** is open 8:15am to 8pm Monday through Friday, and 9am to 3pm on Saturday. In an emergency, it's necessary to travel to the suburbs to **Pharmacie Brunet,** in Les Galeries Charlesbourg, 4250

Première Ave. (1ère or First Ave.), in Charlesbourg (© **418/623-1571**), open 24 hours, 7 days.

Electricity What works in the United States works in Québec.

Emergencies For police or ambulance, call © **911**. Marine Search and Rescue (Canadian Coast Guard), 24 hours a day, © **418/648-3599** (Greater Québec area) or © 800/463-4393 (St. Lawrence River). Poison Control Center, © **800/463-5060** or 418/656-8090.

Liquor & Wine A supermarket-sized **Société des Alcools** store is located at 1059 av. Cartier. Wine and beer can be bought in grocery stores and supermarkets. The legal drinking age in the province is 18.

Mail All mail posted in Canada must bear Canadian stamps. That might seem painfully obvious, but apparently large numbers of visitors use stamps from their home countries, especially the United States.

Newspapers & Magazines Major Canadian and American English-language newspapers and magazines are available in the newsstands of the large hotels, at vending machines on tourist corners in the old town, and at **Maison de la Presse Internationale,** at 1050 rue St-Jean. The leading French-language newspapers are *Le Soleil* and *Le Journal de Québec.*

Pets For emergency pet illnesses or injuries, call © **418/872-5355** 24 hours a day. Pet owners must by law pick up after their animals, and animals must be kept on leashes.

Police For the Québec City police, call © **911**. For the Sûreté du Québec, comparable to the state police or highway patrol, call © **800/461-2131**.

Post Office The main post office *(bureau de poste)* is in the Lower Town, at 300 rue St-Paul near rue Abraham-Martin, not far from Carré Parent (Parent Square) by the port (© **418/694-6175**). Hours are 8am to 5:45pm Monday through Friday. A convenient branch in the Upper Town, half a block down the hill from the Château Frontenac at 3 rue Buade (© **418/694-6102**), keeps the same hours.

Safety Canadian cities are far safer than most of their U.S. counterparts. Still, tourists are particular targets of street criminals, so the usual caveats pertain. Avoid leaving possessions in plain view in your car and stay aware of the behavior of people in your vicinity.

Taxes Most goods and services in Canada are taxed 7% by the federal government. On top of that, the province of Québec has an additional 7.5% tax on goods and services, including those provided by hotels. In Québec, the federal tax appears on the bill as the TPS, and the provincial tax is known as the TVQ. Tourists may receive a rebate on both the federal and provincial tax on items they have purchased but not used in Québec, as well as on lodging. To take advantage of this refund, request the necessary forms at duty-free shops and hotels, and submit them, with the original receipts, within a year of the purchase. Contact the Canadian consulate or Québec tourism office for up-to-the-minute information about taxes.

Telephones The telephone system, operated by Bell Canada, closely resembles the American model. All operators (dial © **00** to get one) speak French and English, and respond in the appropriate language as soon as callers speak to them. Pay phones in Québec require C25¢ (US20¢) for a 3-minute local call. Directory information calls (dial ℂ 411) are free of charge. Both local and long-distance calls usually cost more from hotels—sometimes a lot more, so check. Directories *(annuaires des téléphones)* come in White Pages (residential) and Yellow Pages (commercial).

Time Québec City is on eastern time.

Tipping Waiters, waitresses, and cabbies should be given a 10% to 18% tip, depending upon the quality of the establishment and the service they provide. Bellhops usually get C$1 (US65¢) per bag, slightly more if the bags are heavy or must be carried a long distance. The doorman who hails a cab deserves some coins, up to C$1 (US65¢). Many hotel guests leave C$1 (US65¢) per night for the chambermaid.

Transit Information Call ℂ 418/627-2511 for the transit authority.

Useful Telephone Numbers For Alcoholics Anonymous, call ℂ 418/529-0015, daily 8am to midnight. For Health Info, a 24-hour hot line answered by nurses, call ℂ 418/648-2626. For Tel-Aide, for emotional distress including anxiety and depression, call ℂ 418/686-2433. For information about tides, call ℂ 418/648-7293, 24 hours daily.

12

Where to Stay in Québec City

Staying in one of the small hotels or inns within the walls of the Upper Town can be one of Québec City's memorable experiences. That isn't a guarantee, however, that it will be enjoyable. Standards of comfort, amenities, and prices fluctuate so wildly from one small hotel to another—even within a single establishment—that it is wise to shop around and examine any rooms offered before registering. From rooms with private bathrooms, minibars, cable TVs, and Internet connections, to walk-up budget accommodations with linoleum floors and toilets down the hall, Québec City has a wide enough variety of lodgings to suit most tastes and wallets.

If cost is a prime consideration, note that prices drop significantly from November through April, except for such events as the Winter Festival. If you prefer the conveniences of large chain hotels and the Fairmont Le Château Frontenac is fully booked, you can go outside the ancient walls to the newer part of town. The handful of high-rise hotels out there are within walking distance of the attractions in the old city, or are only a quick bus or taxi ride away. In recent years, a clutch of new boutique hotels and small inns has greatly enhanced the lodging stock.

As a rule, the prices given in the listings below are rack rates. That means you'll rarely, if ever, have to pay that much, unless it's the middle of Winter Carnival and everything else is booked. The higher rates given apply during the warmer months, in the Christmas season, and during the Winter Carnival in February. The cheapest rooms are usually found in smaller establishments, typically converted residences or lodgings carved out of several row houses. Often family-run, they offer fewer of the usual electronic gadgets—air-conditioning and TVs are far from standard at this level—and may have four or five floors, but not have an elevator. In the budget category, even with an advance reservation, always ask to see two or three rooms before making a choice. Unless otherwise noted, all rooms in the lodgings listed below have private bathrooms—*en suite,* as they say in Canada.

Similar in atmosphere and price band to these small hotels are the more than 30 bed-and-breakfasts in and around Vieux-Québec. With rates in the C$75 to C$100 (US$48– US$65) range, they don't represent substantial savings over the small hotels.

They do, however, often provide an opportunity to get to know Quebecois more intimately. When calling to make arrangements, be very clear about your needs and requirements. A deposit is typically required, and minimum stays of 2 nights are common. Credit cards may not be accepted. A very useful *Accommodation Guide,* revised annually, is available at the tourist offices. It lists every member of the Greater Québec Area Tourism and Convention Bureau, from B&Bs to five-star hotels, providing details about number of rooms, prices, and facilities.

Best Hotel Bets

For a roundup of my favorite Québec City hotels, see chapter 1.

1 Haute-Ville (Upper Town)

VERY EXPENSIVE

Fairmont Le Château Frontenac ★★★ *Kids*   Québec City's magical "castle" turned 100 years old in 1993. To celebrate, the management added a new 66-room wing, and because the hotel serves as the very symbol of the city, care was taken to replicate the original architectural style throughout. The hotel has hosted Queen Elizabeth and Prince Philip, and during World War II, Winston Churchill and Franklin D. Roosevelt had the entire place to themselves for a conference. It was built in phases, following the landline, so the wide halls take crooked paths. The highly variable room prices depend on size, location, view or lack of one, and on how recently it was renovated. That makes the rates given below no better than a very rough guide, because day of the week, time of the year, and even the weather, if it has influenced bookings, can determine the range of prices at which the rooms are offered. The casual Café de la Terrasse has dancing on Saturday nights. Two bars overlook the Terrasse Dufferin. If you have occasion to use the concierges, you are likely to be delighted with the experience.

1 rue des Carrières (at rue St-Louis), Québec City, PQ G1R 4P5. © 800/828-7447 or 418/692-3861. Fax 418/ 692-1751. www.cphotels.ca. 618 units. Mid-May to mid-Oct C$409–C$759 (US$264–US$490) double; mid-Oct to mid-May C$210–C$512 (US$135–US$330) double; C$559–C$975 (US$360–US$629) suite year-round. AE, DC, DISC, MC, V. Valet parking C$20 (US$13) per day. **Amenities:** 2 restaurants (International); 2 bars; new indoor pool and kiddie pool; large health club w/ Jacuzzi and sauna; children's programs; video arcade; concierge; car-rental desk; courtesy limo; business center; shopping arcade; limited room service; in-room massage; babysitting; laundry service; same-day dry cleaning; executive floors. *In room:* A/C, TV w/pay movies, dataport, minibar, coffeemaker, hair dryer, iron.

EXPENSIVE

Manoir Victoria ★   The sprawling lobby isn't especially beguiling, but there are two serviceable restaurants on the premises, and the proximity to the St-Jean restaurant and bar scene is a plus for many. An added extra is the indoor pool, rare in this city. The very ordinary hotel sprawls all the way from the main entrance on Côte de Palais to adjacent St-Jean, zigzagging around a couple of stores. A long staircase reaches the lobby, but elevators make the trip to most of the rooms. All 145 rooms were redecorated recently.

Kids Family-Friendly Hotels

Fairmont Le Château Frontenac (see above)   Sleep in a fairy-tale castle with an indoor pool for kids and street performers just outside the door.

L'Hôtel du Vieux-Québec (p. 195)   Popular with families and school groups, it's in a good location for exploring Upper or Lower Town.

Radisson Québec (p. 199)   The rooftop swimming pool is a treat, with its indoor water route to the outside. Winter Carnival activities are a quick and easy walk away.

The Coldest Reception in Town

It takes all kinds. Winter visitors clamor to spend the night—at over US$130 a pop—in a hotel carved from ice. To find out the plans for next winter, check www.icehotel-canada.com.

44 Côte du Palais (rue St-Jean), Québec City, PQ G1R 4H8. *(C)* **800/463-6283** or 418/692-1030. Fax 418/692-3822. www.manoir-victoria.com. 145 units. Mid-May to mid-Oct C$139–C$269 (US$90–US$174) double, C$350–C$600 (US$226–US$387) suite; late Oct to early May C$95–C$215 (US$61–US$139) double, C$250–C$425 (US$161–US$274) suite. Extra person C$30 (US$19). Packages available. AE, DC, DISC, MC, V. Children under 18 stay in parents' room free. Valet parking C$15 (US$9.70). **Amenities:** 2 restaurants (French); 2 bars; heated indoor pool; health club w/ sauna; concierge; car rental; limited room service; babysitting; laundry service; dry cleaning. *In room:* A/C, TV w/pay movies, minibar, hair dryer, iron.

MODERATE

Many of the hotels and inns recommended below are on or near the Jardin des Gouverneurs, immediately south of the Château Frontenac.

Cap Diamant Maison de Touristes   Every room is different in this amiable guest house, its assortment of furniture including brass beds, Victorian memorabilia, and nonspecific retro pieces retrieved from attics. In back of the house, which dates from 1826, there is an enclosed porch and a garden. The Cap Diamant is only 2½ blocks from the Jardin des Gouverneurs. Rooms overlook the rooftops of the old city. Stairs are very steep throughout, including the entrance, and there is no elevator. When reserving, ask about the just-renovated rooms next door. Totally nonsmoking.

39 av. Ste-Geneviève (near de Brébeuf), Québec City, PQ G1R 4B3. *(C)* **418/694-0313.** www.hcapdiamant. qc.ca. 12 units. Summer C$120–C$160 (US$77–US$103) double; winter C$75–C$125 (US$48–US$81) double. Rates include breakfast. Extra person C$15 (US$9.70). MC, V. Parking C$10 (US$6.45) in nearby lot. **Amenties:** Concierge; laundry service; dry cleaning. *In room:* A/C, TV w/pay movies, fridge, coffeemaker.

Château Bellevue   Occupying several row houses at the top of the Jardin des Gouverneurs, this minihotel has a pleasant lobby with leather couches and chairs and a helpful staff, as well as some of the creature comforts that smaller inns in the neighborhood lack. Although the rooms are small and often suffer from unfortunate decorating choices, they are quiet for the most part and have private bathrooms. A few higher-priced units overlook the park. The hotel's private parking is directly behind the building, a notable convenience in this congested part of town, although there are only a few spaces. If you're searching for a room on the spot and this is full, there are 10 other lodgings within a block in any direction.

16 rue Laporte, Québec City, PQ G1R 4M9. *(C)* **800/463-2617** or 418/692-2573. Fax 418/692-4876. www.vieux-quebec.com/bellevue. 58 units. Late Oct to Apr 30 C$99–C$149 (US$64–US$96) double; Winter Carnival and May to late Oct C$119–C$199 (US$77–US$128). Extra person C$10 (US$6.45). AE, DC, MC, V. Free valet parking. *In room:* A/C, TV.

L'Hôtel du Vieux-Québec *Kids*   This century-old brick hotel has been renovated with care. Guest rooms are equipped with sofas, two double beds, and modern bathrooms. Most have kitchenettes. Ask for 1 of the 24 rooms recently redone with new carpeting and furniture; 2 of these are junior suites with Jacuzzis. With these homey layouts, it's understandably popular with families, skiers, and the groups of visiting high-school students who descend upon the

Québec City Accommodations

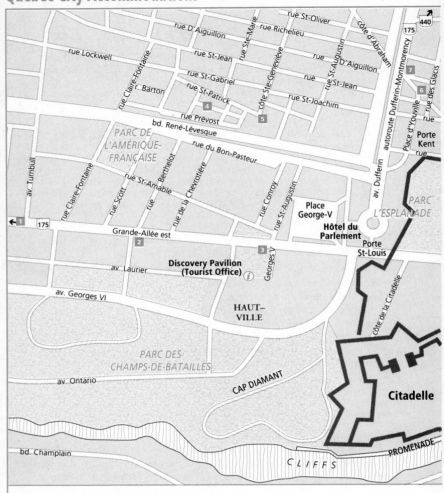

Auberge Saint-Pierre **18**

Auberge Saint-Antoine **19**

Auberge St-Louis **12**

Cap Diamant Maison de Touristes **13**

Château Bellevue **14**

Château Laurier **3**

Dominion 1912 **20**

Fairmont Le Château Frontenac **16**

Hilton Québec **5**

Hôtel des Coutellier **10**

Hôtel Palace Royal **7**

Le Capitole **6**

Le Priori **17**

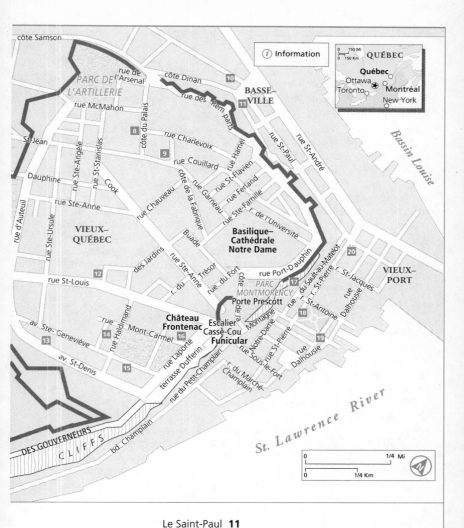

Le Saint-Paul **11**

L'Hôtel du Vieux-Québec **9**

Loews Le Concorde **2**

Manoir Sur-le-Cap **15**

Manoir Victoria **8**

Radisson Québec **4**

Relais Charles-Alexander **1**

city in late spring. In addition to Les Frères de la Côte on the ground floor, there are many moderately priced restaurants and nightspots nearby.

1190 rue St-Jean (at rue de l'Hôtel Dieu), Québec City, PQ G1R 1S6. ℂ **800/361-7787** or 418/692-1850. Fax 418/692-5637. www.hvq.com. 41 units. May to mid-Oct C$135–C$235 (US$87–US$152) double; late Oct to May C$99–C$119 (US$64–US$77) double. Extra person C$20 or C$15 (US$13 or US$9.70). DC, MC, V. *In room:* A/C, TV, fridge, hair dryer.

Manoir Sur-le-Cap All is fresh, painted, and shellacked at this inn on the south side of the Parc des Gouverneurs, opposite the Château Frontenac. Overhauled from top to bottom, all of its bedroom floors gleam, and many have exposed stone or brick walls. Obviously the price is right, unless you require air-conditioning or a phone. Know that these four floors have no elevator. Upgrade to what they call their "condo"—an apartment in a separate building in back—and get an apartment with a working fireplace, a phone, a VCR, and a kitchenette with microwave oven, coffeemaker, and basic crockery. When booking, request parking at one of the nearby lots. This is a nonsmoking facility. English is spoken.

9 av. Ste-Geneviève (near rue Laporte), Québec City, PQ G1R 4A7. ℂ **418/694-1987.** Fax 418/627-7405. www.manoir-sur-le-cap.com. 14 units. May–Oct C$105–C$175 (US$68–US$113) double; C$225 (US$145) suite; Nov–Apr C$75–C$125 (US$48–US$81) double, C$150 (US$97) suite. Additional person C$15 (US$9.70). AE, MC, V. *In room:* TV, coffeemaker, hair dryer, iron, no phone.

2 Outside the Walls

EXPENSIVE

Hilton Québec ★★ Superior on virtually every count to the other mid-rise contemporary hotels outside the old town (excluding Le Capitole, below), this Hilton is entirely true to the breed, the clear choice for executives and those leisure travelers who can't bear to live without their gadgets. And, it was renovated top to bottom as of April 2000. The location—across the street from the city walls and near the Parliament—is excellent. It is also connected to the Place Québec shopping complex, which has 75 shops, 2 cinemas, a 1,000-car parking garage, and the convention center. The public rooms are big and brassy, Hilton-style. Most of the guest rooms have one or two large beds. Upper-floor views of the St. Lawrence River and old Québec are grand. Small pets are accepted.

1100 bd. Rene-Levesque est, Québec City, PQ G1K 7K7. ℂ **800/445-8667** or 418/647-6508. Fax 418/647-2986. www.hilton.com. 571 units. C$154–C$389 (US$99–US$251) double; from C$375 (US$242) suite. Extra person C$20 (US$13). Children stay free in parents' room. Children 7–12 eat for half price. Packages available. AE, DC, DISC, MC, V. Valet parking C$17 (US$11). Head east along Grande-Allée, and just before the St-Louis Gate in the city wall, turn left on rue Honoré-Mercier, then left again as you pass the Parliament building; the hotel is 1 block ahead. **Amenities:** Restaurant (International); bar; heated outdoor pool (year-round); well-equipped health club w/ Jacuzzi and sauna; children's programs; concierge; activities desk; car rental; courtesy limo; substantial business center; limited room service; in-room massage; babysitting; laundry service; same-day dry cleaning; executive floors. *In room:* A/C, TV w/pay movies, dataport, minibar, coffeemaker, hair dryer.

Hôtel Palace Royal ★★ The newest and most luxurious in a small, family-owned Québec hotel group, this hotel elevates the standards of the business hotels outside the walls. Admittedly, it lacks a distinctive personality, perhaps because it's still young. Shooting for a Parisian ambience, lots of bronze statuary and marble are lavished on the lobby areas, while the kidney-shaped pool is at the heart of a virtual tropical garden. Over two-thirds of the units are suites, with unstocked fridges, extra TV sets, and, in many cases, Jacuzzi baths meant for two. Secure underground garage parking is provided.

775 av. Honoré-Mercier (at place d'Youville), Québec City, PQ G1R 6A5. © **800/567-5276** or 418/694-2000. Fax 418/380-2553. www.jaro.qc.ca. 234 units. C$380–C$410 (US$245–US$265). AE, DC, MC, V. Valet parking C$25 (US$16). **Amenities:** Restaurant (steakhouse); bar; indoor pool; decently equipped health club; Jacuzzi; concierge; limited room service; laundry service; same-day dry cleaning. *In room:* A/C, TV w/pay movies, dataport, coffeemaker, hair dryer.

Le Capitole ★★   Le Capitole is as gleefully eccentric as the four business hotels described elsewhere in this section are conventional. The entrance to this hotel is squeezed almost to anonymity between a restaurant and two theaters on Place d'Youville. Rooms, which are all curves and obtuse angles, borrow from Art Deco and incorporate stars into the carpets and clouds onto the ceiling. Most bathtubs have Jacuzzis, and beds have down comforters. All rooms are equipped with VCRs and CD players, with over 100 videos available free of charge.

972 rue Saint-Jean (1 block west of Porte Saint-Jean), Québec City, PQ G1R 1R5. © **800/363-4040** or 418/694-4040. Fax 418/694-1916. www.lecapitole.com. 40 units. Late May to Sept C$200–C$245 (US$129–US$158) double, C$260 (US$168) suite; Oct to early May C$99–C$185 (US$64–US$119) double, C$189–C$215 (US$122–US$139) suite. Packages available. AE, MC, V. **Amenities:** Restaurant (Italian/International); bar; concierge; limited room service; laundry service; dry cleaning. *In room:* A/C, TV/VCR, dataport, minibar, coffeemaker, hair dryer.

Loews Le Concorde ★★   From outside, the skyscraper that houses this hotel is a visual insult to the skyline, rising from a neighborhood of late-Victorian town houses. Enter, and the affront might be forgotten, at least by those who can't be bothered with architectural aesthetics. Standard rooms have marble bathrooms and three telephones. There are spectacular views of the river and the old city, even from the lower floors. A nice touch is the L'Exécutive level, reserved for women only. L'Astral is a revolving rooftop restaurant (see chapter 13), with a bar and live piano music most nights. Of all the hotels listed here, this is the farthest from the old town, about a 10-minute walk to the walls, and then another 10 minutes to the center of the Haute-Ville.

1225 cours du Géneral de Montcalm (at Grande-Allée), Québec City, PQ G1R 4W6. © **800/463-5256** or 418/647-2222. Fax 418/647-4710. www.loewshotels.com. 404 units. May–Oct C$134–C$380 (US$86–US$245) double; Nov–Apr C$105–C$239 (US$68–US$154) double; from C$235 (US$152) suite year-round. Extra person over 17, C$20 (US$13). Children under 17 share parents' room free. Ski and weekend packages available. AE, DC, MC, V. Self-parking C$15 (US$9.70), valet parking C$18 (US$12). **Amenities:** Restaurant (International); 2 bars; heated outdoor pool (Apr–Nov); well-equipped health club w/ sauna; concierge; car-rental desk; business center; shopping arcade; limited room service; in-room massage; babysitting; laundry service; same-day dry cleaning; executive floors. *In room:* A/C, TV w/pay movies, fax, dataport, minibar, coffeemaker, hair dryer, iron.

Radisson Québec ★ *Kids*   Part of Place Québec, a multi-use complex, the hotel is also connected to the city's convention center. It is 2 blocks from Porte (Gate) Kent in the city wall, and not far from the Québec Parliament building, a location likely to fit almost any businessperson's needs. It is, however, an uphill climb from the old city (like all the hotels and inns along or near the Grande-Allée). Some rooms have minibars, and all have video game stations. Every inch has benefited from a $5.2-million renovation completed in 2000. Reception is two levels up.

690 bd. René-Lévesque est, Québec City, PQ G1R 5A8. © **888/884-7777** in Canada, 800/333-3333 from elsewhere, or 418/647-1717. Fax 418/647-2146. www.radisson.com. 377 units. C$145–C$295 (US$94–US$190) double; from C$305 (US$197) suite. Extra adult C$20 (US$13). Children under 16 stay free in parents' room. AE, DC, DISC, MC, V. Parking C$18 (US$12). Turn left off Grande-Allée, and then left again onto Dufferin, just before the St-Louis Gate in the city wall. Once past the Parliament building, take the 1st left. The hotel is 2 blocks ahead. **Amenities:** Restaurant (International); bar; outdoor pool (summer only); fully

---

Tips **Locking Up**

While modern hotels in Montréal and Québec City use card keys and deadbolts, many of the older inns and B&Bs in those cities and out in the country do not. Instead, you may have to (1) insert your room key and turn it twice to lock it upon leaving, or (2) turn the flanged button on the inside doorknob, or (3) push the inside doorknob in, then make a quarter-turn to the left (or, sometimes, the right) and then step outside to close. In any event, always test the door upon leaving.

---

equipped health club w/ sauna and Jacuzzi; concierge; business center; limited room service; babysitting; laundry service; same-day dry cleaning; executive floors. *In room:* A/C, TV w/pay movies, dataport, coffee-maker, hair dryer, iron.

MODERATE

Château Laurier ★★ Anchoring the east end of the Grande-Allée action-filled strip, this old-timer has lifted its formerly dowdy countenance by taking over an adjoining building and adding 65 newer, larger, jazzier units. Some of them have working fireplaces, Jacuzzis, and king beds; all enjoy the comforts and doodads of a first-class hotel. The new rooms are clearly more desirable than those in the plainer and more cramped original wing. A bar and bistro remain in front, down a few steps from Grande-Allée, while the expansive new lobby is located on the Georges V side. The hotel is only 2 blocks west of the St-Louis Gate and across the way from Parliament Hill.

1220 place Georges V ouest (near corner of Grande-Allée), Québec City, PQ G1R 5B8. © 800/463-4453 or 418/522-8108. Fax 418/524-8768. www.vieux-quebec.com/laurier. 154 units. May to mid-Oct C$99–C$259 (US$64–US$167) double; late Oct to Apr C$79–C$169 (US$51–US$109) double. AE, DC, MC, V. Parking C$10 (US$6.65). **Amenities:** Restaurant (bistro); bar; concierge; limited room service; laundry service; dry cleaning. *In room:* A/C, TV w/pay movies, dataport, coffeemaker, hair dryer.

INEXPENSIVE

Relais Charles-Alexander *Value* On the ground floor of this charming brick-faced B&B is an art gallery, which also serves as the breakfast room. This stylish use of space extends to the bedrooms as well, which are crisply maintained and decorated with eclectic antique and wicker pieces and reproductions. Rooms in front are larger; most have showers, not tubs; and some have phones. They are quiet, for the most part, because the inn is just outside the orbit of the sometimes-raucous Grande-Allée terrace bars. Yet the St-Louis Gate is less than a 10-minute walk away from the hubbub. Totally nonsmoking.

91 Grande-Allée est (av. Galipeault), Québec City, PQ G1R 2H5. © 418/523-1220. Fax 418/523-9556. www.quebecweb.com/rca. 23 units. C$87–C$119 (US$56–US$77) double. Rates include breakfast. MC, V. Parking nearby C$8 (US$5.15). **Amenities:** Same-day dry cleaning. *In room:* A/C, TV, hair dryer.

3 Basse-Ville (Lower Town)

VERY EXPENSIVE

Auberge Saint-Antoine ★★ The centerpiece of this uncommonly attractive boutique hotel is the 1830 maritime warehouse that houses the lobby and meeting rooms, with the original dark beams and stone floor still intact. Buffet breakfasts and afternoon wine and cheese are set out in the lobby, where guests can relax in wing chairs next to the hooded fireplace. Canny mixes of antique and reproduction furniture are found in both public and private areas. The bedrooms, in an adjoining modern wing, and a separate, newly remodeled 1727 house are spacious, with such extra touches as custom-made bedsteads and tables. The big bathrooms have robes. Several rooms have private terraces, one of which has a three-hole putting green. A number of suites have kitchenettes and fax machines.

10 rue St-Antoine (Dalhousie), Québec City, PQ G1K 4C9. © 888/692-2211 or 418/692-2211. Fax 418/692-1177. www.saint-antoine.com. 31 units. Late June to late Oct C$229–C$299 (US$148–US$193) double; late Oct to mid-June C$149–C$199 (US$96–US$128) double; C$299–C$399 (US$193–US$257) suite year-round. Extra person C$20 (US$13). Children under 12 stay free in parents' room. AE, DC, DISC, MC, V. Parking C$12 (US$7.75). Follow rue Dalhousie around the Lower Town to rue St-Antoine. The hotel is next to the Musée de la Civilisation. **Amenities:** Concierge; limited room service; in-room massage; babysitting; laundry service; same-day dry cleaning. In room: A/C, TV, fax, dataport, hair dryer, iron.

EXPENSIVE

Auberge Saint-Pierre ★   The doors were only opened in 1997, but the paint was barely dry before this hotel expanded into the adjacent building to add another 13 rooms. The included full breakfasts are special, cooked to order by the chef in the open kitchen. Most of the rooms are surprisingly spacious, and the even more commodious suites are a luxury on a longer visit, especially since they have modest kitchen facilities. All rooms and suites have Jacuzzi baths. The made-to-order furnishings are meant to suggest, rather than replicate, traditional Québec styles. Robes are provided. The new wing is nonsmoking.

79 Saint-Pierre (behind the Musée de la Civilisation), Québec City, PQ G1K 4A3. © 888/268-1017 or 418/694-7981. Fax 418/694-0406. www.auberge.qc.ca. 41 units. Mid-May to Oct C$129–C$329 (US$83–US$212) double; Nov to mid-May C$109–C$299 (US$70–US$193) double. Rates include full breakfast. AE, DC, DISC, MC, V. Parking nearby C$12 (US$7.75). **Amenities:** Bar; access to nearby health club, concierge; breakfast room service; in-room massage; babysitting; laundry service; same-day dry cleaning. In room: A/C, TV, dataport, coffeemaker, hair dryer, iron.

Dominion 1912 ★★★   If there were space enough to recommend only one hotel in the city, this would be it. The owners stripped the inside of the 1912 Dominion Fish & Fruit building down to the studs and pipes and started over. Even the least expensive rooms are large, the queen- or king-size beds heaped with linen-covered pillows and covered with feather duvets. Custom-made bed-side tables swing into place or out of the way. A fruit basket awaits your arrival. Modem outlets are at handy desktop level. Continental breakfast is set out in the handsome lobby along with morning newspapers, and you can munch and read out on the terrace in back. Prices have risen, but even so, this remains one of the most desirable hotels in town.

126 rue Saint-Pierre (at rue Saint-Paul), Québec City, PQ G1K 4A8. © 888/833-5253 or 418/692-2224. Fax 418/692-4403. www.hoteldominion.com. 60 units. Nov–Apr C$169–C$229 (US$109–US$147) double; May–Oct C$205–C$305 (US$132–US$197) double. Rates include breakfast. AE, DC, MC, V. Parking C$12 (US$7.75). **Amenities:** Restaurant (light fare); access to nearby health club; concierge; limited room service; in-room massage; babysitting; laundry service; same-day dry cleaning. In room: A/C, TV/VCR, dataport, mini-bar, coffeemaker, hair dryer, iron.

Le Saint-Paul   This 1854 mid-Victorian near the railroad station is Basse-Ville's latest addition to the hotel scene. While it isn't quite up to the consider-able standards of those recommended above, staying here represents no deprivation. Half the rooms have king-size beds and some have small fridges and/or Jacuzzi baths. Rue St-Paul's antique row is steps away.

229½ rue St-Paul (near rue Lacroix), Québec City, PQ G1K 3W3. © 888/794-4414 or 418/694-4414. Fax 418/694-0889. www.lesaintpaul.qc.ca. 26 units. Late May to Oct C$200–C$270 (US$129–US$174) double; Nov to early May C$120–C$140 (US$77–US$90) double. AE, DC, MC, V. **Amenities:** Restaurant (International); concierge; laundry service; dry cleaning. In room: A/C, TV, dataport.

MODERATE

Hôtel des Coutellier   A few years ago, a small old building was converted into this unpretentious small hotel. The rooms, which include six suites, are large and conventionally fitted out. Those of an independent turn of mind should be pleased. For one thing, the deskperson goes off duty at 11pm and guests let themselves in after that by keying a coded number pad. For another, a breakfast basket waits at the door at 7am in the morning, containing a juice box, yogurt, and muffins (the rooms have coffeemakers).

253 rue St-Paul (near rue Lacroix), Québec City, PQ G1K 3W5. © 888/523-9696 or 418/692-9696. Fax 418/692-4050. www.hoteldescoutellier.com. 24 units. C$99–C$200 (US$64–US$129). Rates include breakfast. Packages available. AE, DC, MC, V. **Amenities:** Restaurant (Belgian); bar; laundry service; dry cleaning. *In room:* A/C, TV, dataport, coffeemaker, hair dryer, iron.

Le Priori   A forerunner of the burgeoning Lower Town hotel scene, Le Priori provides a playful postmodern ambience behind the somber facade of a 1766 house. Designer Philippe Starck inspired the original owners, who installed versions of his conical stainless-steel sinks in the bedrooms and sensual multi-nozzle showers in the small bathrooms. In some rooms, a claw-foot tub sits beside the queen-size beds, which are covered with duvets. New table lamps help enliven the formerly dim lighting. Suites have sitting rooms with wood-burning fireplaces, kitchens, and Jacuzzis. There's a casual restaurant off the lobby.

15 rue Sault-au-Matelot (at rue St-Antoine), Québec City, PQ G1K 3Y7. © 800/351-3992 or 418/692-3992. Fax 418/692-0883. www.hotellepriori.com. 26 units. May–Oct C$159–C$199 (US$103–US$128) double; C$199 (US$128) suite; Nov–Apr C$99–C$139 (US$64–US$90) double, C$199 (US$128) suite. Rates include breakfast. Packages available. AE, DC, MC, V. Self-parking C$10 (US$6.65) per day. **Amenities:** Restaurant (French); bar; concierge; limited room service; laundry service; same-day dry cleaning. *In room:* A/C, TV, dataport, coffeemaker, hair dryer, iron.

4 A Country Hotel in the City

Château Bonne Entente ★★   Cast a line for trout in the pond in front, twirl around the skating rink, get swaddled in seaweed—and still be only a 15-minute drive from Vieux-Québec. Bushels of dollars have elevated the hotel far beyond the folksy boarding house of a half-century ago. For romantics, the choice has to be Art Deco room 358, with a monster tub two steps from the king-size bed. Then there's the "AmeriSpa," where guests are pampered by the hour with a list that only begins with body scrubs and foot massage.

3400 chemin Saint-Foy, Ste-Foy, PQ G1X 1S6. © 800/463-4390 or 418/653-3098. Fax 418/653-3098. www.chateaubonneentente.com. 165 units. May–Oct C$129–$195 (US$83–US$126) double; Nov–Apr C$99–C$149 (US$64–US$96) double; year-round C$229–C$329 (US$149–US$212) suite. Packages available. AE, DC, MC, V. From Montréal on Rte. 40, take the exit onto Autproute Duplessis, shortly turning onto chemin Sainte-Foy; at the light, make a right, go straight and turn right again at the next traffic light. **Amenities:** 3 restaurants (1 only in summer; French, Quebecois, grill); 2 bars; large outdoor pool; golf nearby; tennis; extensive health club and spa; limited room service; massage; babysitting; laundry service; same-day dry cleaning. *In room:* A/C, TV w/pay movies, dataport, minibar, coffeemaker, hair dryer, iron, safe.

13

Where to Dine in Québec City

Once you are within these ancient walls, walking along streets that look to have been transplanted intact from Brittany or Provence, it is understandable if you imagine that you'll have one incredible dining experience after another in Québec City. Hype and expectations aside, the truth is that this gloriously scenic city has no *temples de cuisine* comparable to those of Paris or Manhattan. Although it is easy to eat well in the capital—even, in a few isolated cases, *quite* well—the remembered pleasures of a stay here will likely lie in other areas, absorbed by other senses.

By sticking to any of the many competent bistros, the handful of *nuovo Italiano* trattorias, and a couple of Asian eateries, you will be content. Another step up, two or three ambitious enterprises tease the palate with hints of higher achievement. Even the blatantly touristy restaurants along rue St-Louis and around the Place d'Armes can produce decent meals. The less extravagant among them, in fact, are entirely satisfactory for breakfast or simple lunches, a useful fact to keep in mind if you're staying in one of the many old town guesthouses that serve no meals.

As throughout the province, the best dining deals are the table d'hôte—fixed-price—meals. Virtually all full-service restaurants offer them, if only at lunch. As a rule, they include at least soup or salad, a main course, and a dessert. Some places add in an extra appetizer and/or a beverage, all for the approximate a la carte price of the main course alone.

Curiously, seafood is not given much attention. Mussels and salmon are on most menus, but look for those places that go beyond those staples. Game is popular, and everything from venison, rabbit, and duck to more exotic quail, goose, caribou, and wapiti (North American deer) is available.

At the better places, and even at some of those that might seem inexplicably popular, reservations are all but essential during traditional holidays and during the festivals that pepper the social calendar. Other times, it's usually necessary to book ahead only for weekend evenings. In the listings below, where no mention is made of reservations, they aren't necessary. Dress codes are rarely stipulated, but "dressy casual" works almost everywhere. Remember that for the Quebecois, *dîner* (dinner) is lunch, and *souper* (supper) is dinner, though for the sake of consistency, the word *dinner* below is used in the common American sense. The evening meal tends to be served earlier in Québec City than in Montréal, at 6 or 7pm rather than 8pm.

For a more extended discussion of Québec dining, see "Cuisine Haute, Cuisine Bas: Smoked Meat, Fiddleheads & Caribou," in the appendix.

1 Restaurants by Cuisine

CONTEMPORARY FRENCH
Initiale ✸✸ (Basse-Ville, $$$, p. 209)
Le Paris-Brest ✸ (Grande-Allée, $$$, p. 208)
Le Saint-Amour ✸ (Haute-Ville, $$$, p. 205)

CONTEMPORARY FRENCH/ ITALIAN
Graffiti ✸ (Grande-Allée, $$, p. 208)

CONTEMPORARY ITALIAN
Momento (Grande-Allée, $$, p. 209)

CONTEMPORARY QUEBECOIS
Laurie Raphaël ✸✸ (Basse-Ville, $$$, p. 210)

ECLECTIC
Serge Bruyère ✸✸ (Haute-Ville, $$$, p. 205)
Voodoo Grill ✸ (Grande-Allée, $$, p. 209)

FRENCH BISTRO
L'Ardoise (Basse-Ville, $$, p. 210)
L'Echaudé ✸ (Basse-Ville, $$, p. 210)

Le Marie-Clarisse ✸ (Basse-Ville, $$, p. 211)

FRENCH/INTERNATIONAL
L'Astral (Grande-Allée, $$, p. 208)
Le Café du Monde ✸ (Basse-Ville, $$, p. 210)

LIGHT FARE/CREPES
Le Casse-Crêpe Breton (Haute-Ville, $, p. 208)

MEDITERRANEAN
Les Frères de la Côte (Haute-Ville, $$, p. 205)

QUEBECOIS
Aux Anciens Canadiens ✸ (Haute-Ville, $$$, see below)
Buffet de l'Antiquaire (Basse-Ville, $, p. 211)

SEAFOOD
Le Marie-Clarisse ✸ (Basse-Ville, $$, p. 211)
Poisson d'Avril (Basse-Ville, $$, p. 211)

Key to Abbreviations: $$$$ = Very Expensive $$$ = Expensive $$ = Moderate $ = Inexpensive

2 Haute-Ville (Upper Town)

EXPENSIVE

Aux Anciens Canadiens ✸ QUEBECOIS Smack in the middle of the tourist swarms and inundated by travelers during peak months, this venerable restaurant is in what is probably the oldest (1677) house in the city. Surprisingly, the food at this famous establishment is both fairly priced (at least at lunch) and well prepared. In addition, it's one of the best places in La Belle Province to sample cooking that has its roots in the earliest years of New France. Don't count on the ancient Quebecois recipes tasting this good anywhere else. Caribou and maple syrup figure in many of the dishes, including the meat pie, Lac Brome duck, and a definitive rendering of luscious sugar pie. Servings are large enough to ward off winter for a week. Servers are in costume and there are carved wooden bas-reliefs of regional scenes.

34 rue St-Louis (at rue Haldimand). ☎ **418/692-1627.** Reservations recommended. Main courses lunch C$19–C$45 (US$12–US$29); table d'hôte lunch C$14 (US$9); main courses dinner C$28–C$54 (US$18–US$35). AE, DC, MC, V. Daily noon–10pm.

Le Saint-Amour ⓖ★ CONTEMPORARY FRENCH   This is a restaurant for the coolly attractive and the amorously inclined. Patrons pass through a front room with lace curtains into a covered terrace lit by flickering candles. Easily the most romantic setting for dining in a city that knows about seductive atmosphere, the glass roof reveals splashes of stars. The courtyard has been re-created with mirrors and polished wood paneling. The staff are proud of the caribou filet with a wild mushroom crust, enhanced by dried berries in a pepper sauce. The lobster presented out of its shell looks as good as it tastes, and desserts are dazzlers. Having come this far back to its previous levels of achievement, a final enhancement would be to move the pace of the meal along a little more expeditiously.

48 rue Ste-Ursule (near rue St-Louis). ⓒ 418/694-0667. www.saint-amour.com. Reservations recommended for dinner. Main courses C$24–C$34 (US$15–US$22); table d'hôte lunch C$11–C$16 (US$7.10–US$10), dinner C$29–C$33 (US$18–US$21); tasting dinner C$72 (USD$46). AE, DC, MC, V. Mon–Fri 11:30am–2:30pm and 5:30–11pm; Sat–Sun 5:30–11pm.

Serge Bruyère ⓖ★★ ECLECTIC   No moss grows on this place. The eponymous owner bought the wedge-shaped building in 1979 and set about creating a multilevel dining emporium that had something for everyone. Serge Bruyère, however, died young. His one-time executive chef carries on, along a similar path, serving all meals from informal breakfasts to lavish late dinners. He keeps fiddling with the formula, though. The room in back that served briefly as a German rathskeller is now an Irish pub with live music 4 nights a week.

At ground level in front is the casual Café Bruyère. Up a long staircase at the back is the Bistro Livernois, with three windows looking down on the street. It is especially good for lunches, concentrating on grills and pastas that come with rounds of crusty, chewy bread. Foods are adroitly seasoned. Another flight up is the formal La Grand Table, offering a pricey menu that is both highly imaginative and immaculately presented. Whether the unquestionably showy creations justify the raves and the sedate pace of the meal is up to you. Dress well, and arrive with a healthy credit card.

1200 rue Saint-Jean (Côte de la Fabrique). ⓒ 418/694-0618. Reservations recommended for dinner. Bistro Livernois table d'hôte lunch C$7.95–C$15 (US$5.15–US$9.65), dinner C$18–C$34 (US$12–US$22); Bistro Livernois main courses C$15–C$34 (US$9.70–US$22); La Grand Table main courses C$24–C$35 (US$16–C$23); gastronomic dinners C$85 and C$145 (US$55 and US$94). AE, DC, MC, V. Daily 8am–10:30pm.

MODERATE

Les Frères de la Côte *Kids* MEDITERRANEAN   At the east end of the old town's liveliest nightlife strip, this supremely casual cafe-pizzeria is as loud as any dance club, with patrons shouting over the booming stereo music. None of this discourages a single soul—even on a Monday night. Chefs in straw hats in the open kitchen in back crank out 17 different kinds of pizza—thin-crusted, with unusual toppings that work—and about as many pasta versions, which are less interesting. Bountiful platters of fish and meats, often in the form of brochettes, make appetizers unnecessary. Keep this spot in mind when kids are in tow; there's no way they could make enough noise to bother other customers. Outside tables are available in warm weather. Brunch is served Sundays, 10:30am to 3pm.

1190 rue St-Jean (near Côte de la Fabrique). ⓒ 418/692-5445. Reservations recommended. Main courses C$13–C$14 (US$8.05–US$9); table d'hôte dinner C$19–C$22 (US$12–US$14). AE, DC, MC, V. Daily 11:30am–11pm.

Québec City Dining

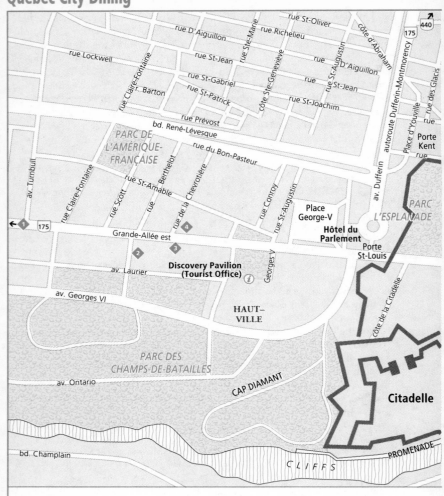

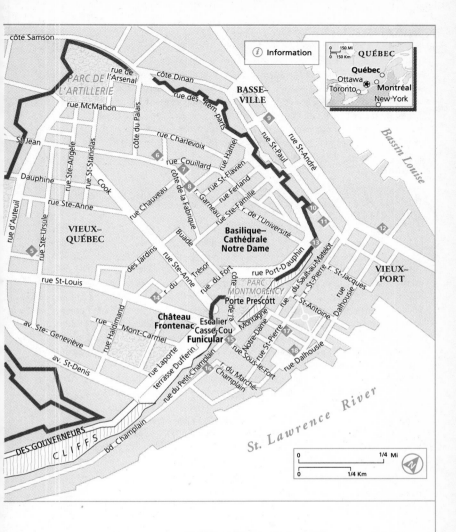

Le Saint-Amour **5**
Les Frères de la Côte **6**
Momento **1**
Poisson d'Avril **9**
Serge Bruyère **8**
Voodoo Grill **3**

INEXPENSIVE

Le Casse-Crêpe Breton *Value* LIGHT FARE/CREPES   Eat at the bar and watch the crêpes being made, or attempt to snag 1 of the 14 tables. These aren't those sissy crêpes named for Suzette, they're pizza-sized monsters. Main-course versions come with two to five ingredients of the customers' choice, usually a combo of ham, cheese, sweet peppers, mushrooms, eggs, or pepperoni. Dessert types are stuffed with jams or fruit and cream. Soups, salads, and sandwiches are as inexpensive as the crêpes. It's open 18 hours a day, which is useful, but when it gets busy, the service is glacial. Beer is served in bottles or on tap.

1136 rue St-Jean (near rue Garneau). ✆ 418/692-0438. Most items under C$6 (US$3.85). MC, V. Daily 7am–1am.

3 On or Near the Grande-Allée

EXPENSIVE

Le Paris-Brest ✿ CONTEMPORARY FRENCH   Named for a French dessert, this is easily one of the best restaurants within or outside the walls, tendering a polished performance from greeting to check. Within minutes after the doors are opened at lunchtime, a happy noise ensues, drowning out the cellphone users. (Dinner is quieter.) A fashionable crowd comes in wearing everything from bespoke suits to designer jeans—tacky T-shirts and children are out of place. They are attended by a comely waitstaff dressed in black who convey as much warmth as the rushed process permits. One sparkling recent appetizer was snow crab tagliatelle. Game and seafood are featured, often including pheasant with honey caramelized pears, crawfish étouffée, and Dover sole. What they do with pasta is impressive: Linguine is tossed in a curry pepper sauce with tiny clams and mussels, as tangy a taste sensation as might be imagined. How odd that the bread is dry and woolly. Find the entrance on rue de la Chevrotière. Free valet parking is available after 5:30pm.

590 Grande-Allée est (at rue de la Chevrotière). ✆ 418/529-2243. Reservations recommended. Main courses C$26–C$30 (US$17–US$20); table d'hôte lunch C$11–C$15 (US$6.75–US$9.85), dinner C$23–C$34 (US$15–US$22). AE, DC, MC, V. Mon–Fri 11:30am–2:30pm; Mon–Sat 6–11:30pm; Sun 5:30–11:30pm.

MODERATE

Graffiti ✿ CONTEMPORARY FRENCH/ITALIAN   These 2 or 3 blocks of rue Cartier off Grand-Allée are just outside the perimeter of tourist Québec, close enough to be convenient. Enthusiasm for this ebullient establishment hasn't flagged a bit, stoked by an attractive male and female staff that hustles about leaving good feelings in their wake. The kitchen blends bistro with trattoria, often on the same plate. Emblematic are the pike with leeks and grilled almonds, and the sautéed rabbit with puréed carrot, broccoli florets, and angel-hair pasta powerfully scented with tarragon. Choice seats are in the glassed-in terrace, the better to scope out the street scene, but there are a variety of booths and banquettes.

1191 av. Cartier (near Grand-Allée). ✆ 418/529-4949. Reservations recommended. Main courses C$9.75–C$20 (US$6.30–US$13); table d'hôte lunch C$11–C$16 (US$6.95–US$10), dinner C$23–C$30 (US$15–US$19). AE, DC, MC, V. Mon–Sat 5–11pm; Sun noon–10pm.

L'Astral FRENCH/INTERNATIONAL   If you share the common conviction that cuisine diminishes and prices rise in direct proportion to the height at which the food is served, you have a legitimate case—especially if your table also moves in a circle. Here's an exception. This restaurant sits atop the Hôtel Loews Le Concorde, and it turns 360° in about an hour. The panorama thus revealed is truly splendid. But here's the double surprise—the food is above average and the cost entirely reasonable. You have the choice of an all-you-can-eat buffet at lunch or dinner or a la carte selections, and the buffet is as good a deal as you're likely to find. Appearances are made by monkfish, lamb, and breast of pheasant, as well as more familiar chicken and beef.

1225 cours du Général-de Montcalm (cor Grande-Allée). ℂ **418/647-2222**. Reservations recommended. Main courses C$20–C$44 (US$13–US$28); lunch buffet C$19 (US$12); dinner buffet C$41 (US$26) adults, C$21 (US$13) children under 12. AE, DC, DISC, MC, V. Daily 11:45am–1am.

Momento CONTEMPORARY ITALIAN   Considering its manic popularity elsewhere on the continent, updated Italian cooking was late arriving in Québec. The city had the usual parlors shoveling overcooked spaghetti with thin tomato sauce, but not the kind of spiffy neo-trattoria that traffics in light-but-lusty dishes meant for lives lived fast. This racy spot is helping to take up the slack, and although it lags somewhat in execution compared to its cross-street rival, Graffiti (see above), it is a welcome antidote to prevailing Franco-Italian clichés. If you don't want a full meal, the 9 pizzas and 14 pastas are uniformly satisfying and of considerable variety. Pizza crusts are almost as thin as crêpes, and the "California" version, with marinated chicken, oranges, mozzarella, sun-dried tomatoes, and sesame seeds on pesto, is a winner.

1144 av. Cartier (cor rue Aberdeen). ℂ **418/647-1313**. Reservations recommended at dinner. Main courses C$15–C$21 (US$9.35–US$14); table d'hôte lunch C$9.25–C$15 (US$5.95–US$9.65), dinner C$15–C$26 (US$9.65–US$17). AE, DC, MC, V. Mon–Fri 11:30am–2pm and 5–10:30pm; Sat–Sun 5–10:30pm.

Voodoo Grill ⭐ ECLECTIC   Of all the unlikely places to expect a decent meal, let alone one that surpasses most of what can be found at more conventional local restaurants, this takes the laurels. African carvings adorn the walls, and a trio of drummers circulate, beating out rapid, insistent rhythms on bongos—a tremendous distraction. It is loud, young, and extremely casual. The menu swings around the Pacific Rim, with stops in Hawaii, Thailand, and Indonesia. Authenticity isn't the point, taste is. Tuna, for only one example, is barely touched by the flame, then set upon a pad of shredded vegetables tossed with linguine and soy sauce. If you're interested, the cover charge for the disco upstairs is waived with proof that you ate at Voodoo.

575 Grand-Allée est (corner of rue de la Chevro tiére). ℂ **418/647-2000**. Reservations recommended. Main courses C$16–C$30 (US$10–US$19). AE, DC, MC, V. Daily 6–11pm.

4 Basse-Ville (Lower Town)

EXPENSIVE

Initiale ⭐⭐ CONTEMPORARY FRENCH   The palatial setting of tall windows, columns, and a deeply recessed ceiling aids in setting a gracious tone. Subdued lighting and the muffled noise level help, too. Cast economy to the winds, choosing from prix-fixe menus of three to six courses. They are changed often, because the chef values freshness of ingredients over novelty, but a recent seasonal dinner started with lobster and crab arrayed with puréed avocado, white asparagus, and truffle. It continued with grilled red tuna supported by sweet garlic, salsify and lemon marmalade, and a swirl of pasta with marguerite leaves. A particular treat was the selection of impressive Québec cheeses, followed by a tart of white wine and maple syrup.

54 rue St-Pierre (corner Côte de la Montagne). ℂ **418/694-1818**. www.restaurantinitiale.com. Reservations recommended on weekends. Main courses C$14–C$39 (US$8.70–US$25); table d'hôte lunch C$12–C$19 (US$7.75–US$12), dinner C$47–C$76 (US$30–US$49). AE, DC, MC, V. Mon–Fri 11:30am–2pm and 6–9pm; Sat–Sun 6–9pm.

Laurie Raphaël ★★ CONTEMPORARY QUEBECOIS   The owners, who named the place after their two children, tinker relentlessly with these glamorous quarters to ensure a suitable arena for the city's most accomplished kitchen. An *amuse-bouche* arrives with cocktails. Appetizers aren't really necessary, because the main course comes with soup or salad, but they're so good that you might wish to share one with your dining companions—the little stack of lightly fried calamari rings, perhaps, with their garnish of edible nasturtium blossoms. Main courses run to caribou and salmon in unconventional guises, often with Asian touches. With an evident concern for "healthy" saucing and exotic combinations, the food closely resembles that associated with serious California restaurants. That includes something of an edifice complex in the towering presentations, held together with skewers and panache. Service falls within the friendly/correct range, only occasionally forgetful. But that's quibbling, for this is a restaurant that is nearly alone at the pinnacle of the local dining pantheon.

117 rue Dalhousie (at rue St-André). ℂ 418/692-4555. www.resto-laurie-raphael.com. Reservations recommended. Main courses C$27–C$45 (US$17–US$29); table d'hôte lunch C$11–C$30 (US$7.10–US$19); gourmet menu C$79 (US$51). AE, DC, MC, V. Tues–Fri 11:30am–2pm and 5:30–10pm; Sat 6–10pm.

MODERATE

L'Ardoise FRENCH BISTRO   This is one of several bistros that wrap around the intersection of rues St-Paul and Sault-au-Matelot. Most are inexpensive and cater more to locals than to tourists. Mussels are staples at Québec restaurants, prepared in the Belgian manner, with bowls of *frites* on the side. Here, they come with 14 different sauces and, with soup or salad, cost only C$18 (US$12)—with free seconds. That the chef cares about what he sends out of his kitchen is evident. His food is vibrant and flavorful, served at banquettes along the walls and at tables both inside and out on the sidewalk. Piaf and Aznavour clones warble laments on the stereo. This is a place to leaf through a book, sip a double espresso, and meet neighbors.

71 rue St-Paul (near Navigateurs). ℂ 418/694-0213. Reservations recommended at dinner. Main courses C$12–C$17 (US$7.70–US$11); table d'hôte lunch C$9.95–C$17 (US$6.40–US$11), dinner C$25–C$33 (US$16–US$21). AE, DC, MC, V. Mon–Thurs 11am–10pm; Fri 11am–10:30pm; Sat 9am–10:30pm; Sun 9am–10pm.

Le Café du Monde ★ FRENCH/INTERNATIONAL   A relentlessly convivial spot, the Café du Monde enjoyed long popularity at its prominent address near the Musée de la Civilisation. In late 2002, it moved to this new location in the Old Port, too late to be properly reviewed for this edition. The new site is on the edge of the river, in Le Terminal de Croisières—the cruise terminal. Presumably, the menu will continue to feature classic patés, quiches, cassoulet, duck confit, and six versions of mussels with *frites,* with pastas and paella among some of the less specifically French preparations. Imported beers are the favored beverages, along with wines by the glass. Service is friendly, but easily distracted given the lively atmosphere.

84 rue Dalhousie (near de la Barricade). ℂ 418/692-4455. www.lecafedumonde.com. Reservations recommended. Main courses C$13–C$18 (US$8.35–US$12); table d'hôte (after 3pm) the price of your main course plus C$6.95 or C$11 (US$4.50 or US$7.05). AE, DC, MC, V. Mon–Fri 11:30am–11pm; Sat–Sun brunch 9:30am–11pm.

L'Echaudé ★ FRENCH BISTRO   The most polished of the necklace of restaurants adorning this Basse-Ville corner, L'Echaudé has sidewalk tables with butcher paper on top and a zinc-topped bar inside the door. The grilled meats and fishes and seafood stews blaze no new trails, but they are very satisfying and an excellent value. Good-deal lunch mains go from cheese omelets to steak tartare, wrapped around with appetizer, dessert, and coffee. Among many classics on the menu are steak frites, ravioli with blue cheese, and salmon tartare. They keep 24 brands of beer on ice and cellar 125 varieties of wine, a generous 10 of which are available by the glass.

73 rue Sault-au-Matelot (near rue St-Paul). (℃) **418/692-1299.** Main courses C$15–C$29 (US$9.65–US$18); table d'hôte lunch C$12–C$18 (US$7.70–US$12), dinner C$25–C$39 (US$16–US$25). AE, DC, MC, V. Mon–Wed 11:30am–2:30pm and 5:30–10pm; Thurs–Fri 11:30am–2:30pm and 5:30–11pm; Sat 5:30–11pm; Sun 10am–2:30pm and 5:30–10pm. Closed 2 weeks in Jan.

Le Marie-Clarisse ★ FRENCH BISTRO/SEAFOOD   This spot, at the bottom of Breakneck Stairs, is where the streets are awash with day-packers and shutterbugs. And yet it serves what many consider to be the best seafood in town, chosen by a finicky owner who makes his selections personally at market. A more pleasant hour cannot be passed anywhere in Québec City than here, over a platter of shrimp or patés, out on the terrace on an August afternoon. In January, cocoon by the stone fireplace inside, indulging in bouillabaisse—a stew of mussels, scallops, tuna, talapia, and shrimp, with a boat of saffron mayo to slather on croutons. Try a Québec wine to wash it down, maybe the l'Orpailleur from Dunham. The two rooms are formed of stone and brick and rafters over 200 years in place.

12 rue du Petit-Champlain (at rue Sous-le-Fort). (℃) **418/692-0857.** Main courses C$9.75–C$31 (US$6.30–US$20); table d'hôte lunch C$15 (US$9.50); dinner is the price of the main course plus C$15 (US$9.50). AE, DC, MC, V. Mon–Sat 11:30am–2:30pm and 6–10pm; terrace open daily Apr 15–Oct 31 11:30am–10pm.

Poisson d'Avril SEAFOOD   Whoever christened this place was having a little joke: Its name means both "April Fool" and "April Fish." Nevertheless, nautical trappings that include model ships, marine prints, and mounted sailfish make the real intent clear. The dinner menu, changed daily, is packed with seafood, including some combinations of costly crustaceans responsible for the stiffer prices noted below. Two of these are the crowded bouillabaisse, which comes with half a lobster, and the "Commodore Platter," laden with snow crabs, giant shrimp, glossy sea scallops, piled mussels, and another half-lobster. Mixed grill is also on the menu, and a sushi bar is operational in the evenings. Lunch is a more modest event, with land-based dishes, pastas, and individual pizzas. In good weather, there's a covered dining terrace.

115 quai Saint-André (in Vieux-Port, near rue St-Thomas). (℃) **418/692-1010.** www.poissondavril.net. Reservations suggested. Main courses C$17–C$30 (US$11–US$19); table d'hôte lunch C$8.95–C$16 (US$5.75–US$10), dinner C$24–C$44 (US$15–US$28). Daily 11am–2pm and 5–10pm.

INEXPENSIVE

Buffet de l'Antiquaire Value QUEBECOIS   Another inhabitant of the rue St-Paul antique row, this is the humblest eating place of the lot, with exposed brick-and-stone walls. And, because it caters mostly to homefolks rather than tourists, reliable versions of native Quebecois cooking are always available, including, but not limited to, pea soup, *poutine*, and *fèves au lard* (beans cooked in lard). Essentially a slightly upgraded luncheonette, it serves sandwiches, salads, and pastries at all hours, backed by full bar service.

95 rue St-Paul (near rue du Sault-au-Matelot). (℃) **418/692-2661.** Most menu items under C$12 (US$5.15), including table d'hôte. AE, MC, V. Daily 7am–11pm.

14

Exploring Québec City

Wandering at random through the streets of Vieux-Québec is a singular pleasure, comparable to exploring a provincial capital in Europe. On the way, you can happen upon an ancient convent, blocks of gabled houses with steeply pitched roofs, a battery of 18th-century cannons in a leafy park, and a bistro with a blazing fireplace on a wintry day. The old city, upper and lower, is so compact that it is hardly necessary to plan precise sightseeing itineraries. Start at the Terrasse Dufferin and go off on a whim, down Breakneck Stairs (Escalier Casse-Cou) to the Quartier du Petit-Champlain and Place Royale, or up to the Citadel and onto the Plains of Abraham, where Wolfe and Montcalm fought to their mutual deaths in a 20-minute battle that changed the destiny of the continent.

Most of what there is to see is within the city walls, or in the Lower Town. It's fairly easy walking. While the Upper Town is hilly, with sloping streets, it's nothing like San Francisco, and only people with physical limitations are likely to experience difficulty. If rain or ice discourages exploration on foot, tour buses and horse-drawn calèches are options.

SUGGESTED ITINERARIES

If You Have 1 Day

Take the walking tour of the Upper Town described in chapter 15, visiting the Citadel or the Musée du Québec or both. Walk down from the Terrasse Dufferin to explore the Lower Town.

If You Have 2 Days

On the second day, take the funicular or descend the Breakneck Stairs from the Terrasse Dufferin to wander through the Lower Town, using the other walk described in chapter 15. Allow at least an hour or two for the Musée de la Civilisation.

If You Have 3 Days

On the third day, make a short excursion north of the city to circle bucolic Ile d'Orléans, isolated from the mainland until a bridge was built in 1935. The island is home to five tranquil hamlets with several middling to good restaurants. It's preferable to drive rather than take a bus tour. Afterward, visit Montmorency Falls and the shrine of Ste-Anne-de-Beaupré, or enjoy the outdoor recreational facilities of Mont Ste-Anne.

If You Have 4 Days or More

Spend your last day driving along the northern bank of the St. Lawrence River and exploring the small villages along the way. Take a whale-watching cruise out of La Malbaie or the ferry from Baie-Ste-Paul, returning to Québec City via the southern bank.

1 The Top Attractions

BASSE-VILLE (LOWER TOWN)

Musée de la Civilisation ★★★   Try to set aside at least 2 hours for a visit to this special museum, one of the most engrossing in all Canada. Designed by Boston-based, McGill University–trained Moshe Safdie and opened in 1988, the Museum of Civilization is an innovative presence in the historic Basse-Ville, near Place Royale. A dramatic atrium-lobby sets the tone with a massive sculpture rising like jagged icebergs from the watery floor, a representation of the mighty St. Lawrence at spring breakup. Through the glass wall in back you can see the 1752 Maison Estèbe, now restored to contain the museum shop. It stands above vaulted cellars, which can also be viewed.

In the galleries upstairs are five permanent exhibitions, supplemented by up to six temporary shows on a variety of themes, many of them interactive. The mission of the museum has never been entirely clear, but never mind. Through highly imaginative display techniques, hands-on devices, computers, holograms, videos, and even an ant farm, the curators have ensured that visitors will be so enthralled by the experience that they won't pause to question its intent. If time is short, definitely use it to take in "Memoires," the permanent exhibit that is a sprawling examination of Québec history, moving from the province's roots as a fur-trading colony to the present. Furnishings from frontier homes, tools of the trappers' trade, worn farm implements, religious garments from the 19th century, and old campaign posters endow visitors with a rich sense of Québec's daily life from generation to generation.

A new permanent exhibition is "Encounter with the First Nations," which examines the products and visions of the aboriginal tribes that inhabit Québec. Exhibit texts are in French and English. There's a cafe on the ground floor.

85 rue Dalhousie (at rue St-Antoine). ✆ 418/643-2158. Admission C$7 (US$4.50) adults, C$6 (US$3.85) seniors, C$4 (US$2.60) students over 16, C$2 (US$1.30) children 12–16, free for children under 12. Tues free to all (except in summer). June 23 to Labour Day daily 9:30am–6:30pm; Sept–June 22 Tues–Sun 10am–5pm.

Place Royale ★★★   This picturesque plaza is the literal and spiritual heart of Basse-Ville. Royal Square is a short walk from the bottom of Breakneck Stairs, via rue Sous-le-Fort. In the 17th and 18th centuries, it was the town marketplace and the center of business and industry. The Eglise Notre-Dame-des-Victoires—the oldest stone church in Québec, built in 1688 and restored in 1763 and 1969—dominates the enclosed square. The paintings, altar, and large model boat suspended from the ceiling were votive offerings brought by early settlers to ensure safe voyages. The church is usually open to visitors during the day, unless a wedding is underway.

Folk dances, impromptu concerts, and other festive gatherings are often held near the bust of Louis XIV in the center of the square. Guided tours in both English and French are available from the interpretation center.

Impressions

The old world rises in the midst of the new in the manner of a change of scene on the stage . . . on its rocky promontory sits the ancient town, belted with its hoary wall and crowned with its granite citadel. . . .
            —Henry James, "Québec" (1871), in *Portraits of Places* (1883)

Québec City Attractions

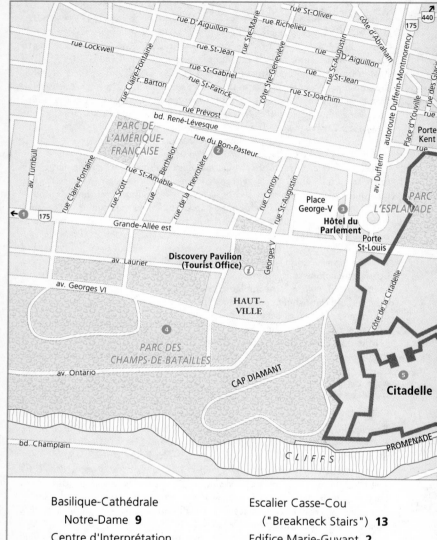

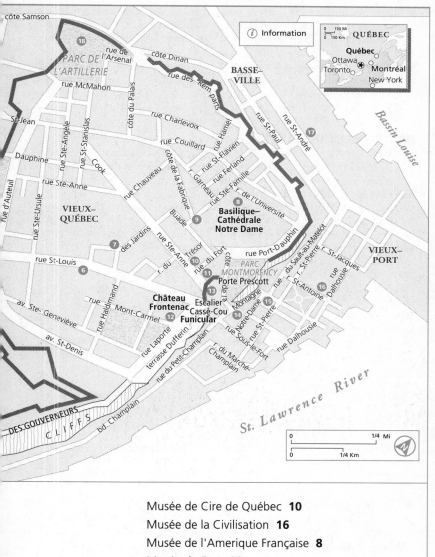

All the buildings on the square have been restored. For years, there was only an empty lot behind the stone facade at the northeast corner, but now it is a whole building again. On the ground floor is the new **Centre d'Interprétation de Place-Royale** (27 rue Notre-Dame; © **418/646-3167**; www.mcq.org). Inside, a multimedia show and other exhibitions detail the nearly 4-century history and development of the plaza.

Admission to Centre d'Interprétation de Place-Royal C$3 (US$1.95) adults, C$2.50 (US$1.60) seniors, C$2 (US$1.30) ages 17 and over, C$1 (US65¢) ages 12 to 16, free under age 12. June 24–Labour Day daily 9:30am–5pm; day after Labour Day to June 23 Tues–Sun 10am–5pm.

HAUTE-VILLE (UPPER TOWN)

La Citadelle ★★ The Duke of Wellington had this partially star-shaped fortress built at the east end of the city walls in anticipation of renewed American attacks after the War of 1812. Some remnants of earlier French military structures were incorporated into the Citadel, including a 1750 magazine. Dug into the Plains of Abraham, the fort has a low profile that keeps it all but invisible until walkers are actually upon it. Never having exchanged fire with an invader, it continues its vigil from the tip of Cap Diamant. British construction of the fortress, now a national historic site, was begun in 1820 and took 30 years to complete. As events unfolded, it proved to be an exercise in obsolescence. Since 1920, it has been home to Québec's Royal 22e Régiment, the only fully Francophone unit in Canada's armed forces. That makes it the largest fortified group of buildings still occupied by troops in North America. As part of a guided tour only, the public may visit the Citadel and its 25 buildings, including the small regimental museums in the former powder house and prison. Despite a couple of spectacular overlooks, the length of the tour and the dry narration are likely to test the patience of younger visitors and the legs of many older people. In those cases, it might be better to attend the ceremonies of the changing of the guard or beating the retreat. Walk or drive up the Côte de la Citadelle (entrance near the St-Louis Gate); there are many parking spaces inside the walls.

1 Côte de la Citadelle (enter off rue St-Louis). © **418/694-2815**. www.lacitadelle.qc.ca. Admission C$6 (US$3.85) adults, C$5 (US$3.25) seniors, C$3 (US$1.95) children 7–17, free for persons with disabilities and children under 7. Guided 55-minute tours daily roughly on the hour, Apr 10am–4pm; May–June 9am–5pm; July–Labour Day 9am–6pm; Sept 9am–4pm; Oct 10am–3pm. Nov–Mar, group reservations only. Changing of the guard (30 min.) June 24–Labour Day daily at 10am; beating the retreat (20 min.) July and Aug Wed–Sat at 6pm. May be cancelled in the event of rain. Walk up the Côte de la Citadelle from the St-Louis Gate.

NEAR THE GRANDE-ALLEE

Musée du Québec ★★ Toward the southern end of the Parc des Champs-de-Bataille (Battlefields Park), just off the Grande-Allée and a half-hour walk or a short bus ride from the Haute-Ville, the Museum of Québec is an art museum that now occupies two buildings, one a former prison, linked together by a soaring glass-roofed "Grand Hall" housing the reception area, a stylish cafe, and a shop.

The original 1933 building houses the permanent collection, the largest aggregation of Québec art in North America, filling eight galleries with works from the beginning of the colony to the present. On the top floor are regional landscapes and canvases of other Québec themes, with some additional examples of North American and British painters. On the ground floor is a splendid assortment of African masks, carvings, musical instruments, and ceremonial staffs. Unfortunately, most descriptive plaques are only in French. Traveling

Room with a View

For a panoramic look at the city, seek out the building that houses Québec's Education Ministry, the **Edifice Marie-Guyart** at 1037 rue de la Chevrotière (© **418/644-9841;** www.observatoirecapitale.org). Enter the tower at the corner of de la Chevrotière and René-Lévesque, and look for signs and elevators directing to the "Observatoire de la Capitale," on the 31st floor. It's the highest overlook in the city. Open late June to mid-October daily 10am to 5pm and late October to late June Tuesday to Sunday 10am to 5pm. Admission is C$4 (US$2.60) adults, C$3 (US$1.95) seniors and students, free for ages 12 and under.

Another place for an overall view is **L'Astral,** the revolving restaurant atop Loews le Concorde Hotel. It isn't necessary to plan a meal there (although the food and prices are more than acceptable), since the bar is as good a vantage point as any. See p. 208 for details.

---

exhibitions and musical events are often arranged. A recent addition to the museum is the 1867 Baillairgé Prison, which in the 1970s became a youth hostel nicknamed the "Petite Bastille." One cell block has been left intact as an exhibit. In this building, four galleries house temporary shows, and the tower contains a provocative sculpture called *Le Plongeur* (The Diver) by the Irish artist David Moore. Also incorporated in the building is the Parc des Champs-de-Bataille Interpretation Centre (see below). There is a children's playroom stocked with toys and books. An accomplished cafe-restaurant serves table d'hôte lunches Monday through Saturday, brunch Sunday, and dinner Wednesday and Saturday nights.

1 av. Wolfe-Montcalm (near av. George VI). © **418/643-2150.** www.mdq.org. Free admission for permanent collection. Admission for special exhibitions C$10 (US$6.45) adults, C$9 (US$5.80) seniors, C$5 (US$3.25) students, C$3 (US$1.95) ages 12 to 16, free for children under 12. June 1–Labour Day daily 10am–5pm (Wed until 9pm); Early Sept–May 31 Tues–Sun 10am–5pm (Wed until 9pm). Bus: 11.

Parc des Champs-de-Bataille ★★
Covering 108 hectares (270 acres) of grassy knolls, sunken gardens, monuments, fountains, and trees, Québec's Battlefields Park stretches over the Plains of Abraham, where Wolfe and Montcalm engaged in their short but crucial battle, resulting in the British troop's defeat of French troops, in 1759. It is a favorite place for all Quebecois when they want some sunshine or a bit of exercise. Free concerts are given during the summer at the bandstand in the park, the Kiosque Edwin-Bélanger. Be sure to see the Jardin Jeanne d'Arc (Joan of Arc Garden), just off avenue Laurier between Loews le Concorde Hôtel and the Ministry of Justice. The statue was a gift from anonymous Americans, and it was here that "O Canada," the country's national anthem, was sung for the first time. Within the park are two Martello towers, cylindrical stone defensive structures built between 1808 and 1812, when Québec feared an invasion from the United States.

Today, Battlefields Park contains almost 5,000 trees representing more than 80 species. Prominent among these are sugar maple, silver maple, Norway maple, American elm, and American ash. There are frequent special activities, including theatrical and musical events, presented in the park during the summer.

Year-round, the park's **Maison de la Découverte** (Discovery Pavilion), at 835 av. Wilfrid Laurier (© **418/648-4071**), provides insights into the significance of the Plains of Abraham to Québec over the years, employing effective multimedia techniques. For C$3.50 (US$2.25), visitors are provided with wireless headsets and directed through several chambers—actually corridors and cells in what was once a prison—to witness dramatic presentations in sound and pictures of episodes in Québec's long history. The narration doesn't fail to describe some of the racier components of that tenure, including a number of elaborate executions, and tales of the prostitutes who serviced the garrison at the Citadelle. It also discusses the landing of Charles Lindburgh on the Plains in 1928. Allow 30 minutes.

The Maison de la Découverte also serves as a starting point for bus and walking tours of the park. In summer, a shuttle bus tours the park in 45 minutes, with narration in French and English.

Discovery Pavilion of the Plains of Abraham, 835 av. Wilfrid Laurier © **418/648-4071.** Free admission to park. Bus tour in summer C$3.50 (US$2.25) for visitors ages 18–64, C$2.75 (US$1.75) ages 13–17 and 65 and over, free for ages 12 and under. Discovery Pavilion open daily 9am–5pm. Park is open at all times. Bus: 3, 11.

2 More Attractions

HAUTE-VILLE (UPPER TOWN)

Basilique-Cathédrale Notre-Dame ★   Notre-Dame Basilica, representing the oldest Christian parish north of Mexico, has weathered a tumultuous history of bombardment, reconstruction, and restoration. Parts of the existing basilica date from the original 1647 structure, including the bell tower and portions of the walls, but most of today's exterior is from the reconstruction completed in 1771. The interior, a re-creation undertaken after a fire in 1922, is flamboyantly neo-baroque, with shadows wavering by the fluttering light of votive candles. Paintings and ecclesiastical treasures still remain from the time of the French regime, including a chancel lamp given by Louis XIV. In summer, the basilica is the backdrop for a 30-minute multimedia sound-and-light show called "Feux Sacrés" (Acts of Faith), which dramatically recalls 5 centuries of Québec's history, as well as the history of this building. The basilica is connected to the group of old buildings that makes up Québec Seminary. To enter that complex, go to 7 rue de l'Université (about a block away).

20 rue Buade (at Côte de la Fabrique). © **418/694-0665.** Free admission to basilica and guided tours. "Feux Sacrés" sound-and-light show C$7.50 (US$4.85) adults, C$5 (US$3.25) seniors, students with ID, and children over 6, free for children under 6. Cathedral daily 7:30am–4:30pm. Guided tours May 1–Nov 1 Mon–Fri 9am–2:30pm, Sat 9am–4:30pm, Sun 12:30pm–4:30pm. The starting times for the tours vary. "Feux Sacrés" sound-and-light show May 1–Oct 15 daily 3:30, 4:30, 5:30, 6:30, 7:30, and 8:30pm; Oct 16–Apr 30, group reservations only.

Chapelle/Musée des Ursulines   The chapel is notable for the sculptures in its pulpit and two richly-decorated alterpieces. They were created by Pierre-Noël Levasseur between 1726 and 1736. Although the present building dates only from 1902, much of the interior decoration is nearly 2 centuries older. The tomb of the founder of this teaching order, Marie de l'Incarnation, is to the right of the entry. She arrived here in 1639 at the age of 40 and was declared blessed by Pope John Paul II in 1980. The museum displays accoutrements of the daily and spiritual life of the Ursulines. On the third floor are exhibits of vestments woven with gold thread by the Ursulines. A cape made of drapes from the bedroom of Anne of Austria and given to Marie de l'Incarnation when she left for New France in

1639 is on display. There are also musical instruments and Amerindian crafts, including the flèche, or arrow sash, still worn during Winter Carnival. Some of the docents are nuns of the still-active order. The Ursuline convent, built originally as a girls' school in 1642, is the oldest in North America.

12 rue Donnacona (des Jardins). (*) 418/694-0694. Chapel free. Museum C$5 (US$3.25) adults, C$4 (US$2.60) seniors, C$3 (US$1.95) students 17 and over, C$2 (US$1.30) ages 12–16, free under age 11. Museum Oct–Apr Tues–Sun 1–4:30pm; May–Sept Tues–Sat 10am–noon and 1–5pm, Sun 1–5pm. Chapel May–Oct same days and hours as museum.

Château Frontenac ⭐   Opened in 1893 to house railroad passengers and encourage tourism, this monster version of a Loire Valley palace is the city's emblem, its Eiffel Tower. The hotel can be seen from almost every quarter, commanding its majestic position atop Cap Diamant. Franklin D. Roosevelt and Winston Churchill held two important summit conferences here in 1943 and 1944. Visitors curious about the interior may wish to take one of the 50-minute guided tours offered daily 10am to 6pm, May 1 to October 15; Saturday and Sunday 1 to 5pm, October 16 to April 30 (departures on the hour). They cost C$6.50 (US$4.20) for adults, C$5.50 (US$3.55) for seniors, and C$3.75 (US$2.40) for children ages 6 to 16. To make reservations, which are required, call (*) **418/691-2166.**

1 rue des Carrières, Place d'Armes. (*) **418/692-3861.**

Musée d'Art Inuit Brousseau   A creation of the people who operate the three most reputable galleries of Inuit art in the city (see chapter 16), this private museum is an extension of the lifelong interest of collector Raymond Brousseau. The permanent collection is supplemented by occasional thematic exhibitions. In addition to carvings in stone and tusk, there are examples of fishing and hunting gear and clothing.

39 rue St-Louis. (*) **418/694-1828.** Admission C$6 (US$3.85) adults, C$4 (US$2.60) seniors and students 13 and older, free for children 12 and under with parent. Daily 9:30am–5pm.

Musée de Cire de Québec   Occupying a 17th-century house, this briefly diverting wax museum, renovated in 1994, skims across the pageant of Québec's history and heroes. Generals Wolfe and Montcalm are portrayed, of course, along with effigies of politicians, singers, Olympic gold medallists, and other newsmakers. Texts are in French and English.

22 rue Ste-Anne (near rue du Trésor). (*) **418/692-2289.** Admission C$3 (US$1.95) adults, C$2 (US$1.30) seniors and students, children under 12 free with parent. May–Oct daily 9am–10pm; rest of year daily 9am–5pm.

Musée de l'Amérique Française   Housed at the site of the Québec Seminary, which dates from 1663, the Museum of French America focuses on the beginnings and the evolution of French culture and civilization in North America. Its extensive collections include paintings by European and Canadian artists, engravings and parchments from the early French regime, old and rare books, coins, early scientific instruments, and even mounted animals and an Egyptian mummy. The mix makes for an engrossing visit.

The museum is located in three parts of the large seminary complex, the Guillaume-Couillard and Jérôme-Demers wings, and the beautiful François-Ranvoyze section, with its trompe l'oeil ornamentation, which served as a chapel for the seminary priests and students. Recent construction has added an annex to the chapel, an underground passage, and a new entrance lobby. Concerts are held in the chapel.

2 Côte de la Fabrique. ☎ **418/692-2843.** www.mcq.org. Admission C$4 (US$2.60) adults, C$3 (US$1.95) seniors and students over 16, C$1 (US65¢) children 12–16, free for children under 12. Late June–Labour Day daily 9:30am–5pm; Sept to mid-June Tues–Sun 10am–5pm. Guided tours (call for reservations) of exhibitions and some buildings daily in summer, Sat and Sun rest of the year.

Musée du Fort   Bordering Place d'Armes, not far from the UNESCO World Heritage monument, this commercial enterprise presents a sound-and-light show using a 120-sq.-m (400-sq.-ft.) panoramic model of the 18th century city and surrounding region. The 30-minute production concerns itself primarily with the six sieges of Québec, including the famous battle on the Plains of Abraham. Commentary is in French or English, in alternating shows. Military and history buffs are the ones most likely to enjoy a visit here.

10 rue Ste-Anne (near Place d'Armes). ☎ **418/692-1759.** Admission C$6.75 (US$4.35) adults, C$5.25 (US$3.40) seniors, C$4 (US$2.60) students. Apr 1–Oct 31 daily 10am–5pm; July–Aug 15 daily 10am–6pm; Dec 26–Jan 2 daily noon–4pm; Feb–Mar Thurs–Sun 12am–4pm; other times by group reservation only.

Parc de l'Artillerie   Fortifications erected by the French in the 17th and 18th centuries enclose the Artillery Park. In addition to protecting the garrison, the defensive works contained an ammunition factory that was functional until 1964. On view are the old officers' mess and quarters, an iron foundry, and a scale model of the city created in 1806. Costumed docents give tours.

It may be a blow to romantics and history buffs to learn that the nearby St-Jean Gate in the city wall was built in 1940, the fourth in a series that begin with the original 1693 entrance, replaced in 1747 and again in 1867.

2 rue d'Auteuil (near Porte St-Jean). ☎ **418/648-4205.** www.parcscanada.gc.ca/artillerie. Admission C$4 (US$2.60) adults, C$3.50 (US$2.25) seniors and students 17 and over, C$2.75 (US$1.75) ages 6–16, free under 6. Early May to mid-Oct Wed–Sun 10am–5pm; rest of year, call for hours.

BASSE-VILLE (LOWER TOWN)

The **Escalier Casse-Cou** connects the Terrasse Dufferin at the top of the cliff with rue Sous-le-Fort at the base. The name translates to "Breakneck Stairs," which is self-explanatory as soon as you see them. They lead from Haute-Ville to the Quartier du Petit-Champlain in Basse-Ville. A stairway has existed here since the settlement began. In 1698, the town council forbade citizens from taking their animals up or down the stairway. If they didn't comply they were punished with a fine.

Maison Chevalier   Built in 1752 for ship owner Jean-Baptiste Chevalier, the existing structure incorporated two older buildings, dating from 1675 and 1695. It was run as an inn throughout the 19th century. The Québec government restored the house in 1960, and it became a museum 5 years later. Inside, with its exposed wood beams, wide-board floors, and stone fireplaces, are changing exhibits on Québec history and civilization, especially in the 17th and 18th centuries. While exhibit texts are in French, guidebooks in English are available at the sometimes-unattended front desk. *Note:* It's also an air-conditioned refuge on hot days.

50 rue du Marché-Champlain (near rue Notre-Dame). ☎ **418/643-2158.** www.mcq.org. Free admission. Late June–Labour Day Tues–Sun 9:30am–5pm; Sept–late Oct and May–late June Tues–Sun 10am–5pm; late Oct–Apr Sat–Sun 10am–5pm.

Centre d'Interprétation du Vieux-Port   A unit of Parks Canada, the four floors of the Old Port Interpretation Center depict the Port of Québec as it was during its maritime zenith in the 19th century. Exhibits illustrate the shipbuilding and lumbering enterprises, employing animated figures and docents in costumes appropriate to the era. The modern port and city can be viewed from the top level, where reference maps identify landmarks. Guided tours of the harbor are available. Texts are in French and English, and most exhibits invite tactile interaction. Guided tours of the Old Port leave from the center.

100 rue St-Andre (at rue Rioux). ✆ **418/648-3300.** www.parkscanada.gc.ca/vieuxport. Admission C$3 (US$1.95) adults, C$2.25 (US$1.45) seniors and students over 17, C$2 (US$1.30) children 5–17, kids under 5 free. May–Aug daily 10am–5pm; Sept to mid-Oct 1pm–5pm.

NEAR THE GRANDE-ALLEE

Hôtel du Parlement   Since 1968, what the Quebecois choose to call their "National Assembly" has occupied this imposing Second Empire château constructed in 1886. Twenty-two bronze statues of some of the most prominent figures in Québec's tumultuous history gaze out from the facade. Highlights are the Assembly Chamber, and the Room of the Old Legislative Council, where parliamentary committees meet. Throughout the building, representations of the fleur-de-lis and the initials VR (for Victoria Regina) remind visitors of Québec's dual heritage. The building can now be toured unaccompanied, but there are free 30-minute guided tours in both French and English. Tour times change without warning so call ahead.

The Restaurant Le Parlementaire (✆ **418/643-6640**) is open to the public. Featuring Québec products and cuisine, it serves breakfast and lunch Monday through Friday most of the year, and dinner Tuesday through Friday in June and December.

Entrance at corner of Grande-Allée est and av. Honoré-Mercier. ✆ **418/643-7239.** Free admission. Guided tours early Sept–June Mon–Fri 9am–4:30pm, Sat, Sun, holidays 10am–4:30pm; June 24–Labour Day Mon–Fri 9am–4:30pm, Sat and Sun 10am–4:30pm.

3 Especially for Kids

Children who have responded to Arthurian tales of fortresses and castles or to the adventures of Harry Potter often delight in simply walking around this storybook city. As soon as possible, head for **Terrasse Dufferin,** which has those coin-operated telescopes that kids are so attracted to. In decent weather, there are always street entertainers, whether they be a Peruvian musical group or men who play saws or wine glasses. A few steps away at Place d'Armes are **horse-drawn carriages,** and not far in the same direction is the **Musée de Cire (Wax Museum),** on Place d'Armes at 22 rue Ste-Anne.

Also at Place d'Armes is the top of **Breakneck Stairs.** Halfway down, across the road, are giant **cannons** ranged along the battlements on rue des Ramparts. The gun carriages are impervious to the assaults of small humans, so kids can scramble over them at will. At the bottom of the Breakneck Stairs, on the left, is a **glass-blowing workshop,** the Verrerie la Mailloche. In the front room, craftsmen give intriguing and informative glass-blowing demonstrations. The glass is melted at 1,395°C (2,545°F) and is worked at 1,092°C (2,000°F). Also in the Lower Town, at 86 rue Dalhousie, the playful **Musée de la Civilisation** (p. 213) keeps kids occupied for hours in its exhibits, shop, and cafe. Military sites are usually a hit, too. The **Citadel** has tours of the grounds and buildings and colorful changing of the guard and beating retreat ceremonies.

The **ferry** to Lévis across the St. Lawrence is inexpensive, convenient from the Lower Town, and exciting for kids. The crossing, over and back, takes less than an hour. To run off the kids' excess energy, head for the **Plains of Abraham,** which is also Battlefields Park. To get there, take rue St-Louis, just inside the

St-Louis Gate, or, more vigorously, the walkway along Terrasse Dufferin and the Promenade des Gouverneurs, with a long set of stairs. Acres of grassy lawn give children room to roam and provide the perfect spot for a family picnic.

Even better is the **Village Vacances Valcartier** (© **418/844-2200;** www. valcartier.com) at 1860 bd. Valcartier in St-Gabriel-de-Valcartier, about 20 minutes' drive north of downtown. In summer, it's a water park, with 23 slides, a huge wave pool, and diving shows. In winter, those same facilities are put to use for snow rafting on inner tubes, ice slides, and skating.

4 Organized Tours

Québec City is small enough to get around quickly and easily with a good map and a guidebook, but a tour is helpful for getting background information on the history and culture of the city, grasping the lay of the land, and seeing those attractions that are a bit of a hike or require wheels to reach, such as the Musée du Québec. **Kiosque Frontenac,** facing the Château Frontenac near the upper terminal of the funicular, can make reservations for most city tours, whether by bus, boat, or foot, and is also a currency exchange. Here are some agencies and organizations that have proved reliable in the past.

BUS TOURS

Buses are obviously convenient if extensive walking is difficult for individual visitors, especially in the hilly and steeply sloping Upper Town. Among the established tour operators **Gray Line** (© **888/558-7668** or 418/649-9226) offers English-only tours, preferable because twice as much information is imparted in the same amount of time as on a bilingual tour. The company's city tours are in small coaches that carry 24 or fewer people, while day trips out of the city, to the casino at Charlevoix and along the south shore, for example, are in full-sized buses. Gray Line also offers a 9½-hour whale-watching excursion by bus to Tadoussac and boat into the St. Lawrence. **Maple Leaf Sightseeing Tours** (© **877/622-3677** or 418/622-3677) picks up passengers at their hotels in a 25-passenger "trolley bus" and embarks on a comprehensive tour of Québec, old and new, Upper and Lower Towns. They also provide walking tours and "step-on" guides—your car or theirs. **La Tournée du Québec Métro** (© **418/ 836-8687** or 800/672-5232) has tours of the city and excursions to Ile d' Orléans and Ste-Anne-de-Beaupré, with hotel pickup.

City tours usually last 2 to 2½ hours and cost from C$22 to C$27 (US$14–US$17) for adults, about half price for children ages 3 to 12. Many of the tour operators also offer half- or full-day (lunch included) tours to Ste-Anne-de-Beaupré, Montmorency Falls, and Ile d'Orléans. These usually cost around C$35 (US$23) for adults.

For more information about bus tours of the city, read the "City Tours" section of the *Greater Québec Area Tourist Guide,* supplied by the tourist office.

HORSE-DRAWN CARRIAGE TOURS

A romantic but expensive way to tour the city is in a horse-drawn carriage, called a *caléche.* They can be hired at Place d'Armes or on rue d'Auteuil, just within the city walls near the St-Louis Gate. The 35-minute guided tour in either French or English costs C$50 (US$32) plus tax and tip. Carriages operate all summer, rain or shine. For information call © **418/683-9222** or 418/624-3062.

WALKING TOURS

Points of departure for walking tours change, so to get up-to-date information on when one is leaving and from where, check at the kiosk on Terrasse Dufferin near the Château Frontenac and beside the funicular entrance. Many tours leave from there. If you want to go at your own pace, an "audio-guide" CD player can be rented at the kiosk for C$10 (US$6.45). Its recorded narration leads past most of the major sites, taking anywhere from 1 to 3 hours.

The **Association des guides touristiques de Québec** (© **418/624-2851**) can provide guides for any length of time, on foot or in your car or theirs. Walking tours of the villages of nearby Ile d'Orléans (see chapter 18) are arranged by **Beau Temps, Mauvais Temps Tours** (© **418/828-2275**).

RIVER CRUISES

A variety of cruise possibilities are offered by **Croisières AML** (© **800/563-4643** or 418/692-1159; www.croisieresaml.com). Weighing in at 900 tons, M/V *Louis Jolliet* is a three-deck 1930s ferry-turned-excursion-vessel. Said to be the largest in Canada, it can carry 1,000 passengers, with bilingual guides, full dining facilities, and bar. Cruises last 1½ hours in the late morning and afternoon, with three daily departures, and 2½ hours in the evening, when dancing and dining are part of the experience. Prices start at C$24 (US$16) for adults, C$22 (US$14) for seniors, C$10 (US$6.45) for children 6 to 16, but are higher for evening cruises and from late June to September.

Meals on the evening dinner and "Love-Boat" cruises are extra, from C$22 to C$32 (US$14–US$21) per person over the cruise fare, tax and service not included. For more information or tickets, drop by the kiosk beside the funicular on Terrasse Dufferin. Board the boat at Quai Chouinard, 10 rue Dalhousie, near Place Royale in the Lower Town.

Croisières AML also has 3-hour **whale-watching cruises** from Baie Ste-Catherine, at the mouth of the Saguenay River. Rates include round-trip bus fare from Québec City, and include a rest stop at the Manoir Richelieu, a resort hotel near Malbaie. The day trip begins at 8:30am and gets back to the city before 8:00pm. Fares are C$79 or C$86 (US$51 or US$56) adults, C$42 or C$56 (US$27 or US$36) children 3 to 16; the higher price applies if you choose to take the small Zodiacs instead of the larger boat. Another cruising and whale-watching tour leaving from Québec City is with **Croisères Dufour** (© **800/463-5250** or 418/692-0222; www.familledufour.com), which picks up passengers at Vieux-Port at 8am and sails downriver to Tadoussac, with three intermediate ports, and spends a couple of hours in the St-Lawrence looking for whales before returning to Québec at about 6:30pm. Fares are C$129 (US$83) adults, C$119 (US$77) seniors, C$65 (US$42) children 6 to 12. Lunch is included. You are most likely to spot whales during the summer.

5 Spectator Sports

Québec has not had a team in any of the professional major leagues since the NHL Nordiques left in 1995, but it is represented by the Capitales baseball club of the Northern League. Home games are played in the Municipal Stadium, 100 rue du Cardinal Maurice-Roy (© **418/521-2255**). Tickets cost from C$6 to C$13 (US$3.85–US$8.40).

Harness races take place at the **Hippodrome de Québec,** 250 bl. Wilfrid-Hamel ExpoCité (© **418/524-5283**). Races take place year-round Thursday to

Tuesday at 1:30 or 7:30pm (times vary from season to season; call ahead). Admission is free. Le Cavallo clubhouse is open year-round.

6 Outdoor Activities

The waters and hills around Québec City provide countless opportunities for outdoor recreation, from swimming, rafting, and fishing, to skiing, snowmobiling, and sleigh rides. There are two centers in particular to keep in mind for most winter and summer activities, both within easy drives from the capital. Thirty minutes from Québec City, off Route 175 north, is the provincial **Parc de la Jacques-Cartier** (© **418/848-3169** or 418/528-8787). Closer by 10 minutes or so is **Parc Mont-Ste-Anne** (© **418/827-4561**), only 40km (24 miles) northeast of the city. Both are mentioned repeatedly in the listings below. From mid-November to late March, taxis participate in a **winter shuttle** program, **HiverExpress,** picking up passengers at 16 hotels at 8:30am, taking them to Mont-Sainte-Anne and Station Stoneham, and returning them to Québec City at about 4:30m. Round-trip fare is C$18 (US$12). Call © **418/525-5191** to make a reservation or ask if your hotel participates when booking a room.

BIKING

Given the hilly topography of the Upper Town, biking isn't a particularly attractive option. But rented bicycles are available at a shop on a hill that descends to the flatter Lower Town. Bikes are about C$8 (US$5.15) an hour or C$30 (US$19) a day. The shop, **Vélo Passe-Sport Plein Air,** at 22 Côte du Palais, also rents in-line skates. It's open daily from 9am to 11pm (© **418/692-3643**). Bikes can also be rented at **Cyclo Services,** at 84 rue Dalhousie in the Vieux-Port (Old Port; © **418/692-4052**), open all year. For more vigorous mountain biking, the **Mont Ste-Anne recreational center** (© **418/827-4561**) has 200km (124 miles) of trails.

CAMPING

There are almost 30 campgrounds in the greater Québec area, with as few as 20 individual campsites and as many as 368. All of them have showers and toilets available. One of the largest is in the **Parc de Mont-Ste-Anne,** and they accept credit cards. One of the smallest, but with a convenience store and snack bar, is **Camping La Loutre** (© **418/846-2201**) on Lac Jacques-Cartier in the park of the same name. It's north of the city, off Route 175. The booklet available at the tourist offices provides details about all the sites.

CANOEING

The several lakes and rivers of **Parc de la Jacques-Cartier** are fairly easy to reach, yet they seem to be in the midst of virtual wilderness. Canoes are available to rent in the park itself.

CROSS-COUNTRY SKIING

Greater Québec has 22 cross-country ski centers with 278 trails. In town, the **Parc des Champs-de-Bataille** (Battlefields Park) has 11km (6 miles) of groomed cross-country trails, a convenience for those who don't have cars or the time to get out of town. Those who do have transportation should consider **Station Mont-Ste-Anne,** which has more than 225km (140 miles) of cross-country trails at all levels of difficulty; equipment is available for rent.

DOG-SLEDDING

Aventures Nord-Bec (© 418/889-8001) at 665 rue Ste-Aimé in Saint-Lambert-de-Lauzon, about 20 minutes south of the city, offers dog-sledding expeditions. While they aren't the equivalent of a 2-week mush across Alaska, there are choices of half-day to 5-day expeditions, and participants obtain a sense of what the experience is like. They get a four-dog sled meant for two passengers and take turns standing on the runners and sitting on the sled. (Shout "Yo" to go left, "Gee" to go right.) Out on the trail it's a hushed world of snow and evergreens. With the half-day trip costing C$69 (US$45) per adult, C$59 (US$38) for students, and C$20 (US$13) for children 12 and under, it's expensive for families, but the memory stays with you. Another firm providing similar experiences is **Aventure Québec** (© 418/827-2227) at 3987 av. Royale at Mont Ste-Anne.

DOWNHILL SKIING

Foremost among the five area downhill centers is the one at **Parc Mont-Ste-Anne,** containing the largest total skiing surface in eastern Canada, with 51 trails (many of them lit for night skiing) and 11 lifts. From November 15 to March 30, a daily HiverExpress shuttle service operates between downtown hotels and alpine and cross-country ski centers. The cars or minivans are equipped to carry ski gear and cost about C$18 (US$12) round-trip per person. For information call © 418/525-5191.

FISHING

From May until early September, anglers can wet their lines in the river that flows through the **Parc de la Jacques-Cartier** and at the national wildlife reserve at **Cap-Tourmente** (© 418/827-3776), on the St. Lawrence, not far from Mont Ste-Anne. Permits are available at many sporting-goods stores.

GOLF

Parc Mont-Ste-Anne has two 18-hole courses, plus practice ranges and putting greens. Reservations are required, and fees are C$60 to C$75 (US$39–US$48), including golf cart. In all, there are two dozen courses in the area, most of them in the suburbs of Ste-Foy, Beauport, and Charlesbourg.

ICE-SKATING

Outdoor rinks are located at Place d'Youville, Terrasse Dufferin, and Parc de l'Esplanade inside the walls, and at Parc des Champs-de-Bataille (Battlefields Park), where rock climbing, camping, canoeing, and mountain biking are also possible. Skates can be rented at **Vélo Passe-Sport Plein Air** (© 418/692-3643), at 22 Côte du Palais in the old town.

SWIMMING

Those who want to swim during their visit should plan to stay at one of the handful of hotels with pools. **Fairmont Le Château Frontenac** has a new one, and the **Radisson** has a heated outdoor pool that can be entered from inside. Other possibilities are the **Hilton, Manoir Victoria,** and **Loews le Concorde.** See chapter 12 for details.

Village Vacances Valcartier, a two-season recreational center in St-Gabriel-de-Valcartier (1860 bd. Valcartier; © 418/844-2200), has an immense wave pool and water slides, as well as 38 trails for snow rafting in winter (kind of like sledding). It's about 20 minutes west of the city.

TOBOGGANING

A toboggan run is created every winter down the stairs at the south end of the Terrasse Dufferin and all the way to the Château Frontenac. Tickets (only C$1 per person) are sold at a temporary booth near the end of the run.

15

Québec City Strolls

The many pleasures of walking in picturesque Québec are entirely comparable to walking in similar *quartiers* in northern European cities. Stone houses huddle close together; carriage wheels creak behind muscular horses; sunlight filters through leafy canopies, falling on drinkers and diners in sidewalk cafes; and childish shrieks of laughter echo down cobblestone streets. Not common to other cities, however, is the bewitching vista of river and mountains that the Dufferin promenade bestows. In winter, Old Québec takes on a Dickensian quality, with lamp glow flickering behind curtains of falling snow. A man who should know—Dickens himself— described the city as having "splendid views which burst upon the eye at every turn."

WALKING TOUR 1	THE UPPER TOWN

Start:	Terrasse Dufferin.
Finish:	Hôtel du Parlement.
Time:	2 hours.
Best Times:	Anytime.
Worst Times:	None.

Start the walk at the:

① Terrasse Dufferin
The boardwalk promenade, with its green-and-white-topped gazebos, looks much as it did 100 years ago, when ladies with parasols and gentlemen with top hats and canes strolled along it on sunny afternoons, with the Château Frontenac as a backdrop. The vistas of river, watercraft, and distant mountains will imprint themselves in your memory.

Stroll south on the Terrasse Dufferin, past the château. If possessed of sufficient energy and leg strength, some people may want to continue up the stairs at the end of the boardwalk to the:

② Promenade des Gouverneurs
This path skirts the sheer cliff wall and climbs up past Québec's Citadel, a 20-minute uphill walk away. Return to the Terrasse Dufferin, walking as far as the battery of ancient (but not original) cannons set up as they were in the old days.

Climb the adjacent stairs into the:

③ Jardin des Gouverneurs
The park, located just west of the Château Frontenac, is so named because it stands on the site of the mansion built to house the French governors of Québec. The house burned in 1834, and the ruins lie buried under the great bulk of the château. The obelisk monument at the lower end of the sloping park is dedicated to both generals in the momentous battle of September 13, 1759, when Wolfe (British) and Montcalm

Walking Tour: The Upper Town

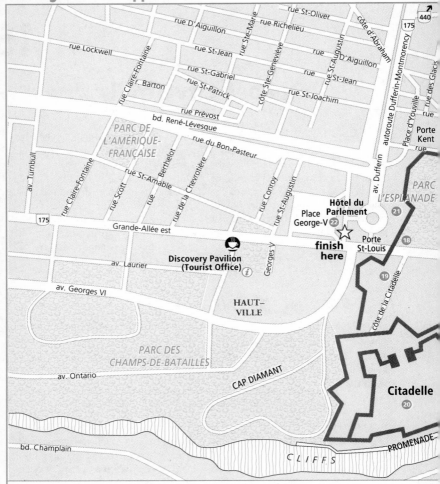

1 Terrasse Dufferin	**9** Château Frontenac
2 Promenade des Gouverneurs	**10** Rue du Trésor
3 Jardin des Gouverneurs	**11** Basilique-Cathédrale
4 Maison Kent	Notre-Dame
5 Maison Jacquet	**12** Séminaire de Québec
6 Maison Maillou	**13** Hôtel-de-Ville (City Hall)
7 Québec Ministry of Finance	**14** Anglican Cathedral of
8 Place d'Armes	the Holy Trinity

(French) fought for what would be the ultimate destiny of Québec and, quite possibly, all of North America. Wolfe, wounded in the fighting, lived only long enough to hear of England's victory. Montcalm died a few hours after Wolfe. Told that he was mortally wounded, Montcalm replied, "All the better. I will not see the English in Québec."

In summer, the park, also known as the Parc des Gouverneurs, is the scene of various shows and musical programs sponsored by the municipal government. The building near the southwest corner of the park is the American consulate.

Walk up rue Mont-Carmel, which runs between the park and the Château Frontenac, and turn right onto rue Haldimand. At the next corner, at rue St-Louis, stands a white house with blue trim called:

④ Maison Kent

Built in 1648, it is possibly the oldest building in Québec. Although it is most famous for being the place in which France signed the capitulation to the British forces, its name comes from the duke of Kent. The duke, Queen Victoria's father, lived here for a few years at the end of the 18th century, just before he married Victoria's mother in an arranged liaison. His true love, it is said, had lived with him in Maison Kent. Today, it houses the consulate general of France, as the tricolor over the door attests.

Diagonally across from Maison Kent, at rue St-Louis and rue des Jardins, is:

⑤ Maison Jacquet

This small white dwelling with crimson roof and trim dates from 1677, and now houses a popular restaurant. Among the oldest houses in the province, it has sheltered some prominent Quebecois, including Philippe Aubert de Gaspé, the author of *Aux Anciens Canadiens,* who lived here from 1815 to 1824. Gaspé's book recounts the history and folklore of Québec.

TAKE A BREAK
Try Quebecois home cooking right here at the restaurant named for de Gaspé's book, *Aux Anciens Canadiens,* 34 rue St-Louis. Consider caribou in blueberry wine sauce or duckling baked in maple syrup, but don't forget the sugar pie floating in cream.

Leaving the restaurant, walk downhill along attractive, if commercialized, rue St-Louis, to no. 17, the:

⑥ Maison Maillou

The house's foundations date from 1736, though the house was enlarged in 1799 and restored in 1959. Note the metal shutters used to thwart weather and unfriendly fire. Now the building houses the Québec Board of Trade and Industry.

The large building across the street from Maison Maillou is the impressive:

⑦ Québec Ministry of Finance

It started out in 1799 as a courthouse, was renovated between 1927 and 1934, and was restored again from 1983 to 1987. Since then it has been Québec's Ministry of Justice, the name on the facade notwithstanding. The architect of the exterior was Eugène-Etienne Tache, Minister of Public Works at that time. The interior of the building is largely Art Deco. The street fronting the Ministry of Finance building is a popular parking spot for calèches, the horse-drawn carriages that tour the city.

Continue down rue St-Louis to arrive at:

⑧ Place d'Armes

This plaza was once the military parade ground outside the governors' mansion (which no longer exists). In the small park at the center of the square is the Monument to the Faith, which recalls the arrival of Recollets monks from France in 1615. The Recollet monks were granted a large plot of land by the king of France in 1681 for their church and monastery. Facing the square is the monument to Samuel de Champlain, who founded Québec in 1608. Created by French artists Paul Chevre and Paul le Cardonel, the statue has stood here since 1898. The statue's pedestal is made from stone that was also used in the Arc de Triomphe and Sacré-Coeur Basilica in Paris.

Near the Champlain statue is the diamond-shaped monument designating Québec City as a UNESCO World Heritage Site, the only city in North America with that distinction. Placed here in 1985, it is made of bronze, granite, and glass. A tourist information center is also at Place d'Armes, at 12 rue Ste-Anne.

Again, up to the right, is the:

9 Château Frontenac

This famous edifice defines the Québec City skyline. The first, lower part was built as a hotel from 1892 to 1893 by the Canadian Pacific Railway Company. The architect, Bruce Price of New York, raised his creation on the site of the governor's mansion and named it after Louis de Buade, Comte de Frontenac. Monsieur le Comte was the one who, in 1690, was faced with the threat of an English fleet under Sir William Phips during King William's War. Phips sent a messenger to demand Frontenac's surrender, but Frontenac replied, "Tell your lord that I will reply with the mouths of my cannons." Which he did. Phips sailed away.

TAKE A BREAK
This is a great part of town to sit and watch the world go by. Grab a sidewalk table and enjoy something to drink or a bite to eat at **Au Relais de la Place d'Armes**, a red-roofed building with a mock-Tudor facade at 16 rue Ste-Anne.

Leaving there, turn right, then right again into the narrow pedestrian lane called:

10 Rue du Trésor

Artists hang their prints and paintings of Québec scenes on both sides of the walkway. In decent weather, it's busy with browsers and sellers. Most prices are within the means of the average visitor. Several of the artists, positioned near adjacent sidewalk cafes, draw portraits or caricatures.

Follow rue du Trésor from rue Ste-Anne down to rue Buade and turn left. On the right, at the corner of rue Ste-Famille is the:

11 Basilique-Cathédrale Notre-Dame (1647)

The basilica has suffered a tumultuous history of bombardment and repeated reconstruction. Its interior is ornate, the air rich with the scent of burning candles. Many artworks remain from the time of the French regime. The chancel lamp was a gift from Louis XIV, and the crypt is the final resting place for most of the bishops of Québec.

Downhill from the basilica on rue Ste-Famille, just past Côte de la Fabrique, is the historic:

12 Séminaire de Québec

Founded in 1663 by Bishop Laval, the first bishop in North America, the seminary had grown into Laval University by 1852, and for many years it occupied the expanded seminary campus. By the middle of the 20th century, however, a new university was constructed west of the city in Sainte-Foy. The entire area is still known as the Latin Quarter—after the language that once dominated university life. An animated neighborhood at night, many visitors will want to return to rues Couillard, Garneau, and St-Jean after the sun goes down. During summer only, tours are given of the old seminary's grounds and some of its stone and wood buildings, revealing lavish decorations of stone, tile, brass, and gilt-framed oil paintings. Call for tour details. The Musée de l'Amérique Française, housed in the seminary, has an entrance at 9 rue de l'Université. It is open year-round.

From here, head back to the basilica. Take a right on rue de Buade and follow it to rue des Jardins to see the:

⑬ Hôtel-de-Ville (City Hall)

The building's lower level, with an entrance at 43 Côte de la Fabrique, houses the Centre d'Interpretation de la Vie Urbaine (Urban Life Interpretation Center), with a large-scale model of Québec City and its suburbs as they were in 1975. It helps strangers to get their bearings, and it might be surprising to see how spread out the city actually is. While the historic Upper and Lower Towns are compact, the city actually covers 92 sq. km (36 sq. miles).

The park next to the City Hall is often converted into an outdoor show area, and in summer, especially during the Festival d'Eté (Summer Festival), concerts, dance recitals, and other programs are staged here.

Continue on rue des Jardins and cross rue Ste-Anne. On the left is the spire of the:

⑭ Anglican Cathedral of the Holy Trinity

This cathedral, said to be modeled after St-Martin-in-the-Fields in London, dates from 1804. The interior is simple but spacious, with pews of solid English oak from the Royal Windsor forest and a latticed ceiling in white with a gilded-chain motif. Visitors may happen upon an organ recital, or at least a rehearsal.

Farther along on rue des Jardins, at rue Donnacona, on the right side of the street, is the:

⑮ Chapelle/Musée des Ursulines

The museum displays the handiwork of the Ursuline nuns from the 17th, 18th, and 19th centuries. There are also Amerindian crafts and a cape that was made for Marie de l'Incarnation, the reverend mother and a founder of

the convent, when she left for New France in 1639.

Be sure to peek into the restored chapel if it's open (May–Oct). It shelters the remains of General Montcalm, who was buried here after he fell in the battle that marked the end of French rule in Québec in 1759. Montcalm's tomb is actually under the chapel and not accessible to the public. His skull, on the other hand, is on display in the Ursuline Museum. The tomb of Marie de l'Incarnation, who died in 1672, is here. The altar, created by sculptor Pierre-Noël Levasseur between 1726 and 1736, is worth a look.

From the museum, turn right on rue Donnacona and walk to the entrance of the Ursuline Convent, built originally in 1642. The present complex is actually a succession of different buildings added and repaired at various times up to 1836, because frequent fires took their toll. A statue of founder Marie de l'Incarnation is outside. The convent is a private girls' school today and is not open to the public.

Continue left up the hill along what is now rue du Parloir to rue St-Louis. Cross the street and turn right. At the next block, rue du Corps-de-Garde, note the tree with a:

⑯ Cannonball

Lodged at the base of the trunk, it purportedly landed here during the War of 1759 and over the years became firmly embraced by the tree.

Continue along St-Louis another 1½ blocks to rue d'Auteuil. The house on the right corner is now the:

⑰ Hôtel d'Esplanade

Notice that many of the windows in the facade facing rue St-Louis are bricked up. This is because houses were once taxed by the number of windows they had, and the frugal homeowner found this way to get around the law, even though it cut down on his view.

Continue straight on rue St-Louis toward the Porte St-Louis, a gate in the walls. Next to it is the Esplanade powder magazine, part of the old fortifications.

Just before the gate is an:

⓲ Unnamed monument

It commemorates the 1943 meeting in Québec of U.S. President Franklin D. Roosevelt and British Prime Minister Winston Churchill, a soft-pedaled reminder to French Quebecois that it was English-speaking nations that rid France of the Nazis.

Cross over St-Louis and turn along Côte de la Citadelle. On the right are headquarters and barracks of a militia district, arranged around an inner court. Near its entrance is a:

⓳ Stone memorial

It marks the resting place of 13 soldiers of General Montgomery's American army, felled in the unsuccessful assault on Québec in 1775. Obviously, the conflicts that swirled around Québec for centuries didn't end with the fateful 1759 battle between the British and the French.

Continue up the hill to:

⓴ La Citadelle

The impressive star-shaped fortress keeps watch from a commanding position on a grassy plateau 108m (360 ft.) above the banks of the St. Lawrence. It took 30 years to complete, by which time it had become obsolete. Since 1920, the Citadel has been the home of the Royal 22e Régiment, which fought in both World Wars and in Korea. With good timing, it is possible to both visit the regimental museum and watch the changing of the guard or the ceremony called "beating the retreat," weather permitting (p. 216).

Return to rue St-Louis and turn left through Porte St-Louis, which was built in 1873 on the site of a gate dating from 1692. Here the street broadens to become the Grande-Allée. To the right is a park that runs alongside the city walls. This is the:

㉑ Site of Winter Carnival

One of the most captivating events in the Canadian calendar, the 11-day celebration takes place every year from the first Thursday to the second Sunday of February. A palace of snow and ice, the centerpiece of the festivities, rises on this spot. Colorfully clad Quebecois come to admire it, climb on it, and sample some maple-syrup candy at the nearby sugar shack set up for the occasion. On the other side of Grand-Allée, ice sculptures are created by 20 teams of artists from around the world participating in the International Snow Sculpture Competition. Each sculpture illustrates an aspect of the culture of the country it represents.

Fronting the park, on avenue Dufferin, stands Québec's stately:

㉒ Hôtel du Parlement

Constructed in 1884, it houses what Quebecois are pleased to call their "National Assembly." Someday the label might actually be accurate. Along the facade are 22 bronze statues of prominent figures in Québec's tumultuous history. The fountain in front of the door, the work of Philippe Hébert (1890), was dedicated to Québec's original Native American, or Amerindian, inhabitants. There are tours of the sumptuous chambers inside, where symbols of the fleur-de-lis and the initials VR (for Victoria Regina) are reminders of Québec's dual heritage. If the crown on top is lit, Parliament is in session.

TAKE A BREAK
Continue along the Grande-Allée 2 more blocks to reach the strip of cafes that cause locals and visitors alike to compare it to another boulevard, the Champs-Elysées. There are plenty of places to stop for a drink or a snack, at outdoor tables in summer. One possibility is **Au Petit Coin Breton**, on the south side of the street, at 655 Grande-Allée est.

From the Grande-Allée, walk or take the no. 11 bus back to the old city. For a longer but scenic hike, continue along Grand-Allée to visit the Musée du Québec, on the left at 1 av. Wolfe-Montcalm; then go into Parc des Champs-de-Bataille (Battlefields Park), picking up the Promenade des Gouverneurs near La Citadelle and proceeding down onto the Terrasse Dufferin and the Château Frontenac.

<table>
<tr><td colspan="2">**WALKING TOUR 2**   **THE LOWER TOWN**</td></tr>
<tr><td>**Start:**</td><td>On the Terrasse Dufferin.</td></tr>
<tr><td>**Finish:**</td><td>Place Royal.</td></tr>
<tr><td>**Time:**</td><td>1½ hours.</td></tr>
<tr><td>**Best Times:**</td><td>Anytime.</td></tr>
<tr><td>**Worst Times:**</td><td>None (except very late at night).</td></tr>
</table>

Descend to the Lower Town by the:

❶ Funicular (Option 1)

Its upper terminus is on Terrasse Dufferin near the Château Frontenac. As the car descends the steep slope, its glass front provides a broad view of the Basse-Ville. The mammoth grain elevators down by the harbor have a capacity of 8 million bushels. Beyond them is the river, with its constant boat traffic, and over to the left, the Laurentides Mountains rise in the distance.

Or, if you prefer a more active (and free) means of descent, use the stairs to the left of the funicular, the:

❶ Escalier Casse-Cou (Option 2)

"Breakneck Stairs" is the self-explanatory name given to this stairway. Stairs have been in place here since the settlement began. In 1698, the town council forbade citizens from taking their animals up or down the stairway.

Both Breakneck Stairs and the funicular arrive at the intersection of rues Petit-Champlain and Sous-le-Fort. At the bottom of the stairs on the left is the:

❷ Verrerie la Mailloche

In the front room, craftsmen give glass-blowing demonstrations—intriguing and informative, especially for children who haven't seen that ancient craft. The glass is melted at 1,395°C (2,545°F) and is worked at 1,092°C (2,000°F). There are displays of the results and a small shop in which to purchase them.

Exiting, walk straight ahead, passing:

❸ Maison Louis Jolliet

Built in 1683, this home belonged to the Québec-born explorer who, with a priest, Jacques Marquette, was the first person of European parentage to explore the upper reaches of the Mississippi River. Jolliet died in 1700 at the age of 55. His former house is now the lower terminus for the funicular and full of tourist trinkets and gimcracks.

Then continue down:

❹ Rue du Petit-Champlain

Allegedly the oldest street in North America, it is usually swarming with restaurant-goers, cafe sitters, strolling couples, and gaggles of schoolchildren ricocheting from one fetching store to another along the way. (See chapter 16 for shopping suggestions.)

At the end of the street, turn left and left again onto boulevard Champlain. A lighthouse from the Gaspé Peninsula used to stand across the street, but it has been returned to its original home, leaving the anchor and

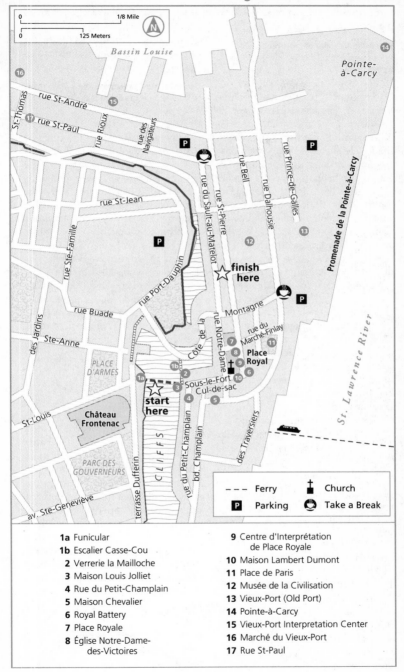

0   1/8 Mile
0   125 Meters

Bassin Louise

Pointe-à-Carcy

rue St-Thomas
rue St-André
rue St-Paul
rue Rioux
rue des Navigateurs

rue Bell

rue Prince-de-Galles

Promenade de la Pointe-à-Carcy

rue St-Jean

rue Ste-Famille

rue du Sault-au-Matelot

rue St-Pierre

rue Dalhousie

rue Port-Dauphin

finish here

rue Buade

Montagne

des Jardins

Ste-Anne

Côte de la

rue Notre-Dame

rue du Marché-Finlay

St. Lawrence River

PLACE D'ARMES

Place Royal

St-Louis

Château Frontenac

Sous-le-Fort
Cul-de-sac

start here

PARC DES GOUVERNEURS

av. Ste-Geneviève

terrasse Dufferin

CLIFFS

rue du Petit-Champlain

bd. Champlain

des Traversiers

| --- Ferry | ✝ Church |
| P Parking | ☕ Take a Break |

1a Funicular
1b Escalier Casse-Cou
2 Verrerie la Mailloche
3 Maison Louis Jolliet
4 Rue du Petit-Champlain
5 Maison Chevalier
6 Royal Battery
7 Place Royale
8 Église Notre-Dame-
   des-Victoires

9 Centre d'Interprétation
   de Place Royale
10 Maison Lambert Dumont
11 Place de Paris
12 Musée de la Civilisation
13 Vieux-Port (Old Port)
14 Pointe-à-Carcy
15 Vieux-Port Interpretation Center
16 Marché du Vieux-Port
17 Rue St-Paul

three cannons that surrounded it looking forlorn and misplaced.

Following the curve of the street, pass more shops and cafes, soon arriving at the crimson-roofed:

⑤ Maison Chevalier

Dating from 1752, this was once the home of merchant Jean-Baptiste Chevalier. Note the wealth of windows in the house, more than 30 in the facade alone. In 1763, the house was sold at auction to ship owner Jean-Louis Frémont, the grandfather of Virginia-born John Charles Frémont (1813–90). John Charles was an American explorer, soldier, and politician who mapped some 10 Western and Midwestern territories. This notable workaholic of French-Canadian heritage was also a governor of California and Arizona, a candidate for president of the United States in 1856, and a general during the Civil War.

The Chevalier House was sold in 1806 to an Englishman, who in turn rented it to a hotelier, who transformed it into an inn. From this time to the end of the century it was known, under various owners, as the London Coffee House. In 1960, the Québec government restored the house, and it became a museum about 5 years later, overseen by the Musée de la Civilisation, which mounts temporary exhibitions here.

Turn left after exiting the house, walking up the short block of rue Notre-Dame to rue Sous-le-Fort. Turn right, and walk 1 more block to the:

⑥ Royal Battery

Erected in 1691, the cannons were added in 1712 to defend the Lower Town. They got the chance in 1759, but the English victory silenced them; the exodus to the Upper Town left them to rust. Sunken foundations were all that remained of the Royal Battery by the turn of the 20th century, and when the time came to restore this area, it had to be rebuilt from the ground up.

From the Royal Battery, return to rue Sous-le-Fort. Here you'll find a good photo opportunity: Up the street, the Château Frontenac is framed between ancient houses.

Go up 1 block to rue Notre-Dame. Turn right. Half a block up the grade is the heart of Basse-Ville, the:

⑦ Place Royale

Occupying the center of the first permanent colony in New France, it served as the town marketplace. The square went into decline around 1860 and by 1950 had become a derelict, run-down part of town. Today it has been restored to very nearly recapture its historic appearance. The prominent bust is of Louis XIV, the Sun King, a gift from the city of Paris in 1928 that was installed here in 1931. The striking 17th- and 18th-century houses around the square once belonged to wealthy merchants. Note the ladders on some of the steep roofs, used to fight snow and fire.

Facing directly onto the square is the small:

⑧ Eglise Notre-Dame-des-Victoires

Named for French naval victories over the British in 1690 and 1711, the oldest stone church in Québec was built in 1688. It was restored in 1763 after its partial destruction by the British in the 1759 siege. The white and gold interior has a few murky paintings and a large model boat suspended from the ceiling, a votive offering brought by early settlers to ensure safe voyages. On the walls, 14 small prints depict the stages of the Passion. The church usually is open to visitors daily from 10am to 4:30pm, unless a wedding is under way.

Walk straight across the plaza, passing the new:

⑨ Centre d'Interprétation de Place-Royale

For decades, this was nothing but a propped-up facade with an empty lot behind it, but it has now been rebuilt to serve as an interpretation center with shows and exhibitions relating the history of this historic district.

At the corner on the right is the:

⑩ Maison Lambert Dumont

Its former function as a wine store is still recalled by the large wine cask spigot jutting from the wall. It's now Geomania, a store selling rocks and crystals.

Walk past the last building on your left about 15m (50 ft.) and turn around. The entire end of that building is a trompe-l'oeil mural of streets and houses and depictions of citizens from the earliest Colonial days to the present, an amusing splash of fool-the-eye trickery.

Return to Place Royale and turn left down rue du Marché-Finlay (in the far-right corner from the church), passing the:

⑪ Place de Paris

The plaza contains an undistinguished white sculpture that resembles a Rubik's Cube. Continue ahead to rue Dalhousie and turn left.

TAKE A BREAK
The immensely popular restaurant, **Le Café du Monde**, 57 rue Dalhousie, at rue de la Montagne, is known for its imported beers, large selection of wines by the glass, and substantial servings of mussels. It's fun, with ingratiating waiters who sometimes sit down at the upright piano to play.

Leaving the cafe, turn left on rue Dalhousie and walk to 85 rue Dalhousie, just past rue St-Antoine, where you'll find:

⑫ Musée de la Civilisation

The museum, which opened in 1988, may be situated among the cobblestone streets in the historic Basse-Ville, but there is nothing traditional about it. Spacious and airy, with ingeniously arranged multidimensional exhibits, it is one of the most innovative museums in Canada, if not in all of North America. If there is no time now, put it at the top of the must-see list for a later visit.

Across the street from the museum is the:

⑬ Vieux-Port (Old Port)

In the 17th century, this 29 hectare (72-acre) riverfront area was the touchdown for European ships bringing supplies and settlers to the new colony. With the decline of shipping and the shifting of economic power to Montréal by the early 20th century, the port fell into precipitous decline. But since the mid-1980s, it has experienced a rebirth, becoming the summer destination for international cruise ships.

Walk across and turn left at the water's edge on the port promenade, soon passing the Naturalium, a privately owned museum of natural sciences that celebrates the biodiversity of the planet, from beetles to bison. Then comes the Agora, an impressive 6,000-seat outdoor theater with a clamshell-shaped stage, and behind it, the city's Customs House, built between 1830 and 1839.

Continue walking along the promenade, past the Agora, to the landscaped:

⑭ Pointe-à-Carcy

From here, look out across Louise Basin to the Bunge of Canada grain elevator, which stores wheat, barley, corn, and soybean crops produced in western Canada before they are shipped to Europe. The bridge to rural Ile d'Orléans can also be seen. Ile d'Orléans is the island that supplies Québec with much of its fresh fruits and vegetables.

Follow the walkway from Pointe-à-Carcy along the Louise Basin. If it is closed, as it may be because of continuing construction, follow the brick walkway toward the Customs House. On the right is the city's new Navy School.

Walk around the Customs House to rue St-André. From here, walk 4 less-than-scenic blocks to rue Rioux. On the right, at 100 rue St-André and rue Rioux (or the left, if the pedestrian walkway along the Louise Basin was the route chosen), is a modern three-story building with blue trim, the:

⑮ Vieux-Port Interpretation Center

This museum illustrates what the Port of Québec was like in the 19th century, during its heyday. Be sure to see the view of the port and the city from the top level of the Interpretation Center. Useful reference maps identify prominent landmarks. The Interpretation Center charges a small admission in summer, but at other times it's free. Texts are in English and French, and visitors are invited to touch most of the exhibits.

From the Vieux-Port Interpretation Center, go to rue St-André, turn right, and walk 1 block to the:

⑯ Marché du Vieux-Port

The market has jaunty green roofs and blue banners. From here look west to see the 1916 train station, designed by New York architect Bruce Price, who designed the Château Frontenac in 1893.

The colorful farmers' market has rows of booths heaped with fresh fruits and vegetables, relishes, jams, handicrafts, flowers, and honey from local hives. Above each booth hangs a sign with the name and telephone number of the seller. A lot of them bear the initials I.O., meaning they come from Ile d'Orléans, 16km (10 miles) outside the city. The market is enclosed, and the central part of it, with meats and cheeses for sale, is heated. There's a little cafe inside at which to order a cup of coffee or a meal, and there is also an ice-cream stand and a bakery.

Leaving the market, cross rue St-André at the light and walk ahead 1 short block to:

⑰ Rue St-Paul

Turn left onto this street, home to a burgeoning number of antique shops and cafes. Most of the shops stretch from rue Rioux, opposite the Interpretation Center, to rue du Sault-au-Matelot. There's a real sense of neighborhood here.

TAKE A BREAK
The busy **Café de Saint-Malo,** at 75 rue St-Paul and rue du Sault-au-Matelot, has low ceilings, rough stone walls, and storefront windows that draw patrons inside. Come for a full meal or, on sunny days, a drink or coffee and dessert at a sidewalk table. From here, meander back toward Place Royale and the funicular along rue du Sault-au-Matelot or rue St-Pierre.

If this walking tour has piqued your interest in Québec's history, the Librairie du Nouveau Monde (New World Bookstore), at 103 rue St-Pierre, can provide an English-language copy of the illustrated and highly readable *An Historical Guide to Québec,* by Yves Tessier.

16

Québec City Shopping

The compact size of the Old Town, with its upper and lower sections, makes it especially convenient for browsing and shopping. Though similar from one place to the next, the merchandise is generally of high quality. There are several art galleries deserving of attention, including an outdoor version in the Upper Town. Antique shops are proliferating along rue St-Paul in the Lower Town.

1 The Shopping Scene

In the Upper Town, wander along **rue St-Jean,** both within and outside the city walls, and on **rue Garneau** and **Côte de la Fabrique,** which branch off the east end of St-Jean. There's a shopping concourse on the lower level of the Château Frontenac. For T-shirts, postcards, and other souvenirs, myriad shops line **rue St-Louis.**

Côte de la Montagne, which leads from the Upper Town to the Lower Town as an alternative to the funicular, has a few stores with more tourist-geared items and some crafts and folk art. The Lower Town itself, particularly the **Quartier du Petit-Champlain,** just off place Royale and encompassing rue du Petit-Champlain, boulevard Champlain, and rue Sous-le-Fort (opposite the funicular entrance), offers many possibilities—clothing, souvenirs, gifts, household items, collectibles—and is avoiding (so far) the trashiness that often afflicts heavily toured areas.

Outside the walls, just beyond the strip of cafes that line Grande-Allée, **avenue Cartier** has shops and restaurants of some variety, from clothing and ceramics to housewares and gourmet foods. The 4 or 5 blocks attract crowds of generally youngish locals, and the hubbub revs up on summer nights and weekends. The area remains outside the tourist orbit.

Most stores are open Monday through Wednesday from 9 or 10am to 6pm, Thursday and/or Friday from 9am to 9pm, and Saturday from 9am to 5pm. Many stores are now also open on Sunday from noon to 5pm.

THE BEST BUYS

Indigenous crafts, handmade sweaters, and **Inuit art** are among the desirable items not seen everywhere else. An official igloo trademark identifies authentic Inuit (Eskimo) art, although the differences between the real thing and the manufactured variety become apparent with a little careful study. Inuit artwork, usually carvings in stone or bone, are "best buys" not because of low prices, but because of their high quality. Expect to pay hundreds of dollars for even a relatively small piece. Apart from a handful of boutiques, Québec City does not offer the high-profile designer clothing often showcased in Montréal.

> (*Tips* **Taxes & Refunds**
>
> Visitors can obtain refunds of taxes incurred for lodgings and shop pur-
> chases. See page 46 for details.

SHOPPING COMPLEXES

In the Upper Town, there's a small complex filled with upscale shops called **Les Promenades du Vieux Québec,** at 43 rue Buade. You'll find a perfumery, a Christmas shop, shops selling Inuit carvings, cafes, a currency exchange, and cloth- ing for men and women, including a Liz Claiborne factory outlet. Just outside the city walls at Porte Kent, **Place Québec** incorporates dozens of shops, a cinema, restaurants, a convention center, and the Hilton hotel, an easy-to-spot landmark. Place Québec is accessible from boulevard Réne-Lévesque and the Hilton. Shop- ping malls on a grander scale aren't found in or near the Old Town. For mall shop- ping, it is necessary to travel to the neighboring municipality of **Sainte-Foy.** The malls there differ little from their cousins throughout North America, in layout and available products. For sheer size, however, you can't beat **Place Fleur de Lys,** at 552 bd. Wilfrid-Hamel (© **418/529-8128**), with 250 retailers, and **Place Lau- rier,** at 2700 bd. Laurier (© **418/651-5000**), with 350 shops.

THE ANTIQUES DISTRICT

Dealers in antiques have gravitated to rue St-Paul in the Lower Town. To get there, follow rue St-Pierre from the Place Royale, and then head west on rue St- Paul. So far, there are more than 20 shops, with more likely to open, filled with brass beds, knickknacks, Québec furniture, candlesticks, old clocks, Victoriana, Art Deco and Art Moderne objects, and even the increasingly sought-after kitsch and housewares of the early post–World War II period.

2 Shopping from A to Z

ARTS & CRAFTS

Abaca   The owners gather their own merchandise on trips abroad. Their inventory includes masks, jewelry, musical instruments, sculpture, and related pieces from Africa, India, Afghanistan, Japan, Korea, China, and a score of other places. Some jewelry and handcrafts by Québec artists are also sold here. The store takes its name from a tree that grows in the Philippines. Another store around the corner also carries the owners' finds: **Origines,** at 54 Côte de la Fab- rique, is filled with jewelry and sculpture. 38 rue Garneau (near rue St-Jean). © **418/ 694-9761.**

Aux Multiples Collections   Inuit, vernacular, and modern Canadian art are on offer in this gallery. The most appealing items, and those given prominence in display, are the Native Canadian carvings in stone, bone, and tusk. The shop ships purchases. Prices are high, but competitive for merchandise of similar quality. Open 7 days. Check out its siblings, the new private museum called Galerie Brousseau et Brousseau at 35 rue St-Louis (© **418/694-1828**), and the Aux Multiples branch at 43 rue de Buade (© **418/692-4298**). 69 rue Ste-Anne (opposite the Hôtel-de-Ville). © **418/692-1230.**

Galerie d'Art du Petit-Champlain   This shop features the superbly detailed carvings of Roger Desjardins, who applies his skills to meticulous renderings of waterfowl. The inventory has been expanded to show lithographs, paintings, and some Inuit art. Open daily. 88 rue du Petit-Champlain (near bd. Champlain). © 418/692-5647.

Galerie d'Art Trois Colombes Quebecois and other Canadian artisans, including Inuits and Amerindians, produce these weavings, carvings, snowshoes, duck decoys, and soapstone sculptures (some by non-Inuits). Upstairs are hand-made hats, coats, sweaters, high-top boots, moccasins, and rag dolls. They ship worldwide. 46 rue St-Louis. © 418/694-1114.

Rue du Trésor Outdoor Gallery Sooner or later, everyone passes this alley near the Place d'Armes. Artists gather along here much of the year to exhibit and sell their work, much like the artists on St-Amable Lane in Vieux-Montréal. Most of the prints on view are of Québec scenes, and one or two might make attractive souvenirs. The artists seem to enjoy chatting with interested passersby. Rue du Trésor (between rue Ste-Anne and rue Buade). No phone.

Version Soleil In the midst of all the antique stores of rue St-Paul, this sun-nily colorful shop traffics in pottery and crafts from many lands, with an evident emphasis on Latin America. 109 rue St-Paul (near Vieux-Port). © 418/692-0032.

BOOKS, MAGAZINES & RECORDS

Archambault This shop has two large floors of recorded music, mostly CDs with some cassettes, and the helpful staff goes to some lengths to find what you want. 1095 rue St-Jean. © 418/694-2088.

Librairie du Nouveau Monde In the Lower Town, this store has a wide variety of books, mostly in French, including the fascinating *Historical Guide to Québec,* by Yves Tessier, a good read (available in English) about the city's past, filled with illustrations, photographs, and a foldout map. 103 rue St-Pierre (behind the Musée de la Civilisation). © 418/694-9475.

Librairie Ulysses Specializing in travel, with guidebooks, travel accessories, and related items, it has smaller branches in the same building as the tourist information office at 12 rue Ste-Anne, opposite Place d'Armes, and at 2600 bd. Laurier in Ste-Foy (© 418/654-9779). 4 bd. René-Lévesque est (near av. Cartier). © 418/529-5349.

Maison de la Presse Internationale As the name says, this large store in the midst of the St-Jean shopping and nightlife bustle stocks magazines, news-papers, and paperbacks from around the world, in many languages. It stays open daily 7am to 11pm or midnight, and it carries the *New York Times,* the *Wall Street Journal,* the *International Herald Tribune,* and many U.S. periodicals. There's another branch in the Place Québec, the mall between the Hilton and Radisson hotels. 1050 rue St-Jean (at the corner of rue Ste-Angèle). © 418/694-1511.

CLOTHING

America A link in the popular chain, this store offers dependably good qual-ity and nice style in casual and dress clothes for men, with intriguing half-twists away from Gap and Banana Republic norms. 1147 rue St-Jean (near rue St-Stanislas). © 418/692-5254.

Excalibor If you arrive in town during Québec's August Medieval Festival, here's the place to purchase doublets and shirts with big floppy sleeves. Fabrics are muslin and velvet and mock brocade. No armor, though. 1055 rue St-Jean. © 418/692-5959.

Ibiza   Replacing a shop that sold toys and kids' things, this leather store sells coats, vests, and handbags. And, oddly enough, knives. 57 Petit-Champlain (in mid-block). ✆ 418/692-2103.

La Maison Darlington   The popular emporium in this ancient house comes on strong with both tony and traditional clothing for men and women produced by such makers as Burberry's, Ballantyne, and Geiger Autrician. Better still are the hand-smocked dresses produced by Quebecois artisans for babies and little girls. 7 rue de Buade (near the Hôtel-de-Ville). ✆ 418/692-2268.

La Maison du Hamac   Although this shop does indeed carry a wide selection of hammocks, as its name asserts, it also has clothing from Latin America and Southeast Asia—colorful hats, shirts, belts, vests, bags, and jewelry from Mexico, Nepal, Guatemala, Indonesia, and Brazil. Kites, too. 91 rue Ste-Anne. ✆ 418/692-1109.

Zazou   This little shop focuses primarily on casual and dressy fashions from Quebecois designers. 31 Petit-Champlain (near the funicular). ✆ 418/694-9990.

A DEPARTMENT STORE

La Maison Simons   The only department store in the old city opened here in 1840. Small by modern standards, Simons has two floors for men's and women's clothing, emphasizing sportswear and household linens. Most of it is pretty basic, and Tommy Hilfiger products are much in evidence. Their stores at Place Ste-Foy (2450 bd. Laurier) and Les Galeries de la Capitale (5401 bd. des Galeries) have a lot of floor space and carry far larger selections of fashions by such designers as Donna Karan and Hugo Boss. Another branch opened in downtown Montréal in 1999. 20 Côte de la Fabrique (near the Hôtel-de-Ville). ✆ 418/692-3630.

FOOD

La Petite Cabane à Sucre   Called the "little sugar shack," it sells ice cream, honey, maple syrup, maple candy, and related products, many in packaging suitable for gifts, including tin log cabins that pour syrup from their chimneys. 94 rue du Petit-Champlain (south end). ✆ 418/692-5875.

Les Halles du Petit-Cartier   This is, in effect, a mall for foodies, containing a collection of merchants in open-fronted shops purveying fresh meats and fish, cheeses, sushi, patés and terrines, glistening produce, deli products, pastries, confections, and fancy picnic items. There are a few fast-food counters and delis that make up sandwiches to order. How about a cooked lobster for your picnic? The mall is open 7 days a week. 1191 av. Cartier (near rue Fraser). No phone.

GIFTS

Artisans Bas-Canada   Crafts and kicky hand-knits predominate, all a little on the expensive side. Duck decoys and burly sweaters for adults and kids are among the most engaging items, supplemented by lots of hats, gloves, mittens, headbands, moccasins, lumberjack coats, soapstone carvings, and Canada-themed books. They tell us they will give a 10% discount to patrons who present a copy of this book. 30 Côte de la Fabrique. ✆ 418/692-2109.

Claude Berry, Inc   Here you'll find hand-painted porcelains from Limoges, jacquard replicas of medieval tapestries, and religious articles—a grab bag that might produce that elusive gift. 6 Côte de la Fabrique. ✆ 418/692-2628.

WINES

Société des Alcools de Québec   A virtual supermarket of wines and spirits, with thousands of bottles in stock. They recently expanded the selling area to incorporate a section of more than 120 kinds of imported beers. There's another SAQ outlet at 888 rue St-Jean (*©* **418/643-4337**). 1059 av. Cartier (near rue Fraser). *©* **418/643-4334.**

17

Québec City After Dark

Although Québec City can't pretend to match the volume of nighttime diversions of exuberant Montréal, there is more than enough after dark activity to occupy your evenings during an average stay. Apart from theatrical productions, almost always in French, knowledge of the language is rarely necessary to enjoy nighttime entertainment.

Drop in at the tourism information office for a list of events, such as the annual **Festival d'Eté** (Summer Festival) in July (② **877/643-8131;** www.infofestival.com/classique), when free concerts and shows are staged all over town in the evenings and the upper portion of rue St-Jean is closed to cars to become a pedestrian promenade. The same holds true for

the **Carnaval d'Hiver** (Winter Carnival) in February (② **418/626-3716;** www.carnaval.qc.ca), when the city salutes the season with a grand ice palace, ice sculptures, and parades.

Concerts and theatrical performances usually begin at 8pm. Most bars and clubs stay open until 2 or 3am. A clear advantage of a night out in Québec City is that cover charges and drink minimums are rare in the bars and clubs that provide live entertainment. Mixed drinks aren't unusually expensive, but neither are they generously poured, which is the reason most people stick to beer, usually Canadian. Some popular brands brewed in Québec are Belle-Gueule, Saint-Ambroise, Boréale, and Maudite (with a winged Satan on the label).

1 The Performing Arts

CLASSICAL MUSIC, OPERA & DANCE

Many of the city's churches host **sacred and secular music concerts,** as well as special **Christmas festivities.** Among the churches are the Anglican Cathedral of the Holy Trinity, Eglise St-Jean-Baptiste, historic Chapelle Bon-Pasteur, and, on Ile d'Orléans, the Eglise Ste-Pétronille. Outdoor performances in summer are staged beside City Hall in the Jardins de l'Hôtel-de-Ville, in the Pigeonnier at Parliament Hill, on the Grande-Allée, and at Place d'Youville.

L'Orchestre Symphonique de Québec, Canada's oldest symphony, performs at the Grand Théâtre de Québec from September to May. The **Québec Opéra** mounts performances there in the spring and fall, as does, more occasionally, the **Danse-Partout** ballet company.

CONCERT HALLS & PERFORMANCE VENUES

Agora   This 6,000-seat amphitheater at the Vieux-Port is the scene of rock and occasional classical concerts, and a variety of other shows in the summer. Iron Maiden, Jethro Tull, Joe Cocker, and Johnny Winter have all appeared here. The city makes a dramatic backdrop. The box office, at 84 rue Dalhousie, is open daily 10am to 6pm in season. 120 rue Dalhousie (Vieux-Port). ② 418/692-4672.

Colisée Pepsi   Rock concerts by name acts on the order of Phil Collins and Led Zeppelin and newer bands like New Radicals and Fun Loving Criminals are often held in this arena, located in a park on the north side of the St-Charles River. The box office is open in summer Monday through Friday 9am to 4pm, in winter 10am to 5pm. 250 bd. Wilfrid-Hamel (ExpoCité). ℭ **418/691-7110.**

Grand Théâtre de Québec   Classical music concerts, opera, dance, and theatrical productions are performed in two halls, one of them containing the largest stage in Canada. Visiting conductors, orchestras, and dance companies often perform here when resident organizations are away. The Trident Theatre troupe performs in French in the Salle Octave-Crémazie. Québec's Conservatory of Music lies underneath the theater. The box office is open Monday through Saturday 10am to 6pm. 269 bd. René-Lévesque est (near av. Turnbull). ℭ **418/643-8131;** www.grandtheatre.qc.ca.

Kiosque Edwin-Bélanger   The bandstand at the edge of the Battlefields Park is the site of a 10-week summer music season, from mid-June to late August. Performances are Wednesday through Sunday and range from operas, chorales, and classical recitals to jazz, pop, and blues. All are free. 390 av. de Bernières (near the Musée de Québec). ℭ **418/648-4050.**

Le Capitole   Various shows are offered on an irregular schedule in this historic 1,262-seat theater. Dramatic productions and comedic performances are in French, but they also host rock groups and occasional classical recitals. An ongoing production, from June to October, is the "Elvis Story," if that's your cup of tea. 972 rue St-Jean (near Porte St-Jean). ℭ **800/261-9903** for tickets, or 418/694-9903 for information.

2 The Club & Music Scene

ROCK, FOLK, BLUES & JAZZ

Most bars and clubs stay open until 2 or 3am, closing earlier if business doesn't warrant the extra hour or two. Cover charges and drink minimums are all but unknown in the bars and clubs that provide live entertainment. There are three principal streets to choose among for nightlife: the Grande-Allée, rue St-Jean, and the emerging avenue Cartier.

Café des Arts   Recently moved from above a store on rue St-Jean, this unusual enterprise puts on a variety of offbeat theatrical pieces, mime, poetry readings, dance, jazz, and *chanson* (the French cabaret singing style). Admission charges are as low as C$3 (US$1.95) and as high as C$16 (US$10). Shows usually start around 8:30pm. 870 ave. de Salaberry (near rue St-Jean). ℭ **418/694-1499.**

Chez Son Père   A musical institution in Québec since 1960, this is the place where French-Canadian folk singers often get their start. The stage is on the second floor, with the usual brick walls and sparse decor. A young, friendly crowd can be found here. The club is a few steps uphill from bustling rue St-Jean. 24 rue St-Stanislas (near rue St-Jean). ℭ **418/692-5308.** No cover.

D'Orsay   Visitors whose complexions have cleared up and who are well into their mortgages will want to keep this chummy pub-bistro in mind. Most of the clientele is on the far side of 35, and they start up conversations easily—two active bars help. There's a small dance floor with a DJ, and in summer afternoons and evenings, entertainers sometime perch on a stool on the terrace out back. There is a full menu of conventional international dishes, from onion soup and fajitas to burgers and mussels. 65 rue de Buade (opposite Hôtel-de-Ville). ℭ **418/694-1582.**

Tips **Finding Out What's On**

Check the "Culture and Entertainment" section of the *Greater Québec Area Tourist Guide* for suggestions. A weekly information leaflet called *L'Info-Spectacles,* listing headline attractions and the venues in which they are appearing, is found at concierge desks and in many bars and restaurants, as is the tabloid-sized giveaway *Voir,* which provides greater detail. Also widely available is *Le Guide Québec Scope,* a free monthly. The *Greater Québec Area Tourist Guide* has both French and English editions, while the rest of the guides are in French, but salient points (time, place, price) aren't difficult to decipher.

Fourmí Atomik   Up the hill from rue St-Jean is this *bar coopérative* populated exclusively by people born after 1975. The large terrace is filled every less-than-frigid afternoon and evening with a group concerned primarily with drinking, talking, smoking, and connecting. Food, while available, is way down the list. Live bands put in appearances from time to time. 33 rue d'Auteil (south of Porte Kent). ✆ **418/694-1473.** No cover.

Kashmir   Upstairs, over the Pizzeria d'Youville, this bar puts on an eclectic variety of musical and artistic presentations, including rock, blues, and art exhibitions, with the added attraction of dancing to a deejay 3 or 4 nights a week. Scheduling is erratic. Pass the time before the evening's performances at the pool tables or poker machines. 1018 rue St-Jean (near rue St-Stanislas). ✆ **418/694-1648.** Cover depends upon performer, usually about C$3 (US$1.95).

L'Emprise   Live jazz, usually of the mainstream or fusion variety, is a long-standing tradition in this agreeable room. The bar, off the lobby of the venerable Hôtel Clarendon, has large windows and Art Deco touches. Seating is at tables and around the bar. It has a mellow atmosphere and attracts serious jazz fans. Music is nightly, from about 10pm. 57 rue Ste-Anne (at des Jardins). ✆ **418/ 692-2480.** No cover.

Les Yeux Bleus   At the end of an alleyway off rue St-Jean, it looks tumble-down from the outside but isn't intimidating inside. The music is mostly Quebecois *chanson,* partly international pop. 1117½ rue St-Jean. ✆ **418/694-9118.** No cover.

Palais Montcalm   The main performance space is the 1,100-seat Raoul-Jobin theater, which presents a mix of dance programs, classical music concerts, and plays. More intimate recitals and jazz groups are found in the much smaller Café-Spectacle. 995 place d'Youville (near Porte Saint-Jean). ✆ **418/691-2399** for tickets.

Théâtre du Petit-Champlain   Quebecois and French singers alternate with jazz groups in this roomy cafe-theater in the Lower Town. Have a drink on the patio before the show. The box office is open Monday through Friday 1 to 5pm, to 7pm the night of a show. Ticket prices range from C$15 to C$30 (US$9.65–US$19) depending on the artist. Performances are usually Tuesday through Saturday. 68 rue du Petit-Champlain (near the funicular). ✆ **418/692-4744.**

DANCE CLUBS

Le Bistro Plus   A bistro by day, things change at night when the dance floor in back fills with dancing young bodies—very young, in many cases. During the week, the music is recorded, with live Latin groups on weekends on the ground floor, a disco on the second floor. It gets frat-house raucous and messy, especially after the 4-to-7pm happy hour, but congenial, too, with darts, a pool table, and TVs tuned to sports to keep people entertained. 1063 rue St-Jean (near rue St-Stanislas). ☎ 418/694-9252. No cover.

Le Dagobert   Long the top disco in Québec City, this three-story club has an arena arrangement on the ground floor for live bands, with raised seating around the sides. Upper floors have a large dance floor, more bars, TV screens to keep track of sports events, and video games. The sound system, whether emitting live (mostly homage or alternative bands) or recorded music, is just a decibel short of bedlam; more than a few habitués are seen donning earplugs. Things don't start jamming until well after 11pm. The crowd divides into students and their more fashionably attired older brothers and sisters. A whole lot of eye-balling and approaching goes on. 600 Grande-Allée (near av. Turnbull). ☎ 418/522-2645. No cover.

Liquid Bar   With a Grande-Allée address but an entrance a few steps down rue de la Chevrotière, Liquid Bar's doors are clogged every weekend with under-25 celebrants eager to gain entrance. Lights rotate and flash across the dance floor, underscoring rap and house music. 580 Grande-Allée. ☎ 418/524-1367.

Living Lounge   One of the newest clubs on Grand-Allée, Living Lounge has two grungy floors—pool tables, foosball, and a bar downstairs, and a dance space upstairs with a couple of bars and house and hip-hop played at the sound levels of jets taking off. The median age is about 8 years below Dagobert and Maurice. 690 Grande-Allée est. No phone. Sometimes a cover of up to C$5 (US$3.25).

Maurice   Successfully challenging Le Dagobert (across the street) at the top rung of the nightlife ladder, this triple-tiered enterprise occupies a converted mansion at the thumping heart of the Grand-Allée scene. It includes a surpris-ingly good restaurant, a couple of bars, and a dance room that rotates live Latin and blues bands, filling the gaps with DJ music. Downstairs, the Charlotte Bar has a variety of live music most nights. Theme nights are frequent, and the bal-conies and bars overflow with up to 1,000 post-boomers. Happy hour means two-for-one drinks. 575 Grande-Allée est. ☎ 418/647-2000. No cover.

Vogue/Sherlock Holmes   This pair of double-decked bars is less frenetic than the Monkey Bar, next door, with a small disco upstairs in Vogue, and the pubby eatery Sherlock below, with a pool table and dart board. Grad students and Gen-Xers spending the disposable income of first jobs make up most of the clientele. 1170 d'Artgny (off Grande-Allée). ☎ 418/529-9973. No cover.

Moments Only in Québec City

The **Basilique Notre-Dame** schedules *son et lumière* (sound-and-light) shows inside the city's loveliest church eight times daily, May 1 to October 15. Tickets cost C$7.50 (US$5).

An after-dinner stroll and a lounge on a bench on **Terrasse Dufferin,** the boardwalk above the Lower Town, may well be your most memorable night on the town. Ferries glide across the river burnished by moonglow, and the stars haven't seemed that close since childhood.

3 The Bar & Cafe Scene

The strip of the **Grande-Allée** between place Montcalm and place George V, near the St-Louis Gate, has been compared to the Boulevard St-Germain in Paris. That's a stretch, but it is lined on both sides with cafes, giving it a resemblance. Many cafes have terraces abutting the sidewalks, so cafe-hopping is an active pursuit. Eating is definitely not the main event. Meeting and greeting and partying are aided in some cases by glasses of beer so tall they require stands to support them. This leads, not unexpectedly, to a beery collegiate atmosphere that can get sloppy and dumb as the evening wears on. But early on, it's fun to sit and sip and watch. The following bars are removed from the Grande-Allée mêlée.

Aviatic Club   A favorite for after-work drinks since 1945, it's located in the front of the city's restored train station. The theme is aviation (odd, given the venue), signaled by two miniature planes hanging from the ceiling. Food is served, ranging from sushi to Tex-Mex, along with local and imported beers. 450 de la Gare-du-Palais (near rue St-Paul, Lower Town). ℂ **418/522-3555.**

L'Astral   Spinning slowly above a city that twinkles below like tangled necklaces, this restaurant and bar atop the Hôtel Loews le Concorde unveils a breathtaking 360° panorama. Many people come for dinner, but you can come just for drinks and the view. 1225 place Montcalm (at the Grande-Allée). ℂ **418/647-2222.**

Le Pape-Georges   This cozy stone-and-beamed wine bar features blues and *chanson* (a French cabaret singing style), along with other styles, usually from Thursday through Sunday at 10pm. Light fare—plates of mostly Québec cheeses, assorted cold meats, and smoked salmon—is served during the day. Although it's in the middle of a tourist district, most of the patrons appear to be locals. 8 rue Cul-de-Sac (near bd. Champlain, Lower Town). ℂ **418/692-1320.**

Saint Alexandre Pub   Roomy and sophisticated, this is one of the best-looking bars in town. It's done in British pub style, with polished mahogany, exposed brick, and a working fireplace that's a particular comfort during the 8 cold months of the year. It serves 40 single-malt scotches and more than 200 beers, 24 of them on tap, along with hearty victuals that complement the brews. Sometimes it presents jazz duos and trios, usually on Monday nights from 7:30 to 11:30pm. Large front windows provide easy observation of the busy St-Jean street life; open daily 5pm to 2am. 1087 rue St-Jean (near St-Stanislas). ℂ **418/ 694-0015.**

GAY BARS

The gay scene in Québec City is a small one, centered in the Upper Town just outside the city walls, on **rue St-Jean** between **avenue Dufferin** and **rue St-Augustin,** and also along rue St-Augustin and nearby **rue d'Aiguillon,** which runs parallel to rue St-Jean. One popular bar and disco, frequented by both men and women (and by men who appear to be women), is **Le Ballon Rouge,** at 811 rue St-Jean (ℂ **418/647-9227**). Upstairs is the **Lazyboy** lounge, with a bathroom you have to see. Nearby is a club called **Le Drague** ("The Drag"), at 815 rue St-Augustin (ℂ **418/649-7212**), which has a dance room, pool tables, and—you guessed it—drag shows on Sunday. There are live performances of other kinds Thursdays through Saturdays.

18

Side Trips from Québec City

The first four excursions described below can be combined and completed in a day. Admittedly, it will be a breakfast-to-dark undertaking, especially if much time is taken to explore each destination, but the farthest of the four destinations is only 40km (25 miles) from Québec City.

The famous shrine of Ste-Anne-de-Beaupré and the Mont Ste-Anne ski area are only about half an hour from the city by car, while bucolic Ile d'Orléans, with its maple groves, orchards, farms, and 18th- and 19th-century houses, is a mere 15 minutes away. With 2 or more days available, you can continue along the northern shore to Charlevoix, where inns and a gambling casino invite an overnight stay, and then take the ferry across the river and drive back toward Québec City, exploring the villages along the St. Lawrence's southern bank as you make your way.

Although it is preferable to drive in this region, tour buses go to Montmorency Falls and the shrine of Ste-Anne-de-Beaupré, and circle the Ile d'Orléans.

For more information, log on to **www.quebecregion.com**.

1 Ile d'Orléans

16km (10miles) NE of Québec City

Until 1935, the only way to get to Ile d'Orléans was by boat (in summer) or over the ice (in winter). The highway bridge since built has allowed the fertile fields of the island to become Québec City's primary market-garden. During harvest periods, fruits and vegetables are picked fresh on the farms and trucked into the city daily. In mid-July, hand-painted signs posted by the main road on the island announce FRAISES: CUEILLIR VOUS-MEME (Strawberries: Pick 'em yourself). The same invitation is made during apple season, September through October. Farmers hand out baskets and quote the price, paid when the basket's full. Bring along a bag or box to carry away the bounty.

ESSENTIALS
GETTING THERE
BY BUS   There are no local buses. For organized bus tours, contact **La Tournée du Québec Métro** (© 418/836-8687), **Old Québec Tours** (© 418/624-0460), or **Gray Line** (© 418/649-9226).

BY CAR   It's a short drive from Québec City to the island. Follow avenue Dufferin (in front of the Parliament building) to connect with Autoroute 440 east, in the direction of Ste-Anne-de-Beaupré. In about 15 minutes, the Ile d'Orléans bridge is seen on the right. If you'd like a guide, **Maple Leaf Guide Services** (© 418/622-3677) can provide one in your car or theirs.

VISITOR INFORMATION

After arriving on the island, turn right on Route 368 East toward Ste-Pétronille. The **Bureau d'Information Touristique** (© **418/828-9411**) is in the house on the right, and it has a useful guidebook (C$1, US65¢) for the island. It's open June 24 to mid-October Sunday through Thursday 8:30am to 7:30pm, Friday and Saturday 8:30am to 8pm; the rest of the year Monday through Friday 9am to 5pm, Saturday 10am to 5pm, Sunday 10am to 4pm. A good substitute for the Ile d'Orléans guide is the *Québec City and Area* guide, which describes a short tour of Ile d'Orléans. A driving-tour cassette can be rented or purchased at the tourist office, and cycling maps are available there.

The lodgings recommended below for the Ile d'Orléans are all of the *auberge* type, meaning they have six or more rooms and have full-service dining rooms open to both guests and nonguests. But there are also many bed-and-breakfast inns and *gîtes* (homes with a room or two available to travelers). Cheaper and less elaborate than the auberges, many of them provide leaflets and photos to the tourist office so that you can check them out there.

EXPLORING THE ISLAND

The island was long isolated from the mainland, as is evident in the three **stone churches** that date from the days of the French regime. There are only seven such churches left in all of Québec, so this is a point of pride for Ile d'Orléans. A firm resistance to development has kept many of its old houses intact as well. Though this could easily have become just another sprawling bedroom community, it has remained a rural farming area—and island residents work to keep it that way. They even hope to bury their telephone lines and to put in a bicycle lane to cut down on car traffic.

A coast-hugging road circles the island, 39km (21 miles) long and 8km (5 miles) wide, and another couple of roads bisect it. Farms and picturesque houses dot the east side of the island, and abundant apple orchards enliven the west side.

There are six tiny villages on Ile d'Orléans, each with a church as its focal point. It's possible to do a quick circuit of the island in half a day, but a full day may be justified if you eat in a couple of restaurants, visit a sugar shack, skip stones from the beach, and stay the night in one of the several waterside inns. If you're strapped for time, drive as far as St-Jean, then take Route du Mitan across the island, and return to the bridge, and Québec City, via Route 368 West.

STE-PETRONILLE

The first village reached on the recommended counterclockwise tour is Ste-Pétronille, only 3km (2 miles) from the bridge. With 1,050 inhabitants, it is best known for its Victorian inn, **La Goéliche** (see below), and also claims the northernmost stand of **red oaks** in North America, dazzling in autumn. The houses were once the summer homes of wealthy English in the 1800s; the church dates from 1871. Even if you don't stay at the inn, drive down to the water's edge, where a small public area with benches is located. Strolling down the picturesque **rue Laflamme** is another pleasant way to while away an hour or two.

Where to Stay & Dine

La Goéliche ⭐ On a rocky point of land at the southern tip of the island stands this country inn and restaurant with a wraparound porch. Actually, this is a virtual replica of the 1880 Victorian house that stood here until 1996. That one burned to the ground, leaving nothing but the staircase. This one was completed in record time and manages to retain the period flavor with tufted

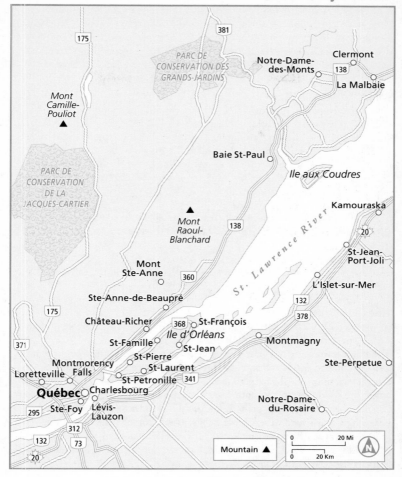

chairs, Tiffany-style lamps, and a few antiques. Only the two suites have TVs. The river slaps at the foundation of the glass-enclosed terrace dining room, which is a grand observation point for watching cruise ships and Great Lakes freighters steaming past.

22 Chemin du Quai, Ste-Pétronille, PQ G0A 4C0. ℂ **888/511-2248** or 418/828-2248. Fax 418/828-2745. www.goeliche.ca. 18 units. C$157–C$197 (US$105–US$131) double. Rates include breakfast. Meal plan available. AE, DC, DISC, MC, V. Free parking. **Amenities:** Restaurant (Contemporary French); bar; heated outdoor pool; golf and tennis nearby; massage; babysitting. *In room:* Minibar, coffeemaker, hair dryer.

ST-LAURENT

From Ste-Pétronille, continue on Route 368 East. After 6km (4 miles), you'll arrive at St-Laurent, once a boat-building center turning out 400 craft per year. To learn more about the town's maritime history, visit **Le Parc Maritime de St-Laurent** (ℂ **418/828-9672**), an active boat yard from 1908 to 1967. Before the bridge was built, it provided islanders the means to get across the river to

Québec City. The Maritime Park incorporates the old Godbout Boatworks and offers demonstrations of the craft. It's open daily mid-June to Labour Day, 10am to 5pm.

The town's church was erected in 1860, and there are a couple of picturesque roadside chapels as well. You'll find good views of farmlands and the river from the St-Laurent golf course—follow signs from the main road.

Where to Stay & Dine

Le Canard Huppé   A roadside inn reminiscent of those found in the motherland, this tidy young establishment takes considerable pride in its kitchen. Consider this one menu item: crimson raviolis stuffed with duck confit and smoked snails and drizzled with lobster butter. All meals are served; breakfast and lunch can be had in the bistro/bar or out on the terrace under the linden tree, while dinner is presented in the main dining room where the service meets professional standards. Rooms upstairs don't have TVs or phones, but they are attractively decorated, with firm mattresses.

In addition, the owners have opened an annex down the road, directly on the river. Five of its six rooms have electric fireplaces, three have whirlpool tubs, and all have TVs.

2198 Chemin Royal, St-Laurent, PQ G0A 3Z0. (C) **800/838-2292** or 418/828-2292. Fax 418/828-2292. www.canard-huppe.qc.ca. 10 units in inn, 6 units in villa. C$100–C$155 (US$65–US$100) double. Rates include full breakfast. Packages available. AE, DC, MC, V. **Amenities:** Restaurant (Contemporary French); bar; small outdoor pool. *In room:* A/C, no phone in inn, TV in villa.

Where to Dine

Le Moulin de Saint-Laurent ✦ COUNTRY FRENCH   This former flour mill, in operation from 1720 to 1928, has been transformed into one of the island's most romantic restaurants. Rubble-stone walls and hand-wrought beams form the interior, with candlelight glinting off hanging copper and brass pots. On a warm day, sit on the shaded terrace beside the waterfall, and be sure to wander upstairs to see the Quebecois antiques. Lunch can be light—an omelet or a plate of assorted patés or cheeses, perhaps. The light, dry cider made on the island is a refreshing alternative to wine. On weekends, a small combo plays in the evenings.

The owners also have cottages for rent at the shore. Two-night/3-day packages are C$225 to C$249 (US$145–US$161) per person, including breakfast, dinner, and either a 1½-hour cruise or 1-day bike rental.

754 Chemin Royal. (C) **888/629-3888** or 418/829-3888. Fax 418/829-3716. www.moulinstlaurent.qc.ca. Reservations recommended at dinner. Main courses lunch C$9.95–C$19 (US$6.40–US$12), dinner C$13–C$24 (US$8.35–US$15); table d'hôte, add C$13 (US$8.35) to the price of the main course. AE, DC, MC, V. Daily 10:30am–2pm and 6–9pm. Closed mid-Oct to May 1.

ST-JEAN

St-Jean, 6km (4 miles) from St-Laurent, was home to sea captains. That might be why the houses in the village appear more luxurious than others on the island. The yellow bricks in the facades of several of the homes were ballast in boats that came over from Europe. The village church was built in 1732, and the walled cemetery is the final resting place of many fishermen and seafarers.

On the left as you enter the village is one of the largest and best-preserved houses on the island: **Manoir Mauvide-Genest,** 1451 av. Royale ((C) **418/ 829-2630**). Completed in 1752 and thoroughly restored in 2001, it is filled with period furnishings. Guided tours are provided by costumed docents. A "beggar's bench" on view was so named because a homeless person who appeared at the door late in the day would be offered a bed for the evening (otherwise, he might cast a spell on the house). A small chapel was added in 1930; Huron Indians made the altar. Open hours vary, so call ahead. Admission is C$5 (US$3.25) for adults, C$2 (US$1.30) for children under 11.

If you're pressed for time, pick up **Route du Mitan,** which crosses Ile d'Orléans from here to St-Famille on the west side of the island. Route du Mitan, not easy to spot, is on the left just past the church in St-Jean. A detour down the road is a diverting drive through farmland and forest. Return to St-Jean and proceed east on Route 368 to St-François.

ST-FRANCOIS

The 9km (5½-mile) drive from St-Jean to St-François exposes vistas of the Laurentian Mountains off to the left on the western shore of the river. Just past the village center of St-Jean, **Mont Ste-Anne** can be seen, its slopes scored by ski trails. At St-François, home to about 500 people, the St. Lawrence, a constant and mighty presence, is 10 times wider than when it flows past Québec City. Regrettably, the town's original church (1734) burned in 1988. The 1992 replacement can be visited. At St-François, 24km (15 miles) from the bridge, the road becomes Route 368 West.

Where to Stay & Dine

Auberge Chaumonot QUEBECOIS   At this riverside inn, the food reflects what farmers have eaten on this island for generations—pork chops, lamb, salmon, meatball stew, pheasant paté, tomato-and-onion relish, and plenty of warm bread. The kitchen mixes in a few relatively modern touches, such as quiche Lorraine and shrimp and duck paté. Picture windows look out on the river.

The inn has eight tidy rooms available, all with air-conditioning and TV. They are quite ordinary, but if you wish to stay the night, doubles with breakfast go for C$89 to C$149 (US$57–US$96). There's also an outdoor pool.

425 av. Royale, St-François. © 418/829-2735. Fax 418/829-0483. www.aubergechaumonot.specialistes. com. Reservations recommended. Main courses C$18–C$27 (US$12–US$17); table d'hôte lunch C$9.95–C$19 (US$6.40–US$12), dinner C$24–C$32 (US$16–US$21). AE, MC, V. Daily 11am–3pm and 5–9pm (until 10pm July–Aug). Closed Nov–Apr.

STE-FAMILLE

Founded in 1661 at the northern tip of the island, Ste-Famille is the oldest parish on the island. With 1,660 inhabitants, it is 8km (5 miles) from St-François and 19km (12 miles) from the bridge. Across the road from the triple-spired church (1743) is the convent of **Notre-Dame Congregation,** founded in 1685 by Marguerite Bourgeoys, one of Montréal's prominent early citizens. This area supports dairy and cattle farms and apple orchards.

Anglers might wish to swing by **Etang Richard Boily,** 4739 Chemin Royal (© 418/829-2874), where they can cast their lures for speckled or rainbow trout in a stocked pond, daily 9am to sunset. It isn't *entirely* like fishing in a rain barrel. Poles and bait are supplied—no permit is required—and customers pay only for what they catch, about C45¢ (US30¢) per inch; the fish run 9 to 12 inches. They'll clean, cut, and pack what you catch. Some island restaurants can even be persuaded to cook the fish for you. For more passive activity, buy a handful of fish pellets, toss them in the water, and watch the ravenous trout jump.

On the same property is a *cabane à sucre,* the traditional "sugar shack" where maple syrup is made. See demonstrations of the equipment and get debriefed on the process that turns the sap of a tree into syrup. Free tastes are offered and several types of products are for sale in a shop on the premises.

Farther along, near the village church, you might wish to visit the **Boulangerie G.H. Blouin,** 3967 Chemin Royal (✆ **418/829-2590**), run by a family of bakers who have lived on the island for 300 years. You'll also find a little shop called **Le Mitan** (✆ **418/829-3206**) that stocks local crafts and books about the island.

ST-PIERRE

By Ile d'Orléans standards, St-Pierre is a big town, with a population of about 2,000. Its central attraction is the island's oldest church (1717). Services are no longer held there; it contains a large handicraft shop in the back, behind the altar, which is even older than the church (1695). The pottery, beeswax candles, dolls, scarves, woven rugs, and blankets aren't to every taste but are worth a look.

Thousands of migrating snow geese, ducks, and Canada geese stop by in the spring, a spectacular sight when they launch themselves into the air in flapping hordes so thick they almost blot out the sun.

Where to Stay & Dine

Le Vieux Presbytère   Down the street running past the front of the church, this former 1790 rectory has been converted to a homey inn. Filled with antiques and other old pieces, its sitting and dining rooms and glassed-in sun porch coax strangers into conversation. For privacy, choose one of the cottages 30m (100 ft.) from the main house; for more space and enough beds for a family of five, ask for room number one.

A fireplace warms the dining room much of the year. The kitchen is fond of game, including ostrich, bison, and wapiti (deer). Main courses run from about C$15 to C$28 (US$9.65–US$18), with a table d'hôte of C$30 (US$19). They have ostriches, elk, and bison in the adjoining lot, an unexpected sight.

1247 av. Mgr. d'Esgly, St-Pierre, PQ G0A 4E0. ✆ **888/828-9723** or 418/828-9723. Fax 418/828-2189. www.presbytere.com. 8 units (2 share a bathroom). C$65–C$125 (US$42–US$81) double. Rates include breakfast. Meal plan available. AE, DC, MC, V. **Amenities:** Restaurant (Regional); bike rental; limited room service; laundry service. *In room:* No phone.

2 Montmorency Falls

11km (7 miles) NE of Québec City

At 83m (274 ft.), the falls, named by Samuel de Champlain for his patron, the duke of Montmorency, are 30m (100 ft.) higher than Niagara—a boast no visitor is spared. They are, however, far narrower. The waterfall is surrounded by the provincial Parc de la Chute-Montmorency, where, from early May through late October, visitors can stop to take in the view or have a picnic. In winter, the plunging waters contribute to a particularly impressive sight: The freezing spray sent up by the falls builds a mountain of white ice at the base called the "Sugarloaf," which sometimes grows as high as 30m (100 ft.). On summer nights the falls are illuminated, and toward the end of July and into August, there is an international fireworks competition overhead, **Les Grands Feux Loto-Québec.** The yellow cast of the waterfall results from the high iron content of the riverbed.

ESSENTIALS
GETTING THERE

BY BUS   Programs are subject to frequent change, so check with **La Tournée du Québec Métro** (✆ **418/836-8687**), **Old Québec Tours** (✆ **418/664-0460**), or **Gray Line** (✆ **418/649-9226**) to see what's currently available.

BY CAR   Take Autoroute 40, north of Québec City, going east. At the end of the autoroute, where it intersects with Route 360, the falls come into view.

VISITOR INFORMATION

A **tourist information** booth is located beside the parking area at the falls, just after the turnoff from the highway (© **418/663-2877;** www.chute montmorency.qc.ca). It's open early June to early September 9am to 7pm, and early September to mid-October 11am to 5pm. Admission to the falls is free.

VIEWING THE FALLS

In 1759, General Wolfe and his army of 4,000 hauled 30 heavy cannons to the heights east of the cataract, aiming them at French troops deployed on the opposite side. The British lost the ensuing firefight but 6 weeks later won the decisive battle on the Plains of Abraham. One of the earthen strongholds they constructed survives.

There are a variety of platforms from which the falls can be viewed, including a footbridge that spans the river just where it flows over the cliff, stairs that descend one side from the top to near the bottom, and a cable car (not for the vertiginous) that runs from the parking lot to a terminal near a manor house that contains an interpretation center, a cafe-bar, and a restaurant. **Manoir Montmorency,** above the falls, was opened in 1994, replacing an earlier structure that burned down. Lunches and dinners of notably improved quality are served there daily, all year, except Monday and Tuesday January through March, when only lunches are served. The dining room and porch have a side view of the falls.

Round-trip fares on the cable car cost C$7.50 (US$4.85) for adults, C$4.50 (US$2.90) for ages 6 to 16.

3 Ste-Anne-de-Beaupré

35km (22 miles) NE of Québec City, 24km (15 miles) NE of Montmorency Falls

Legend has it that French mariners were sailing up the St. Lawrence River in the 1650s when they ran into a terrifying storm. They prayed to their patroness, St. Anne, to save them, and when they survived they dedicated a wooden chapel to her on the north shore of the St. Lawrence, near the site of their perils. Not long afterward, a laborer on the chapel was said to have been cured of lumbago, the first of many documented miracles. Since that time, pilgrims have made their way here—over a million a year—to pay their respects to St. Anne, the mother of the Virgin Mary and grandmother of Jesus.

ESSENTIALS
GETTING THERE

BY BUS   An intercity bus to Ste-Anne-de-Beaupré leaves the Québec City bus station three times a day, at around 9:15am, 3pm, and 6:15pm. Return trips are at 2:25pm and 6pm Monday through Saturday and 8pm Sunday. Always call ahead to confirm departure times (© **418/525-3000**). The round-trip fare is C$12 (US$7.75). Also check with **La Tournée du Québec Métro** (© **418/ 836-8687**), **Old Québec Tours** (© **416/664-0460**), or **Gray Line** (© **418/ 649-9226**).

BY CAR   From Montmorency Falls, it's a 20-minute drive along Route 138 East to the little town of Ste-Anne-de-Beaupré. The highway goes right past the basilica, with an easy entrance into the large parking lot.

VISITOR INFORMATION

An **information booth** at the southwestern side of the basilica, 10018 av. Royale (© **418/827-3781**), is open year-round, daily 8:30am to 4:30pm. The basilica itself is open year-round. Admission is free. Masses are held daily but hours vary.

EXPLORING THE BASILICA

The towering **basilica** is the most recent building raised on this spot in St. Anne's honor. After the sailors' first modest wooden chapel was swept away by a flood in the 1600s, another chapel was built on higher ground. Floods, fires, and the ravages of time dispatched later buildings, until a larger, presumably sturdier structure was erected in 1887. In 1926, it, too, lay in ruins, gutted by fire. As a result of a lesson finally learned, the present basilica is constructed in stone, following an essentially neo-Romanesque scheme.

Note that the church and the whole town of Ste-Anne-de-Beaupré are particularly busy on days of saintly significance: the first Sunday in May, mid- through late July, the fourth Sunday in August, and early September.

Other attractions in Ste-Anne-de-Beaupré include the **Way of the Cross**, with life-size bronze figures, on the hillside opposite the basilica; the **Scala Santa Chapel** (1891); and the **Memorial Chapel** (1878), with a bell tower and altar from the late 17th and early 18th centuries, respectively. More commercial than devotional are the Cyclorama, a 360° painting of Jerusalem, and the Musée Sainte-Anne, featuring art dedicated to Saint Anne. Admission to the Musée Sainte-Anne is C$4 (US$2.60) adults, C$3 (US$1.95) children 6 to 13; to the Cyclorama, it's C$6 (US$3.85) adults, C$3 (US$1.95) children 6 to 15.

Driving north on Route 138 toward Mont Ste-Anne, about 2km (1½ miles) from Ste-Anne-de-Beaupré, on the left, is a factory-outlet strip mall—about as far from the divine as you can get—called **Promenades Ste-Anne** (© **418/827-3555**). It has shops selling discounted merchandise from Dansk, Liz Claiborne, Mondi, Marikita (crafts), and Benetton, as well as a bistro serving California-style food. The mall is open 7 days a week.

WHERE TO STAY & DINE

Auberge La Camarine ⭑   Why they named it after a bitter berry is uncertain, but this inn has a kitchen that is equaled by only a handful of restaurants in the entire region. The cuisine bears a resemblance to the variety of fusion cookery that joins French, Italian, and Asian techniques and ingredients. Rabbit stuffed with sweetbreads and spinach, and joined with two-mushroom risotto, is illustrative of the style. Presentation is of the edifice variety, too often employing upright groves of rosemary and thyme. Never mind. The contrasting colors, flavors, and textures are made to work magically together. The owners are justly proud of their wine cellar. Only dinner is served (overnight guests can get breakfast and a light lunch), daily from 6 to 8:30pm. The pace of a meal is leisurely. Reservations are required. The restaurant is open nightly for 10 months a year, and closed Sunday and Monday in November and May.

Guest rooms blend antique and contemporary notions, and some have fireplaces and/or Exercycles. Two have Jacuzzis. The ski slopes of Mont Ste-Anne are a short drive away by car or regular shuttle.

10947 bd. Ste-Anne, Beaupré, PQ G0A 1E0. © **800/567-3939** or 418/827-5703. Fax 418/827-5430. www.camarine.com. 31 units. C$105–C$149 (US$68–C$96) double. Many packages available. AE, DC, MC, V. Go past the Promenades Ste-Anne outlet center, turning left off Route 138. **Amenities:** Restaurant (Fusion); outdoor pool; bar; golf nearby; access to nearby health club; babysitting; coin-op laundry. *In room:* A/C, TV, coffeemaker.

4 Mont Ste-Anne

40km (25 miles) NE of Québec City, about 10km (6 miles) NE of Ste-Anne-de-Beaupré

Like Montréal, Québec City has its Laurentian hideaways. But there are differences: The Laurentians sweep down quite close to the St. Lawrence at this point, so Quebecois need drive only about 30 minutes to be in the woods. And since Québec City is much smaller than Montréal, the Québec City resorts are more modest in size and fewer in number, but their facilities and amenities are equal to those of resorts elsewhere in the Laurentian range.

Mont Ste-Anne is a four-season getaway offering the best skiing near Québec City as well as a plethora of outdoor activities during the summer, including golf, mountain biking, hiking, and paragliding.

ESSENTIALS
GETTING THERE
BY BUS   The **HiverExpress** (© **418/525-5191**) shuttle service from Québec City carries passengers to the slopes at Mont Ste-Anne, making it possible to stay in the city at night and ski the mountain by day. The round-trip fare is C$18 (US$12). Lodging is available (© **800/463-1568**).

BY CAR   Continue along Route 138 from Ste-Anne-de-Beaupré, turning onto secondary Route 360 to the recreation area.

PARC MONT STE-ANNE
The park entrance is easy to spot from the highway. For information and rates for mountain-bike or ski rentals, call © **418/827-4561** or 418/827-3121.

Parc Mont Ste-Anne, 49 sq. km (30 sq. miles) surrounding a 788m (2,625-ft.) high peak, is an outdoor enthusiast's dream. In summer, there is camping, golfing, in-line skating, cycling, hiking, jogging, paragliding, and a 242km (150-mile) network of mountain biking trails (bikes can be rented at the park). An eight-passenger gondola to the top of the mountain operates every day between late June and early September, weather permitting, for the benefit of cyclists. Gondola ticket prices are C$10 (US$6.45) for adults, C$8 (US$5.15) for ages 14 to 20, C$6 (US$3.85) for seniors and children 7 to 13, and free for children under 7.

In winter, the park is Québec's largest and busiest ski area. Twelve lifts, including the gondola and three quad chair lifts, transport downhill skiers to the starting points of 50 trails and slopes. More than 210km (130 miles) of cross-country trails lace the park, dotted with eight heated rest huts. Cross-country skiers pay day rates of about C$16 (US$10) for an adult, less for students and seniors. Paragliding instruction is available in winter as well as summer.

The park is an easy commute from the city, which is what most people do. An additional nearby inn is Auberge La Camarine, described above.

WHERE TO STAY & DINE
Château Mont Sainte-Anne ✿   Settled in at the base of its namesake mountain, the resort, opened in 1979, continues to grow, adding more and more rooms as you read this. While the management is succeeding in its efforts to increase summer business, focusing on the resort's two golf courses, kid's day camp, and horseback and cycling trails, its real identity is as a ski center. (As a result, summer rates are significantly cheaper than winter rates.) It is well-suited in its role as a ski lodge, with comprehensive facilities that include cable-car lifts, two summit chalets, downhill trails on both the north and south faces of the

mountain, a fleet of 15 snowmobiles, ample snowmaking equipment, and related diversions—ice-skating and dog-sledding among them. Many years they boast skiing into mid-May. What's more, the menu in the main dining room is unusually inventive for a mass feeding operation, and the two bars provide satisfying pub grub. A free shuttle van carries guests to and from Vieux-Québec.

500 bd. Beau-Pré, Beaupré, PQ G0A 1E0. ℰ **800/463-4467** or 418/827-1862. Fax 418/827-5072. www.chateaumontsainteanne.com. 240 units plus 185 condos. C$119–C$219 (US$77–US$141). Children under 17 stay free in parents' room. Many packages available. AE, DC, MC, V. **Amenities:** 2 restaurants (Eclectic, International); 2 bars; indoor and outdoor pools; golf on premises; health club and spa; children's programs; game room; activities desk; courtesy van; massage; babysitting; laundry service; dry cleaning. *In room:* A/C, TV, dataport, kitchenette, fridge, coffeemaker, hair dryer.

5 Canyon Ste-Anne & Ste-Anne Falls

40km (25 miles) NE of Québec City, about 60km (37 miles) NE of Ste-Anne-de-Beaupré

A short drive off Route 138 is the deep gorge and powerful waterfall created by the Ste-Anne-du-Nord River. Unseen from the main road, it's worth a detour and only takes about an hour to visit.

ESSENTIALS
GETTING THERE
BY CAR   Continue along Route 138 from Ste-Anne-de-Beaupré.

CANYON STE-ANNE
Driving north, the marked entrance is on the left. A dirt road leads through the trees to a parking lot. On the far side of the adjacent picnic ground is a building containing a cafeteria and the ticket booth. Admission is C$7 (US$4.50) ages 13 and up, C$2 (US$1.30) ages 6 to 12. The site is open daily May to June 23 and the day after Labour Day through October from 9am to 5pm; and June 24 to Labour Day daily 8:30am to 5:45. It's closed the rest of the year. To confirm these hours, which are subject to change due to weather and season, call ℰ **418/827-4057.**

An open-sided shuttle bus takes you to the first bridge, which crosses the river just above the thundering falls, 74m (243 ft.) high. At the turn of the 20th century, the river was used to float logs from lumbering operations, and part of the dramatic gorge was created by dynamiting around 1917. Trails descend both sides to a second bridge, 55m (180 ft.) above the yellowish iron-tinged water that crashes over massive rock walls. From there, a trail follows the northern rim to a third and final bridge, ending in an observation platform.

The woods that surround the gorge are privately owned, and were only opened to the public in 1973. Management has wisely avoided commercial intrusions along the trails and the few descriptive signs are muted, letting the undeniable natural beauty of the site speak for itself. Visitors who have difficulty walking can get the effect of the falls without going too far from the bus, and those who suffer acrophobia can easily avoid the bridges.

6 Charlevoix

Baie-St-Paul: 98km (61 miles) NE of Québec City; La Malbaie: 149km (92 miles) NE of Québec City; St-Siméon: 182km (113 miles) NE of Québec City

The Laurentians move closer to the shore of the St. Lawrence as they approach what used to be called Murray Bay at the mouth of the Malbaie River. While we can't pretend that the entire length of Route 138 from Beaupré is fascinating, the Route 362 detour from Baie-St-Paul is scenic, with wooded hills interrupted by narrow riverbeds and billowing meadows, ending in harsh cliffs plunging down to the river. The air is scented by sea salt and rent by the shrieks of gulls.

Baie-St-Paul is an artists' colony, and there are several good-to-memorable inns between there and Cap à l'Aigle, a few miles beyond La Malbaie. St-Siméon, where travelers catch the ferry to the southern shore of the St. Lawrence, affords summer visitors numerous opportunities for whale-watching.

ESSENTIALS
GETTING THERE
BY CAR   Take Route 138 as far as Baie-St-Paul, then pick up Route 362 to La Malbaie, merging once again with Route 138 to reach the ferry at St-Siméon.

VISITOR INFORMATION
Baie-St-Paul has a year-round **tourist office** at 444 bd. Mgr-de Laval (℗ **418/435-4160**), open mid-June through Labour Day daily 9am to 7pm, and from September to early June daily 9am to 5pm. La Malbaie also has a tourist office, at 630 bd. de Comporté (℗ **418/665-4454**), with the same hours. St-Siméon has seasonal tourist offices at 494 rue St-Laurent and at the ferry landing, open mid-June through Labour Day daily 9am to 7pm. Check out **www.tourisme-charlevoix.com**.

EXPLORING THE AREA
In addition to the country inns dotting the region from Baie-St-Paul to Cap à l'Aigle to La Malbaie and beyond, nearby Pointe-au-Pic has a casino, a newer, smaller offshoot of the one in Montréal. The northern end of the region is marked by the confluence of the Saguenay River and the St. Lawrence. These waters attract six species of whales, many of which can be seen from shore from mid-June through late October, and **whale-watching cruises** are increasingly popular. In 1988, Charlevoix was named a UNESCO World Biosphere Reserve. Though only 1 of 325 such regions in the world, it was the first one to include a human settlement.

BAIE-ST-PAUL
The first town of any size reached in Charlevoix via Route 138, this attractive community of 6,000 holds on to a reputation as an artist's retreat that began at the start of the 20th century. More than a dozen boutiques and galleries and a couple of small museums show the work of local painters and artisans. Given the setting, it isn't surprising that many of the artists are landscapists, but other styles and subjects are represented. Although some of their production is of the hobbyist level, much is highly professional. To see selections, check the **Maison Reneé Richard,** at 58 rue St-Jean-Baptiste (℗ **418/435-5571**); the **Galerie d'Art,** 1 rue Forget (℗ **418/435-3429**); and **Le Centre d'Art,** 4 rue Ambroise-Fafard (℗ **418/435-3681**), which specialize in landscape artists from Québec.

A Local Museum
Le Centre d'Exposition   Opened in 1992, this brick-and-glass museum has three floors of work primarily by regional artists, both past and present. Inuit sculptures are included, and temporary one-person and group shows are mounted throughout the year.

23 rue Ambroise-Fafard. ℗ **418/435-3681**. www.centre-bsp.qc.ca. Admission C$3 (US$1.95) adults, C$2 (US$1.30) seniors and students, free for children under 12. Sept–May daily 10am–5pm; June–Aug daily 10am–6pm.

Where to Stay & Dine

La Maison Otis   A wide range of facilities and amenities allow guests who reserve far enough in advance to customize their lodgings. Combinations of fireplaces, whirlpools, stereo systems, VCRs, four-poster beds, and suites that sleep four are all available, distributed among three buildings. Housekeeping is meticulous. A long porch fronts the colorful main street, and a kidney-shaped indoor pool and sauna are on the premises, as is a jovial piano bar. The required meals are no sacrifice, served in a room with a stone fireplace and shaded candlesticks on pink tablecloths. Excellent clam chowder, salmon tartare, and pheasant have been notable in the past.

23 rue St-Jean-Baptiste, Baie-St-Paul, PQ G0A 1B0. ℂ 800/267-2254 or 418/435-2255. Fax 418/435-2464. www.quebecweb.com/maisonotis. 30 units. C$70–C$200 (US$45–US$126) double. AE, DC, MC, V. Pets accepted. **Amenities:** Restaurant (Regional); bar; indoor pool; golf nearby; exercise room; Jacuzzi; sauna; massage; babysitting. *In room:* A/C, TV, hair dryer.

CAP-A-L'AIGLE

Route 362 rejoins Route 138 in La Malbaie, the largest town in the area, with almost 4,000 inhabitants. It serves as a provisioning center, with supermarkets, hardware stores, and gas stations. There is a **tourist information office** at 495 bd. de Comporté (ℂ **418/665-4454**), open mid-June through Labour Day daily 9am to 9pm, the rest of the year daily 8:30am to 4:30pm. Continue through the town center and cross the bridge on the right, making a sharp right again on the other side. This is Route 138, with signs pointing to Cap-à-l'Aigle.

Where to Stay & Dine

La Pinsonnière ★★★   This is one of only eight hostelries in the prestigious Relais & Châteaux organization in all of Canada. Properties in that organization offer limited size, bedrooms that often border on princely luxury, but most of all, an obsessive emphasis on excellent food and wine. Bedrooms here come in several categories, the priciest of which are equipped with Jacuzzis and gas fireplaces. A substantial renovation of the entire facility has been completed. Packages include whale-watching cruises, dog-sled runs, and skiing at Mont Grand-Fonds. There's access to the river, but the water is *very* cold.

You'll know where the owners focus their laserlike attention when you're seated in the serene dining room beside the picture window, anticipating a dinner that will become the evening's entertainment. With drinks and menus comes the *amuse-bouche*—say, quail leg on a bed of slivered asparagus—immediately followed by soup. The main event might be a succulent veal chop with a nest of shaved carrots, fiddleheads, and purple potatoes. A piano is played on summer evenings. Wines are a particular point of pride here, and the owner needs no urging to conduct tours of his impressive cellar.

124 rue St-Raphaël, La Malbaie (secteur Cap-à-l'Aigle), PQ G5A 1X9. ℂ **800/387-4431** or 418/665-4431. Fax 418/665-7156. www.lapinsonniere.com. 25 units. May–Oct 30 and Christmas–New Year C$150–C$465 (US$97–US$300) double; Nov–Apr (with the exception of the Dec holiday week) C$125–C$465 (US$81–US$300) double. Meal plan available but not required. Packages available. Minimum 2-night stay on weekends, 3 nights on holiday weekends. AE, DISC, MC, V. **Amenities:** Restaurant (Creative French); bar; heated indoor pool; golf nearby; tennis court; access to nearby health club; spa; sauna; concierge; limited room service; massage; babysitting; dry cleaning. *In room:* A/C, TV, hair dryer.

ST-SIMEON

Rejoin Route 138 and continue 32km (20 miles) to St-Siméon. If you've decided to cross to Rivière-du-Loup on the other side of the St. Lawrence, returning to Québec City along the south shore, the ferry departs from here.

With discretionary time left, I recommend continuing on to Baie-Ste-Catherine and Tadoussac, but if that isn't an option, it's only 150km (93 miles) back to the city the way you came on the north shore.

In St-Siméon, signs direct cars and trucks down to the ferry terminal. Boarding is on a first-come, first-served basis, and ferries leave on a carefully observed schedule, weather permitting, from April to early January. Departure times of the two to five daily sailings vary substantially from month to month, however, so get in touch with the company, **Clarke Transport Canada** (© 418/ **638-2856**), to obtain a copy of the schedule. For current fares, call © 418/ **862-5094** or check the website at www.travrdlstsim.com. Always subject to change, round-trip fares for passengers remaining on board are C$14 (US$8.85) ages 12 to 64 years, C$12 (US$7.95) seniors, C$9.20 (US$5.95) children 5 to 11. For cars, the one-way fare is C$29 (US$19). MasterCard and Visa accepted. Arrive at least 30 minutes before departure, 1 hour ahead in summer. Voyages take 65 to 75 minutes.

From late June through September, passengers may enjoy a bonus on the ferry trip. Those are the months when the **whales** are most active. They are estimated at more than 500 in number when pelagic (migratory) species join the resident minke and beluga whales. They prefer the northern side of the Estuary, roughly from La Malbaie to Baie-Ste-Catherine, at the mouth of the Saguenay River. Because that is the area the ferry steams through, sightings are an ever-present possibility, especially in summer.

BAIE STE-CATHERINE

To enhance your chances of seeing whales, continue northeast from St-Siméon on Route 138, arriving 32km (20 miles) later in Baie-Ste-Catherine, near the estuary of the Saguenay River. A half dozen companies offer cruises to see whales or the majestic Saguenay Fjord from here or from Tadoussac, on the opposite shore. The cruise companies use different sizes and types of watercraft, from powered inflatables called Zodiacs that carry 10 to 25 passengers up to stately catamarans and cruisers that carry up to 500. The zodiacs don't provide food, drink, or narration, while the larger boats have snack bars and naturalists on board to describe the action. The small boats, though, are more maneuverable, darting about at each sighting to get closer to the rolling and breaching behemoths.

Zodiac passengers are issued life jackets and waterproof overalls, but should expect to get wet anyway. It's cold out there, too, so layers and even gloves are a good idea. People on the large boats sit at tables inside or ride the observation bowsprit, high above the waves. Big boats are the wimp's choice for whale-watching. Mine, too.

Most cruises last 2 to 3 hours. One of the most active companies offering trips is **Croisières AML,** with offices in Québec City (© **800/563-4643** all year, 418/692-1159 in season). From June through mid-October, they have up to four departures daily. Fares on the larger boats are C$45 (US$29) for adults, C$20 (US$13) for children 6 to 12, while zodiac fares are C$52 (US$34) for adults, C$30 (US$19) for children. Excursions of comparable duration and with similar fares are provided on the catamaran maintained by **Famille Dufour Croisières** (© **800/463-5250** or 418/692-0222). Departures are from the Tadoussac and Baie-Ste-Catherine wharves.

From Baie Ste-Catherine, it's less than a half-hour drive back to St-Siméon and the ferry across to the opposite shore. Alternatively, continue north to the ferry, **Traverse Tadoussac** (© **418/235-4395**), at the mouth of the dramatic Saguenay River. Palisades rise sharply from both shores, the reason this area is often referred to as a fjord. The ferry can board up to 400 passengers and 75 vehicles for the trip across to Tadoussac, which takes only 10 minutes. Departure times vary according to season and demand, of course, but in summer figure every hour from midnight to 6am, every 40 minutes from 6:20am to 8am, every 20 minutes from 8am to 8pm, and every 40 minutes from 8:20pm to midnight.

TADOUSSAC

Known as "The Cradle of New France," the oldest permanent European settlement north of Florida was established in 1600 at the point where the Saguenay and St. Lawrence Rivers meet. Missionaries followed and stayed until the middle of the 19th century. The hamlet might have vanished soon after, had a resort hotel not been built there in 1864. A steamship line brought vacationers downriver from Montréal and points farther west and deposited them here for stays that often lasted all summer. Apart from the hotel—the current building was erected in 1942—a few small support businesses, a post office, a marina, and more than a dozen small motels and B&Bs constitute the town. Its port is an important starting point for whale-watching and Saguenay cruises. Tadoussac is the southernmost point of the tourist region designated as Manicouagan.

For 4 days in early June, the town hosts a **Festival de la Chanson,** a song festival with more than a dozen concerts. Call © **866/861-4108** or 418/235-1421 or check www.fjord-best.com/festival-tadoussac.

Where to Stay & Dine

Hôtel Tadoussac   From the opposite shore, the bright-red mansard roof of this sprawling hotel dominates the point of land that slopes down to the river. (You might recognize it as the centerpiece in the film *Hotel New Hampshire*.) The lawn has a *pétanque* (lawn bowling) court, as well as groupings of chairs from which to watch the comings and goings of boats and zodiacs. Inside, the public spaces and bedrooms have a shambling, country-cottage appearance—no pretense of luxe here. Maple furnishings and hand-woven rugs and bedspreads are all made in Québec. Meals in the large dining room are better than might be expected, while falling short of impressive. Reservations must be made for dinner, with the earlier seating drawing older guests and most of the families with children.

165 rue Bord de l'Eau, Tadoussac, PQ G0T 2A0. © **800/463-5250** or 418/235-4421. Fax 418/235-4607. www.familledufour.com. 149 units. C$195–C$250 (US$126–US$161) double. Rates include breakfast. Meal plan, golf, and whale-watching cruise packages available. AE, DC, DISC, MC, V. Closed mid-Oct to early May. **Amenities:** Restaurant (Regional); bar; heated outdoor pool; golf nearby; tennis court; babysitting; laundry service. *In room:* TV.

Appendix: Montréal & Québec City in Depth

As important to your enjoyment of a new destination as deciding where you'll stay or eat is learning something about its history and culture.

1 A Look at French Canada: Now & Then

THE FOUNDING OF MONTREAL **Paul de Chomedey, sieur de Maisonneuve** arrived in 1642 to establish a colony and to plant a crucifix atop the hill he called Mont-Royal. He and his band of settlers came ashore and founded **Ville-Marie,** dedicated to the Virgin Mary, at the spot now marked by Place Royale. They built a fort, a chapel, stores, and houses, and the energetic **Jeanne Mance** made her indelible mark by founding the hospital named Hotel-Dieu-de-Montréal, which still exists today.

Life was not easy. Unlike the friendly Algonquins who lived in nearby regions, the Iroquois in Montréal had no intention of living in peace with the new settlers. Fierce battles raged for years, and the settlers were lucky that their numbers included such undauntable souls as la Salle, du Luth, de la Mothe Cadillac, and the brothers Lemoyne.

At **Place d'Armes** stands a statue of de Maisonneuve, marking the spot where the settlers defeated the Iroquois in bloody hand-to-hand fighting, with de Maisonneuve himself locked in mortal combat with the Iroquois chief. De Maisonneuve won.

From that time the settlement prospered, though in 1760, the year after Wolfe defeated Montcalm on the Plains of Abraham in Québec, it fell to the British. Until the 1800s the city was contained in the area known today as **Vieux-Montréal.** Its ancient walls no longer stand, but its long and colorful past is preserved in the streets, houses, and churches of the Old City.

ENGLAND CONQUERS NEW FRANCE In the 1750s the struggle between Britain and France had escalated, after a series of conflicts beginning in 1689 that had embroiled both Europe and the New World. The latest episode was known as the **French and Indian War** in North America, an extension of Europe's Seven Years' War. Strategic Québec became a valued prize. The French sent **Louis Joseph, marquis de Montcalm,** to command their forces in the town. The British sent an expedition of 4,500 men in a fleet under the command of a 32-year-old general, **James Wolfe.** The ensuing battle for Québec, fought on the **Plains of Abraham** southwest of the city on September 13, 1759, is one of the most famous battles in North American history, because it resulted in a continent that was under to British influence for centuries to come.

Both generals perished as a result of the 20-minute battle on the Plains of Abraham. Wolfe lived just long enough to hear that he had won. Montcalm died a few hours later. Today a memorial to both men overlooks Terrasse Dufferin in Québec City, the only statue in the world commemorating both victor and vanquished of the same battle. The inscription, in neither French nor English but Latin, says simply, COURAGE WAS FATAL TO THEM.

THE UNITED STATES INVADES   The capture of Québec determined the course of the war, and the **Treaty of Paris** in 1763 ceded all of French Canada to England. In a sense, this victory led to Britain's worst defeat. If the French had held Canada, the British government might have been more judicious in its treatment of the American colonists. As it was, the British decided to make the colonists pay the costs of the French and Indian War, on the principle that it was their homes being defended. They slapped so many taxes on all imports that the infuriated colonists openly rebelled against the Crown.

But if the British misjudged the temper of the colonists, the Americans were equally wrong about the mood of the Canadians. **George Washington** felt sure that French Canadians would want to join the revolution, or at least be supportive. He was mistaken on both counts. The Quebecois detested their British conquerors, but they were also staunch Royalists and devout Catholics, and saw their contentious neighbors as godless Republicans. Only a handful supported the Americans, as often as not to sell them supplies, and three of Washington's most competent commanders came to grief in attacks against Québec. Thirty-eight years later, in the **War of 1812,** another U.S. army marched up the banks of the Richelieu River where it flows from Lake Champlain to the St. Lawrence. And once again the French Canadians stuck by the British and drove back the invaders. The war ended essentially in a draw, but it had at least one encouraging result: Britain and the young United States agreed to demilitarize the Great Lakes and to extend their mutual border along the 49th parallel to the Rockies.

MONTREAL & QUEBEC CITY TODAY   The ancient walls that protected Québec City over the centuries are still in place today, the town within their embrace little changed, preserving for posterity the heart of New France. Montréal, though, has gone through a metamorphosis. It was "wet" when the United States was "dry" due to Prohibition. Bootleggers, hard drinkers, and prostitutes flocked to this large city situated so conveniently close to the American border and mixed with rowdy people from the port, much to the distress of Montréal's mainly upstanding citizenry. For half a century the city's image was decidedly racy, but in the 1950s a cleanup began, with a boom in high-rise construction and eventual restoration of much of the derelict Old Town. In **1967** Montréal welcomed the world to Expo. The great gleaming skyscrapers and towering hotels, the superb Métro system, and the highly practical underground city, so much a part of this modern city, date mostly from the past 40 years.

All this activity helped to fuel a phenomenon later labeled the **"Quiet Revolution."** It was to transform the largely rural, agricultural province into an urbanized, industrial entity with a pronounced secular outlook. French Canadians, long denied access to the upper echelons of desirable corporate careers, started to insist upon equal opportunity with the powerful Anglophone minority. Inevitably, a radical fringe movement of separatists emerged, signaling its intentions by bombing Anglophone businesses. The **FLQ,** as it was known, was behind most of the terrorist attacks, reaching its nadir with the kidnapping and murder of a cabinet minister, **Pierre Laporte.**

Most Quebecois separatists were not violent, and most Quebecois were not even separatists. **Pierre Trudeau,** a bilingual Quebecois, became prime minister in 1968. As flamboyant, eccentric, and brilliant as any Canadian who ever held the post, he necessarily devoted much of his time trying to placate voters on both sides of the issue. In 1969, the **Official Languages Act** mandated that all federal agencies provide services in both French and English. Yet by 1980, a provincial referendum on separation from the confederation was defeated by only 60% of the vote. Subsequent attempts to assuage the chafed sensibilities of French Quebecois failed again and again, as often at the hands of other provincial premiers as by the Quebecois, hounding at least three prime ministers from office.

In 1993, the governing Tories were defeated by the opposition Liberals. The new prime minister, **Jean Chrétien,** a federalist, was not aided in his task of national reconciliation by representation in the House of Commons of the militantly separatist **Bloc Quebecois,** which became the largest opposition party in the same election. And in Québec the following year, the **Parti Quebecois** won provincial elections to end 9 years of Liberal control. The new premier, **Jacques Parizeau,** vowed to hold an early referendum on sovereignty, which was held in late October 1995 and was narrowly defeated by a bare 1% of the total vote. Parizeau resigned the day after, after making intemperate remarks about the negative role of ethnic voters in the results. Recent polls suggest that pro-confederation sentiments are gaining ground over separatism, but fluctuations have been the rule. Contention over the intractable issue isn't going to end anytime soon, but conversations with ordinary Quebecois suggest they are so weary of the seemingly endless sovereignty argument they no longer care what happens as long as it is decided one way or the other.

2 The Politics of Language

The defining dialectic of Canadian life is language, the thorny issue that might yet tear the country apart. Many Quebecois believe that a separate independent state is the only way to maintain their culture in the face of the Anglophone ocean that envelops them. The role of Québec within the Canadian federation is the most debated and volatile issue in Canadian politics.

One attempt to smooth ruffled Francophone fur was made in 1969, when federal legislation stipulated that all services were henceforth to be offered in both English and French, in effect declaring the nation bilingual. That didn't long assuage militant Quebecois. Having made the two languages equal in the rest of the country, they undertook to guarantee the primacy of French in their own province. To prevent dilution by newcomers, the children of immigrants are required to enroll in French-language schools, even if English or a third language is spoken in the home. Bill 101 was passed in 1977, which all but banned the use of English on public signage. Stop signs now read ARRET, a word that actually refers to a stop on a bus or train route. (Even in France, the red signs read STOP, but then, Quebecois like to believe they speak a purer—by which they mean older—form of the language than is spoken in the mother country today.) The bill funded the establishment of enforcement units, virtual language police who let no nit go unpicked.

As a result of this backlash, which has resulted in the flight of an estimated 400,000 Anglophones to other parts of Canada, Canadian Prime Minister Brian Mulroney met with the 10 provincial premiers in April 1987 at a retreat at Québec's Meech Lake to cobble together a collection of constitutional reforms. The Meech Lake Accord, as it came to be known, addressed a variety of issues, but most important to the Quebecois it recognized Québec as a "distinct society" within the federation. In the end, however, Manitoba and Newfoundland failed to ratify the accord by the June 23, 1990, deadline. As a result, support for the secessionist cause burgeoned in Québec, and the separatist Parti Quebecois now controls the provincial government. A referendum held in 1995 was narrowly won by those Québec residents who favored staying within the union, but the vote settled nothing. The issue continues to divide families and dominate all political discourse.

In the midst of the unshakable fray, Québec remains committed to ensuring, one way or another, the survival of the province's culture and language, its bedrock loyalty to its Gallic roots. France may have relinquished control of Québec in 1763, but its influence, after its century and a half of rule, remains powerful to this day. The Quebecois continue to look across the Atlantic for inspiration in fashion, food, and the arts. Culturally and linguistically, it is that tenacious French connection that gives the province its special character, which is a source of great regional pride and considerable national controversy.

There are reasons for the festering intransigence of the Quebecois, about 240 years' worth. After what they unfailingly call "The Conquest," their English rulers made a few concessions to French-Canadian pride, including allowing them a Gallic version of jurisprudence. But a kind of linguistic exclusionism prevailed, with wealthy Scottish and English bankers and merchants denying French-Canadians access to upper levels of business and government. The present strife, and the frequent foolishness and small-mindedness that attends it on both sides, is as much payback as it is pride in the French heritage.

None of this should deter potential visitors. The Quebecois are exceedingly gracious hosts. While Montréal may be the largest French-speaking city outside Paris, most Montréalers grow up speaking both French and English, switching effortlessly from one language to the other as the situation dictates. Telephone operators go from French to English the instant they hear an English word out of the other party, as do most store clerks, waiters, and hotel staff. This is less the case in country villages and in Québec City, but there is virtually no problem that can't be solved with a few French words, some expressive gestures, and a little goodwill.

3 Cuisine Haute, Cuisine Bas: Smoked Meat, Fiddleheads & Caribou

French cuisine has prevailed since the arrival of Québec's earliest white settlers. At first, the food of the colony was the country cooking of the motherland adapted to the ingredients found in New France: **root vegetables, dried legumes, apples, maple sugar and syrup,** and whatever catchable **fish and game** were available. Dishes native to the region evolved, many of which are still savored by the Quebecois today. Among these are *cretons,* a paté of minced pork, allspice, and parsley; a meat pie called *tourtière,* beans and pork baked in maple syrup; and *tarte au sucre,* maple sugar pie. As time passed and food became more than sustenance, the gastronomic fervor of the old country was imported to Québec, and replications of Parisian bistros and manifestations of the epicurean teachings of Brillat-Savarin arrived and multiplied. The entire range of Gallic cuisine was then available, from lowbrow to upper-crust. Game is still highly popular, with wild boar, venison, pheasant, quail, hare, and even caribou and wapiti (deer) appearing frequently on menus. Oddly, for a region whose identity is shaped in large part by the great river that runs through it, fish is seen less often. When it is, it is almost invariably salmon. Extremely popular shellfish are **scallops** (*peétoncles,* pronounced "pay-*tonk*"); **mussels** *(moules),* served in the Belgian manner with thin French fries *(frites),* and **lobster** *(homard),* which comes at remarkable bargain prices during the summer festival celebrating its availability.

Le Dining Terms

A little knowledge of local restaurant terminology will help you avoid confusion when dining in Québec. An *entrée* is an appetizer, not the main course, which is *le plat principal.* In fancier places, where a pre-appetizer nibble is proffered, it is an *amuse-gueule* or *amuse-bouche,* and the little plate of cookies and sweets that comes with coffee contains *les mignardises.* A tip left at the end of a meal is a *pourboire.*

Vegetables are largely those familiar to Americans, increasingly provided by organic or hydroponic farms, especially in winter. An exception is **fiddleheads**—*têtes des violon*—the tightly curled tips of wild ferns picked in spring just before they unfold into fronds. Their season is short, usually the last half of May and early June, and they appear on plates all over the province, usu-ally sautéed and tossed in butter or oil with garlic. Cheese-lovers can rejoice in the delicious reality that more than 75 distinct *fromages* are produced in Québec. Many of them equal some of the best French varieties, in part because the Quebecois versions are also unpasteurized. For that reason, they cannot be imported into the United States, so this is the place to sample them.

The culinary revolution that rolled across the continent from California in the 1980s swallowed up Vancouver, Toronto, Chicago, and New York; but it barely touched Montréal, and it bypassed Québec City entirely. That is now changing, quite dramatically. **Cal-Ital, New Canadian,** and **fusion** have arrived and are taking their place at the head of the table. The most honored restaurants in the province are making their own rules, improvising, inventing new combi-nations of textures, tastes, and ingredients. The traditional kitchens remain, but they are lightening their sauces, rethinking their assumptions, and even tossing out old recipes. More Italian, Mediterranean, and Asian restaurants are opening every year. Cosmopolitan Québec has become even more sophisticated, with remarkable restaurants found even in relatively remote rural areas.

The Quebecois enjoy their comfort foods as much as anyone. In Montréal, these include **smoked meat,** a maddeningly tasty sandwich component that hovers in the neighborhood of pastrami and corned beef but is somehow differ-ent. And the Montréal rendition of the **bagel** is thinner, chewier, and better than the more famous New York prototype. Take it from someone born in *Le Bronx.*

Many lower-priced restaurants in Montréal allow patrons to bring their own wine, indicated by signs in the window that show a red hand holding a bottle or carry the words APPORTEZ VOTRE VIN. To buy wine or spirits outside a bar or restaurant, go to an outlet of the Québec Société des Alcools (SAQ), the gov-ernmental monopoly that holds the exclusive right to sell all strong liquor in the province. Licensed grocery stores may sell wine, beer, and alcoholic cider, but the Société des Alcools stores have the largest selections of wines. A subcategory of stores, *maisons des vins,* also carry old, rare, and special wines.

In restaurants, wine is often offered by the liter, half-liter, quarter-liter, and glass *(verre).* The quarter-liter contains two glasses, usually a small saving over glasses ordered separately. Imported wines and spirits are very expensive, encour-aging experimentation with Canadian efforts with the grape. Some are appalling, a few are . . . not bad. Excellent Québec beers include **Belle Gueule, Boréal,** and the darker **St-Amboise.**

Index

See also Accommodations and Restaurant indexes, below.

RESTAURANTS: QUEBEC CITY & ENVIRONS

FROMMER'S® COMPLETE TRAVEL GUIDES

Alaska
Alaska Cruises & Ports of Call
Amsterdam
Argentina & Chile
Arizona
Atlanta
Australia
Austria
Bahamas
Barcelona, Madrid & Seville
Beijing
Belgium, Holland & Luxembourg
Bermuda
Boston
Brazil
British Columbia & the Canadian
   Rockies
Budapest & the Best of Hungary
California
Canada
Cancún, Cozumel & the Yucatán
Cape Cod, Nantucket & Martha's
   Vineyard
Caribbean
Caribbean Cruises & Ports of Call
Caribbean Ports of Call
Carolinas & Georgia
Chicago
China
Colorado
Costa Rica
Denmark
Denver, Boulder & Colorado
   Springs
England
Europe
European Cruises & Ports of Call
Florida

France
Germany
Great Britain
Greece
Greek Islands
Hawaii
Hong Kong
Honolulu, Waikiki & Oahu
Ireland
Israel
Italy
Jamaica
Japan
Las Vegas
London
Los Angeles
Maryland & Delaware
Maui
Mexico
Montana & Wyoming
Montréal & Québec City
Munich & the Bavarian Alps
Nashville & Memphis
Nepal
New England
New Mexico
New Orleans
New York City
New Zealand
Northern Italy
Nova Scotia, New Brunswick &
   Prince Edward Island
Oregon
Paris
Philadelphia & the Amish Country
Portugal
Prague & the Best of the Czech
   Republic

Provence & the Riviera
Puerto Rico
Rome
San Antonio & Austin
San Diego
San Francisco
Santa Fe, Taos & Albuquerque
Scandinavia
Scotland
Seattle & Portland
Shanghai
Singapore & Malaysia
South Africa
South America
South Florida
South Pacific
Southeast Asia
Spain
Sweden
Switzerland
Texas
Thailand
Tokyo
Toronto
Tuscany & Umbria
USA
Utah
Vancouver & Victoria
Vermont, New Hampshire &
   Maine
Vienna & the Danube Valley
Virgin Islands
Virginia
Walt Disney World® & Orlando
Washington, D.C.
Washington State

FROMMER'S® DOLLAR-A-DAY GUIDES

Australia from $50 a Day
California from $70 a Day
Caribbean from $70 a Day
England from $75 a Day
Europe from $70 a Day

Florida from $70 a Day
Hawaii from $80 a Day
Ireland from $60 a Day
Italy from $70 a Day
London from $85 a Day

New York from $90 a Day
Paris from $80 a Day
San Francisco from $70 a Day
Washington, D.C. from $80 a Day

FROMMER'S® PORTABLE GUIDES

Acapulco, Ixtapa & Zihuatanejo
Amsterdam
Aruba
Australia's Great Barrier Reef
Bahamas
Berlin
Big Island of Hawaii
Boston
California Wine Country
Cancún
Charleston & Savannah
Chicago
Disneyland®
Dublin
Florence

Frankfurt
Hong Kong
Houston
Las Vegas
London
Los Angeles
Los Cabos & Baja
Maine Coast
Maui
Miami
New Orleans
New York City
Paris
Phoenix & Scottsdale

Portland
Puerto Rico
Puerto Vallarta, Manzanillo &
   Guadalajara
Rio de Janeiro
San Diego
San Francisco
Seattle
Sydney
Tampa & St. Petersburg
Vancouver
Venice
Virgin Islands
Washington, D.C.

FROMMER'S® NATIONAL PARK GUIDES

Banff & Jasper
Family Vacations in the National
   Parks
Grand Canyon

National Parks of the American
   West
Rocky Mountain

Yellowstone & Grand Teton
Yosemite & Sequoia/ Kings Canyon
Zion & Bryce Canyon

FROMMER'S® MEMORABLE WALKS

Chicago	New York	San Francisco
London	Paris	Washington, D.C.

FROMMER'S® GREAT OUTDOOR GUIDES

Arizona & New Mexico	Northern California	Vermont & New Hampshire
New England	Southern New England	

SUZY GERSHMAN'S BORN TO SHOP GUIDES

Born to Shop: France	Born to Shop: Italy	Born to Shop: New York
Born to Shop: Hong Kong,	Born to Shop: London	Born to Shop: Paris
Shanghai & Beijing		

FROMMER'S® IRREVERENT GUIDES

Amsterdam	Los Angeles	San Francisco
Boston	Manhattan	Seattle & Portland
Chicago	New Orleans	Vancouver
Las Vegas	Paris	Walt Disney World®
London	Rome	Washington, D.C.

FROMMER'S® BEST-LOVED DRIVING TOURS

Britain	Germany	Northern Italy
California	Ireland	Scotland
Florida	Italy	Spain
France	New England	Tuscany & Umbria

HANGING OUT™ GUIDES

Hanging Out in England	Hanging Out in France	Hanging Out in Italy
Hanging Out in Europe	Hanging Out in Ireland	Hanging Out in Spain

THE UNOFFICIAL GUIDES®

Bed & Breakfasts and Country	Southwest & South Central	Mid-Atlantic with Kids
Inns in:	Plains	Mini Las Vegas
California	U.S.A.	Mini-Mickey
Great Lakes States	Beyond Disney	New England and New York with
Mid-Atlantic	Branson, Missouri	Kids
New England	California with Kids	New Orleans
Northwest	Chicago	New York City
Rockies	Cruises	Paris
Southeast	Disneyland®	San Francisco
Southwest	Florida with Kids	Skiing in the West
Best RV & Tent Campgrounds in:	Golf Vacations in the Eastern U.S.	Southeast with Kids
California & the West	Great Smoky & Blue Ridge Region	Walt Disney World®
Florida & the Southeast	Inside Disney	Walt Disney World® for Grown-ups
Great Lakes States	Hawaii	Walt Disney World® with Kids
Mid-Atlantic	Las Vegas	Washington, D.C.
Northeast	London	World's Best Diving Vacations
Northwest & Central Plains		

SPECIAL-INTEREST TITLES

Frommer's Adventure Guide to Australia &	Frommer's Italy's Best Bed & Breakfasts and
New Zealand	Country Inns
Frommer's Adventure Guide to Central America	Frommer's New York City with Kids
Frommer's Adventure Guide to India & Pakistan	Frommer's Ottawa with Kids
Frommer's Adventure Guide to South America	Frommer's Road Atlas Britain
Frommer's Adventure Guide to Southeast Asia	Frommer's Road Atlas Europe
Frommer's Adventure Guide to Southern Africa	Frommer's Road Atlas France
Frommer's Britain's Best Bed & Breakfasts and	Frommer's Toronto with Kids
Country Inns	Frommer's Vancouver with Kids
Frommer's Caribbean Hideaways	Frommer's Washington, D.C., with Kids
Frommer's Exploring America by RV	Israel Past & Present
Frommer's Fly Safe, Fly Smart	The New York Times' Guide to Unforgettable
Frommer's France's Best Bed & Breakfasts and	Weekends
Country Inns	Places Rated Almanac
Frommer's Gay & Lesbian Europe	Retirement Places Rated